Palgrave Macmillan Studies in Banking and Financial Institutions

Series Editor
Philip Molyneux, Bangor University, Bangor, UK

The Palgrave Macmillan Studies in Banking and Financial Institutions series is international in orientation and includes studies of banking systems in particular countries or regions as well as contemporary themes such as Islamic Banking, Financial Exclusion, Mergers and Acquisitions, Risk Management, and IT in Banking. The books focus on research and practice and include up to date and innovative studies that cover issues which impact banking systems globally.

Santiago Carbó-Valverde ·
Pedro J. Cuadros-Solas
Editors

New Challenges
for the Banking
Industry

Searching for Balance Between Corporate
Governance, Sustainability and Innovation

Editors
Santiago Carbó-Valverde
Department of Economic Analysis,
Facultad de Economía
University of Valencia
Valencia, Spain

Pedro J. Cuadros-Solas
Department of Economics
CUNEF Universidad
Madrid, Spain

ISSN 2523-336X   ISSN 2523-3378   (electronic)
Palgrave Macmillan Studies in Banking and Financial Institutions
ISBN 978-3-031-32930-2   ISBN 978-3-031-32931-9   (eBook)
https://doi.org/10.1007/978-3-031-32931-9

This Palgrave Macmillan imprint is published by the registered company Springer Nature Switzerland AG
The registered company address is: Gewerbestrasse 11, 6330 Cham, Switzerland

CONTENTS

NOTES ON CONTRIBUTORS

Selena Aureli, Ph.D. is Associate Professor at Bologna University (Italy) where she teaches Financial Reporting and Analysis to Master students and Managerial Accounting to Undergraduate students. She was formerly enrolled by the University of Urbino. Her main research interests are in financial and sustainability reporting, managerial accounting, and performance measurement. She has extensive experience in collaborative research, in conjunction with other universities and private industry. She visited Tampere University in Finland, the Higher School of Economics of Moscow, and the University of Zaragoza in Spain. Among latest publications on ESG aspects, she co-authored the article "The value relevance of Environmental, Social, and Governance disclosure: Evidence from Dow Jones Sustainability World Index listed companies," published in the Corporate Social Responsibility and Environmental Management Journal in 2020.

Federico Beltrame is Associate Professor of Corporate Finance in the Department of Economics and Statistics, University of Udine, Italy. He holds a Ph.D. in Business Science from the same University. His main research interests are related to SMEs' cost of capital, banks' capital structure, and mutual guarantee credit institutions.

Paola Brighi is Associate Professor of Banking and Finance at the Department of Management at the University of Bologna, Italy. She obtained her M.A. from the University of Louvain-la-Neuve and her Ph.D. from the University of Ancona. She has been a Visiting Scholar at the University of Wisconsin and the University of Essex. She has published articles in international journals and contributed chapters to books. She has also presented her works at many international conferences (Financial Management Association, European Financial Management Association, International Finance, and Banking Society, etc.). Her research interests relate to ESG topics, bank efficiency, cooperative banks, relationship lending, bank geographic diversification, and SME finance.

Santiago Carbó-Valverde is Professor of Economics at the Universidad de Valencia (Spain), and formerly at the Universidad de Granada, Bangor University (UK) and CUNEF. He is the Head of Financial Studies and Executive Director of the Financial Digitalization Observatory at the Spanish think-tank Funcas. He was President of IBEFA (International Banking, Economics, and Finance Association). He has served as Consultant for various central banks and international institutions. He has written over 200 articles and other publications on the financial system. He has published articles in peer-reviewed journals, such as *Review of Economics and Statistics, Nature-Scientific Reports, European Economic Review, Review of Finance, Journal of Corporate Finance, Journal of Money Credit and Banking, and Journal of Banking and Finance*. He also frequently contributes to press journals and media.

Fatima Cardias Williams holds Ph.Ds. in Economics and Finance, and Forest Products and Agricultural Sciences. Her research interests include corporate governance and the impact of faultlines in boards, executive remuneration in banking, and ESG; she has examined M&As in banking sectors in Latin American countries. From her doctoral research, she wrote a module on Executive Compensation which has been delivered to M.B.A. and Masters' students in Bangor University. Formerly, a Researcher and Head of the Pathology Laboratory at the Forest Products Research Center at the National Institute of Amazonian Research (INPA) in Manaus, Brazil, a Research Scientist at the BioComposites Centre, Bangor University, and Plant Scientist for Marishal Thompson & Co (Environmental) Ltd at the European Plant Science Laboratory, she has produced a body of research papers and reports and is currently investigating how a deeper knowledge of science might benefit the financial and economic sectors of society.

Andrea Cerri, Ph.D. in Management, is Academic Fellow of the Department of Finance at Università Bocconi and at SDA Bocconi. He currently holds the course of Finance Lab at Università Bocconi. He also teaches International Financial Markets and then Venture Capital and managerial entrepreneurship for IES Abroad, Milan Center. He carried out post-doctoral research activities at the Faculty of Business Economics of Università Cattolica in Milan. He is author of national and international articles and publications on financial topics. As a professional, he is enrolled as Chartered Professional Accountant, Statutory Auditor, and he is enrolled ad Technical Consultant of the Court of Milan. As professional he serves in some boards of statutory auditors, he supports firms and financial institutions in litigations, operates as firms' technical consultant, and provides services like firms' valuation or business plan implementation or restructuring plans.

Giuseppina Chesini is Associate Professor of Banking and Finance at the Department of Management, University of Verona, Italy. She received her Ph.D. in Financial Markets and Institutions from the University of Bergamo, Italy. She is a charter member of ADEIMF (Italian Association of University Teachers of Financial Intermediaries and Markets) and a member of the European Association of University Teachers in Banking and Finance, Wolpertinger Club. Her main research interests include empirical banking, financial regulation, financial markets, and sustainable finance. She is author of about 70 scientific publications, including papers, chapters, and monographs. She has been Visiting Professor at the Baruch College (City University), New York (USA) and at the Kyushu University, Fukuoka (Japan). She has been involved in several national and international research projects.

Georgios Chortareas is a Professor in Economics at King's Business School. His principal research interests are in monetary policy and in international finance. He has published on topics including monetary policy delegation, central banking, real exchange rates, current accounts, and banking.

Pedro J. Cuadros-Solas is Associate (tenured) Professor of Economics and Banking at CUNEF Universidad. Ph.D. in Economics from the Universidad de Granada. He is Economist at Funcas and the Funcas Observatory of Financial Digitalization. His research interests lie in banking, financial digitalization, corporate finance (underwriting), financial intermediation, and financial crises. His research work has been published in international journals, such as the *Journal of Corporate Finance, Journal of Financial Stability, Journal of International Financial Markets, Institutions & Money, European Journal of Finance, Financial Innovation, Research in International Business and Finance, International Review of Economics & Finance, PLOS ONE,* and *Global Policy.* He has been awarded the second prize for research (twice) by the FEF (Financial Studies Foundation) and the research award for the best thesis in Economics by the RADE (Royal Academy of Doctors in Spain). He is the leading researcher in several national research projects for Spanish Ministry of Science.

Antonio Carlo Francesco Della Bina is Assistant Professor of Corporate Finance at the Department of Management at the University of Bologna, Italy. He received a Ph.D. in Finance from the University of Bologna, with a dissertation on financial analysis. He was Visiting Scholar at the Haas School of Business, University of California, Berkeley. His research has been published in finance, economics, and corporate governance journals and book chapters. His research interests are in the fields of corporate finance, financial analysts, corporate valuation, empirical asset pricing, market efficiency, investors' behavior, and ESG.

Kristaps Freimanis is a 4th year Ph.D. student in Macroeconomics and Scientific Assistant of Riga Technical University. He received his Master's in Economics in 2017 and Bachelor's in Financial Engineering in 2014 from Riga Technical University. He has more than 10 years long industry experience in various financial and risk management positions. Currently, he is Financial Planning and Analysis Unit Manager in the biggest electricity distribution system operator in Latvia.

His research interests include state economic policy, market failures, and regulation. His research results have been published in peer-reviewed journals, the chapter in the book, and international scientific conferences.

Enrico Fioravante Geretto is an Associate Professor at the University of Udine, Department of Economics and Statistics. In the past, he was a Lecturer of Banking Operations Technique, Insurance Operations Technique, Financial Instruments Technique, Asset Management Economics, Intermediaries, and Financial Markets. Currently, he is a Professor of

Economics and Management of the Bank (Master's Degree in Banking and Finance) and Economics of Financial Intermediaries.

Gimede Gigante, Ph.D. in Banking and Finance, is Director of the Innovation and Corporate Entrepreneurship Center at SDA Bocconi School of Management and Deputy Director of the Bachelor Degree Program in Economics and Finance at Bocconi University, where he has been Course Director of Principles of International Finance since 2017 and has served as Academic Director of the Bocconi Summer School since 2019. He has held visiting positions at the Finance Department of Columbia Business School and at the Salomon Brothers Center (Stern School of Business, NYU). Member of the Harvard Business Review advisory council, he is also a Fellow of the Research Unit on Investment Banking and Structured Finance at the Baffi Carefin Center. His main areas of research are international finance, financial markets, corporate valuation, investment banking, fintech, and private equity.

Cristina Gonnella is Ph.D. in Business Administration and Management at the Department of Economics and Management, University of Pisa. She has been visiting student at CUNEF Universidad in Madrid. Her research fields are related to banking. She focuses on corporate governance (board of directors composition and structure) and CSR (the intra-organizational integration of socio-environmental issues). She is particularly interested in studying Management Control Systems for socio-environmental sustainability in Banks. She also collaborates with the University of Florence and the Italian Forum for Sustainable Finance to search for the determinants (e.g., board, ESG governance structures) and the effects (e.g., financial performance) of ESG integration in Italian pension funds' investment choices.

Priscilla Greggio works as Associate Consultant at Bain & Company (Milan) since 2021, where she has gained experience primarily in the Energy and Renewables sector. She graduated in the double-degree CEMS Master in International Management from Bocconi University and London School of Economics. She gained knowledge in the startup field working for Eatfirst in Berlin, focusing on Finance and Product Development. Her main areas of interest are sustainability, energy, sustainable finance, and emerging markets.

Fangyuan Kou is a Ph.D. Researcher in the Banking and Finance Department of King's Business School. She graduated with a B.Sc. degree in

xii   NOTES ON CONTRIBUTORS

International Trade and Economics from the University of International Business and Economics (UIBE), and an MSc in Banking and Finance from King's College London. Her main research interests are empirical banking, corporate finance, and climate finance.

Ted Lindblom is a Professor at the School of Business, Economics, and Law at the University of Gothenburg, Sweden. His current research concerns the field of industrial and financial management with particular focus on technological innovations and firms' strategic behavior and pricing in a game-theoretic setting, corporate finance, and banking. In the banking area, he has for almost 40 years studied the effects of market structural changes and regulation of banks as well as banks' risk management, pricing of payment services, and the growing use of various trade financing arrangements in international supply chains. He has authored and co-authored several articles and books regarding these issues.

Muddassar Malik is a Doctoral Researcher at the Department of Accounting and Finance—Turku School of Economics of University of Turku, Finland. His areas of research interests include bank risk governance, bank risk, financial performance, and banking regulation. He is an International Researcher with an academic background from several European countries, research visits to universities in Europe, Australia, and United States, and is actively engaged in research activities in Europe and Australia.

Aineas Mallios is a Lecturer at the School of Business, Economics, and Law at the University of Gothenburg, Sweden. He focuses on industrial organization, law and economics, banking and finance, and the economics of innovation. He teaches industrial organization, corporate finance, risk management, and private equity at the undergraduate and graduate levels.

Egidio Palmieri is a Research Fellow in bank risk management at the University of Udine, Department of Economics and Statistics and Visiting Researcher at Bangor Business School, UK. He deals with risk management in banks and the implications of ESG issues within the financial system.

Maurizio Polato is Full Professor of Banking and Finance at Udine University, Italy. His research fields mainly relate to the securities and exchange industry and bank performance. He is the author of various publications on the topic, which address issues related to the industry's structure, performance, and value measurement for securities trading and regulation.

Francisco Rodríguez-Fernández is Full Professor of Economics at the University of Granada (Spain) Ph.D. in Economics (University of Granada). He is Senior Economist at Funcas and the Funcas Observatory of Financial Digitalization. He has been Consultant and/or Visiting Researcher at the Universities of Modena and Bologna, as well as at the World Bank, the ECB, and the Federal Reserve Bank of Chicago. He has been a leading Researcher in several national and international research projects for the European Commission, the Spanish Ministry of Science and a number of international bodies. He has been also Consultant for financial institutions and payment market participants. He is Vice-President of the International Banking, Economics, and Finance Association. He has published articles in peer-reviewed journals such as the *Review of Economics and Statistics*, *Nature-Scientific Reports*, *European Economic Review*, *Review of Finance*, *Journal of Money*, *Credit and Banking*, *Journal of Corporate Finance*, or *Journal of Banking and Finance*.

Hannu Schadewitz is Professor in Charge of Doctoral Studies in Accounting and Finance subject. His primary areas of research interest include discretionary corporate reporting, international accounting, ESG reporting, and governance. His current research analyzes how accounting quality varies within European Union countries, dynamicity in corporate governance, and its impact on reporting. He is also interested in causes and realizations of ESG in various market regimes. He is a member of the Editorial Boards of CGIR, SUSTAINABILITY, and Highlights of Sustainability. His teaching areas are financial accounting theory and financial reporting. He is also member of the Board, Graduate School of Accounting (GSA).

Maija Šenfelde holds a Doctor degree in Economics (1993). She has been working for Riga Technical University (Latvia) in different positions. Since 2003 Maija Šenfelde is a Professor of Faculty of Engineering Economics and Management, from 1997 to 2007 she was a Deputy Dean for Studies, from 2009 to 2014 she was a Director of Institute of National and Regional Economy, since 2014 she is a Head of Department of Territorial Development Management and Urban Economics. Her main fields for research are macroeconomics, international and regional economics.

She has published scientific papers in peer-reviewed journals and is the author of scientific monographs and study books as well. She is an Expert of Latvian Science Council, Member of Promotion Council, Member of the editorial boards of several scientific journals.

Stefan Sjögren is a Professor in Industrial and Financial Management at the School of Business, Economics, and Law at the University of Gothenburg, Sweden. His research interests are within the corporate finance field covering capital budgeting, international finance, capital structure, and valuation. He also conducts research on regulation, patent valuation, risk capital, and valuation of ideas.

Alexia Ventouri is an Associate Professor (Senior Lecturer) in Banking and Finance at King's Business School. Her research areas include empirical finance and banking, corporate and climate finance, performance, risk, the industrial structure of banking and financial regulation. Her publications appear in internationally recognized journals, such as *British Journal of Management*, the *Journal of Banking and Finance*, *Journal of Business Research*, *Journal of Financial Stability*, and *Journal of Empirical Finance*, among others.

Valeria Venturelli is Associate Professor of Banking and Finance in the Marco Biagi Department of Economics at the University of Modena and Reggio Emilia, Italy. She graduated in Economics from the University of Modena and Reggio Emilia and received a Ph.D. in Financial Markets and Institutions from the Catholic University of Milan, Italy. She has published articles in leading academic journals and contributed chapters to books. Her research interests relate to ESG, bank business model, regulation and supervision, SME financing.

Giulio Velliscig is Adjunct Professor in Tools of Financial Informatics and Research Fellow in the Department of Economics and Statistics of the University of Udine in Italy. He holds a Ph.D. in Managerial and Actuarial Sciences from the same University. His main research interests include banking regulation, bank capital structure, and bond markets.

Jonathan Williams is Professor of Finance and Accounting at Surrey Business School. A banking and finance specialist, he is a Visiting Professor at the University of Turin, the University of Malta, and Zhejiang University of Finance and Economics. He is the Chair of the European Association of Teachers of Banking and Finance (The Wolpertinger

Group), Treasurer of the Financial Markets and Institutions Special Interest Group of BAFA (British Accounting and Finance Association), and a member of the Chartered Banker Institute's Quality and Standards Committee. He has published in leading international journals including the *Journal of Corporate Finance*, *Journal of Banking and Finance*, *Journal of Financial Stability*, and *Regional Studies* among others. He has presented his research at institutions including the World Bank and Deutsche Bundesbank and at conferences and universities in countries across the world. His current research interests include executive compensation and corporate governance, financial deregulation and competitiveness, and fintech.

Gianni Zorzi is Adjunct Professor of Corporate Finance at Ca' Foscari University, Venice. He holds a Ph.D. in Finance from the University of Trieste. His main research interests include credit ratings and credit scoring models, asset management, multinational business finance, as well as risk management for non-financial firms.

LIST OF FIGURES

LIST OF TABLES

CHAPTER 1

Introduction

Santiago Carbó-Valverde and Pedro J. Cuadros-Solas ⓘ

The energy transition and the digital transformation are reshaping how large parts of society live, work, and do business. Financial intermediation, which is at the center of the economic activity of households and companies, represents a key gearwheel of economic growth. Therefore, it is not exempt from the disruptive influence of these two major trends. In particular, the banking industry is facing challenges and opportunities on many fronts, from the pandemic recovery and growing competition from technological companies to the role of banks in the long-term existential threats of climate change and changes to financial infrastructure.

The main objective of this book is to contribute to the banking and finance literature by providing insights into new research topics which are being undertaken in the aftermath of the COVID-19 pandemic. The studies included in the book mainly comprise empirical investigations

S. Carbó-Valverde
University of Valencia, Valencia, Spain
e-mail: santiago.carbo@uv.es

P. J. Cuadros-Solas (✉)
CUNEF Universidad, Madrid, Spain
e-mail: pedro.cuadros@cunef.edu

S. Carbó-Valverde and P. J. Cuadros Solas (eds.), *New Challenges for the Banking Industry*, Palgrave Macmillan Studies in Banking and Financial Institutions, https://doi.org/10.1007/978-3-031-32931-9_1

and cover many major research fields in finance and banking. This book is structured in different chapters covering recent research studies on banking and finance. These chapters are written by a selection of experienced academics from a range of European universities and institutions. All these papers benefited from the discussion during the 2022 Wolpertinger Conference organized by the European Association of University Teachers of Banking and Finance held in September 2022.

Over the last 5 years, the finance literature has focused on the implications of ESG improvements. In this volume, we aim to reflect some of these lines including outstanding papers dealing with interesting issues. The research topics covered in this volume can be structured into different blocks:

- Corporate Governance:
    Effective corporate governance is critical to the proper functioning of the banking sector and the economy as a whole. Banks' safety and soundness are key to financial stability, and how they conduct their business, therefore, is central to economic health. Governance weaknesses at critical credit institutions can result in poor financial intermediation that causes problems across the banking sector and the real economy. Several aspects of corporate governance are covered in the volume. Especially, what is the impact of banks' corporate governance practices on their performance.
- Sustainability and Green Finance:
    Sustainability is important for banks because it helps them mitigate the impacts of climate change. Sustainable banks favor investments in renewable energies and socially responsible businesses over destructive businesses such as fossil fuel companies, helping them fund the future low-carbon economy. In this part of the book, the specific chapter will examine how banks are conducting their green transition.
- Innovation:
    Technological innovation triggers a structural change in all areas of the global economy, and banking is no exception. Digitalization and innovative technologies are creating unprecedented disruption in the banking sector, and the rate of change is accelerating. Unlike what happened in the past, several technologies have all emerged at

the same time (e.g., cloud computing, blockchain, artificial intelligence, biometrics, and/or big data). Banks face crucial decisions as technology shifts customer expectations and changes the regulatory landscape. Digital transformation is not just an option any longer for banks, but a necessity to remain competitive.

The second chapter, after this Introduction, "*Compensation Policy in Banking: The Case of Tournament Incentives Pay Gaps, Incentives, and Bank Performance*", by Fatima Cardias Williams and Jonathan Williams examines the impact of tournament incentives on firm performance. These authors find that high-powered tournament incentives lead to higher levels of firm profitability after controlling for the level of pay and other executive and firm-level characteristics. Their findings are relevant to inform the design of firms' compensation policies. In this sense, these results argue in favor of using vertical pay practices to motivate effort and realize firms' organizational goals.

The third chapter "*The effect of board diversity and ESG engagement on banks' profitability and risk*" by Selena Aureli, Paola Brighi, Muddassar Malik, and Hannu Schadewitz investigates the impact of board diversity on bank performance assuming that board diversity shapes environmental, social, and governance (ESG) engagement. Using data from public commercial banks from OECD countries from 2008 to 2019, they find that board diversity has an impact on bank performance. In general, better board diversification implies greater returns.

In Chapter 4, "*ESG Default Risk Mitigation Effect: A Time-Sectorial Analysis*" by Egidio Palmieri, Enrico Geretto, and Maurizio Polato explores whether ESG pillar scores impact the firms' probability of default on longer time horizons. Using a difference-in-difference regression for 1.991 European-listed companies, the authors confirm the existence of a ESG risk mitigation effect, even for short-medium term probabilities of default. Additionally, they also reveal that environmental score produces a remarkable impact on short-medium term default probabilities, while governance score improvements are consistent in the medium-long run.

Chapter 5, "*Principles of the Optimal Government Regulation in the Financial Market*" by Kristaps Freimanis and Maija Šenfelde reviews the literature on the principles of regulation. The authors identify 12 principles of optimal government regulation, including the recently highlighted topic of climate-related risks. In particular, 68% of sources refer to the following 5 principles: (a) Cost-benefit balanced, (b) Risk-based, (c) Consistency and competitive neutrality, (d) High quality, transparent decision-making, and enforcement, and (e) International coordination, convergence, and implementation in policy and rulemaking.

The next chapter *"Firm Pollution and Reputational Risk: Where Do We Stand?"* by Alexia Ventouri, Georgios Chortareas, and Fangyuan Kou analyzes the links between reputational risk and polluting activities, focusing on the driving factors of corporate reputation risk and CSR. Based on an exploratory analysis of reputational risk in U.S. companies from 2007 to 2019, the authors find a significant association between firm pollution and reputational rating. Moreover, they also find that firms' average reputational risk rating levels are relatively lower for firms with poorer corporate governance and higher financial risk.

Chapter 7 *"Is all that glitters that "green"? An Empirical Investigation of the magnitude of greenwashing in banking and its determinants"* by Gimede Gigante, Priscilla Greggio, and Andrea Cerri investigates the reliability of banks' "green finance" active commitments and their greenwashing behaviors. Using a novel methodology to quantify the magnitude of greenwashing for a cross-country dataset in the period 2016–2020, they find that big and more profitable banks located in advanced economies are more likely to engage in greenwashing and that this behavior has reduced over time. These findings confirm the urgent need for stringent surveillance by a global governing body to check the reliability of banks' sustainable data disclosed.

Chapter 8 "Sovereign Green Bonds in Europe: Are they Effective in Supporting the Green Transition?" by Giuseppina Chesini examines the issuance of sovereign green bonds in Europe. In particular, the research investigates whether sovereign green bonds contribute to the management of climate risks, accelerating the transition to sustainability and carbon neutrality. The author shows that the European sovereign green bond market has increased steadfastly in the last few years. However, there are two main obstacles previously preventing European countries from paving the way in issuing green bonds. First, most sovereign debt legal frameworks do not allow the earmarking of proceeds to specific green projects because of fungibility requirements. Second, there is no uniform green bond standard within the EU, which can prevent growth in the green bond market.

In Chapter 9, *"The Impact of ESG Score and Controversy on Stock Performance"* by Paola Brighi, Antonio Carlo Francesco Della Bina, and

Valeria Venturelli investigates whether a high overall ESG score improves firm value and decreases risk and to what extent ESG controversies may negatively affect a firm's financial performance. Using an extensive international dataset of 7,175 companies from 2002 to 2018, the authors find evidence of an improvement in value and risk associated with a better ESG score. These results underline that higher ESG performance significantly increases market value while decreasing idiosyncratic and total risk.

Chapter 10 *"The digitalization of the European banking industry: some evidence"* by Santiago Carbó, Pedro Cuadros, Cristina Gonnella, and Francisco Rodríguez explores the digital transformation of the European banking industry by focusing on the annual banks' expenses on information technology (IT). Using a representative sample of European banks from 2017 to 2021, the authors find that the ratio of IT expenses to total operating expenses and the ratio of IT expenses to total operating income have increased by 1.02 percentage points (+10.34%) and 0.95 percentage points (+15.82%), respectively. Moreover, they also find that less capitalized, riskier, more profitable, and less efficient, and those banks that exhibit a lower growth of total assets spend more on IT.

Chapter 11 *"The Relation between Patent Pledgeability and Credit Rationing"* by Aineas Mallios, Ted Lindblom, and Stefan Sjögren examines the role of patent-backed loans as a contracting device to reduce credit rationing in loan markets characterized by imperfect information. This chapter provides a theoretical foundation showing how the information asymmetry (adverse selection problem) between borrowing firms and banks can be also solved by offering intangible collateral—patent pledging—in addition to tangible collateral. Their findings suggest that patent pledging can be used to minimize credit rationing, which may lead to more investment in innovation and more growth.

The final chapter *"Increasing the predictive power of financial distress models – the case of the new alert system proposed by the Italian NCCAAE"* by Federico Beltrame, Giulio Velliscig, Gianni Zorzi, and Maurizio Polato develops and tests an alternative alert system to predict firms' financial distress which combines the benefits of the Z-score's multivariate discriminant model and the National Council of Chartered Accountants and Accounting Experts' predictors. Using a sample of 43 viable and 43 non-viable Italian SMEs, the authors compare the predictive accuracy of the mentioned models over the period 2015–2019. They show that the Z-score overperforms the alert system in predicting non-viable firms, whereas the opposite emerged on viable firms. However, the revised versions showed enhanced predictive accuracy.

We hope this collective work contributes to the recent banking literature covering the critical issues of energy transition and digitalization. We also hope the reader enjoys the book as much as those that have contributed.

Acknowledgements The authors wish to thank all the contributors for preparing such interesting chapters for this book. It has been a pleasure to work with an amazing group of respected academics to bring this book to fruition. We could not have produced this book without the editor at Palgrave Macmillan, Ellie Duncan, and the production team headed by Geetha Chockalingam. We also want to thank the Wolpertinger European Association of University Teachers of Banking and Finance, especially Professor Jon Williams, Chair of the Wolpertinger Committee, for trusting us in organizing the 2022 Wolpertinger Conference at CUNEF Universidad (Madrid, Spain).

PART I

Corporate Governance

CHAPTER 2

Compensation Policy in Banking: The Case of Tournament Incentives

Fatima Cardias Williams and Jonathan Williams◉

2.1 An Introduction to Compensation and the Role of Incentives

A famous phrase contends that "it's not how much you pay, but how" (Jensen and Murphy 1991). It stresses the importance of incentives inherent in the structure of executive compensation contracts, which should align the interests of principal (shareholders) and agents (executives). We consider a different incentive, namely tournament incentives, which are created by large pay gaps between the highest paid and others. Tournament theory posits that incentives created by disproportionately large pay gaps motivate effort leading to superior firm performance outcomes. Thus, we examine vertical compensation policy through use of pay gaps in the C-suite of firm executives.

Banking is an appropriate lens through which to examine executive compensation policy given the ire that faulty compensation contracts

F. C. Williams · J. Williams (✉)
Surrey Business School, University of Surrey, Guildford, UK
e-mail: jon.williams@surrey.ac.uk

S. Carbó-Valverde and P. J. Cuadros Solas (eds.), *New Challenges for the Banking Industry*, Palgrave Macmillan Studies in Banking and Financial Institutions, https://doi.org/10.1007/978-3-031-32931-9_2

drew for incentivising excessive risk-taking prior to the Global Financial Crisis (GFC).[1] A frank assessment of compensation policy should consider the evolution of executive pay given the furore over *levels* of pay awarded to bank executives (see Murphy 2013; Edmans et al. 2017). In the 1980s and 1990s, executive pay in the financial services sector caught up with and far exceeded non-financial sector pay as financial firms hired talented individuals to manage increasingly global and complex business models (Malmendier and Tate 2009; Mishel and Davis 2015; Quigley and Hambrick 2015). Relatively quickly, banking evolved into a high-skill-wage industry with corporate boards using compensation policy to encourage executives to exploit new growth opportunities (DeYoung et al. 2013). Boards created larger incentives for executives by increasing the weight of incentive or variable pay. The rationale is the premise that (higher) pay for (better) performance reduces potential agency conflicts by aligning the interests of principal and agents (Murphy 1986; Frydman and Saks 2010; Frydman and Jenter 2010).

Notwithstanding, compensation contracts can incorporate moral hazard. Since shareholders cannot observe the actions of their executives, they can only infer *if* executives took appropriate actions based on realised outcomes, for instance, movements in firms' share prices (Holmstrom 1979). This information asymmetry suggests monitoring costs are prohibitively high leaving executives to shirk and free ride thereby constituting the hidden action or moral hazard (Jensen and Meckling 1976; Gibbons and Murphy 1990). This prospect deals a hard blow to the notion of pay-for-performance that informs compensation policy at many firms.

Our first objective is to classify executives into distinct roles and employ pairwise comparisons to identify developments in executive pay across intervals and between cohorts of banks. Our second objective is to measure the size of pay gaps and compare between cohorts—to

---

[1] Several authors discuss claims that flawed incentives played a causal role in the "excessive" risk-taking which led to the GFC (Brunnermeier 2009; Ellul and Yeramilli 2013; Bolton et al. 2015). Others add managerial power to the list of causal factors (Bebchuk et al. 2010; Bhagat and Bolton 2014), the influence of institutional investors with short-term preferences (Cheng et al. 2015), and bad luck (Fahlenbrach and Stulz 2011; Beltratti and Stulz 2012). Bebchuk and Spamann (2010) caution that allowing bank executives to cash large amounts of equity-based and bonus pay before the long-run consequences of their decisions are realised, creates an incentive for executives to focus on short-term results without redress to the consequences of risk-taking for long-term firm value.

reflect country-level practices in compensation policy—and across time. We construct an indicator we term the "CEO pay gap". For this, we rank executives by pay and measure the pay gap as the pay differential between the highest-ranking executive (normally the CEO) and each individual executive at bank j in time t (Vieito 2012). Our executive-level indicator has advantages over variables like the *payslice*, which measures the CEO's share in the total pay of the leading three (Burns et al. 2017) or five (Bebchuk et al. 2011) highest paid executives.[2]

Our third objective is to establish the impact of vertical pay practices through the effect of pay gaps on firm performance. In doing so, we test the propositions of tournament theory, which contends that tournament incentives induce executives to exert optimal effort because disproportionately large pay gaps create a high-powered incentive to compete for the top prize (becoming CEO) and greater rewards, both monetary and non-monetary, leading to better firm performance (Lazear and Rosen 1981; Rosen 1982, 1986; O'Reilly et al. 1988; Main et al. 1993; Baker et al. 1988; Lambert et al. 1993; Hannan et al. 2008; Connelly et al. 2014). Whereas tournament theory offers a solution to problems associated with contracting and does create incentives, relatively few studies have investigated the impact of tournaments in the C-suite (Kale et al. 2009; Ang et al. 2002)[3] and at banks (Ang et al. 2002; Srivastava and Insch 2007; Burns et al. 2017).[4]

For our purposes, we construct a rich dataset containing the compensation and biographical features of individual executives, which we combine with firm-level accounting and markets data. Our sample contains mostly large, international, and systemically important banks, which are complex

---

[2] The CEO pay slice measures the relative importance of CEOs to other executives in terms of power, abilities, and contribution to the firm. Using a large sample of US public firms, Bebchuk et al. (2011) report a negative association between the pay slice and firm value.

[3] Kale et al. (2009) examine equity-based tournament incentives for CEOs and Vice-Presidents. The relationship between tournament incentives and firm performance increases in intensity when CEOs near retirement, but loses intensity when firms appoint new CEOs or hire outside CEOs. Ang et al. (2002) find US banks operated two tiers of compensation for CEOs and other executives between 1993 and 1996.

[4] Burns et al. (2017) sample over 8,300 firms in 52 countries; using alternative pay slice and pay gap indicators, they find tournaments are associated with greater firm value. Similarly, Srivastava and Insch (2007) support tournament propositions at their sample of 100 US banks.

firms with high coordination requirements requiring executives function as a collaborative unit. We posit that high-powered tournament incentives proxied by the CEO pay gap motivate effort, and we assume effort correlates with collaboration. Thus, tournament incentives lead to improvements in firm performance measured by return on equity (ROE). Hence, our first hypothesis:

> *H1: Tournament incentives created through larger CEO pay gaps lead to superior firm performance.*

Tournaments define a prize that only one winner can win, and the motivating factor is the prospect of greater monetary reward (Rosen 1982, 1986; Main et al. 1993; Conyon and Sadler 2001). Yet, such incentives might not surmount socio-psychological and socio-political factors affecting behaviour. Winner-takes-all outcomes can create perceived injustices that impair collaboration and cause self-serving behaviour; this weakens commitment to organisational goals and retards firm performance (Lazear and Rosen 1981; Rosen 1986; Lazear 1989; Henderson and Fredrickson 2001).[5] Furthermore, tournament incentives might not work in industries with high coordination needs like banks.[6] The prospect that vertical pay policy could adversely impact effort and weaken cooperation leads to hypothesis two:

> *H2: Tournament incentives impair effort and collaboration causing firm performance to deteriorate.*

Our analysis shines a light on how incentives affect the workings of top management teams. We estimate the relationship between ROE and CEO pay gaps to establish the effect of tournament incentives on bank profitability. For this purpose, we employ the System GMM estimator because

---

[5] Should large pay gaps induce effort, a contestant might split their effort between cooperation and self-service. Incentive exists for politicking (Lazear 1989; Milgrom and Roberts 1988) or sabotage if the allocation of prizes depends on contestants' relative performance; the probability of winning is increased by boosting one's own performance or damaging other contestants' (Harbring and Irlenbusch 2011; Chowdhury and Gürtler 2015).

[6] Tournament incentives are reportedly less effective in industries with high coordination needs, such as high-tech firms and banks (Lin et al. 2013).

firms' compensation policy and performance are potentially endogenously determined.

To the best of our knowledge, ours is the first study to quantify pay differentials among C-suite officers in banking and to test the effect of high-powered tournament incentives on bank ROE. In contrast to much of the compensation literature on banks, our analysis extends beyond CEOs to the C-suite of executives (Chava and Purnanandam 2010).

In addition to the CEO pay gap, we construct alternative pay gap indicators. The "inter-rank pay gap" quantifies pay differentials between first and second rank, second and third rank, and third and fourth rank etcetera at bank j in time t. To proxy industry tournament incentives (Coles et al. 2017), namely the effect of higher pay in other firms, we construct the "industry pay gap" by identifying the highest paid executive in the sample for each year and subtracting the pay of executives. Lastly, and based also on industry-wide pay, the "roles pay gap" measures the dispersion between, say the highest-earning Chief Risk Officer in the sample and all other CROs by year.

In preview, our evidence shows that high-powered incentives proxied by the CEO pay gap positively affect bank performance. This result provides insights for practitioners and policymakers interested in the effect that the design of compensation policy can exert on bank performance.

2.2   Executive Pay and Tournament Incentives in Banking

The difficulties in compiling executive-level compensation data for international firms are a challenge we manage to overcome. From BoardEx, we collect the annual pay of executives in the sample firms to construct pay gaps. Our rich dataset comprises over 4,200 executive-year observations from 1999 to 2016 and houses compensation data and biographical information on executives at 68 banks. Over half (57.61%) of the observations cover executives at 34 US banks with fewer (42.39%) on executives at 34 European banks.[7] We categorise the status of C-suite officers where "C" stands for Chief. This is not straightforward. Management hierarchies vary across firms and BoardEx reports nearly 350 director titles as they appear

---

[7] Of the European cohort, 16.66% are British banks (12 banks). The remainder are in France (4), Germany (3), Ireland (2), Italy (5), the Netherlands (2), Spain (3), Sweden (1), and Switzerland (2).

in annual reports. Our status classification identifies thirteen comparable roles: CEO; Deputy CEO; Divisional CEO; President; Vice President; Executive Director (no specific title); Chief Legal Officer (CLO); Chief Administrative Officer (CAO); Chief Risk Officer (CRO); Chief Operating Officer (COO); Chief Financial Officer (CFO); Chair; and Deputy Chair.

Next, we rank the annual total pay of executives within firms and by year. Total pay comprises salary, bonus, equity-linked pay, and deferred compensation. From the ranking, we identify the highest paid executive in each bank observing that the CEO is not always the highest paid. Our dataset contains 181 unique CEOs and 874 CEO-year observations; in roughly 75% of cases, the CEO is the highest paid. In explanation, we find cases when another executive, say the head of an investment banking division, earns more than the CEO does.[8] Also, instances occur when CEOs take a haircut and receive salary only.[9]

We fit a model of pay against status; it specifies year effects and clusters standard errors by firm. Then, we use pairwise comparisons to contrast average pay by status (see upper panel, Table 2.1). The column "Margin" shows average pay while "Groups" identifies whether pay differs significantly by status. CEOs are the highest paid with average pay of $13.4 million followed by the Chief Operating Officer (COO) ($11.6 m) and Divisional CEO ($10.1 m). Margins sharing a letter in the group label are not significantly different at the five per cent level. For example, the letter "F" indicates there is some overlap in the pay of CEOs and COOs. While a significant pay differential exists between CEOs and other C-suite officers, we do not observe significant difference between COOs and Presidents, Vice Presidents, Chief Administrative Officers, Chairs, and Deputy Chairs (letter "D"). We decompose our analysis by interval to capture "pre-crisis", "crisis", and "post-crisis" periods. It shows pay was much higher before the GFC. For instance, the average CEO earned $16.1 million per annum between 1999 and 2006. This figure fell to $11.6 million during the GFC (2007 to 2009) and declined marginally

---

[8] At Barclays, the compensation of Bob Diamond, Head of Barclays Capital, the investment banking division, considerably exceeded CEO John Varley from 2006 to 2008.

[9] Our dataset includes cases when CEOs did not receive equity-related pay during the GFC. For instance, Lloyd Blankfein at Goldman Sachs and Jamie Dimon at JP Morgan and Chase in 2009; Vikram Pandit at Citi in 2009 and 2010 and Brian Moynihan at Bank of America in 2010.

to $10.3 million post-crisis (2010 to 2016). This pattern extends to other C-suite officers and supports claims that before the crisis executive pay was excessive.

We assess banks' corporate governance practices by comparing CEO pay when CEOs perform only the CEO role; CEOs are also Chair or President (duality), and CEOs are also Chair and President (triple titled). Bebchuk et al. (2011) and Song and Wan (2019) claim a CEO is more powerful when performing additional roles and this can cause rent-seeking behaviour and appropriation. We fit a model of pay using our rich data to differentiate banks led by single, dual, and triple-titled CEOs (see Table 2.2). The upper panel shows average pay for sole, dual, and triple-titled bank CEOs; the middle and lower panels show contrasts in pay and T-statistics from the null hypothesis that contrasts between pairs are equal to zero. Table 2.2 shows average pay across time and three intervals. While dual and triple-titled CEOs receive significantly higher pay than sole CEOs, the magnitude of the contrasts declines over time. Whereas the sole CEO earns more post-crisis ($7.4 m $c.f.$ $5.7 m), dual and triple CEOs earn substantially less ($10.5 m $c.f.$ $21.7 m for dual; $13.1 m $c.f.$ $20.8 m for triple). One might reasonably deduce that corporate governance has improved in terms of a reduction in CEO power.

Table 2.3 shows pay across cohorts of banks and intervals. The three cohorts are EU (European Union) banks, US banks, and GSIBs (Global Systemically Important Banks).[10,11] It shows a much higher level of average pay at GSIBs; the average GSIB executive earned $13 million per annum between 1999 and 2016, exceeding average pay at US banks ($6.5 m) and European banks ($2.1 m) by significant margins ($6.6 m and $10.9 m, respectively). The inter-temporal analysis affirms findings in Table 2.1 that average pay was higher pre-GFC; whereas pay did rebound

[10] The GSIB sub-sample includes 24 (of 30 as at November 2015) banks. Sixteen GSIBs have headquarters in Europe, eight in the US (with three in Japan and one in China). On average in 2015, the balance sheet total of a GSIB was around €1,392,060 million with the largest banks around €2.0 trillion (HSBC and Barclays in the UK; BNP Paribas and Crédit Agricole in France; JPMorgan Chase and Bank of America in the US; and Deutsche Bank in Germany). Statistics help to illustrate the complexity of the GSIBs, which, on average in 2015 have 90 shareholders and 2,084 subsidiaries.

[11] Previously, the Bank of England and the IMF had identified 16 Large Complex Financial Institutions (LCFIs) (Herring and Carmassi 2010). We include in our sample of GSIBs some former LCFIs that failed or were taken over following the crisis, for example, Lehman Brothers, Merrill Lynch, and ABN AMRO.

Table 2.1 Total pay, $; by executive status and interval

Status	1999–2016 Margin	Groups	1999–2006 Margin	Groups	2007–2009 Margin	Groups	2010–2016 Margin	Groups
CEO	13,400,000	F	16,100,000	E	11,600,000	F	10,300,000	F
Deputy CEO	3,788,323	A	5,647,171	AB	1,842,537	A	2,261,222	A
Divisional CEO	10,100,000	E	12,900,000	CDE	7,170,784	DE	8,156,218	DEF
President	7,839,426	CDE	7,667,859	BC	8,654,101	CDEF	7,174,190	CDEF
Vice President	6,632,022	ABCDE	8,102,153	BCD	4,943,910	ABCD	5,156,180	ABCDE
Executive	3,626,000	A	4,090,584	A	2,503,106	AB	7,725,836	ABCDEF
Chief Legal Officer	4,388,115	A	5,164,618	AB	4,897,184	BCD	2,911,543	AB
Chief Admin Officer	6,552,540	ABCDE	8,318,551	ABCDE	5,615,666	CD	3,947,181	ABC
Chief Risk Officer	5,034,701	AB	5,057,118	AB	4,063,522	ABC	4,421,616	BC
Chief Finance Officer	6,455,824	BC	6,195,094	AB	6,491,532	CD	6,194,059	CD
Chief Operating Officer	11,600,000	DEF	14,100,000	DE	9,268,975	ABCDEF	8,880,691	EF
Chair	6,320,144	ABCD	6,561,536	AB	10,200,000	ABCDEF	3,996,980	ABC
Deputy Chair	8,529,307	BCDE	7,110,755	AB	10,300,000	EF	11,200,000	BCDEF

This Table presents results from the model: Total Pay$_{ijt}$ = α_0 + β_kStatus$_{ijt}$ + η + ε_{ijt} where Status$_{ijt}$ is a vector of k binary indicators of the status of executive i in firm j at time t; η are year effects. "Margin" reports average pay. "Groups" shows results from pairwise comparisons. There are six groups in total from A, lowest amount of total pay, to F, highest amount of pay. Margins with the same letter are not significantly different at the 95% interval. For instance, pay across CEOs are not significantly different. However, there is overlap in pay between some CEOs and some Chief Operating Officers (Group F) with pay of other COOs belonging to groups D and E, which has some overlap with pay for other roles

Table 2.2 Total pay, $; by CEO status and interval

	1999–2016	1999–2006	2007–2009	2010–2016
Margin				
Non-CEO executives	7,208,078	7,858,741	6,281,116	6,731,337
CEO sole	6,417,208	5,746,357	6,705,577	7,361,544
Duality	16,900,000	21,700,000	14,200,000	10,500,000
Triple	16,400,000	20,800,000	13,200,000	13,100,000
Contrast				
Sole v Non-CEO	−790,870	−2,112,383	424,461	630,206
Dual v Non-CEO	9,721,417	13,800,000	7,897,179	3,801,981
Triple v Non-CEO	9,187,147	12,900,000	6,954,597	6,416,966
Dual v Sole	10,500,000	16,000,000	7,472,718	3,171,774
Triple v Sole	9,978,017	15,000,000	6,530,137	5,786,760
Triple v Dual	−534,270	−918,666	−942,582	2,614,985
***T*-statistic**				
Sole v Non-CEO	−0.64	−1.63	0.32	0.36
Dual v Non-CEO	3.97	3.23	3.54	2.76
Triple v Non-CEO	4.98	3.81	2.67	3.85
Dual v Sole	3.76	3.42	2.55	1.22
Triple v Sole	4.26	3.89	2.16	2.41
Triple v Dual	−0.16	−0.16	−0.25	0.97

The upper section presents results from the model: Total Pay$_{ijt} = \alpha_0 + \beta_k \text{CEO}_{ijt} + \eta + \varepsilon_{ijt}$ where CEO_{ijt} is a vector of k binary indicators classifying if a CEO i in firm j at time t is single titled, dual titled, or triple titled; η are year effects. "Margin" reports average pay. The middle and lower sections show contrasts in average pay and T-statistics to test the null that a contrast is equal to zero

post-crisis at European banks, it did not do so at US banks and GSIBs though their pay levels remained significantly higher than that paid by European banks.

After ranking pay by firm and year to construct the CEO pay gap, we perform pairwise comparisons. To deepen our analysis, we decompose the sample into EU and US banks that are not GSIBs, and EU and US which are GSIBs. This enables a more precise assessment of pay practices. Table 2.4 shows the results. For the full period, the average CEO pay gap is considerably larger at US GSIBs ($21.1 m) and smallest at EU non-GSIBs ($1.9 m). Across intervals, the pay gap at US non-GSIBs and GSIBs is larger than at European counterparts. However, the pay gap for US GSIBs decreases substantially over time (from $31.3 m in 1999 to 2006, to $9.2 m in 2010 to 2016), and we observe a similar trend at

Table 2.3 Total pay, $; by cohort and interval

Cohort	1999–2016	1999–2006	2007–2009	2010–2016
EU Banks	2,138,712	2,236,568	1,877,932	2,138,980
US Banks	6,456,043	7,695,314	5,320,040	5,193,580
GSIBs	13,000,000	14,700,000	12,100,000	11,100,000
Contrast				
GSIBs v EU	10,900,000	12,500,000	10,200,000	8,928,569
US v EU	4,317,331	5,458,746	3,442,108	3,054,600
US v GSIBs	−6,561,181	−7,040,992	−6,744,840	−5,873,969
T-statistic				
GSIBs v EU	16.1	10.64	10.41	12.05
US v EU	6.33	4.61	3.5	4.07
US v GSIBs	−12.51	−7.34	−8.35	−11.96

The upper section presents results from the model: Total Pay$_{ijt} = \alpha_0 + \beta_k \text{Bank}_{jt} + \eta + \varepsilon_{ijt}$ where Bank$_{ijt}$ is a vector of k binary indicators that identifies if firm j at time t is EU, US, or GSIB; η are year effects. "Margin" reports average pay. The middle and lower sections show contrasts in average pay and T-statistics to test the null that a contrast is equal to zero

US non-GSIBs. In contrast, pay gaps appear more consistent at European banks, which are reflected in the decreasing magnitude of contrasts between US and European cohorts. However, the contrasts between each group remain significant in post-crisis.

2.3   DATA AND SUMMARY STATISTICS

Our data sources are BoardEx for executive pay and biographical information, Orbis Bank Focus for bank financial statements, and Eikon for market-based data. Internet searches were used to locate missing data on biographical characteristics. Our dataset houses information on 971 unique executives at 68 banks giving 4,203 executive-year observations. The panel is unbalanced due to firm failure and merger and acquisition activity. All values are denominated in US dollars at 2013 prices.

In our model of the effect of tournament incentives on firm performance, we select return on equity (ROE) to proxy performance because it indicates returns to bank shareholders. Since ROE is an accounting-based measure, and for robustness, we re-estimate models using annual average share returns as the dependent variable. Table 2.5 reports the results of pairwise comparisons by ROE. It shows a pre-crisis strong performance with mean ROE exceeding 20% for each cohort although

Table 2.4 CEO pay gap, $; by cohort and interval

	1999–2016	1999–2006	2007–2009	2010–2016
Margin				
EU non-GSIB	1,949,697	1,904,085	2,385,240	1,592,038
US non-GSIB	7,882,863	9,382,434	6,801,270	6,192,022
EU GSIB	5,762,274	5,668,739	7,177,184	5,069,005
US GSIB	21,100,000	31,300,000	17,900,000	9,160,756
Contrast				
US non v EU non	5,933,167	7,478,349	4,416,030	4,599,984
EU GSIB v EU non	3,812,577	3,764,654	4,791,944	3,476,967
US GSIB v EU non	19,100,000	29,400,000	15,500,000	7,568,717
EU GSIB v US non	−2,120,589	−3,713,695	375,914	−1,123,017
US GSIB v US non	13,200,000	21,900,000	11,100,000	2,968,733
US GSIB v EU GSIB	15,300,000	25,600,000	10,700,000	4,091,751
T-statistic				
US non v EU non	5.28	3.72	3.79	6.81
EU GSIB v EU non	3.02	1.67	3.6	4.66
US GSIB v EU non	15.01	12.59	11.26	10.38
EU GSIB v US non	−2.05	−1.94	0.32	−2.08
US GSIB v US non	12.56	10.94	9.12	5.77
US GSIB v EU GSIB	12.78	11.38	7.79	6.77

The upper section presents results from the model: CEO Pay Gap$_{ijt}$ = α_0 + β_kBank$_{jt}$ + η + ε_{ijt} where Bank$_{ijt}$ is a vector of k binary indicators that identifies if firm j at time t is EU non-GSIB, US non-GSIB, EU GSIB, or US GSIB; η are year effects. "Margin" reports average pay. The middle and lower sections show the contrasts and the T-statistics to test the null that a contrast is equal to zero

in terms of significance only the ROE at GSIBs is larger. Table 2.5 documents the collapse in ROE in the GFC. During this interval, the variation in performance across cohorts increases as evidenced by the significance of the contrasts. Post-crisis ROE deteriorates at European non-GSIBs and European GSIBs. In contrast, profitability rebounds for US banks and US GSIBs although remaining considerably below pre-crisis levels. Table 2.6 repeats the analysis for stock market returns. It confirms the impact of the GFC and the continuing post-crisis distress of European banks.

Table 2.5   ROE, %; by cohort and interval

	1999–2016	1999–2006	2007–2009	2010–2016
Margin				
EU non-GSIB	12.17	20.38	3.35	0.80
US non-GSIB	13.21	20.92	−2.60	10.08
EU GSIB	14.79	21.01	9.89	7.00
US GSIB	15.67	22.99	5.04	10.76
Contrast				
US non v EU non	1.04	0.54	−5.96	9.28
EU GSIB v EU non	2.62	0.63	6.54	6.20
US GSIB v EU non	3.50	2.61	1.69	9.96
EU GSIB v US non	1.58	0.09	12.49	−3.09
US GSIB v US non	2.46	2.07	7.64	0.68
US GSIB v EU GSIB	0.88	1.98	−4.85	3.77
T-statistic				
US non v EU non	1.48	1.12	−2.24	10.58
EU GSIB v EU non	3.36	1.19	2.20	6.44
US GSIB v EU non	4.32	4.63	0.54	10.33
EU GSIB v US non	2.38	0.20	4.80	−4.04
US GSIB v US non	3.52	4.13	2.74	0.89
US GSIB v EU GSIB	1.14	3.61	−1.57	4.37

The upper section presents results from the model: $\text{ROE}_{jt} = \alpha_0 + \beta_k \text{Bank}_{jt} + \eta + \varepsilon_{ijt}$ where Bank_{ijt} is a vector of k binary indicators that identifies if firm j at time t is EU non-GSIB, US non-GSIB, EU GSIB, or US GSIB and η are year effects. "Margin" reports average ROE. The middle and lower sections show the contrasts and the T-statistics to test the null that a contrast is equal to zero

We select variables to explain variation in ROE from the compensation and banking literatures. Since our main objective is to determine the relationship between ROE and tournament incentives, the covariate of most interest is the pay gap indicator. To gauge the impact of tournament incentives, in separate regressions we control for the effects of the *level* of executives *Total Pay*, incentives arising from executives' holdings of *Inside Debt*, and an estimated measure of *Excess Pay* reflecting claims of excesses. Holdings of inside debt constitute typically unfunded and unsecured claims on the firm and imply holders (executives) face default risk like outside creditors do. To reduce possible agency costs of debt, Jensen and Meckling (1976) advocate an optimal incentive structure whereby executives' personal holdings of their bank's debt and equity occur in

Table 2.6 Share price returns, %; by cohort and interval

	1999–2016	1999–2006	2007–2009	2010–2016
Margin				
EU non-GSIB	−8.00	4.23	−42.77	−8.37
US non-GSIB	0.53	8.43	−46.81	14.99
EU GSIB	−1.21	7.11	−19.18	−4.97
US GSIB	3.68	10.86	−32.46	11.06
Contrast				
US non v EU non	8.53	4.20	−4.04	23.36
EU GSIB v EU non	6.79	2.88	23.58	3.40
US GSIB v EU non	11.68	6.63	10.31	19.43
EU GSIB v US non	−1.74	−1.32	27.62	−19.96
US GSIB v US non	3.15	2.43	14.35	−3.92
US GSIB v EU GSIB	4.89	3.75	−13.27	16.04
T-statistic				
US non v EU non	5.00	3.07	−0.68	8.69
EU GSIB v EU non	3.60	1.91	3.57	1.15
US GSIB v EU non	5.96	4.13	1.48	6.57
EU GSIB v US non	−1.08	−0.99	4.78	−8.54
US GSIB v US non	1.86	1.69	2.31	−1.67
US GSIB v EU GSIB	2.60	2.39	−1.93	6.06

The upper section presents results from the model: $\text{Returns}_{jt} = \alpha_0 + \beta_k \text{Bank}_{jt} + \eta + \varepsilon_{ijt}$ where Bank_{ijt} is a vector of k binary indicators that identifies if firm j at time t is EU non-GSIB, US non-GSIB, EU GSIB, or US GSIB and η are year effects. "Margin" reports average share price returns. The middle and lower sections show the contrasts and the T-statistics to test the null that a contrast is equal to zero

a ratio that mirrors the bank's overall external capital structure. Wei and Yermack (2011) introduced the relative incentive ratio that measures how a unit change in firm value increases the value of executives inside debt versus equity claims, scaled by a similar measure of how the same unit rise in firm value would lead to changes in firms' external debt versus external equity claims (see the k indicator of Edmans and Liu 2011). A ratio greater (lower) than unity suggests executives would follow conservative (riskier) strategies in favour of debt (equity) holders. Tung and Wang (2012) compute the relative incentive ratios of CEOs at US bank holding companies pre-GFC; banks run by CEOs with greater inside debt were less exposed to risk and consequently reported higher stock market returns during the GFC. We follow Core et al. (2008) and measure excess pay as the difference between actual total pay and predicted total pay where the latter is estimated from a regression of total pay on tenure, bank size, the ratio of book-to-market equity,[12] return on assets, and fixed time effects. The correlation coefficient between total pay and excess pay is 0.4478 and significant at the one per cent level.

We account for executive-level characteristics because of compelling evidence of the benefits of heterogeneity in top management teams at complex firms (Hambrick and Mason 1984; Pitcher and Smith 2001). Whereas *Tenure* (years in firm) can proxy entrenchment, it could also signal human capital and salient firm-specific knowledge. We use a binary variable to indicate the year of a *New CEO* appointment. It equals unity for all bank executives in the year of a new appointee, zero otherwise. New appointments can result from retirements and/or effective dismissal. Thus, the first year of a new broom could affect firm performance in either direction because of changes in the composition and relationships within leadership teams.

Our covariates include a vector of bank-level indicators. *Bank Size* is the log of total assets plus off-balance-sheets and is proxy for complexity. Talented individuals are likelier to self-select to work at larger; complex firms that offer generous remuneration. While this scenario implies a positive relation between size and performance, we note consolidation is associated with larger banks losing competitive zeal (Boyd and De Nicolo 2005). Although successful banks survive and grow market share, the empirical record is ambiguous on whether larger banks are more efficient (Stiroh and Strahan 2003). Two indicators proxy banks' business models. Bank boards had encouraged CEOs to pursue new growth opportunities like securitisation that arose from financial deregulation (DeYoung et al. 2013). While such actions can create value, a greater exposure to more volatile activities may offset any gains and reduce risk-adjusted bank performance (Stiroh 2006; Stiroh and Rumble 2006; LePetit et al. 2008). *Loan intensity* is measured by the ratio of net loans-to-total assets, and *Non-core funding* captures the proportion of liabilities considered more volatile (compared to customer deposits). Indeed, the GFC episode witnessed distress at banks engaged in funding long-dated assets with short-term funds, which caused a liquidity crunch. To proxy the *risk*

---

[12] Book-to-market is constructed as the ratio of the book value of firms' total assets-to-the book value of liabilities plus the market value of equity.

intensity of banks', we specify the proportion of risk weighted assets-to-total assets with higher values signalling greater risk and vice-versa. We use the ratio of loan loss reserves-to-total assets to measure asset quality and the net interest margin to proxy value added.

Anderson et al. (2011) note the association between how diverse a board is and how complex a firm is. While complex factors of cognition, culture, and risk-taking attitudes influence boardroom composition, limited empirical evidence exists on how board diversity affects firm performance. *A priori* heterogeneity enhances a board's functional ability, such as its ability to engage in complex problem solving, decision-making, and management monitoring (Forbes and Milliken 1999). However, board diversity could increase decision-making costs and raise the likelihood of conflicts between members.

Since the effects of diversity on firm performance are unclear (Adams et al. 2015), our board diversity variables also signal on banks' corporate governance structures. We specify *Board size* based on findings that very small or very large boards are more effective. While small boards can minimise coordination problems and monitor managers more effectively, large complex firms benefit from a higher number of members as advisors, which infers a convex relationship between firm performance and board size (Yermack 1996; Jensen 1993; Bhagat and Black 1999; Coles et al. 2008). As good governance practice implies greater board independence, we specify *Board monitoring* as the ratio of supervisory directors-to-executive directors. A larger proportion of outside directors could improve the monitoring of executives on behalf of shareholders (John and Senbet 1998). While outside directors bring additional skills and experience, contributing towards more effective decision-making, independent boards have been associated with weaker firm performance and less risk-taking at banks (Pathan 2009; Pathan and Faff 2013), and as having no effect on risk-taking during the GFC (Erkens et al. 2012).

Anderson et al. (2011) consider boards' social and occupational diversity. Social diversity encompasses gender, ethnicity, and age. We specify *Gender* as the ratio of the number of female directors-to-board size. Standard arguments view males as prone to overconfidence and aggressive behaviour rendering them less risk-averse and less conservative. Indeed, the likelihood of small bank default in the US during the GFC was lower when the CEO or chair was female (Palvia et al. 2015). However, Adams and Funk (2012) and Berger et al. (2014) find female aversion to risk dissipates and increases if more females sit on boards when females access male-dominated environments, like banking. Our proxy indicator of diversity is the ratio of foreign directors-to-board size. Studies report an inter-generational impact that culturally inherited attitudes towards risk and uncertainty exert over behaviour and economic outcomes like firm performance (Guiso et al. 2006; Pan et al. 2017). *Experience* is the number of boards directors have sat on to date-to-board size. Our motivation is to proxy experiences gleaned away from the firm while acknowledging that too much outside experience could indicate busy boards leading to unintended consequences for firm performance. Lastly, we calculate *Age* as the coefficient of variation of executive's ages. Age helps to shape an executive's strategic actions that affect firm performance. While knowledge and experience increase with age, mature executives are more risk-averse (Rhodes 1983; Lewellen et al. 1987; MacCrimmon and Wehrung 1990). In contrast, younger executives face larger incentives to increase job security by taking on riskier activities, which could jeopardise firm performance (Nguyen et al. 2015).

Table 2.7 provides descriptive statistics while Appendix A offers a detailed description of the variables.

2.4   METHODOLOGY FOR ESTIMATING THE EFFECT OF CEO PAY GAPS ON BANK PERFORMANCE

Potentially, some unobserved time-varying omitted variables jointly affect firms' performance and compensation policy (Kale et al. 2009). The relation can be dynamically endogenous with causation running in both directions, which implies that past performance determines current compensation policy and performance. Dynamic endogeneity can arise in two ways in our setting. First, a highly profitable bank with low default probability sets high-powered incentives to motivate executives, maintain, and attract talent implying a positive association between firm performance and pay gap. Second, a firm's culture determines both how it structures a tournament and the attitudes of executives towards effort; each affects performance (Burns et al. 2017). *A priori* high-powered incentives can be motivational or may induce behaviour antagonistic of firms' goals. The relationship between performance and incentives can follow either direction; it is dynamic as past performance proxies' unobserved culture, which influences compensation policy and future performance.

Table 2.7   Descriptive statistics: Covariates in pay gap regressions

Variable	N	Mean	Std dev	Lower quartile	Median	Upper quartile	CV
Total pay, $ m	3952	8.496	15.500	1.840	4.319	9.751	1.83
Inside debt	2733	0.88	27.06	−0.05	0.00	0.13	30.78
Excess pay	3930	0.01	0.99	−0.53	0.03	0.58	195.15
Tenure, years	4188	10.75	9.68	3.60	7.80	14.80	0.90
New CEO	4188	0.14	0.34	0.00	0.00	0.00	2.53
Bank size $ b	4166	935	1,179	150	508	1,174	1.26
Loans-to-assets, %	4166	49.95	21.90	37.68	55.15	66.96	0.44
Non-core deposits, %	4166	40.78	25.61	20.53	36.66	55.78	0.63
RWA-to-TA, %	3806	61.13	23.11	44.17	60.12	80.52	0.38
LLT-to-TA, %	4018	1.01	0.96	0.47	0.86	1.26	0.96
NIM, %	4166	2.28	1.20	1.21	2.27	3.19	0.53
Board size, #	4188	18.13	4.85	15.00	18.00	21.00	0.27
SD-to-ED, ratio	4188	2.62	1.85	1.71	2.33	2.86	0.71
Gender diversity	4186	0.13	0.08	0.07	0.13	0.19	0.62
Diversity, %	4182	0.08	0.11	0.00	0.05	0.13	1.34
Experience, %	4188	8.55	3.69	6.18	7.88	9.93	0.43
Age—CV	4184	0.13	0.04	0.11	0.13	0.15	0.28

We use the two-step System GMM estimator to account for potential endogeneity through use of instruments. Whereas difference GMM corrects endogeneity by transforming regressors through differencing (Arellano and Bond 1991) system, GMM corrects endogeneity by introducing more instruments to improve efficiency and transforming the instruments to make them uncorrelated (exogenous) with the fixed effects (Arellano and Bover 1995; Blundell and Bond 1998). The system includes a first equation in levels with first differences as instruments, and a second equation in first differences with levels as instruments. System GMM is a dynamic estimator; it controls for endogeneity of the lagged dependent variable, omitted variable bias, observed panel heterogeneity, and measurement errors. Specifying lag(s) of firm performance as covariate(s) captures the effects of possible dynamic endogeneity. If previous performance affects performance positively, then past levels of performance constitute a basis for future strategic choices on compensation policy. An advantage of system GMM is it draws instruments from within the panel dataset. We use orthogonal deviations that subtract the average of all future available observations of a variable to minimise data loss, appropriate for unbalanced panels.

We specify our model as $Y_{jt} = \alpha Y_{jt-1} + \beta X1_{ijt} + \gamma X2_{jt} + \theta_t + \mu_i + \epsilon_{ijt}$. Y is bank performance (RoE); $X1$ the CEO pay gap; $X2$ a vector of covariates described in Sect. 2.3; θ a vector of year effects; μ_i unobserved bank-specific time-invariant effect that allows for heterogeneity in the means of the Y_{jt} series across banks; and ε_{jit} a disturbance term that is independent across executives within banks. We treat compensation policy (pay gap), total pay, inside debt, excess pay, tenure, and bank-level indicators as endogenous variables and other covariates exogenous. The Windmeijer adjustment corrects standard errors for downward bias.

We apply Arellano and Bond diagnostic tests to check for autocorrelation of the error term. We test the null that the differenced error term is first order and second order serially correlated. Failure to reject the null of no second-order serial correlation implies that the original error term is serially uncorrelated, and the moment conditions are correctly specified. The Hansen test for over-identification tests the null hypothesis of the overall validity of the instruments used; failure to reject the null implies supports for the choice of instruments.

2.5   Results on the Relationship Between Tournament Incentives and Bank Performance

Our estimates of the effects on banks' ROE of CEO pay gaps is obtained using System GMM. The tests reported at the foot of the tables show our models are correctly specified and not subject to second-order serial correlation (In some cases, we specify a second-order lag of the dependent variable to satisfy the condition). In addition, Hansen test statistics lie in the appropriate range, and we reject the null at the five per cent level (except in two instances).

Table 2.8 shows the estimated relationship between ROE and CEO pay gap for all banks across 1999 to 2016. Our estimates of the effect of the CEO pay gap control for the level of *total pay* (column 1), *inside debt* (column 2), *total pay* and *inside debt* (column 3), and *excess pay* (column 4). In each specification, the CEO pay gap is economically meaningful and statistically significant at one per cent (except column three at five per cent). We observe that tenure positively affects ROE (at 10%) in two of four models. In comparison, ROE is significantly lower in years when new CEOs accede, banks' asset quality is poorer, and boards are larger whereas

ROE is significantly higher when net interest margins are wider. Table 2.8 provides compelling support for claims that CEO pay gaps create superior firm performance outcomes leading us to accept hypothesis 1.

We construct alternative pay gap indicators and report results in Table 2.9 and Tables 2.12 and 2.13. Table 2.9 shows the estimated relationship between ROE and the Inter-rank pay gap, which measures rank-order pay differentials, first minus second, second minus third. It creates an incentive to expend effort to accede to the next highest-ranking position. Alternatively, if the gaps between status are large, it might induce feelings of deprivation leading to reduced effort and adverse effects on firm performance. Table 2.9 shows the Inter-rank pay gap positively and significantly impacts ROE in two models (at 10%). Although supporting using tournament incentives between executive levels, we caution that the evidence is not as robust as for CEO pay gaps.

We construct two industry-level pay gap indicators. The industry-pay gap measures the differential between the highest paid in the sample and others by year (Table 2.12). The industry roles pay gap measures the differences between, for example, the highest-ranking Chief Risk Officer and other CROs by year (Table 2.13). The results reveal a positive and economically meaningful relationship between the industry pay gap and ROE in two models (significant at 10 and 5%), which further supports arguments favouring tournament incentives. Pay differences between roles do not affect firm profitability.

We examine cohorts of European (EU) banks, US banks, and GSIBs (Samples of European and US banks include their respective GSIBs). The GSIB cohort of large, complex, and geographically diversified banking firms includes some of the world's largest banks; the Financial Stability Board classifies 24 sample banks as Global Systemically Important Banks. The decomposition let us assess whether compensation policy affects firm performance differently across jurisdictions. Evidence reported elsewhere shows compensation practices differ between executives at US and European firms; US firms pay more and make greater use of incentive pay compared to Europeans (Conyon et al. 2011; Fernandes et al. 2013).

Table 2.10 shows the effects of tournament incentives on ROE are consistent geographically although their relative importance varies. Incentives exert a much greater effect on profitability at US banks; the relationship between the ROE and CEO pay gap is economically meaningful (1.330) and very highly significant (at 1%, see column 2). Although the economic importance of pay gaps is not as marked at EU banks

Table 2.8 Estimated relationship between ROE and CEO pay gap; all banks—1999–2016

	(1)	(2)	(3)	(4)
ROE_{t-1}	0.411***	0.366***	0.330***	0.484***
	(6.72)	(5.01)	(4.33)	(7.36)
ROE_{t-2}	–	–	–	0.033
	–	–	–	(0.59)
CEO pay gap	1.119***	1.352***	0.894**	1.873***
	(3.63)	(4.21)	(2.30)	(4.46)
Total pay	−0.00389	–	1.723	–
	(−0.00)	–	(1.46)	–
Inside debt	–	0.226	0.246	–
	–	(1.36)	(1.54)	–
Excess pay	–	–	–	−3.006***
	–	–	–	(−3.14)
Tenure	0.162	0.681*	0.667*	−0.182
	(0.44)	(1.94)	(1.81)	(−0.44)
New CEO	−2.347***	−2.337***	−2.105***	−2.893***
	(−3.30)	(−3.35)	(−2.94)	(−3.33)
Bank size	0.392	1.074*	0.540	0.216
	(0.70)	(1.67)	(0.81)	(0.34)
Loan intensity	−0.0133	0.0421	0.0539	−0.0421
	(−0.19)	(0.67)	(0.75)	(−0.61)
Non-core funding	0.0810	0.0102	0.0308	0.0900
	(1.39)	(0.20)	(0.54)	(1.39)
Risk intensity	0.0184	−0.0500	−0.0695	0.0409
	(0.38)	(−0.81)	(−1.20)	(0.77)
Asset quality	−4.155***	−4.201***	−4.524***	−3.467***
	(−3.71)	(−2.92)	(−2.96)	(−2.87)
Net interest margin	2.186**	2.409**	2.624**	1.980**
	(2.25)	(2.37)	(2.19)	(2.00)
Board Size	−3.963**	−5.041**	−4.096**	−6.794***
	(−2.20)	(−2.56)	(−1.99)	(−3.14)
Board monitoring	−2.126**	−1.519	−1.815	−2.341*
	(−2.09)	(−1.17)	(−1.25)	(−1.95)
Gender diversity	−6.262	−3.042	−3.552	0.0272
	(−1.43)	(−0.78)	(−0.89)	(0.01)
Diversity	−3.029	−5.635	−5.178	−5.019
	(−0.94)	(−1.44)	(−1.22)	(−1.54)

(continued)

Table 2.8 (continued)

	(1)	(2)	(3)	(4)
Board experience	0.127	0.0939	0.0659	0.138
	(0.95)	(0.59)	(0.40)	(0.965)
Age CV	9.894	8.649	3.742	5.271
	(1.03)	(0.74)	(0.31)	(0.46)
Intercept	0	0	−30.30*	−6.973
	(.)	(.)	(−1.96)	(−0.73)
Year FE	*Yes*	*Yes*	*Yes*	*Yes*
N	2052	1877	1877	1510
2nd order auto	0.146	0.105	0.113	0.126
Instruments, #	146	76	79	103
Hansen test	0.155	0.224	0.121	0.151

t statistics in parentheses
$^{*}p < 0.10$, $^{**}p < 0.05$, $^{***}p < 0.01$

(0.692, column 1) and GSIBs (0.718, column 3), the effects of tournament incentives on ROE are statistically important (at 5 and 10% levels, respectively). Referencing Sect. 2.2, the use of tournament incentives and effectiveness of pay gaps is greater at US banks. Our general result, however, affirms the positive association between tournament incentives and bank profitability and justifies the acceptance our first hypothesis.

The dynamic nature of bank performance is confirmed by the significant lagged dependent variable (ROE_{t-1}) for cohorts of EU banks and GSIBs. The covariates reveal some interesting insights on factors affecting bank profitability though findings do not necessarily generalise across cohorts. *Tenure*, for example, adversely influences ROE at EU banks (−0.808 at 10%) while exerting an economically meaningful effect (1.562 at 1%) at US banks. Whereas the EU result implies a detrimental impact of entrenchment, the US result suggests a human capital perspective of service. The economically meaningful and very highly significant relation between ROE and *New CEO* shows ROE deteriorates in years of new CEO appointments (bar US banks albeit economically important). Further research is required on the impact of changes in CEO on tournament incentives.

Of the bank-level variables, our findings show larger (*bank size*) EU and US banks and EU and US banks with wider *net interest margins* are more profitable while EU and US banks experiencing weaker *asset quality*

Table 2.9 Estimated relationship between ROE and inter-rank pay gap; all banks—1999–2016

	(1)	(2)	(3)	(4)
ROE_{t-1}	0.420***	0.348***	0.306***	0.431***
	(6.76)	(4.72)	(4.04)	(5.75)
ROE_{t-2}	–	–	–	0.0789
	–	–	–	(1.36)
Inter-rank pay gap	0.0653	0.167*	0.0706	0.214*
	(0.92)	(1.87)	(0.73)	(1.86)
Total pay	0.549	–	2.036**	–
	(0.73)	–	(1.98)	–
Inside debt	–	0.225	0.272	–
	–	(1.24)	(1.59)	–
Excess pay	–	–	–	−3.076***
	–	–	–	(−2.91)
Tenure	0.270	0.835**	0.787**	−0.246
	(0.76)	(2.34)	(2.07)	(−0.59)
New CEO	−2.684***	−2.539***	−2.312***	−3.967***
	(−3.67)	(−3.78)	(−3.24)	(−4.91)
Bank size	0.401	1.404**	0.784	0.420
	(0.73)	(2.37)	(1.29)	(0.68)
Loan intensity	−0.0310	0.0128	0.0372	−0.179**
	(−0.52)	(0.20)	(0.53)	(−2.16)
Non-core funding	0.101	0.00244	0.0257	0.0382
	(1.53)	(0.04)	(0.44)	(0.57)
Risk intensity	0.0458	−0.0281	−0.0604	0.0334
	(0.94)	(−0.43)	(−1.06)	(0.59)
Asset quality	−4.227***	−4.786***	−4.993***	−5.734***
	(−3.70)	(−3.29)	(−3.36)	(−3.04)
Net interest margin	2.903***	3.739***	3.598***	4.287***
	(2.89)	(3.51)	(2.85)	(4.06)
Board Size	−3.282*	−4.687**	−4.297**	−5.447**
	(−1.77)	(−2.50)	(−2.11)	(−2.28)
Board monitoring	−2.605**	−1.882	−1.904	−3.794***
	(−2.54)	(−1.46)	(−1.34)	(−3.29)
Gender diversity	−5.770	−2.370	−4.027	0.112
	(−1.23)	(−0.65)	(−1.00)	(0.02)
Diversity	−2.279	−3.845	−4.653	−5.878*
	(−0.72)	(−1.00)	(−1.11)	(−1.68)

(continued)

Table 2.9   (continued)

	(1)	(2)	(3)	(4)
Board experience	0.185	0.194	0.127	0.308*
	(1.41)	(1.23)	(0.75)	(1.79)
Age CV	10.04	10.06	5.395	1.750
	(1.03)	(0.98)	(0.47)	(0.14)
Intercept	6.995	0	−26.75*	19.79**
	(0.60)	(.)	(−1.74)	(2.53)
Year FE	*Yes*	*Yes*	*Yes*	*Yes*
N	2051	1876	1876	1510
2nd order auto	0.116	0.0914	0.118	0.207
Instruments, #	146	76	79	75
Hansen test	0.139	0.143	0.132	0.114

t statistics in parentheses
$^{*}p < 0.10$, $^{**}p < 0.05$, $^{***}p < 0.01$

are less profitable. For GSIBs, the sole significant bank-level variable is *loan intensity* (at 10%); GSIBs holding larger volumes of loans are not as profitable.

For firms' corporate governance practices, we observe an economically meaningful and very highly significant inverse relationship between *board size* and profitability at US banks and GSIBs. It suggests relatively smaller boards face fewer coordination problems. In addition, relatively more diverse US banks and GSIBs are less profitable. However, relatively more gender diverse EU banks realise higher levels of ROE. Our findings affirm that board room diversity matters albeit not in a uniform way.

For robustness, in Table 2.11, we change the indicator of firm performance to returns calculated from daily share prices. Second, and to account for differences in the magnitude of pay gaps, we scale the pay gap by firm equity. Specifying returns as the dependent variable, the CEO pay gap increases in economic importance compared to the baseline ROE model (see columns 1 and 3) and is significant (at 1%). In models specifying the scaled CEO pay gap, results confirm the significant economic and statistical relationship between tournament incentives and each performance indicator. Thus, our evidence supporting tournament incentives becomes even more compelling.

	EU	US	GSIB
Table 2.10 Estimated relationship between ROE and CEO pay gap; by cohort—1999–2016			
ROE_{t-1}	0.386***	0.0524	0.307***
	(4.72)	(0.61)	(3.92)
ROE_{t-2}	–	–	0.114*
	–	–	(1.92)
CEO pay gap	0.692**	1.330***	0.718*
	(2.14)	(4.01)	(1.78)
Total pay	−0.0579	−0.240	0.363
	(−0.07)	(−0.29)	(0.48)
Tenure	−0.808*	1.562***	0.514
	(−1.69)	(3.58)	(1.05)
New CEO	−4.464***	−1.481	−3.285***
	(−5.57)	(−1.58)	(−3.84)
Bank size	1.165*	2.677***	0.101
	(1.92)	(3.61)	(0.09)
Loan intensity	0.0495	0.0818	−0.0926*
	(0.79)	(1.08)	(−1.66)
Non-core funding	0.0448	0.0189	−0.0092
	(0.76)	(0.31)	(−0.15)
Risk intensity	0.0277	0.0150	−0.0228
	(0.58)	(0.22)	(−0.46)
Asset quality	−3.044***	−11.78***	−0.0456
	(−2.94)	(−4.94)	(−0.04)
Net interest margin	4.480***	2.738**	1.401
	(5.90)	(2.45)	(1.39)
Board Size	−1.447	−8.961***	−6.108***
	(−0.73)	(−3.08)	(−3.03)
Board monitoring	0.455	1.772	−1.407
	(0.39)	(0.79)	(−1.04)
Gender diversity	11.24**	−9.344	7.231
	(2.25)	(−1.65)	(1.30)
Diversity	−3.243	−14.61**	−7.830***
	(−1.22)	(−2.21)	(−2.71)
Board experience	−0.0967	−0.555	0.248
	(−0.87)	(−1.62)	(1.52)
Age CV	17.61	6.097	−15.91

(continued)

Table 2.10
(continued)

	EU	*US*	*GSIB*
	(1.18)	(0.42)	(−1.11)
Intercept	−19.92	−10.79	19.64
	(−1.34)	(−0.81)	(1.28)
Year FE	*Yes*	*Yes*	*Yes*
N	888	1164	643
2nd order auto	0.152	0.892	0.130
Instruments, #	134	130	88
Hansen test	0.647	0.514	0.266

t statistics in parentheses
$^{*}p < 0.10$, $^{**}p < 0.05$, $^{***}p < 0.01$

2.6   Discussion

The complexity and systemic importance of large banks underscores the importance of examining executive compensation and incentives facing executives. We consider if incentives created by pay differentials affect firm performance. While competition between executives for prizes (promotion) could facilitate risk-taking rather than risk sharing, we conjecture that the high coordination needs, and complexity of banks necessitates that executives exert effort *and* collaborate. Tournament theorists believe high-powered incentives set by large pay gaps are the vehicle to incentivise effort and collaboration and/or risk sharing. Our results speak to this narrative.

Notwithstanding, tournament incentives may prove to be damaging if winner-takes-all outcomes impair collaboration and cause departures and loss of skills thereby hurting firms' retention policy and adversely affecting performance. Hence, disproportionately large pay gaps can affect firms' social-psychological and socio-political context and create feelings of deprivation thereby weakening commitment to organisational goals. A political economy perspective suggests individuals face three choices: how much effort to expend; how to split effort between cooperation and self-service; and whether to engage in politicking (Lazear 1989; Milgrom and Roberts 1988). Although large gaps can incentivise effort, they could facilitate self-serving actions and sabotage (Harbring and Irlenbusch 2011; Chowdhury and Gürtler 2015). To avoid these two problems, firms could set a horizontal compensation policy and compress pay leading to

Table 2.11 Robustness checks

	ROE	ROE & scaled pay gap	Returns	Returns & scaled pay gap
ROE$_{t-1}$	0.411***	0.397***	−0.0249	−0.0139
	(6.72)	(6.42)	(−0.64)	(−0.38)
CEO pay gap	1.119***	–	5.386***	–
	(3.63)	–	(3.16)	–
CEO pay gap scaled	–	1.003***	6.927*	3.280**
	–	(3.24)	(1.72)	(2.14)
Total pay	−0.00389	0.0308	0.456	6.034*
	(−0.00)	(0.04)	(0.38)	(1.91)
Tenure	0.162	0.188	3.592	0.471
	(0.44)	(0.53)	(1.56)	(0.41)
New CEO	−2.347***	−2.300***	−9.082***	2.052
	(−3.30)	(−3.18)	(−3.48)	(0.92)
Bank size	0.392	1.276**	0.201	−5.094*
	(0.70)	(2.08)	(0.76)	(−1.81)
Loan intensity	−0.0133	−0.0186	0.0704	−0.00725
	(−0.19)	(−0.29)	(0.33)	(−0.03)
Non-core funding	0.0810	0.0953	0.184	0.120
	(1.39)	(1.41)	(0.78)	(0.61)
Risk intensity	0.0184	0.0294	−12.74*	0.325
	(0.38)	(0.61)	(−1.78)	(1.58)
Asset quality	−4.155***	−4.377***	−7.822*	−11.45*
	(−3.71)	(−3.86)	(−1.73)	(−1.92)
Net interest margin	2.186**	2.517**	10.88	−5.491
	(2.25)	(2.48)	(1.36)	(−1.37)
Board Size	−3.963**	−4.177**	3.332	6.798
	(−2.20)	(−2.27)	(0.80)	(0.97)
Board monitoring	−2.126**	−1.935*	−15.79	3.115
	(−2.09)	(−1.93)	(−0.80)	(0.77)
Gender diversity	−6.262	−7.512	−22.06*	−11.46
	(−1.43)	(−1.58)	(−1.70)	(−0.69)

(continued)

Table 2.11 (continued)

	ROE	*ROE & scaled pay gap*	*Returns*	*Returns & scaled pay gap*
Diversity	−3.029	−3.031	1.382**	−18.46
	(−0.94)	(−1.01)	(2.57)	(−1.63)
Board experience	0.127	0.150	−23.49	1.290**
	(0.95)	(1.14)	(−0.58)	(2.58)
Age CV	9.894	10.18	5.386***	−22.96
	(1.03)	(1.08)	(3.16)	(−0.60)
Intercept	0	0	−84.05	0
	(.)	(.)	(−1.61)	(.)
Year FE	*Yes*	*Yes*	*Yes*	*Yes*
N	2052	2052	2052	2052
2nd order auto	0.146	0.149	0.378	0.341
Instruments, #	146	146	88	111
Hansen test	0.155	0.116	0.00109	0.00747

t statistics in parentheses
*$p < 0.10$, **$p < 0.05$, ***$p < 0.01$

smaller pay gaps, which are expected to engineer greater commitment to firms' goals leading to improvements in performance (Cowherd and Levine 1992; Henderson and Fredrickson 2001). Notwithstanding, our econometric evidence does not support this conjecture.

2.7 CONCLUSIONS AND IMPLICATIONS FOR COMPENSATION POLICY

We examine executive pay at mainly large, complex banks. We estimate average pay across C-suite roles and use pairwise comparisons to identify significant differences. On average, the CEO is the highest paid followed by the Chief Operating Officer. We compare pay at banks run by single titled CEOs to dual titled and tripled titled CEOs, which provides insights into corporate governance and CEO power. Pre-GFC CEO power was at its highest. Post-GFC the average pay of dual and triple-titled CEOs fell considerably, while increasing moderately for sole titled CEOs.

Bankers' pay was excessive pre-GFC. Post-crisis average pay has declined often quite substantially. Comparing pay levels between cohorts reaffirms findings elsewhere that larger and more complex firms (GSIBs) reward executives with significantly higher pay. In addition, we find evidence of pay differential across borders as US banks pay more on average than their European counterparts.

We construct the CEO pay gap to proxy tournament incentives. Like observed differences in pay across cohorts, pay gaps are largest for US GSIBs and US banks (not GSIB) and particularly pre-GFC. The sizes of pay gaps have diminished post-GFC and especially at US GSIBs. Our findings imply that corporate governance practices in banking are improving.

Does the use of high-powered tournament incentives yield superior firm performance? Our robust evidence supports the premise of tournament theory; large pay gaps lead to higher levels of profitability after controlling for the level of pay, inside debt, excess pay, corporate governance practices, and financial characteristics including banks' size and choice of business model. We find limited evidence that both Inter-rank and industry pay gaps positively impact bank performance.

Our findings have implications for compensation policy. The results provide unambiguous proof that compensation policy can deliver beneficial firm performance outcomes across borders and after controlling for the *level* of pay. Our main result offers compelling evidence that vertical pay practices lead to higher levels of realised profits and returns. Thus, we advocate inclusion of high-powered tournament incentives in the design of compensation policy to induce effort and collaboration in the C-suites of large, complex firms with high coordination needs.

APPENDIX A: VARIABLE DEFINITIONS

ROE—ratio of profit before tax-to-equity.

CEO pay gap—natural logarithm of the total pay of the highest rank executive less the pay of other individual executives.

Total pay—sum of salary, bonus, equity-linked pay, and deferred compensation.

Inside debt—deferred pay-to-total liabilities scaled by the change in accumulated wealth-to-change in equity.

Excess pay—%Residual $\text{Pay}_{ijt} = \log(\text{Pay}_{ijt}) - \log(\text{Expected Pay}_{ijt})$.

Tenure—number of years spent in the firm.

New CEO—equals 1 for executives in the year when a firm appoints a new CEO, zero otherwise.

Bank Size—natural logarithm of the sum of total assets and off-balance-sheet assets.

Loan intensity—ratio of net loans-to-total loans to proxy a bank's business model with respect to asset structure.

Non-core funding—ratio of short-term and other interest-bearing liabilities-to-total purchased funds to proxy a bank's business model with respect to funding.

Risk intensity—ratio of risk weighted assets-to-total assets.

Asset quality—ratio of loan loss reserves-to-total assets.

Net interest margin—ratio of net interest revenue-to-total earning assets.

Board size—number of directors on the board.

Board monitoring—ratio of independent directors-to-executive directors.

Gender diversity—ratio of female directors-to-board size.

Diversity—number of foreign directors-to-board size.

Experience—number of boards' directors sit on to date-to-board size.

Age—coefficient of variation of the age of executive directors (Tables 2.12 and 2.13).

Appendix B: Additional Tables

Table 2.12 Estimated relationship between ROE and industry pay gap; all banks—1999–2016

	(1)	(2)	(3)	(4)
ROE_{t-1}	0.422***	0.338***	0.362***	0.469***
	(6.94)	(6.36)	(6.42)	(7.68)
ROE_{t-2}	–	–	0.0932*	−0.0135
	–	–	(1.72)	(−0.28)
Industry pay gap	6.252**	−2.625*	7.998**	−3.952
	(2.07)	(−1.74)	(2.24)	(−1.63)
Total pay	3.409***	–	3.895***	–
	(3.43)	–	(3.06)	–
Inside debt	–	0.174*	0.177	–
	–	(1.70)	(0.99)	–
Excess pay	–	–	–	−2.629***
	–	–	–	(−3.02)
Tenure	−0.239	0.589*	0.0465	0.181
	(−0.61)	(1.80)	(0.11)	(0.46)
New CEO	−2.189***	−3.176***	−1.680**	−2.877***
	(−3.90)	(−5.50)	(−2.33)	(−3.80)
Bank size	−0.718	1.118**	−0.793	0.453
	(−1.28)	(2.18)	(−1.23)	(0.89)
Loan intensity	−0.0444	0.000862	−0.0230	−0.0288
	(−0.74)	(0.01)	(−0.37)	(−0.45)
Non-core funding	0.0980*	0.0582	0.0430	0.137*
	(1.70)	(1.00)	(0.76)	(1.85)
Risk intensity	0.0207	−0.0351	−0.0286	0.0423
	(0.48)	(−0.70)	(−0.56)	(0.91)
Asset quality	−4.051***	−6.026***	−3.745***	−3.860***
	(−4.52)	(−5.36)	(−3.40)	(−3.67)
Net interest margin	1.992**	4.387***	2.429**	3.450***
	(2.54)	(4.52)	(2.15)	(4.07)
Board Size	−1.771	−6.375***	−1.746	−5.162**
	(−1.06)	(−3.20)	(−0.99)	(−2.50)
Board monitoring	−1.440*	−0.0556	−1.084	−2.698***
	(−1.89)	(−0.05)	(−1.15)	(−2.82)
Gender diversity	−7.141*	−5.345	0.324	0.0240
	(−1.79)	(−1.48)	(0.10)	(0.01)
Diversity	0.655	−1.907	1.850	−1.696
	(0.25)	(−0.67)	(0.55)	(−0.59)

(continued)

Table 2.12 (continued)

	(1)	(2)	(3)	(4)
Board experience	0.101	0.167	0.206	0.0725
	(1.00)	(1.36)	(1.49)	(0.60)
Age CV	6.922	2.227	−0.437	2.013
	(0.84)	(0.23)	(−0.04)	(0.24)
Intercept	−138.4**	0	0	0
	(−2.02)	(.)	(.)	(.)
Year FE	*Yes*	*Yes*	*Yes*	*Yes*
N	2702	2472	1915	2052
2nd order auto	0.434	0.433	0.533	0.320
Instruments, #	160	159	86	159
Hansen test	0.174	0.129	0.132	0.0577

t statistics in parentheses
$^{*}p < 0.10$, $^{**}p < 0.05$, $^{***}p < 0.01$

Table 2.13 Estimated relationship between ROE and industry roles pay gap; all banks—1999–2016

	(1)	(2)	(3)	(4)
ROE_{t-1}	0.444***	0.342***	0.301***	0.472***
	(7.53)	(5.98)	(5.30)	(8.36)
ROE_{t-2}	0.0104	–	–	0.000492
	(0.23)	–	–	(0.01)
Ind. roles pay gap	0.0965	0.00647	0.138**	−0.0541
	(1.57)	(0.15)	(2.37)	(−0.80)
Total pay	1.477*	–	2.911***	–
	(1.91)	–	(3.72)	–
Inside debt	–	0.200*	0.224*	–
	–	(1.85)	(1.94)	–
Excess pay	–	–	–	−2.092***
	–	–	–	(−2.73)
Tenure	−0.115	0.762**	0.385	0.272
	(−0.30)	(2.31)	(1.01)	(0.75)
New CEO	−2.278***	−2.747***	−2.476***	−2.731***
	(−3.39)	(−4.63)	(−4.38)	(−3.60)
Bank size	−0.388	1.404***	0.489	0.403
	(−0.72)	(2.71)	(0.90)	(0.91)
Loan intensity	−0.0469	0.0216	0.0361	−0.0189
	(−0.83)	(0.39)	(0.62)	(−0.34)
Non-core funding	0.112*	0.0159	0.0660	0.0998
	(1.75)	(0.26)	(1.14)	(1.44)
Risk intensity	0.0443	−0.0422	−0.0516	0.0356
	(1.02)	(−0.86)	(−1.22)	(0.88)
Asset quality	−3.966***	−5.872***	−5.948***	−3.766***
	(−3.94)	(−5.15)	(−5.45)	(−3.47)
Net interest margin	2.358***	4.023***	3.434***	2.905***
	(2.80)	(4.37)	(3.88)	(3.82)
Board Size	−2.012	−5.933***	−5.027***	−4.145**
	(−1.17)	(−3.14)	(−2.80)	(−2.58)
Board monitoring	−1.700*	−0.614	−0.463	−2.281**
	(−1.90)	(−0.67)	(−0.47)	(−2.24)
Gender diversity	−2.766	−4.254	−5.702	0.471
	(−0.82)	(−1.28)	(−1.57)	(0.15)
Diversity	−2.005	−1.651	−1.753	−1.745
	(−0.67)	(−0.61)	(−0.54)	(−0.62)

(continued)

Table 2.13 (continued)

	(1)	(2)	(3)	(4)
Board experience	0.176	0.181	0.0655	0.111
	(1.51)	(1.37)	(0.51)	(0.97)
Age CV	5.473	5.610	5.854	2.684
	(0.62)	(0.66)	(0.60)	(0.31)
Intercept	−12.26	−9.714	0	9.355
	(−1.08)	(−1.40)	(.)	(1.31)
Year FE	*Yes*	*Yes*	*Yes*	*Yes*
N	2063	2485	2485	2063
2nd order auto	0.639	0.417	0.460	0.391
Instruments, #	159	159	173	159
Hansen test	0.143	0.323	0.438	0.112

t statistics in parentheses
$^{*}p < 0.10$, $^{**}p < 0.05$, $^{***}p < 0.01$

REFERENCES

Adams, R.B., de Haan, J., Tersesen, S., Ees, H.V. (2015). Board diversity: Moving the field forward. Corporate Governance: An International Review, 23(2): 77–82.

Adams, R.B., Funk, P. (2012). Beyond the glass ceiling: Does gender matter? Management Science, 58(2): 219–235.

Anderson, R.C., Reeb, D.M., Upadhyay, A., Zhao, W. (2011). The economics of director heterogeneity. Financial Management, 40(1): 5–38.

Ang, J., Lauterbach, B., Schreiber, B.Z. (2002). Pay at the executive suite: How do US banks compensate their top management teams? Journal of Banking and Finance, 26: 1143–1163.

Arellano, M., Bond, S.R. (1991). Some tests of specification for panel data: Monte Carlo evidence and an application to employment equations. Review of Economics Studies, 58: 277–297.

Arellano, M., Bover, O. (1995). Another look at the instrumental variable estimation of error component models. Journal of Econometrics, 68: 29–51.

Baker, G.P., Jensen, M.C., Murphy, K.J. (1988). Compensation and incentives: Practice vs. theory. Journal of Finance, 43 (3): 593–616.

Bebchuk, L.A., Cohen, A., Spamann, H. (2010). The wages of failure: Executive compensation at Bear Stearns and Lehman 2000–2008. Regulating Bankers' Pay. Yale Journal on Regulation, 27: 257–282.

Bebchuk, L.A., Cremers, M.K.J., Peyer, U.C. (2011). The CEO pay slice. Journal of Financial Economics, 102: 199–221.

Bebchuk, L.A., Spamann, H. (2010). Regulating bankers' pay. Georgetown Law Journal, 98: 247–287.

Beltratti, A., Stulz, R. (2012). The credit crisis around the globe: Why did some banks perform better? Journal of Financial Economics, 105: 1–17.

Berger, A.N., Kick, T., Schaeck, K. (2014). Executive board composition and bank risk taking. Journal of Corporate Finance, 28: 48–65.

Bhagat, S., Black, B. (1999). The uncertain relationship between board composition and firm performance. Business Lawyer, 54: 921–963.

Bhagat, S., Bolton, B. (2014). Financial crisis and bank incentive compensation. Journal of Corporate Finance, 25: 313–341.

Blundell, R., Bond, S. (1998). Initial conditions and moment restrictions in dynamic panel data models. Journal of Econometrics, 87: 115–143.

Bolton, P., Mehran, H., Shapiro, J. (2015). Executive compensation and risk taking. Review of Finance, 19(6): 2139–2181.

Boyd, J.H., de Nicolò, G. (2005). The theory of bank risk taking and competition revisited. Journal of Finance, 60(3): 1329–1343.

Brunnermeier, M.K. (2009). Deciphering the liquidity and credit crunch 2007–08. Journal of Economic Perspectives, 23: 77–100.

Burns, N., Minnick, K., Starks, L. (2017). CEO tournaments: A cross-country analysis of causes, cultural influences and consequences. Journal of Financial and Quantitative Analysis, 52(2): 519–551.

Chava, S., Purnanandam, A. (2010). CEOs versus CFOs: Incentives and corporate policies. Journal of Financial Economics, 97: 263–278.

Cheng, I.H., Hong, H., Scheinkman, J.A. (2015). Yesterday's heroes: Compensation and risk at financial firms. Journal of Finance, 70: 839–879.

Chowdhury, S.M., Gürtler, O. (2015). Sabotage in contests: A survey. Public Choice, 164: 135–155.

Coles, J.L., Daniel, N.D., Naveen, L.N. (2008). Boards: Does one size fit all? Journal of Financial Economics, 87: 329–356.

Coles, J.L., Li, Z.F., Wang, A.Y. (2017). Industry tournament incentives. The Review of Financial Studies, 31(4): 1418–1459.

Connelly, B.L., Tihanyi, L., Crook, T.R., Gangloff, K.A. (2014). Tournament theory: Thirty years of contests and competitions. Journal of Management, 40(1): 16–47.

Conyon, M.J., Fernandes, N., Ferreira, M.A., Matos, P., Murphy, K.J. (2011). The Executive Compensation Controversy: A Transatlantic Analysis. Fondazione Rodolfo de Benedetti.

Conyon, M., Sadler, G. (2001). Executive pay, tournaments and corporate performance in UK Firms. International Journal of Management Review, 3(2): 141–168.

Core, J.E., Guay, W., Larcker, D.F. (2008). The power of the pen and executive compensation. Journal of Financial Economics, 88: 1–25.

Cowherd, D.M., Levine, D.I. (1992). Product quality and pay equity between lower-level employees and top management: An investigation of distributive justice theory. Administrative Science Quarterly, 37(2): 302–320.

DeYoung, R., Peng, E.Y., Yan, M. (2013). Executive compensation and business policy choices at U.S. commercial banks. Journal of Financial and Quantitative Analysis, 48(1): 165–196.

Edmans, A., Gabaix, X., Jenter, D. (2017). Executive compensation: A survey of theory and evidence. ECGI Working Paper Series in Finance, Working Paper No 514/2017.

Edmans, A., Liu, Q. (2011). Inside debt. Review of Finance, 15: 75–102.

Ellul, A., Yerramilli, V. (2013). Stronger risk controls, lower risk: Evidence from US bank holding companies. Journal of Finance, 68: 1757–1803.

Erkens, D.H., Hung, M., Matos P. (2012). Corporate governance in the 2007–2008 financial crisis: Evidence from financial institutions worldwide. Journal of Corporate Finance, 18: 389–411.

Fahlenbrach, R., Stulz, R. (2011). Bank CEO incentives and the credit crisis. Journal of Financial Economics, 99: 11–26.

Fernandes, N., Ferreira, M.A., Matos, P., Murphy, K.J. (2013). Are U.S. CEOs paid more? New international evidence. Review of Financial Studies, 26(2): 323–367.

Forbes, D.P., Milliken, F.J. (1999). Cognition and corporate governance: Understanding boards of directors as strategic decision-making groups. The Academy of Management Review, 24(3): 489–505.

Frydman, C., Jenter, D. (2010). CEO compensation. Annual Review of Financial Economics, 2(1): 75–102.

Frydman, C., Saks, R.E. (2010). Executive compensation: A new view from a long-term perspective, 1936–2005. Review of Financial Studies 23: 2099–2138.

Gibbons, R., Murphy, K.J. (1990). Relative performance evaluation for chief executive officers. Industrial and Labor Relations Review, 43: 30–51.

Guiso, L., Sapienza, P., Zingales, L. (2006). Does culture affect economic outcomes? Journal of Economic Perspectives, 20(2): 23–48.

Hambrick, D.C., Mason, P. (1984). Upper echelons: The organisation as a reflection of its top managers. Academy of Management Review, 9(2): 193–206.

Hannan, R.L., Krishnan, R., Newman, A.H. (2008). The effects of disseminating relative performance feedback in tournament and individual performance compensation plans. Accounting Review, 83(4): 893–913.

Harbring, C., Irlenbusch, B. (2011). Sabotage in tournaments: Evidence from a laboratory experiment. Management Science, 57(4): 611–627.

Henderson, A.D., Fredrickson, J.W. (2001). Top management team coordination needs and the CEO pay gap: A competitive test of economic and behavioural views. Academy of Management 44(1): 96–117.

Herring, R., Carmassi, J. (2010). The corporate structure of international financial conglomerates: Complexity and its implications for safety and soundness. In: Berger, A., Molyneux, P. and Wilson, J. (eds), The Oxford Handbook of Banking (1st edition), Oxford University Press, 195–229.

Holmstrom, B. (1979). Moral hazard and observability. The Bell Journal of Economics, 10(1): 74–91.

Jensen, M.C. (1993). The modern industrial revolution, exit, and the failure of internal control systems. Journal of Finance, 48(3): 831–880.

Jensen, M.C., Meckling, W.H. (1976). Theory of the firm: Managerial behaviour, agency costs, and ownership structure. Journal of Financial Economics, 3: 305–360.

Jensen, M.C., Murphy, K.J. (1991). CEO incentives—It's not how much you pay, but how. Harvard Business Review, May–June, No. 3, 138–153.

John, K., Senbet, L.W. (1998). Corporate governance and board effectiveness. Journal of Banking and Finance, 22: 371–403.

Kale, J., Reis, E., Venkateswaran, A. (2009). Rank-order tournaments and incentive alignment: The effect on firm performance. Journal of Finance, 64: 1479–1512.

Lambert, R.A., Larcker, D.F. and Weigelt, K. (1993). The structure of organizational incentives. Administrative Science Quarterly, 38: 438–461.

Lazear, E.P. (1989). Pay equality and industrial politics. Journal of Political Economy, 97: 561–580.

Lazear, E.P., Rosen, S. (1981). Rank-order tournaments as optimum labor contracts. Journal of Political Economy, 89(5): 841–864.

LePetit, L., Nys, E., Rous, P., Tarazi, A. (2008). Bank income structure and risk: An empirical analysis of European banks. Journal of Banking and Finance, 32(8): 1452–1467.

Lewellen, W., Loderer, C., Martin, K. (1987). Executive compensation contracts and executive incentive problems: An empirical analysis. Journal of Accounting and Economics, 9(3): 287–310.

Lin, Y-F., Yeh, Y.M.C., Shih, Y-T. (2013). Tournament theory's perspective of executive pay gaps. Journal of Business Research, 66(5): 585–592.

Main, B.G.M., O'Reilly, C.A., Wade, J. (1993). Top executive pay: Tournament or teamwork? Journal of Labor Economics, 11(4): 606–628.

MacCrimmon, K.R., Wehrung, D.R. (1990). Characteristics of risk taking executives. Management Science, 36(4): 422–435.

Malmendier, U., Tate, G. (2009). Superstar CEOs. Quarterly Journal of Economics, 124(4): 1593–1638.

Milgrom, P., Roberts, J. (1988). An economic approach to influence activities in organizations. American Journal of Sociology, 94: 154–179.

Mishel, L., Davis, A. (2015). Top CEOs make 300 times more than typical workers. EPI—Economic Policy Institute, Issue Brief #399, June 21.

Murphy, K.J. (1986). Incentives, learning, and compensation: A theoretical and empirical investigation of managerial labor contracts. The RAND Journal of Economics, 17(1): 59–76.

Murphy, K.J. (2013). Executive compensation: Where we are, and how we got there. In Constantinides, G., Harris, M. and Stulz, R. (eds) Handbook of the Economics of Finance, Vol. 2, Part A, 211–356.

Nguyen, D.D., Hagendorff, J., Eshraghi, A. (2015). Which executive characteristics create value in banking? Evidence from appointment announcements. Corporate Governance: An International Review, 23: 112–128.

O'Reilly III, C.A., Main, B.G., Crystal, G.S. (1988). CEO compensation as tournament and social comparison: A tale of two theories. Administrative Science Quarterly, 33(2): 257–274.

Palvia, A., Vähämaa, E., Vähämaa, S. (2015). Are female CEOs and chairwomen more conservative and risk averse? Evidence from the banking industry during the financial crisis. Journal of Business Ethics, 131(3): 577–594.

Pan, Y., Siegel, S., Wang, T.Y. (2017). Corporate risk culture. Journal of Financial and Quantitative Analysis, 52(6): 2327–2367.

Pathan, S. (2009). Strong boards, CEO power and bank risk-taking. Journal of Banking and Finance, 33: 1340–1350.

Pathan, S., Faff, R. (2013). Does board structure in banks really affect their performance? Journal of Banking and Finance, 37: 1573–1589.

Pitcher, P., Smith, A.D. (2001). Top management team heterogeneity: Personality, power, and proxies. Organization Science, 12(1): 1–18.

Quigley, T.J., Hambrick, D.C. (2015). Has the "CEO effect" increased in recent decades? A new explanation for the great rise in America's attention to corporate leaders. Strategic Management Journal, 36: 821–830.

Rhodes, S.R. (1983). Age-related differences in work attitudes and behavior: A review and conceptual analysis. Psychological Bulletin, 93: 328–367.

Rosen, S. (1982). Authority, control and distribution of earnings. Bell Journal of Economics, 13: 311–323.

Rosen, S. (1986). Prizes and incentives in elimination tournaments. American Economic Review, 76: 701–715.

Song, W-L., Wan, K-M. (2019). Does CEO compensation reflect managerial ability or managerial power? Evidence from the compensation of powerful CEOs. Journal of Corporate Finance, 56: 1–14.

Srivastava, A., Insch, G. (2007). Executive compensation differentials: Testing tournament theory. International Journal of Business Research, 7(2): 187–193.

Stiroh, K.J. (2006). A portfolio view of banking with interest and non-interest activities. Journal of Money, Credit and Banking, 38(5): 1351–1361.

Stiroh, K.J., Rumble, A. (2006). The dark side of diversification: The case of US financial holding companies. Journal of Banking and Finance, 30: 2131–2161.

Stiroh, K.J., Strahan, P.E. (2003). Competitive dynamics of deregulation: Evidence from U.S. banking. Journal of Money, Credit and Banking, 35(5): 801–828.

Tung, F., Wang, X. (2012). Bank CEOs, inside debt compensation, and the global financial crisis. Social Science Research Network. Boston Univ. School of Law Working Paper No. 11–49.

Vieito, J.P.T. (2012). Gender, top management compensation gap, and company performance: Tournament versus behavioural theory. Corporate Governance: An International Review, 20(1): 46–63.

Yermack, D. (1996). Higher market valuation of companies with a small board of directors. Journal of Financial Economics, 40: 185–211.

Wei, C., Yermack, D. (2011). Investors reactions to CEOs' inside debt incentives. The Review of Financial Studies, 24(11): 3813–3840.

CHAPTER 3

The Effect of Board Diversity and ESG Engagement on Banks' Profitability and Risk

Selena Aureli⊙, *Paola Brighi*⊙, *Muddassar Malik*⊙, *and Hannu Schadewitz*⊙

3.1 Introduction

Climate change, social issues and sustainable development are at the forefront of worldwide academic and government discussions (ECB 2020; EBA and ESMA 2021; EBA 2021a; Hansen 2022). Broadly speaking, any economic actor and businesses in all sectors are called to take action towards sustainable development goals, banks included (Avrampou

S. Aureli · P. Brighi
Department of Management, University of Bologna, Bologna, Italy
e-mail: selena.aureli@unibo.it

P. Brighi
e-mail: paola.brighi@unibo.it

P. Brighi
CEFIN - Centro Studi Banca e Finanza, University of Modena and Reggio, Modena, Italy

47

S. Carbó-Valverde and P. J. Cuadros Solas (eds.), *New Challenges for the Banking Industry*, Palgrave Macmillan Studies in Banking and Financial Institutions, https://doi.org/10.1007/978-3-031-32931-9_3

et al. 2019; Bruno and Lagasio 2021; Birindelli et al. 2022). Accordingly, a growing strand of literature is investigating how environmental, social and governance (ESG) aspects are addressed by businesses and their impact of financial performance. In fact, as highlighted by the World Economic Forum (2020), it is widely recognized that ESG factors generate sustainable value and economic effectiveness.

Corporate governance (CG) is the most strategically oriented dimension in ESG because it guides managerial decision-making and has a great impact on the propensity of organizations to adopt more sustainable strategies to generate profits (Hahn and Figge 2011; Cardoni et al. 2020). For this reason, CG is highly investigated in academic literature. CG has the responsibility to help companies meet the grand challenges that contemporary society faces like sustainable development (Scherer and Voegtlin 2020; Veldman et al. 2016). It is a variable that impacts both financial performance (how managers assess strategies' effectiveness) and the decision to incorporate social and environmental aspects within strategy. For this reason, it affects both short and long term organizational performance (Manning et al. 2019; Jacoby et al. 2019).

A key element of CG is the composition of the board of directors. Boards are responsible for providing oversight, insight and foresight (Mueller et al. 2009). To ensure that organizations are capable to respond to recent calls for more sustainability, experts have pointed out the necessity to have boards with a variety of backgrounds, knowledge and skills often defined as board diversity (BD). Not only gender differences but also "aspects such as age, nationality, expertise, work and educational background, professional qualifications" (Veldman et al. 2016) because they can pick different external signals and improve discussions within the management board and supervisory board. BD is a crucial factor that impacts board's effectiveness and is receiving an increasing attention especially from the banking literature attempting to explain financial

M. Malik (✉) · H. Schadewitz
Department of Accounting and Finance, Turku School of Economics,
University of Turku, Turku, Finland
e-mail: muddassar.m.malik@utu.fi

H. Schadewitz
e-mail: hannu.schadewitz@utu.fi

performance (Love and Rachinsky 2015; Zagorchev and Gao 2015; Tarchouna et al. 2017; Al-Hadi et al. 2019; Gulati et al. 2020; Aslam and Haron 2020; Shakil et al. 2019; Birindelli et al. 2022).

In the banking sector, governance has increasingly received researchers' attention because of companies' excessive risk-taking and acts of corporate misconduct that have demonstrated the failures of past models of CG. The banking sector is a case in point when talking about CG. Critics on the role of bankers in the US corporate scandals of 2001 and the 2008 financial crisis (Bryant et al. 2014) have engendered new empirical research on the benefits of more stringent CG rules and greater diversity in the board of directors, who are responsible for managing the bank (Shakil et al. 2019). The relevance of governance and board composition in ensuring financial stability (Ayadi et al. 2021) is supported by the intense regulation on governance compared to the other ESG dimensions: from the Sarbanes–Oxley Act in 2002 and the national laws setting gender quotas in the Boards of directors to the continuous update of governance rules set by Stock Exchanges and the issuance of principles and guidelines for enhancing CG in banks (EBA and ESMA 2021; EBA 2021b).

The intensive regulation development for banks is understandable because of their significant role in collecting funds from small savers and accelerating the economic development in economies through the lending function. Banks have a wide reach in economies; therefore, the general public is substantially influenced by banks existence. This, in turn, makes banks' responsibilities greater compared to other industries, including ESG matters. Since banks have very significant role in societies at large, it is essential that they pay attention to and promote good corporate citizenship in its all three dimensions: environment, social and governance. Moreover, considering that during financial distress times of banks, taxpayers' money is used to rescue banks; stakeholders should have right to know banks' situation and how taxpayers' money is spent (Khan et al. 2021).

Given the above, banks' boards should have ability and willingness to challenge bank management and engage a dialogue to ensure that bank's decisions consider relevant factors that could affect stakeholders' interests (John et al. 2016). This ability seems to strongly depend on BD. However, it is not always clear how BD impacts on ESG strategies and financial performance. Hence, the present chapter investigates the impact of BD on bank performance expressed by ROA (Return on Assets), SROA

(Risk-adjusted ROA) and Z-SCORE (insolvency risk measure) by developing several models that allow to assess the direct and indirect impact, i.e., mediated by the ESG scores, of BD on banks profitability and risk.

The rest of the chapter is structured as follows. Section 3.2 reviews the literature dealing with CG and BD, then followed by a review on ESG aspects and their impact on bank performance. Section 3.3 describes data and methods applied in this chapter. Section 3.4 displays the main results, while the last Sect. 3.5 concludes.

3.2   Literature Review

3.2.1   Corporate Governance and the Relevance of Board Diversity

Corporate governance (CG) is used to be defined as a set of principles and rules informing the way a company is directed, administered and/or controlled by managers in the best interests of shareholders. However, in the latest decades, this definition devoted to solve shareholders' control issues due to information asymmetries and agency problem has been substituted by a more comprehensive concept of CG as mechanisms to create value for both investors and other stakeholders. According to the stakeholder theory an organization's effectiveness is measured by its ability to satisfy not only the shareholders, but also those agents who have a stake in the organization (Freeman 1984). This more comprehensive perspective is highly relevant in bank context because high leverage of banks and related debtholders' (depositors') claims. Good governance could restrict potential risk shift incentive of managers on behalf of shareholders (John et al. 2016). The more holistic stakeholder approach extends the scope of CG by considering all stakeholders, including shareholders, subjects with equal rights (Money and Schepers 2007; Shahzad et al. 2016). Therefore, this more ample approach strongly links CG to Corporate Social Responsibility and sustainability (Kolk and Pinkse 2010; Garcia-Torea et al. 2016).

One of the key mechanisms of CG is represented by Board of Directors as they are responsible for monitoring the management, providing it with strategic advice (Van den Berghe et al. 2004). Board diversity is crucial because it creates value by enhancing the decision-making process (Anderson et al. 2011).

In the past, research on board diversity mainly focused on gender (Adams and Ferreira 2009), demonstrating that the presence of female directors typically improves performance and reduce the risk of failure (Palvia et al. 2015; Farag and Mallin 2017; Bennouri et al. 2018; Schadewitz and Spohr 2022) and fraud (Cumming et al. 2015). While recent professional forums and research indicate to investigate the value of differences in other board members' capabilities, the more studied and also easy-to identify differences relate to gender, age, nationality and race (Cumming and Leung 2021). Other also attempted to include task-related differences (Adams et al. 2015) such as educational or functional background and professional qualifications because they are important in making the board less homogeneous. Soft factors are held important by the corporate governance self-discipline code. Among others, the UK code states, for example, that "diversity of skills, background and personal strengths is an important driver of a board's effectiveness, creating different perspectives among directors, and breaking down a tendency towards group think (point no.16)" (Financial Reporting Council 2018). Social backgrounds, cognitive and personal strengths are considered to bring unique perspectives and increase the capability of the Board to identify innovative solutions together with factors of structural diversity like board independence and CEO non-duality (Adams et al. 2015).

However, the literature on CG also found negative impacts of board diversity on performance. Diversity may increase the degree of internal frictions and conflicts (Lount et al. 2015) and prolong decision-making, which means higher costs (Adams and Ferreira 2009). Female gender quotas on boards have sometimes negative impacts (Ferreira 2015), and the relationship between director experience and financial firm performance is not uniform (De Haan and Vlahu 2016). In general, studies on the relationship between board diversity and performance have led to mixed results because it is still not clear which attributes of diversity are important and when they have a positive and desired impact on board functionality (Hillman 2015).

In addition, prior conflicting evidence is related to the different research approaches and controls for types of diversity. While some authors study the individual effect of single diversity aspects (e.g., only the impact of gender on banks profitability), others call for including several aspects of diversity simultaneously (Adams et al. 2015). Following this trend, Ararat et al. (2015) have developed a composite index for capturing and measuring the diversity of boards.

While the latter, simultaneous, method has the advantage to take into account multiple attributes taking place in real life board working, it has the drawback to reduce comparability of results as different authors may use different variables and approaches to create a measure (typically an index) to capture the relevant diversity dimensions. For example, as Adegboye et al. (2020), researchers have employed principal component analysis or adopt a more theoretically driven approach like Al-Hadi et al. (2019). The latter study utilized prior research to identify the constructing variables and construct a corporate governance index as the sum of individual variables scores (1 or 0) divided by the maximum expected index score. Some authors use more practically-oriented frameworks like Moalla et al. (2020) that create a governance index drawn from the OECD principles of corporate governance. Bearing in mind all these relevant aspects, in the methods and sample section we describe how we created our index for board diversity.

3.2.2   ESG and Performance in the Bank Sector

A vast literature has tried to empirically prove the relationship between corporate financial performance and ESG firm's orientation, but many authors limited their scope of analysis to specific geographical areas and mainly addressed non-financial companies. There is a gap in the literature for studies investigating the phenomenon at the international level (Aouadi and Marsat 2018; Buallay 2020) and considering the financial and banking sectors (Buallay 2020; Shakil et al. 2019).

With reference to the bank sector, most of the existing studies report a positive impact of ESG engagement with respect to financial performance and typically on profitability (e.g., Simpson and Kohers 2002; Shen et al. 2016; Brogi and Lagasio 2019; Brighi et al. 2022), which might be expected to increase bank value (Bolton 2013). However, also mixed results emerge. For example, Nizam et al. (2019) analyse the impact of social and environmental sustainability on 713 banks' financial performance over the period 2013–2015 and found out that a positive impact on financial performance. Contrary to that, splitting ESG into its components generate mixed results on the performance (Buallay 2019). The environmental dimension is positively associated with ROE and Tobin's Q, the social pillar is negatively associated with ROA, ROE and Tobin's Q, and governance is positively associated with Tobin's Q but negatively associated with ROA and ROE.

The majority of the studies focus on the European context. Buallay (2019) reports a positive association between ESG and financial performance (measured in terms of ROA, ROE and Tobin's Q) in the European Union. La Torre et al. (2021), who analyse 44 European banks between 2009 and 2019, indicate a positive relationship between ESG performance and EVA spread. However, the relationship between the ESG performance and bank's market performance measures is negative. This finding means that the market is not incentivizing banks to voluntarily engage significant ESG actions. Due to this result, banking authorities' supervisory perspectives on bank ESG risk is necessary to drive banks adopting ESG practices. Also Bătae et al. (2021), who investigate the relationship between ESG and financial performance of 39 European banks for the period 2010–2019, offer several interesting results from the theoretical viewpoint. Their results indicate that banks with high ESG performance evidence resource efficiency and environmental innovation (environment-aware products and services process digitization). However, these ESG-related resources are not useful to gain competitive advantage and record positive financial performance as predicted by resource-based view theory (Sharma, et al. 2019; Andries and Stephan 2019). The obtained negative relationship between corporate social responsibility and financial performance is also against the prediction of stakeholder theory. Furthermore, against the agency theory prediction, CG quality contributes negatively to accounting performance and market valuation. Bătae et al. (2021) put forward the idea that investors do not value a bank's involvement in social responsibility and best governance practices. According to the authors these findings support the view that boards and managers are following investors 'preferences' for short term returns, which downplay governance improvements and corporate social responsibility (CSR) strategies.

Stakeholder theory (Freeman 1984) proposes that ESG investments shift attention from shareholder-focused to stakeholder-focused governance, which, in turn, leads to a reduction in management risk with a positive impact on the firm value. Broader stakeholder-focused governance has guided the latest research to investigate ESG's impact on both bank value and risk-taking. For example, Di Tommaso and Thornton (2020) examine performance of 81 banks headquartered in 19 European countries over 2007–2018 and found that ESG detracts banks' value but it has a beneficial impact on bank risk-taking. High ESG is associated with reduced bank risk-taking (Z-SCORE, CDS (Credit Default Swap) spread and Nonperforming loans). Risk-taking is mitigated by boards that are smaller, independent and gender diverse. Authors point out that considering ESG promotion is a trade-off between reduced bank risk-taking, a more stable financial system and bank value. Similarly, Chiaramonte et al. (2022) study whether ESG strategies enhance bank stability during financial turmoil. Their sample includes European banks in 21 countries observed over 2005–2017. The authors adopt two opposite views for explaining the relationship between CSR and risk: (i) the risk mitigation view (based on stakeholder theory, value created by moral capital) and (ii) the overinvestment view (rooted in agency theory, opportunistic management behaviour). Overall, more ESG engaged banks receive economic advantages such as lower risk, higher stability and benefits from Non-Financial Reporting Directive. Finally, Gangi et al. (2019) investigate if more environmentally friendly banks are less risky. Their sample, which comprises 142 banks, 35 countries, covering years 2011–2015, allow to state that banks with effective CG mechanisms are more likely to be engaged in environmentally friendly actions, but this engagement and CG mechanisms are negatively associated with banks' risks (measured by the Z-SCORE). Indeed, CG mechanisms are often accounted for when researchers investigate ESG impacts on banks' risk and performance. For example, García-Meca et al. (2015) studies the composition of the board of directors and its effects on bank performance for 159 banks, 9 countries and covering period 2004–2010. Performance measures are Tobin's Q and ROA. Results show that board's gender diversity increases bank performance, while national diversity inhibits it. However, such results are context-dependent: in regimes with weaker regulation and lower investor protection board diversity has less influence on the performance of banks.

In sum, prior literature found that investments in ESG aspects positively contribute to bank performance, but their evidence is mixed. Variety of results might be attributed to different performance variables used but also to empirical analyses often limited to single countries and/or specific types of banks or specific timeframe. Another limitation of several studies is the simplistic assessment of ESG engagement of banks. For example, Galletta et al. (2021) merely identify the presence or absence of specific social and environmental policies using a dummy variable (coded 1 if the bank engages with stakeholders and/or policies of gas emission reduction) in regression models.

This paper attempts to offer a more detailed and comprehensive analysis of the relationship between ESG practices and bank performance looking at the diversity of the board as the key driver. Our approach in this paper resembles that in Harjoto and Laksmana (2018), who report, with a US firm sample, that CSR serves as a control mechanism to curb excessive risk with the impact on firm risk-taking decisions contributing to greater firm value. Therefore, we investigate how board diversity (BD) affects directly or indirectly via ESG to bank performance.

3.3   Data and Methods

3.3.1   Sample and Data Sources

The sample refers to Organization for Economic Co-operation and Development (OECD) commercial banks, whose financial and ESG performance were obtained over the period 2008–2019. Data were retrieved from three datasets. The first one is BoardEx collecting information on directors' characteristics. The second one is Bankfocus, which offers information on the banks' consolidated financial statements. The third one is Refinitiv (Thomson Reuters) database that infers information on the ESG scores. Refinitiv provides a score for 10 categories that contribute to generate the three ESG pillar scores—environmental, social and corporate governance. ESG pillar scores evaluate a company's relative environmental, social and corporate governance performance, commitment and effectiveness. The three pillar scores are then aggregated in order to obtain the overall Refinitiv ESG score. Each pillar score as well as the overall ESG score varies between 0 (lowest performer) and 100 (best performer).

We exclude banks with missing data. We utilize an unbalanced panel dataset. However, to limit the effects of the problem of sporadically missing data, that is to say, incomplete panels, we choose only banks that have data for at least 4 continuous balance-sheet years (Baltagi 2005). The final dataset includes 3,159 bank-year observations.

3.3.2   Board Diversity Variable Measurement

While most of past studies link bank performance to gender diversity in the board (Galletta et al. 2022), the authors believe that diversity is a wider multidimensional concept. Drawing from management literature, we know that diversity in race, nationality, culture, religion, professional mindsets within the board and in the workforce in general, can be a lever for innovation and successful solutions (Cumming and Leung 2021). Thanks to the plurality of views freely expressed in decision-making (Aghazadeh 2004), board diversity potentially allows to better understand global markets, leads to more effective problem-solving and reduces group think. All these capabilities should head to better performance and reduce financial fragility of banks (Farag and Mallin 2015, 2017).

In order to investigate the relationship between BD and banks performance, the authors performed a quantitative analysis based on the creation of an index capable to synthesize relevant board characteristics, named Governance Diversity (GD). Following the study of Adegboye et al. (2020), we computed the following variables to create our index: (i) GENDER, which measures the presence of women in the board; (ii) AGE, which accounts for the different age of the board members; (iii) NATIONALITY, which describes the country of the director's nationality; and also (iv) NED, which refers to the presence of non-executive directors that measures the degree of independence of the board. GD index was obtained using Principal Component Analysis (PCA). It can be considered an alternative measure of the quality of the bank board governance, for example, if compared to the Refinitiv governance score, but focusing on specific social (gender, age and nationality) and occupational (role) characteristics.

The validity of PCA is tested through Kaiser–Meyer–Olkin (KMO), which is a measure of sampling adequacy. By this measure, if KMO is greater than 0.5 then it validates the suitability of using PCA. In our test, KMO is 0.5572 which validates PCA analysis. In order to find the correct component of GD, authors ran K-fold cross validation. K-fold helps through Root Mean Square Error (RMSE) to find the best component, which is selected based on lowest RMSE. The K-fold measures ROA, SROA and Z-SCORE of this study provided the first component as suitable, which has the lowest RMSE. Following lowest RMSE, authors employed the first component as GD in regression analyses.

3.3.2.1 *Performance Measures*

To investigate the relationship between the BD and bank performance, in this paper, we propose alternative proxies for bank performance. We first use the bank return on average assets (ROA) to then construct a risk-adjusted profitability measure, named SROA, following Stiroh (2004b), Chiorazzo et al. (2008) and Brighi and Venturelli (2014). SROA is defined as the ratio of net results from ordinary activities to total asset for a given year to the standard deviation of ROA in a rolling way over the last three years. Analytically,

$$\text{SROA}_{i,t} = \frac{\text{ROA}_{i,t}}{\sigma(\text{ROA}_{i,t})} \tag{3.1}$$

where $\text{SROA}_{i,t}$ indicates risk-adjusted returns for the bank i in the year t. Finally, as in Stiroh (2004a), we introduce a measure of insolvency risk computed in terms of the Z-SCORE as follows:

$$\text{Z-SCORE}_{i,t} = \frac{\left(\text{ROA}_{i,t} + \frac{\text{E}_{i,t}}{\text{TA}_{i,t}}\right)}{\sigma(\text{ROA}_{i,t})} \tag{3.2}$$

The Z-SCORE is a measure for insolvency risk widely used in recent empirical research (Stiroh 2004a, 2004b; Mercieca et al. 2007; Laeven and Levine 2008; Demirgüç-Kunt and Huizinga 2010; Brighi and Venturelli 2014). It is related to the probability of failure and quantifies how many standard deviations profits must fall below its mean to bankrupt the firm. Higher values of SROA and the Z-SCORE are desirable as they indicate higher bank profitability and lower insolvency risk.

3.3.2.2 Control Variables

Both external and internal factors affect the profitability and risk of banks over time. The external variables reflect environmental factors that are expected to affect the financial institutions return and risk. The internal determinants include bank-specific variables. Among the bank-specific determinants, we focus on bank size, capital ratio and board size, which build our vector of control variables. Since there are many ways to measure bank size, whose effects are important to capture, we clarify that in this paper we utilize the continuous variable SIZE, which is equal to the natural logarithm of total assets, where total asset is the year-end total assets (Stiroh 2004a; Stiroh and Rumble 2006; De Young and Rice 2004; Chiorazzo et al. 2008; Brighi and Venturelli 2014, 2016). The continuous variable, expressed as Ln (Total asset), is normally expected to be a superior regressor than some arbitrary size dummies, except the case when there is a non-monotonic relationship between size and performance. Yet, we also added SIZE SQ.

Table 3.1 displays a summary of all the variables included in the analysis. While Table 3.2 provides the key statistics, Table 3.3 describes the structure of the sample in terms of geographical distribution (covering 16 countries) and years of observation. Table 3.4 reports the correlation matrix. Visual inspection of the correlation matrix shows no multicollinearity between independent variables, which validates the stability of our regression results (see Mintah and Schadewitz 2015).

Table 3.1 Variables and definitions

Name	Definition
Dependent variables	
ROA	Net results from ordinary activity over total asset
SROA	Annual ROA over its standard deviation calculated in a rolling way over the last three years
Z-SCORE	$\dfrac{\left(\mathrm{ROA}_{i,t}+\frac{\mathrm{E}_{i,t}}{\mathrm{TA}_{i,t}}\right)}{\sigma\left(\mathrm{ROA}_{i,t}\right)}$ where E: Equity and TA: Total Assets
Independent variables	
Board characteristics	
NED	It is a dummy variable indicating if the director is independent $= 1$ or not $= 0$
GENDER	It measures the number of male board directors over the total number of board directors
NATIONALITY	Proportion of directors from different countries at the Annual Report date selected
AGE	It measures the directors' age
GD	It is an index measuring the diversity of the board, as mechanism of Corporate Governance. It has been generated through the Principal Component Analysis using the following variables: AGE, GENDER, NED and NATIONALITY
BOARD_SIZE	It measures the number of board directors
ESG characteristics	
ESG	The overall company ESG score measures the company's performance on environmental, social and corporate governance pillars. Source: Refinitiv ESG

(continued)

Table 3.1 (continued)

Name	Definition
ESGC	The overall company ESG score with ESG controversies to provide a comprehensive evaluation of the company's sustainability impact and conduct over time. Source: Refinitiv ESG
E	The weighted average relative rating of a company based on the reported environmental information and the resulting three environmental category scores. Source: Refinitiv ESG
G	The weighted average relative rating of a company based on the reported social information and the resulting four social category scores. Source: Refinitiv ESG
S	The weighted average relative rating of a company based on the reported governance information and the resulting three governance category scores. Source: Refinitiv ESG
Bank-specific determinants	
SIZE	Ln (Total Asset)
SIZE_SQ	The square of total asset
CAP_RATIO	The capital ratio defined as the ratio between Equity and Total Assets

Table 3.2 Summary statistics for all banks, on average over the period 2008–2019

VARIABLES	(1) N	(2) mean	(3) sd	(4) min	(5) max
ROA	3,159	0.470	1.109	−11.548	3.134
SROA	3,159	0.009	0.017	0.000	0.211
Z-SCORE	3,159	0.092	0.747	−0.001	11.447
GENDER	3,159	0.771	0.121	0.500	1.000
NED	3,159	0.488	0.500	0.000	1.000
AGE	3,159	65.298	9.110	47.000	83.000
NATIONALITY	3,159	0.312	0.251	0.000	0.900
BOARD_SIZE	3,159	16.326	6.102	9.000	29.000
ESG	3,004	66.203	16.925	8.855	94.246
ESGC	3,004	57.967	15.017	8.855	87.169
E	3,004	73.823	23.650	3.175	97.475
S	3,004	65.374	20.181	4.559	97.576
G	3,004	67.606	19.477	2.407	94.891
GD	3,180	−0.010	1.176	−2.602	3.318
ESG_GD	3,004	10.246	81.889	−193.094	237.667
SIZE	3,159	19.637	2.102	14.082	28.203
SIZE_SQ	3,159	390.030	84.964	198.298	795.385
CAP_RATIO	3,159	6.856	0.036	0.011	0.202

Table 3.3 The sample structure

	2008	2009	2010	2011	2012	2013	2014	2015	2016	2017	2018	2019	Total
Australia	10	11	9	11	11	9	10	10	11	9	9	8	118
Canada				1	1	1	1	1	1	1	1	2	10
Chile	10	7	7	7	7	6	7	7	10	10	8	10	96
Colombia						3	3	3	3	3	3	3	21
Denmark						10	10	11	11	10	11	10	73
Finland	14	13	14	11	14	12	12	12	15	14	13	15	159
France	16	14	17	16	16	15	15	14	14	14	14	14	179
Germany	47	51	51	51	52	46	46	46	48	50	52	51	591
Greece	32	14	15	15	14	14	15	10	10	8	8	7	162
Israel	13	13	13	28	29	27	29	27	28	22	18	17	264
Italy	31	22	23	19	18	18	29	34	35	34	32	29	324
Japan						10	11	11	11	11	21	21	96
Poland	33	32	32	30	30	32	31	30	29	14	13	8	314
Spain	39	42	45	42	40	38	38	41	40	39	40	42	486
Sweden	15	16	16	17	17	19	18	17	18	18	17	17	205
Turkey					9	8	9	8	8	7	5	7	61
Total	260	235	242	248	258	268	284	282	292	264	265	261	3159

3.3.3   Models

The models can be described by the following equation, in which $y = $ [ROA, SROA, Z-SCORE] are the dependent variables:

$$y_{i,t} = \alpha_{i,t} + \beta_1 \text{GD}_{i,t} + \beta_2 \text{ESG Score}_{i,t}$$

$$+ \beta_3 \text{GD}_{i,t} * \text{ESG Score}_{i,t} + \sum_{k=1}^{4} \varphi_k X'_{i,t} + \varepsilon_{i,t} \qquad (3.3)$$

where i represents the individual firm observation belonging to the sample ($i = 1, 2, 3, \ldots, 31560$); t indicates time ($t = 2002, \ldots, 2019$); β represents the parameters to be estimated; and X' is a vector of control variables that includes board and bank characteristics based on findings in the previous literature. Both constant and error terms are included in the model. The multivariate panel models incorporate bank and year fixed effects. Regressions are estimated separately for ROA (Table 3.5), SROA (Table 3.6) and Z-SCORE (Table 3.7) measures.

The first part of the equation aims to measure the effects of diversity on performance by using the GD index and its individual different measures

Table 3.4 Correlation matrix

	ROA	SROA	Z-SCORE	GENDER	NED	AGE	NATIONALITY	BOARD_SIZE	ESG
ROA	1								
SROA	−0.6286*	1							
Z-SCORE	0.0078	−0.061	1						
GENDER	0.0822*	0.2116*	−0.0596	1					
NED	−0.0511	−0.039	−0.0364	−0.1287*	1				
AGE	−0.0272	0.0083	0.0759*	0.1168*	0.2328*	1			
NATIONALITY	0.0244	−0.0889*	−0.0142	−0.2735*	0.1581*	−0.0970*	1		
BOARD_SIZE	−0.2420*	0.0107	−0.0484	−0.0455	−0.1348*	−0.0938*	0.0773*	1	
ESG	−0.3506*	−0.0378	−0.0627	−0.3851*	0.1971*	0.0912*	0.2139*	0.3234*	1
ESGC	−0.2233*	−0.0216	−0.0311	−0.1449*	0.1700*	0.1666*	0.0447	−0.0387	0.6716*
E	−0.3681*	−0.0961*	−0.0476	−0.4156*	0.1434*	0.0878*	0.1641*	0.4303*	0.7684*
S	−0.3549*	−0.0874*	−0.02	−0.4300*	0.1415*	0.0618	0.0311	0.3647*	0.8985*
G	−0.1143*	0.0858*	−0.0692	−0.0561	0.1844*	0.1032*	0.3905*	0.0069	0.6600*
GD	−0.0463	−0.1769*	0.0046	−0.7427*	0.4883*	−0.1222*	0.7609*	0.0277	0.3823*
SIZE	−0.0493	−0.0137	−0.0499	−0.0546	0.0812*	0.0997*	0.1428*	0.2066*	0.2075*
SIZE_SQ	−0.0355	−0.0099	−0.0508	−0.0313	0.0764*	0.0932*	0.1122*	0.1728*	0.1599*
CAP_RATIO	0.4869*	0.1486*	−0.004	0.3185*	−0.0853*	−0.0351	−0.1345*	−0.3980*	−0.4777*

(continued)

Table 3.4 (continued)

	ESGC	E	S	G	GD	SIZE	SIZE_SQ	CAP_RATIO
ESGC	1							
E	0.5085*	1						
S	0.5495*	0.7139*	1					
G	0.5291*	0.2849*	0.2963*	1				
GD	0.1466*	0.3527*	0.2896*	0.2983*	1			
SIZE	−0.0417	0.0685	0.1238*	0.2300*	0.1276*	1		
SIZE_SQ	−0.0675	0.0115	0.0785*	0.2120*	0.0972*	0.9946*	1	
CAP_RATIO	−0.2724*	−0.6655*	−0.5099*	−0.0509	−0.2719*	−0.1710*	−0.1359*	1

* indicates statistical significance at the 10%

This table provides information on multicollinearity. Visual inspection of the table shows no correlation between independent variables

Table 3.5 Results on governance diversity, ESG factors and ROA

	Model 1	Model 2	Model 3	Model 4	Model 5	Model 6	Model 7
GENDER	−1.0863***						
	(0.2283)						
NED	−0.0023						
	(0.0285)						
AGE	−0.0020						
	(0.0016)						
NATIONALITY	−0.1392						
	(0.1326)						
GD		0.0491**			0.0831***	0.0694***	
		(0.0247)			(0.0264)	(0.0261)	
E			−0.0026*		−0.0026*		
			(0.0015)		(0.0015)		
S			−0.0010		−0.0008		
			(0.0016)		(0.0017)		
G			−0.0080***				
			(0.0017)				
ESG				−0.0196***		−0.0189***	
				(0.0030)		(0.0030)	
ESGC				0.0095***		0.0093***	0.0031**
				(0.0019)		(0.0019)	(0.0015)
GD_ESG							0.0018***
							(0.0004)
controls	controls	controls	controls	controls	controls	controls	controls
SIZE	6.0049***	6.4129***	9.7651***	9.4304***	9.8298***	9.8183***	9.6909***
	(0.5800)	(0.5529)	(0.7804)	(0.7639)	(0.7930)	(0.7770)	(0.7776)
SIZE_SQ	−0.1358***	−0.1457***	−0.2301***	−0.2232***	−0.2310***	−0.2316***	−0.2280***

(continued)

Table 3.5 (continued)

	Model 1	Model 2	Model 3	Model 4	Model 5	Model 6	Model 7
BOARD_SIZE	-0.0405***	-0.0506***	-0.0499***	-0.0440***	-0.0411***	-0.0410***	-0.0372***
	(0.0139)	(0.0133)	(0.0192)	(0.0188)	(0.0194)	(0.0190)	(0.0191)
	(0.0099)	(0.0097)	(0.0097)	(0.0096)	(0.0098)	(0.0097)	(0.0098)
CAP_RATIO	42.5640***	41.4792***	45.6608***	45.2045***	45.2385***	45.4413***	45.7541***
	(1.1396)	(1.1202)	(1.2148)	(1.1927)	(1.2119)	(1.1948)	(1.1993)
Constant	52.1858***	55.2851***	88.4203***	85.6539***	88.0912***	88.8104***	86.4066***
	(5.4116)	(5.1813)	(7.4986)	(7.3400)	(7.5720)	(7.4282)	(7.4197)
Observations	3,159	3,159	2,982	2,982	2,982	2,982	2,982
Adjusted R-squared	0.5900	0.5872	0.6091	0.6118	0.6074	0.6126	0.6095
Bank Fixed Effect	YES	YES	YES	YES	YES	YES	YES
Year Fixed Effect	YES	YES	YES	YES	YES	YES	YES

***, ** and * indicates statistical significance at the 1%, 5% and 10%, respectively

Notes: This table reports the results of a panel data regression fixed effect. Regression coefficients are reported with SE in parenthesis. The dependent variable is ROA

Table 3.6 Results on governance diversity, ESG factors and SROA

	Model 1	Model 2	Model 3	Model 4	Model 5	Model 6	Model 7
GENDER	0.0109***						
	(0.0039)						
NED	−0.0000						
	(0.0005)						
AGE	0.0000						
	(0.0000)						
NATIONALITY	0.0043*						
	(0.0022)						
GD		−0.0003			−0.0005	−0.0002	
		(0.0004)			(0.0004)	(0.0004)	
E			0.0001***		0.0001***		
			(0.0000)		(0.0000)		
S			0.0000		0.0000		
			(0.0000)		(0.0000)		
G			0.0001***				
			(0.0000)				
ESG				0.0004***		0.0004***	
				(0.0000)		(0.0000)	
ESGC				−0.0002***		−0.0002***	−0.0001***
				(0.0000)		(0.0000)	(0.0000)
GD_ESG							−0.0000**
							(0.0000)
controls	controls	controls	controls	controls	controls	controls	controls

(continued)

Table 3.6 (continued)

	Model 1	Model 2	Model 3	Model 4	Model 5	Model 6	Model 7
SIZE	−0.0430***	−0.0508***	−0.0678***	−0.0591***	−0.0630***	−0.0603***	−0.0542***
	(0.0098)	(0.0093)	(0.0131)	(0.0128)	(0.0134)	(0.0130)	(0.0131)
SIZE_SQ	0.0008***	0.0010***	0.0013***	0.0012***	0.0012***	0.0012***	0.0010***
	(0.0002)	(0.0002)	(0.0003)	(0.0003)	(0.0003)	(0.0003)	(0.0003)
BOARD_SIZE	0.0008***	0.0009***	0.0009***	0.0008***	0.0008***	0.0008***	0.0008***
	(0.0002)	(0.0002)	(0.0002)	(0.0002)	(0.0002)	(0.0002)	(0.0002)
CAP_RATIO	−0.6018***	−0.5881***	−0.6781***	−0.6726***	−0.6669***	−0.6734***	−0.6783***
	(0.0192)	(0.0189)	(0.0204)	(0.0200)	(0.0204)	(0.0201)	(0.0203)
Constant	−0.2862***	−0.3494***	−0.4918***	−0.4193***	−0.4362***	−0.4292***	−0.3497***
	(0.0913)	(0.0873)	(0.1261)	(0.1231)	(0.1276)	(0.1247)	(0.1254)
Observations	3,159	3,159	2,982	2,982	2,982	2,982	2,982
Adjusted R-squared	0.5079	0.5063	0.5389	0.5450	0.5349	0.5449	0.5353
Bank Fixed Effect	YES	YES	YES	YES	YES	YES	YES
Year Fixed Effect	YES	YES	YES	YES	YES	YES	YES

***, **, and * indicates statistical significance at the 1%, 5% and 10%, respectively

Notes: This table reports the results of a panel data regression fixed effect. Regression coefficients are reported with SE in parenthesis. The dependent variable is SROA

Table 3.7 Results on governance diversity, ESG factors and Z-SCORE

	Model 1	Model 2	Model 3	Model 4	Model 5	Model 6	Model 7
GENDER	−1.0236***						
	(0.2147)						
NED	−0.0517*						
	(0.0268)						
AGE	0.0011						
	(0.0015)						
NATIONALITY	0.7642***						
	(0.1247)						
GD		0.0842***			0.0725***	0.0638**	
		(0.0233)			(0.0255)	(0.0251)	
E			−0.0033**		−0.0031**		
			(0.0014)		(0.0014)		
S			−0.0108***		−0.0109***		
			(0.0016)		(0.0016)		
G			−0.0138***				
			(0.0016)				
ESG				−0.0326***		−0.0320***	
				(0.0028)		(0.0028)	
ESGC				0.0044**		0.0043**	−0.0067***
				(0.0018)		(0.0018)	(0.0015)
GD_ESG							0.0013***
							(0.0003)
controls	controls	controls	controls	controls	controls	controls	controls

(continued)

Table 3.7 (continued)

	Model 1	Model 2	Model 3	Model 4	Model 5	Model 6	Model 7
SIZE	−0.5535	−1.3537***	−1.6387**	−1.7066**	−1.9546**	−1.3503*	−2.0074***
	(0.5455)	(0.5218)	(0.7483)	(0.7327)	(0.7671)	(0.7453)	(0.7580)
SIZE_SQ	0.0128	0.0304**	0.0388**	0.0406**	0.0465**	0.0328*	0.0486***
	(0.0130)	(0.0125)	(0.0184)	(0.0180)	(0.0188)	(0.0183)	(0.0186)
BOARD_SIZE	−0.0195**	−0.0249***	−0.0348***	−0.0297***	−0.0227**	−0.0269***	−0.0257***
	(0.0093)	(0.0092)	(0.0093)	(0.0092)	(0.0095)	(0.0093)	(0.0095)
CAP_RATIO	1.7810*	1.6256	1.3904	0.7267	0.4138	0.9442	1.2258
	(1.0719)	(1.0572)	(1.1648)	(1.1440)	(1.1725)	(1.1461)	(1.1692)
Constant	−4.2185	−11.4880**	−12.5970*	−13.3239*	−16.6928**	−10.4242	−18.0778**
	(5.0899)	(4.8899)	(7.1898)	(7.0400)	(7.3255)	(7.1253)	(7.2330)
Observations	3,159	3,159	2,982	2,982	2,982	2,982	2,982
Adjusted R-squared	0.1997	0.1889	0.2228	0.2276	0.2052	0.2290	0.1974
Bank Fixed Effect	YES	YES	YES	YES	YES	YES	YES
Year Fixed Effect	YES	YES	YES	YES	YES	YES	YES

***, ** and * indicates statistical significance at the 1%, 5% and 10%, respectively

Notes: This table reports the results of a panel data regression fixed effect. Regression coefficients are reported with SE in parenthesis. The dependent variable is Z-SCORE

used to create the index: AGE, GENDER, NATIONALITY and NED. Then, the equation estimates the effect of the ESG score as provided by Refinitiv on firm's performance. In the models, we use different measures of ESG: ESG, ESGC and E, S and G separately (for variable definitions, see Table 3.1). The latter refer to the single pillars (E, S and G), while the first two measures refer to the cumulative ESG score with or without the controversies score. Finally, it has been estimated the impact of the inter-action effect between the GD and the ESG score on the three dependent variables, ROA SROA and Z-SCORE.

3.4   RESULTS

Results are presented in Tables 3.5, 3.6 and 3.7. We first investigate (model 1) the effect of board diversity focusing on individual measures related to variables AGE, GENDER, NATIONALITY and NED. The single board characteristics are not statistically significant expect for the GENDER suggesting a negative impact in terms of less return (Table 3.5) and more risk (Table 3.7), but greater performance adjusted for the risk (Table 3.6). So, we cannot just equate the presence of female members in the board with reduced risk as some studies did in the past. Female directors contribute to curb the risk given certain performance objectives. Then, we included the GD index developed with the PCA (model 2). Results are statistically significant suggesting that board diversity is important in the influence of the bank risk-performance strategies. A better board diversification implies greater return (Table 3.5) and less risk (Table 3.7).

As for the ESG analysis, we first consider separately the E, S and G scores (model 3) to then substitute them with the comprehensive ESGC and ESG scores provided by Refinitiv (model 4). The results suggest that the single E, S and G pillars have a negative impact in terms of minor return (ROA) and more risk (Z-SCORE). Differently, when we consider the impact in terms of performance adjusted by the risk (SROA) the result reverse to positive, i.e., as the single E, S and G scores improve the firm benefits in terms of greater performance adjusted for the risk. However, S dimension is not statistically significant here. Similarly, results hold in the case of the composite ESG score but they are reversed when we pass to consider the combined ESGC score, i.e., the ESG scores corrected by the negative effect of the controversies. In this last case results suggest an increase in the return, a decrease in the risk but a reversed effect in terms of performance adjusted by the risk. These undefined and not conclusive results suggest that further investigation becomes necessary.

We also investigate how the results of model 3 could change by substituting the measure of governance provided by Refinitiv with the GD index by creating model 5. Results suggest that our measure of corporate governance diversity becomes positive and significant in the case of the ROA, i.e., as the GD increases the firm registers a positive impact in terms of more return. The results appear positive and statistically significant also in the case of the risk measured by the Z-SCORE, i.e., as the GD increases the risk of the firm decreases.

Then, we proceed to verify if the same model holds considering at the same time the ESG and the ESGC scores, i.e., the scores without and with the controversies, respectively (model 6). Results suggest that the GD index also in this case contributes to improve the return and to decrease the risk of the firm. As for the ESG scores results suggest that ESG produces a negative impact in terms of a decreased return and increased risk. The contrary holds for the ESGC score. The results are coherent given that in the case of ESG the score is not corrected for the negative effect due to controversies. When we pass to consider the score netted by the controversies the sign is simply and coherently reversed.

Finally, we further investigate the interaction between a bank's ESG orientation and its attitude towards GD (computed as the combined effect of the firm ESG score and the GD index). We find an interesting result both in terms of return and risk (model 7). The GD index outweighs the negative impact on the profitability due to the controversies. A good governance can spur the bank to mitigate the ESG negative controversies effects. An adequate GD can more than outweigh a controversy negative effect, in fact the interaction between GD and ESG generates the desired multiplier effect of the corporate governance on ESG as suggested in the literature (Manning et al. 2019) with a final positive impact both in terms of increased profitability (ROA) and risk reduction (Z-SCORE).

The controls behave as expected. As for the BOARD_SIZE results suggest that as the number of board directors increases, we observe both a decrease in the return and an increase in the risk. Results appear however reversed when considering the performance adjusted by the risk.

This result is in line with agency theory that associates better financial performance to smaller board size because they more easily communicate and coordinate actions compared to larger boards. At the same time, it refuses the proposition of resource dependence theory, which is in favour of larger boards, as more directors offer greater linkages and networks, reducing a bank's dependency on external resources.

3.5   Conclusions

The most recent discipline on the corporate governance and board effectiveness (Financial Reporting Council 2018; EBA and ESMA 2021; EBA 2021b) suggests that an increasing degree of diversification among the board members—gender, age, competence and independence—could improve the board dialectic spurring the bank to adopt more performant strategies.

Past literature has often operationalized board diversity as a single variable: most contributions focus on gender or they measure the impacts of single aspects of the governance (e.g., board independence). This chapter tries to contribute to this stream of literature by enclosing in a single index different aspects of the board diversity and then to investigate its effects in terms of risk and performance. The evidence suggests that board diversity have any statistically significant effects in terms of bank-risk performance.

These results are robust to the inclusion in the model of the variables summarizing the firm ESG orientation. The GD variable continues to be firm value increasing even considering the negative effect produced by the controversies in the ESG dimension. Moreover, a good governance can spur the bank to mitigate the ESG negative controversies effects. An adequate GD can more than outweigh a controversy negative effect. In this sense, a good board diversification becomes more effective in presence of ESG controversies, i.e., the board can more than outweigh the negative effects linked to the ESG controversies dimension.

References

Adams, Renée B.; Ferreira, Daniel. Women in the boardroom and their impact on governance and performance. *Journal of Financial Economics*, 2009, 94.2: 291–309.

Adams, Renee B.; De Haan, Jakob; Terjesen, Siri; Van Ees, Hans. Board diversity: Moving the field forward. *Corporate Governance: An International Review*, 2015, 23.2: 77–82.

Adegboye, Alex; Ojeka, Stephen; Adegboye, Kofo. Corporate governance structure, Bank externalities and sensitivity of non-performing loans in Nigeria. *Cogent Economics & Finance*, 2020, 8.1: 1816611.

Aghazadeh, Seyed-Mahmoud. Managing workforce diversity as an essential resource for improving organizational performance. *International Journal of Productivity and Performance Management*, 2004.

Al-Hadi, A.; Al-Yahyaee, K.H.; Hussain, S.M.; Taylor, G. Market risk disclosures and corporate governance structure: Evidence from GCC financial firms. *The Quarterly Review of Economics and Finance*, 2019, 73: 136–150.

Anderson, R.C.; Reeb, D.M.; Upadhyay, A.; Zhao, W. The economics of director heterogeneity. *Financial Management*, 2011, 40.1: 5–38.

Andries, Petra; Stephan, Ute. Environmental innovation and firm performance: How firm size and motives matter. *Sustainability*, 2019, 11.13: 3585.

Aouadi, Amal; Marsat, Sylvain. Do ESG controversies matter for firm value? Evidence from international data. *Journal of Business Ethics*, 2018, 151.4: 1027–1047.

Ararat, Melsa; Aksu, Mine; Tansel Cetin, Ayse. How board diversity affects firm performance in emerging markets: Evidence on channels in controlled firms. *Corporate Governance: An International Review*, 2015, 23.2: 83–103.

Aslam, Ejaz; Haron, Razali. Does corporate governance affect the performance of Islamic banks? New insight into Islamic countries. *Corporate Governance: The International Journal of Business in Society*, 2020.

Avrampou, A.; Skouloudis, A.; Iliopoulos, G.; Khan, N. Advancing the sustainable development goals: Evidence from leading European banks. *Sustainable Development*, 2019, 27.4: 743–757.

Ayadi, R.; Bongini, P.; Casu, B.; Cucinelli, D. Bank business model migrations in Europe: Determinants and effects. *British Journal of Management*, 2021, 32.4: 1007–1026.

Baltagi, Badi H. *Econometric analysis of panel data*, John Wiley & Sons Ltd, West Sussex, England, 2005.

Bătae, Oana Marina; Dragomir, Voicu Dan; Feleagă, Liliana. The relationship between environmental, social, and financial performance in the banking sector: A European study. *Journal of Cleaner Production*, 2021, 290: 125791.

Bennouri, M.; Chtioui, T.; Nagati, H.; Nekhili, M. Female board directorship and firm performance: What really matters? *Journal of Banking & Finance*, 2018, 88: 267–291.

Birindelli, G.; Bonanno, G.; Dell'atti, S.; Iannuzzi, A.P. Climate change commitment, credit risk and the country's environmental performance: Empirical evidence from a sample of international banks. *Business Strategy and the Environment*, 2022, 31.4: 1641–1655.

Bolton, Brian J. Corporate social responsibility and bank performance. Available at SSRN 2277912, 2013.

Brighi, Paola; Venturelli, Valeria. How do income diversification, firm size and capital ratio affect performance? Evidence for bank holding companies. *Applied Financial Economics*, 2014, 24.21: 1375–1392.

Brighi, Paola; Venturelli, Valeria. How functional and geographic diversification affect bank profitability during the crisis. *Finance Research Letters*, 2016, 16: 1–10.

Brighi, Paola; Della Bina, Antonio Carlo Francesco; Venturelli Valeria. Do ESG investments mitigate ESG controversies? Evidence from international data. *CEFIN Working Papers*, 2022, 1–34.

Brogi, Marina; Lagasio, Valentina. Environmental, social, and governance and company profitability: Are financial intermediaries different? *Corporate Social Responsibility and Environmental Management*, 2019, 26.3: 576–587.

Bruno, Michelangelo; Lagasio, Valentina. An overview of the European policies on ESG in the banking sector. *Sustainability*, 2021, 13.22: 12641.

Bryant, Murray; Sigurjonsson, Throstur Olaf; Mixa, Már Wolfgang. Restoring trust in public institutions and the financial system. *International Journal of Economics and Accounting*, 2014, 5.4: 306–319.

Buallay, Amina, Is sustainability reporting (ESG) associated with performance? Evidence from the European banking sector. *Management of Environmental Quality*, 2019, 30.1: 98–115.

Buallay, Amina Mohamed. Sustainability reporting and bank's performance: Comparison between developed and developing countries. *World Review of Entrepreneurship, Management and Sustainable Development*, 2020, 16.2: 187–203.

Cardoni, Andrea; Kiseleva, Evgeniia; Lombardi, Rosa. A sustainable governance model to prevent corporate corruption: Integrating anticorruption practices, corporate strategy and business processes. *Business Strategy and the Environment*, 2020, 29.3: 1173–1185.

Chiaramonte, L.; Dreassi, A.; Girardone, C.; Piserà, S. Do ESG strategies enhance bank stability during financial turmoil? Evidence from Europe. *The European Journal of Finance*, 2022, 28.12: 1173–1211.

Chiorazzo, Vincenzo; Milani, Carlo; Salvini, Francesca. Income diversification and bank performance: Evidence from Italian banks. *Journal of Financial Services Research*, 2008, 33.3: 181–203.

Cumming, Douglas; Leung, Tak Yan; Rui, Oliver. Gender diversity and securities fraud. *Academy of Management Journal*, 2015, 58.5: 1572–1593.

Cumming, Douglas; Leung, Tak Yan. Board diversity and corporate innovation: Regional demographics and industry context. *Corporate Governance: An International Review*, 2021, 29.3: 277–296.

De Haan, Jakob; Vlahu, Razvan. Corporate governance of banks: A survey. *Journal of Economic Surveys*, 2016, 30.2: 228–277.

Demirgüç-Kunt, Asli; Huizinga, Harry. Bank activity and funding strategies: The impact on risk and returns. *Journal of Financial Economics*, 2010, 98.3: 626–650.

DeYoung, Robert; Tara, Rice. Non-interest income and financial performance at US commercial banks. *Financial Review*, 2004, 39(1): 101–127.

Di Tommaso, C., & Thornton, J. Do ESG scores effect bank risk taking and value? Evidence from European banks. *Corporate Social Responsibility and Environmental Management*, 2020, 27(5): 2286–2298.

EBA-European Banking Authority. Report on management and supervision of ESG risks for credit institutions and investment firms, 2021a, EBA/REP/2021/18.

EBA-European Banking Authority. Final Report on Guidelines on internal governance under Directive 2013/36/EU, July 2021b, Communication EBA/GL/2021/05 2.

EBA-European Banking Authority and ESMA—European Securities and Markets Authority. Final Report on Guidelines on the assessment of the suitability of members of the management body and key function holders under Directive 2013/36/EU and Directive 2014/65/EU, 2021, ESMA35-36-2319 EBA/GL/2021/06.

ECB—European Central bank. Guide on climate-related and environmental risks Supervisory expectations relating to risk management and disclosure, 2020, https://www.bankingsupervision.europa.eu/ecb/pub/pdf/ssm.202011finalguideonclimate-relatedandenvironmentalrisks~58213f6564.en.pdf.

Farag, Hisham; Mallin, Christine. Corporate governance and diversity in Chinese banks. In: *Sustainable entrepreneurship in China*. Palgrave Macmillan, New York, 2015. pp. 23–54.

Farag, Hisham; Mallin, Chris. Board diversity and financial fragility: Evidence from European banks. *International Review of Financial Analysis*, 2017, 49: 98–112.

Ferreira, Daniel. Board diversity: Should we trust research to inform policy? *Corporate Governance: An International Review*, 2015, 23.2: 108–111.

Financial Reporting Council—FRC. Guidance on Board effectiveness, 2018. https://www.frc.org.uk/getattachment/61232f60-a338-471b-ba5a-bfed25 219147/2018-guidance-on-board-effectiveness-final.pdf

Freeman, R.E. *Strategic management: A stakeholder approach.* Pitman Publishing, Boston (1, 4), 1984.

Galletta, S.; Mazzù, S.; Naciti, V.; Vermiglio, C. Gender diversity and sustainability performance in the banking industry. *Corporate Social Responsibility and Environmental Management*, 2022, 29.1: 161–174.

Gangi, F.; Meles, A.; D'angelo, E.; Daniele, L.M. Sustainable development and corporate governance in the financial system: Are environmentally friendly banks less risky? *Corporate Social Responsibility and Environmental Management*, 2019, 26.3: 529–547.

García-Meca, Emma; García-Sánchez, Isabel-María; Martínez-Ferrero, Jennifer. Board diversity and its effects on bank performance: An international analysis. *Journal of Banking & Finance*, 2015, 53: 202–214.

Garcia-Torea, Nicolas; Fernandez-Feijoo, Belen; De La Cuesta, Marta. Board of director's effectiveness and the stakeholder perspective of corporate governance: Do effective boards promote the interests of shareholders and stakeholders? *BRQ Business Research Quarterly*, 2016, 19.4: 246–260.

Gulati, Rachita; Kattumuri, Ruth; Kumar, Sunil. A non-parametric index of corporate governance in the banking industry: An application to Indian data. *Socio-Economic Planning Sciences*, 2020, 70: 100702.

Hahn, Tobias; Figge, Frank. Beyond the bounded instrumentality in current corporate sustainability research: Toward an inclusive notion of profitability. *Journal of Business Ethics*, 2011, 104.3: 325–345.

Hansen, Lars Peter. Central banking challenges posed by uncertain climate change and natural disasters. *Journal of Monetary Economics*, 2022, 125: 1–15.

Harjoto, Maretno; Laksmana, Indrarini. The impact of corporate social responsibility on risk taking and firm value. *Journal of Business Ethics*, 2018, 151.2: 353–373.

Hillman, Amy J. Board diversity: Beginning to unpeel the onion. *Corporate Governance: An International Review*, 2015, 23.2: 104–107.

Jacoby, G.; Liu, M.; Wang, Y.; Wu, Z.; Zhang, Y. Corporate governance, external control, and environmental information transparency: Evidence from emerging markets. *Journal of International Financial Markets, Institutions and Money*, 2019, 58: 269–283.

John, Kose; de Masi, Sara; Paci, Andrea. Corporate governance in banks. *Corporate Governance: An International Review*, 2016, 24.3: 303–321.

Khan, Habib Zaman, Sudipta Bose, Abu Taher Mollik and Harun Harun. "Green washing" or "authentic effort"? An empirical investigation of the quality of sustainability reporting by banks. *Accounting, Auditing & Accountability Journal*, 2021, 34.2: 338–369.

Kolk, Ans; Pinkse, Jonatan. The integration of corporate governance in corporate social responsibility disclosures. *Corporate Social Responsibility and Environmental Management*, 2010, 17.1: 15–26.

Kuang, Y.F.; Liu, X.K.; Paruchuri, S.; Qin, B. Cfo social ties to non-CEO senior managers and financial restatements. Accounting and Business Research, 2022, 52.2: 115–149.

La Torre, Mario; Leo, Sabrina; Panetta, Ida Claudia. Banks and environmental, social and governance drivers: Follow the market or the authorities? *Corporate Social Responsibility and Environmental Management*, 2021, 28.6: 1620–1634.

Laeven, Luc; Levine, Ross. Complex ownership structures and corporate valuations. *The Review of Financial Studies*, 2008, 21.2: 579–604.

Lount, R.B.J.; Sheldon, O.; Rink, F.; Phillips, K.W. Biased perceptions of racially diverse teams and their consequences for resource support. Organization Science, 2015, 26.5: 1351–1364.

Love, Inessa; Rachinsky, Andrei. Corporate governance and bank performance in emerging markets: Evidence from Russia and Ukraine. *Emerging Markets Finance and Trade*, 2015, 51.sup2: S101-S121.

Malik, Muhammad Shaukat; Ali, Huma; Ishfaq, Anwar. Corporate social responsibility and organizational performance: Empirical evidence from banking sector. *Pakistan Journal of Commerce and Social Sciences (PJCSS)*, 2015, 9.1: 241–247.

Manning, Bart; Braam, Geert; Reimsbach, Daniel. Corporate governance and sustainable business conduct—Effects of board monitoring effectiveness and stakeholder engagement on corporate sustainability performance and disclosure choices. *Corporate Social Responsibility and Environmental Management*, 2019, 26.2: 351–366.

Mercieca, Steve; Schaeck, Klaus; Wolfe, Simon. Small European banks: Benefits from diversification? *Journal of Banking & Finance*, 2007, 31.7: 1975–1998.

Mintah, A.P.; Schadewitz, H. Audit Committee and its impact on the financial performance of a firm: An empirical investigation of UK financial institutions during the pre/post financial crisis, Working Paper. 2015.

Moalla, Marwa; Salhi, Bassem; Jarboui, Anis. An empirical investigation of factors influencing the environmental reporting quality: evidence from France. *Social Responsibility Journal*, 2020.

Money, Kevin; Schepers, Herman. Are CSR and corporate governance converging?: A view from boardroom directors and company secretaries in FTSE100 companies in the UK. *Journal of General Management*, 2007, 33.2: 1–11.

Mueller, Jens; Cocks, Graeme; Ingley, Coral. The seesaw of governance: getting the balance right. International *Journal of Business Strategy*, 2009, 9.1: 137–146

Nizam, Esma, et al. The impact of social and environmental sustainability on financial performance: A global analysis of the banking sector. *Journal of Multinational Financial Management*, 2019, 49: 35–53.

Palvia, Ajay; Vähämaa, Emilia; Vähämaa, Sami. Are female CEOs and chairwomen more conservative and risk averse? Evidence from the banking industry during the financial crisis. *Journal of Business Ethics*, 2015, 131.3: 577–594.

Schadewitz, Hannu; Spohr, Jonas. Gender diverse boards and goodwill changes: association between accounting conservatism, gender and governance. *Journal of Management and Governance*, 2022, 26.3: 757–779.

Scherer, Andreas Georg; Voegtlin, Christian. Corporate governance for responsible innovation: Approaches to corporate governance and their implications for sustainable development. *Academy of Management Perspectives*, 2020, 34.2: 182–208.

Shahzad, Ali M.; Rutherford, Matthew A.; Sharfman, Mark P. Stakeholder-centric governance and corporate social performance: A cross-national study. *Corporate Social Responsibility and Environmental Management*, 2016, 23.2: 100–112.

Shakil, Mohammad Hassan; Mahmood, Nihal; Tasnia, Mashiyat; Munim, Ziaul Haque. Do environmental, social and governance performance affect the financial performance of banks? A cross-country study of emerging market banks. *Management of Environmental Quality: An International Journal*, 2019, 30.6: 1331–1344.

Sharma, Dipasha; Bhattacharya, Sonali; Thukral, Shagun. Resource-based view on corporate sustainable financial reporting and firm performance: evidences from emerging Indian economy. *International Journal of Business Governance and Ethics*, 2019, 13.4: 323–344.

Shen, C.-H.; Wu, M.-W.; Chen, T.-H.; Fang, H. To engage or not to engage in corporate social responsibility: Empirical evidence from global banking sector. *Economic Modelling*, 2016, 55: 207–225.

Simpson, W. Gary; Kohers, Theodor. The link between corporate social and financial performance: Evidence from the banking industry. *Journal of Business Ethics*, 2002, 35.2: 97–109.

Stiroh, Kevin J. Diversification in banking: Is noninterest income the answer? *Journal of Money, Credit and Banking*, 2004a, 36.5: 853–882.

Stiroh, Kevin J. Do community banks benefit from diversification? *Journal of Financial Services Research*, 2004b, 25.2: 135–160.

Stiroh, Kevin J; Adrienne, Rumble. The dark side of diversification: The case of US financial holding companies. *Journal of Banking & Finance*, 2006, 30: 2131–2161.

Tarchouna, Ameni; Jarraya, Bilel; Bouri, Abdelfettah. How to explain non-performing loans by many corporate governance variables simultaneously? A corporate governance index is built to US commercial banks. *Research in International Business and Finance*, 2017, 42: 645–657.

Van den Berghe, Lutgart A.A.; Levrau, Abigail. Evaluating boards of directors: what constitutes a good corporate board? *Corporate Governance: An International Review*, 2004, 12.4: 461–478.

Veldman, Jeroen; Gregor, Filip; Morrow, Paige. Corporate governance for a changing world: Report of a global roundtable series. Brussels and London: Frank Bold and Cass Business School, 2016.

World Economic Forum. Measuring stakeholder capitalism: Towards common metrics and consistent reporting of sustainable value creation. Retrieved, 2020, https://www.weforum.org/reports/measuring-stakeholder-capitalism-towards-common-metrics-and-consistent-reporting-of-sustainable-value-cre ation/.

Zagorchev, Andrey; Gao, Lei. Corporate governance and performance of financial institutions. *Journal of Economics and Business*, 2015, 82: 17–41.

Zhang, Dana. Top management team characteristics and financial reporting quality. *The Accounting Review*, 2019, 94.5: 349–375.

ESG Default Risk Mitigation Effect: A Time-Sectorial Analysis

Egidio Palmieri, Enrico Fioravante Geretto, and Maurizio Polato

4.1 INTRODUCTION

Integrating environmental, social, and governance (ESG) issues into risk-taking policies and firms' strategic planning have become a topic of interest for banks, managers, researchers, and policymakers. As a result, the entire financial industry focused its attention on sustainability matters, and more than $30 trillion of assets under management are invested according to environmental-friendly criteria (Christensen et al. 2021).

E. Palmieri (✉) · E. F. Geretto · M. Polato
Department of Economics and Statistics, University of Udine, Udine, Italy
e-mail: egidio.palmieri@uniud.it

E. F. Geretto
e-mail: enrico.geretto@uniud.it

M. Polato
e-mail: maurizio.polato@uniud.it

S. Carbó-Valverde and P. J. Cuadros Solas (eds.), *New Challenges for the Banking Industry*, Palgrave Macmillan Studies in Banking and Financial Institutions, https://doi.org/10.1007/978-3-031-32931-9_4

Jointly to the introduction of IFRS 9, banks are required to assess the lifetime probability of default when a credit position deteriorates at least to stage two, noted as the underperforming stage. In this optic, the inclusion of ESG scoring will provide a tool for banks to correctly assess the probability of default with time horizons more significant than one year (Gubareva 2021). This approach has been becoming a standard for the financial sector following the loan origination and monitoring guidelines issued in 2021 by EBA. Firms that take care of sustainability issues can contribute to durable development and, at the same time, benefit from a reduction of the cost of capital charged by banks and financial markets. The decrease in the cost of capital is a consequence of improved creditworthiness.

In order to enlarge the knowledge matured in the previous literature, we developed two research questions at which we respond: (RQ1) Does each ESG pillar score impact with the same magnitude firms' probability of default on longer time horizons? (RQ2) Does the ESG risk mitigation effect changes in the function of the sector firms belong to?. The former research question is a topic of interest for banks and regulators. Credit institutions in an appliance to the EBA guidelines mentioned and IFRS 9 are interested in evaluating the impact of ESG performance variation on default probability for different time frames. At the same time, regulators are interested in the effect of capital allocation consequently to the firms' risk mitigation effect on time spans greater than one year. The second research question will interest banks due to the relevance of risk diversification strategies. Banks that integrate ESG performance in their risk appetite framework can dynamically adjust their capital allocation in the function of macroeconomic variables sectorial and geo-graphical areas.

Given this broad interest in the topic, researchers have studied the benefits of introducing ESG performance on creditworthiness assessment procedures exploiting market values, balance sheet items, and the ESG reports that specialized rating agencies publish for an ever-growing number of companies (Stubbs 2013; Berg et al. 2019; Gibson et al. 2021; Barth et al. 2022). In addition, a default risk mitigation effect has been discovered for firms that implement environmental, social, and governance policies (Devalle et al. 2017). Despite this evidence, there are currently problems regarding rating uniformity and transparency among rating agencies worldwide (Stubbs 2013). This "rating divergence" constitutes a deterrent for a systematic adoption of ESG metrics in assessing creditworthiness.

The first contribution of the present work consists of the confirmation of the existence of risk mitigation effect, even for short-medium term probabilities of default. Furthermore, we reveal that environmental score produces a remarkable impact on short-medium term default probabilities, while governance score improvements are consistent in the medium-long run. In the end, we quantify the sectorial impact on ESG risk mitigation effect for a subset of ten sectors.

To provide a reply to the mentioned research question, we structured the present chapter as follow: (i) Sect. 4.2, and it is provided a review of the literature concerning environmental, social, and governance issues, the relationship among ESG and firms' riskiness; (ii) in Sect. 4.3 we introduce the dataset, a brief description of the variables, the selection criteria, and we discuss the theoretical model applied for the development of the econometric model; (iii) in Sect. 4.4 the results of the econometric analysis are presented; (v) in Sect. 4.5 the conclusions are exposed.

4.2   LITERATURE REVIEW

Whether companies' default probabilities are affected by ESG performance is widely discussed in the literature. The research field can be firstly split according to the variable used as a proxy of firms' default likelihood: (i) estimates on probabilities of default directly gathered by information providers such as Bloomberg, Thomson Reuters, or Refinitiv Datastream; (ii) credit default swap spreads (CDSs), available on the market.

For the former research stream, it is possible to count the contribution of Höck et al. (2020): exploiting a sample of European non-financial firms demonstrates the ESG performance capability to decrease companies' credit risk. Another study always focused on European non-financial firms confirms these results, and they point out that an improvement in ESG score can generate a contraction of idiosyncratic risk (Sassen et al. 2016). Even Devalle et al. (2017) and De Santis et al. (2020) convey the existence of the risk mitigation effect in charge of any enhancement of ESG performance (Yang et al. 2020). Furthermore, other authors underline the benefits of ESG strategies in downside risk reduction.

Based on CDS spread, the latter research stream supports a u-shape relationship among firms' riskiness and ESG scores (Devalle et al. 2017). They also proved a negative association between credit risk and ESG performance. Additionally, the authors underline that firms starting from poor or modest ESG performance take more advantages from the risk mitigation effect; in fact, the latter is characterized by a decreasing marginal risk reduction.

A second research stream is focused on country regulation. According to them, environment safeguard and governance best practices could magnify the risk mitigation effect of environmental, social, and governance issues. Hübel (2020) provides a valuable contribution in this sense: the risk reduction effect is more consistent in countries characterized by relevant attention to ESG issues. ESG strategies are more effective in improving firms' creditworthiness, in civil law countries are more oriented on stakeholders than common law ones mainly concerned with free-market paradigms (Liang and Renneboog 2017; Kim and Li 2021). Risk mitigation is more prominent in countries where the protection of the environment, social development, and fair governance structures are topics of interest for the legislator and society. Typically, these countries reward ESG improvements with a lower cost of capital due to the increased creditworthiness. Coherently with this position, Breuer et al. (2018) affirm that countries distinguished by high levels of investor protection reward ESG compliant firms with a lower cost of capital. However, this dynamic can be observed only for firms with significant creditworthiness: the market reward marginally unreliable companies in terms of risk mitigation (Höck et al. 2020). In conclusion, in this section, European firms' overall credit risk reduction is more consistent than American ones when companies enhance ESG performance (Barth et al. 2022).

A third research stream can be observed as a function of the effectiveness of each ESG individual pillar in increasing firms' creditworthiness. According to Sassen et al. (2016) and Gibson et al. (2021), the contribution of environmental performance is more remarkable in credit risk reduction concerning all the other ESG dimensions. An opposite perspective suggests that social score improvements provide a solid signal to the market regarding lower riskiness because any social development reinforces a firm's reputation (Kim and Li 2021; Bhattacharya and Sharma 2018; Stellner et al. 2015). Finally, other authors attribute to governance score increases the most significant impact on reducing companies' riskiness (Cash 2018; Kiesel and Lücke 2019). According to this view, governance policies provide a managerial stimulus towards long-term decisions, and they affect firms' reputations in the medium-long term (Henisz and McGlinch 2019). Following this opinion, the ESG-driven risk mitigation effect is noticeably remarkable in the long run rather than in other time frames (Hübel 2020).

In opposition to all the previous contributions, a research stream is focused on the problems that affect the implementation of ESG strategies in reducing firms' riskiness. First, exist a problem in terms of rating uniformity and transparency. The former is represented by the situation in which two or more rating agencies assessing the same ESG firms for the same company employ a different subset of indicators and metrics. This problem is believed to be the cause of rating incomparability. With similar effects, the lack of transparency in ESG rating assessing methodology prevents any ESG rating from comparison. The lack of uniformity is generated by the tendency for which rating agencies, in the elaboration of sustainability reports, use a subset of ESG ratings tailored to customers' needs. On the other side, lack of transparency is triggered by a low tendency for rating agencies to share their know-how (Stubbs 2013; Avetisyan and Hockerts 2017). Scarcity of uniformity in charge of ESG indicators has been articulated in three different types of divergence: (i) scope divergence, which occurs when two rating agencies choose the same ESG metric in explaining two different phenomena; (ii) measurement divergence, which takes place when two rating agencies choose different ESG metric in explaining the same phenomena; and (iii) weight divergence, it occurs when two rating agencies define different weight matrix in the composition of overall ESG scores at pillar level (Berg et al. 2019; Christensen et al. 2021).

Furthermore, rating agencies tend to be biased by the rater effect. Once, an agency assigns a firm a positive score in one ESG area; all the other scores are positively affected and vice-versa. In addition, the existence of score divergence has been empirically demonstrated in a paper based on a sample of American firms listed in the S&P 500 index; moreover, they come up with the conclusion that rating divergence is directly related to stock returns (Gibson et al. 2021). In conclusion, rating divergence undermines comparability and induces market participants to study the dissimilarities among rating agencies' reports, compromising information efficiency (Ingo 2020). Definitively, we must point out that there is a need to adapt the current legal framework to increase the interest in ESG issues and ensure the complete comparability of the ratings and the transparency of the methodologies underlying which the reports are created (Olmedo et al. 2019).

4.3   DATA AND METHODS

In the first section, we introduce the dataset composition and statistics; in the second segment, the methodology used in the present paper is exposed.

4.3.1   Data

We collected data of 335 European listed companies on Bloomberg for 2010–2020. Variables are gathered on an annual basis, and the index market composition is provided in the Table 4.1. Firms characterized by uncomplete ESG scoring disclosure or missing probabilities of default and Z-score have been excluded to ensure data consistency and continuity. The unavailability of data referring to the Z-score and the ESG report for two periods after 2015 represents the trigger for missing observation elimination. Furthermore, companies subject to double listing have been removed. After applying these filters, the initial set of firms has been reduced to 211 elements.

To develop a sectorial-based analysis, we collected the information regarding each sector firms belong to exploiting Bloomberg Industry Classification Systems (BICS). Coherently with the purpose of the present work, we have decided to use the only first level of classification, and the financial sector has been excluded from our analysis. All the nine sectors considered are listed as follows in Table 4.2.

We considered the Altman Z-Score as a proxy of firms' idiosyncratic riskiness. Its value is derived from the analysis of balance sheet and income statement voices: (i) working capital; (ii) total assets; (iii) retention of

Table 4.1 Dataset composition by stock market index

Number of firms	Index	N. firms (%)
50	EUROSTOXX	15
20	BEL 20	6
40	CAC40	12
30	DAX30	9
100	FTSE100	30
35	IBEX	10
20	SMI	6
40	FTSE MIB	12
335	**Sum**	**100**

Table 4.2   Dataset composition by sector

Code	Sectors	N	%
COM	Communication	17	8
CON	Consumer Staples	28	13
DIS	Consumer Discretionary Products	21	10
ENE	Energy	28	13
HEA	Health care	19	9
IND	Industrials	28	13
MAT	Materials	21	10
TEC	Technology	30	14
UTI	Utilities	19	9
	Sum	**211**	**100**

profits; (iv) EBIT; (v) market capitalization; (vi) total liabilities; and (vii) turnover (Altman **1968**).

The dependent variable is the Bloomberg probability of default with a time horizon from 1 to 5 years. These measures are based on Merton's distance from default, preventing endogeneity biases.

ESG performance has been assessed for each pillar: (i) environmental, this dimension takes into consideration firms' annual emissions, exploitation of resources, and innovation level; (ii) social, this pillar concerns workforce condition, respect of human rights, contribution to the community and product responsibility; and (iii) governance, this component analyses quality of management, implementation of corporate social responsibility strategies, shareholders rights, and hostile takeovers. The overall ESG score proposed by Bloomberg is the weighted average of each pillar score adjusted to the controversies score that refers to the company object of study. Bloomberg does not provide the weights matrix or the ESG score methodology. However, the list of variables is provided as follows in Table 4.3.

An unbalanced panel dataset represents the final sample due to a temporal mismatch that characterized the residual firms after applying the filter selection. As a result of the filters, the analysis is based on 1.991 different observations. Table 4.4 represents the principal summary statistics: mean; variance; standard deviation; and quartiles.

Table 4.3 List of variables

Code	Variable	Source
ZSC	Altman Z-Score	Bloomberg
B1Y	Bloomberg PD 1 year	Bloomberg
B2Y	Bloomberg PD 2 years	Bloomberg
B3Y	Bloomberg PD 3 years	Bloomberg
B4Y	Bloomberg PD 4 years	Bloomberg
B5Y	Bloomberg PD 5 years	Bloomberg
ENV	Environment Disclosure	Bloomberg
GOV	Governance Disclosure	Bloomberg
SOC	Social Disclosure	Bloomberg
ESG	ESG Total Disclosure	Bloomberg
MKT	Market Capitalization	Bloomberg
LEV	Leverage	Bloomberg
ETA	Earning to Total Asset Ratio	Bloomberg
BIC	Bloomberg Industry Classification System	Bloomberg

4.3.2   Methods

Intending to assess the diversified sectorial contribution of ESG performance on firms' probability of default, we implemented a set of difference-in-difference analyses. We developed a difference-in-difference regression for each probability of default described above, evaluating the impact of the introduction of ESG metrics into the default likelihood assessment process.

According to Fama (1970), we assume that the European stock market benefits from solid efficiency, so market prices and values express a good approximation of firms' characteristics and probabilities of default. In this sense, the inclusion of ESG metrics into the difference-in-difference analysis grant us to discover a differential risk observed among treatment and control groups (Wooldridge and Imbens 2009). We attribute each firm to a control or treatment group through a pseudo-random algorithm. As an exogenous event, we consider the Paris Climate Agreement held in December 2015. We assume that after that occurrence, a broader interest in sustainability spreads on the market, affecting the estimation of firms' default probabilities.

Table 4.4 Dataset main statistics

	ZSC	B1Y (%)	B2Y (%)	B3Y (%)	B4Y (%)	B5Y (%)	ENV	GOV	SOC	ESG	MKT	LEV	ETA (%)
Mean	3.15	0.21	0.67	1.23	1.76	2.29	43.48	61.53	51.66	49.60	301.79	4.99	7.16
Variance	7.88	0.01	0.03	0.05	0.07	0.08	227.08	84.16	201.40	135.60	14,979.40	223.56	0.42
St. Dev	2.81	1.21	1.79	2.26	2.60	2.82	15.07	9.17	14.19	11.64	387.04	14.95	6.50
Minimum	0.05	0.00	0.01	0.06	0.15	0.33	2.33	26.79	8.77	11.57	2.15	1.10	−24.27
1st quartile	1.55	0.00	0.07	0.25	0.49	0.83	34.11	57.14	43.86	43.39	61.65	2.14	3.65
Median	2.55	0.02	0.25	0.63	1.06	1.55	44.72	62.50	54.39	50.83	156.69	2.76	6.34
3rd quartile	3.94	0.09	0.64	1.35	2.02	2.65	55.81	67.86	61.40	57.85	405.55	3.97	10.01
Maximum	38.63	25.59	33.71	38.52	41.44	43.04	79.07	96.24	85.96	77.27	3118.25	22.40	48.15

HYP1: ESG individual pillars do not contribute equally to the ESG risk mitigation effect.

HYP2: ESG risk mitigation effect is affected by sector firms belong to.

We developed a set of hypotheses to provide an answer to our research questions:

A difference-in-difference model applied to our dataset can assess changes in the probability of default as a function of the risk expressed by financial statements, corrected for the time factor, and adjusted for ESG performance. We present in the Table 4.5 the logic model implemented. The time effect represents the coefficients of interest (γ_1), the treatment effect connected to ESG performance (γ_2), and the interaction among ESG score and time effect (λ_1). This latter will be computed for each yearly probability of default and comparing the values of λ_1 it is possible to validate or reject hypothesis 1.

$$\begin{aligned} PD_{it} = {} & \alpha + \beta_1 * ZSC_{it} + \beta_2 * ENV_{it} + \beta_3 * SOC_{it} \\ & + \beta_4 * GOV_{it} + \gamma_1 * D_{\text{time}_{it}} + \gamma_2 * D_{\text{trm}_{it}} \\ & + \lambda_1 * D_{\text{trm}_{it}} * D_{\text{time}_{it}} + u_{it} \end{aligned}$$

with: (i) PD_{it} = probability of default with yearly time frame t ($t = 1; 2; 3; 4; 5$); (ii) α = constant; (iii) ZSC_{it} = Z-Score; (iv) ENV_{it} = environmental score; (v) SOC_{it} = social score; (vi) GOV_{it} = governance score; (vii) $D_{\text{time}_{it}}$ = dummy which takes a value of 1 for the years after 2014 and 0 in the other cases; (viii) $D_{\text{trm}_{it}}$ = dummy which takes value 1 in the group of companies treated and 0 in the rest; and (ix) $D_{\text{trm}_{it}} * D_{\text{tm}_{it}}$ = interaction variable that assumes a value of 1 in the case of companies

Table 4.5   Difference-in-difference model framework

	Before ESG (2010–2015)	After ESG (2015–2020)	After–Before
Control firms	α	$\alpha + \gamma_1$	γ_1
Treatment firms	$\alpha + \gamma_2$	$\alpha + \gamma_1 + \gamma_2 + \lambda_1$	$\gamma_1 + \lambda_1$
Control—treatment	γ_2	$\gamma_2 + \lambda_1$	λ_1

belonging to the treatment group for the years after 2014; (x) u_{it} = error term.

$$
\begin{aligned}
\text{PD}_{it} = {} & \alpha + \beta_1 * \text{ZSC}_{it} + \beta_2 * \text{ENV}_{it} + \beta_3 * \text{SOC}_{it} \\
& + \beta_4 * \text{GOV}_{it} + \delta_1 * \text{MAT}_{it} + \delta_2 * \text{DIS}_{it} \\
& + \delta_3 * \text{IND}_{it} + \delta_4 * \text{HEA}_{it} + \delta_5 * \text{TEC}_{it} \\
& + \delta_6 * \text{CON}_{it} + \delta_7 * \text{COM}_{it} + \delta_8 * \text{ENE}_{it} \\
& + \gamma_1 * D_{\text{time}_{it}} + \gamma_2 * D_{\text{trm}_{it}} + \lambda_1 * D_{\text{trm}_{it}} * D_{\text{time}_{it}} + u_{it}
\end{aligned}
$$

with: (i) PD_{it} = probability of default with yearly time frame t (t = 1; 2; 3; 4; 5); (ii) α = constant and utility sector given the omission of a sector; (iii) ZSC_{it} = Z-Score; (iv) ESG_{it} = ESG Score; (v) COM_{it} = dummy for communication sector; (vi) CON_{it} = dummy for consumer staple sector; (vii) DIS_{it} = dummy for discretionary product sector; (viii) ENE_{it} = dummy for energetic sector; (ix) HEA_{it} = dummy for health sector; (x) IND_{it} = dummy for industrial sector; (xi) MAT_{it} = dummy for materials sector; (xii) TEC_{it} = dummy for technology sector; (xiii) MKT_{it} = control variable that refers to market capitalization; (xiv) LEV_{it} = control variable that refers to leverage; (xv) ETA_{it} = control variable that refers to earning to total asset ratio; (xvi) $D_{\text{time}_{it}}$ = dummy which takes a value of 1 for the years after 2014 and 0 in the other cases; (xvii) $D_{\text{trm}_{it}}$ = dummy which takes value 1 in the group of companies treated and 0 in the rest; and (xviii) $D_{\text{trm}_{it}} * D_{\text{tm}_{it}}$ = interaction variable that assumes a value of 1 in the case of companies belonging to the treatment group for the years after 2014; (ix) u_{it} = error term.

4.4   RESULTS

In the first section, we introduce the results of the empirical models: (i) *difference-in-difference* that consider the effect of each ESG pillar on the probabilities of default; (ii) *difference-in-difference* that consider the effect of the overall ESG score on the probabilities of default considering the influence of the sector firms belong to.

The second section consists of the robustness test implemented to verify the correctness of the methodology applied to the present paper.

4.4.1   *Empirical Results*

Empirical results suggest that the environmental pillar accounts for the most in reducing firms' probability of default, with a confidence interval that grows as the time horizon expands (Table 4.6). A statistical significance characterizes yearly probabilities of default at 90%, while 5-year default likelihood has a 99% significance. Environmental pillar coefficients assume negative values that grow following a *u-shaped* expansion. This phenomenon means that each improvement in environmental performance significantly reduces default probabilities for two- and three-year time frames. Each environmental policy implementation carries out a set of benefits that occur with a delay and require time to be observed on the market. Therefore, credit institutions should consider default probabilities with time horizons longer than one year to better assess firms' creditworthiness.

There is no statistical significance regarding the social pillar, even if it is considered a 90% confidence interval. So social strategies cannot be considered a risk mitigation factor.

In opposition to previous results, governance score improvements can reduce firms' default probabilities only for time horizons greater or equal to three years (Chang et al. 2021; Bruno and Lagasio 2021). The existence of a more remarked delay for the effects produced by any change in governance strategies suggests that environmental pillar improvements produce a significant reduction of default likelihood in the short term. In contrast, governance score improvements are more consistent in the medium-long term.

Considering the entire *difference-in-difference* model, it is possible to observe that λ_1, the coefficient expression of the interaction among time and treatment assumes negative values and a statistical significance of 99%. These values can be interpreted as the risk mitigation effect between enterprises that do not implement ESG strategies before the exogenous shock and firms that realize ESG policies after the event represented by the *Paris agreement on climate*. Furthermore, the coefficient increases, in absolute values, along with the expansion of the time horizon considered. This means that the risk mitigation effect is more prominent for the medium-long term than the short term.

The F-test is statistically more remarkable than the critical value for each regression considered rejecting the multiple null hypotheses on all the regressors considered. Moreover, the adjusted R-squared improves

Table 4.6 Difference-in-difference model 1

	PD1	PD2	PD3	PD4	PD5
Intercept	0.078*	0.422***	0.225***	0.328***	0.419***
	(0.141)	(0.086)	(0.113)	(0.156)	(0.175)
ZSC	0.01	0.009	0.013	−0.006	−0.02
	(0.012)	(0.028)	(0.041)	(0.051)	(0.057)
ENV	−0.016*	−0.043**	−0.032**	−0.024***	−0.028***
	(0.0093)	(0.019)	(0.008)	(0.009)	(0.010)
SOC	0.006	0.015	0.031	0.028	0.052
	(0.007)	(0.016)	(0.023)	(0.029)	(0.032)
GOV	0.002	−0.024	−0.052	−0.021*	−0.026*
	(0.009)	(0.021)	(0.029)	(0.012)	(0.016)
MKT	−0.012***	−0.013***	−0.016***	−0.019***	−0.021***
	(0.001)	(0.001)	(0.002)	(0.004)	(0.005)
LEV	−0.016	−0.013	−0.023	−0.033	−0.042
	(0.018)	(0.011)	(0.017)	(0.021)	(0.023)
ETA	4.817***	9.123***	3.183***	3.667***	3.922***
	(0.3417)	(0.2087)	(0.3073)	(0.3825)	(0.4261)
time (γ_1)	0.129*	0.173**	0.169**	0.152**	0.124**
	(0.071)	(0.081)	(0.084)	(0.097)	(0.104)
treatment (γ_2)	−0.016	−0.046	−0.127	−0.146	−0.176
	(0.037)	(0.083)	(0.122)	(0.151)	(0.169)
$\lambda_1 = (\gamma_1 * \gamma_2)$	−0.119***	−0.225***	−0.292***	−0.336***	−0.369***
	(0.084)	(0.052)	(0.076)	(0.094)	(0.105)
R^2	0.1231	0.171	0.1934	0.2057	0.2149
R^2 Adj	0.1187	0.1668	0.1894	0.2017	0.211
F-Statistic on	27.79*** (df = 10; 1979)	40.83*** (df = 10; 1979)	47.47*** (df = 10; 1979)	51.26*** (df = 10; 1979)	54.19*** (df = 10; 1979)
N. Observations	1991	1991	1991	1991	1991

Note $*p < 0.1$; $**p < 0.05$; $***p < 0.01$

as the time interval expands, reinforcing the relevance of the risk mitigation effect on longer time horizons more significantly than one year. Regarding the second model of regression, it is possible to observe that the coefficient of the overall ESG score is negative and follows the same u-shape expansion observed for the environmental pillar in the first difference-in-difference model. This means that the effect produced by any improvement on charge of the overall ESG score manifests a more consistent reduction of the probability of default for the two years default likelihood. Furthermore, the magnitude of the reduction increase along with the time frame as can be observed for the governance pillar coefficient. The overall ESG score presents a statistical relevance of 99% for each PD extension (Table 4.7).

We remind you that we omitted the dummy variable referred to the utility sector concerning the sector-based analysis. In this sense, it

Table 4.7 Difference-in-difference model 2

	PD1	PD2	PD3	PD4	PD5
Intercept	0.081	0.184*	0.400**	0.169***	0.229***
	(0.125)	(0.077)	(0.113)	(0.139)	(0.156)
ZSC	0.012	0.011	0.020	−0.004	−0.017
	(0.013)	(0.028)	(0.042)	(0.051)	(0.058)
ESG	−0.025***	−0.056***	−0.028***	−0.036***	−0.042***
	(0.009)	(0.014)	(0.011)	(0.013)	(0.016)
COM	0.120	0.077	0.122	0.16	0.191
	(0.102)	(0.062)	(0.092)	(0.114)	(0.127)
CON	0.051	0.063	0.117	0.159	0.190
	(0.093)	(0.057)	(0.084)	(0.103)	(0.116)
DIS	0.044	0.083	0.104	0.107	0.102
	(0.104)	(0.063)	(0.093)	(0.115)	(0.129)
ENE	0.069	0.1904*	0.299*	0.376*	0.426*
	(0.050)	(0.096)	(0.165)	(0.197)	(0.234)
HEA	0.007	−0.011	0.063	0.093	0.112
	(0.099)	(0.06)	(0.089)	(0.113)	(0.123)
IDS	0.120	0.101	0.170*	0.203*	0.266*
	(0.093)	(0.057)	(0.096)	(0.117)	(0.136)
MAT	0.126	0.113	0.190*	0.252*	0.293*
	(0.098)	(0.06)	(0.098)	(0.129)	(0.152)
TEC	0.029	0.164	0.083	0.115	0.136
	(0.105)	(0.064)	(0.095)	(0.117)	(0.132)
MKT	−0.012***	−0.015***	−0.016***	−0.017***	−0.021***
	(0.001)	(0.001)	(0.003)	(0.005)	(0.005)
LEV	−0.020	−0.017	−0.029	−0.041*	−0.052*
	(0.019)	(0.011)	(0.017)	(0.021)	(0.028)
ETA	4.915***	9.475***	3.392***	3.947***	4.260***
	(0.3416)	(0.2087)	(0.3073)	(0.3803)	(0.4261)
time (γ_1)	0.127*	0.168**	0.163**	0.145**	0.136**
	(0.061)	(0.084)	(0.079)	(0.073)	(0.063)
treatment (γ_2)	0.056	0.053	0.094	0.13	0.159

(continued)

Table 4.7   (continued)

	PD1	PD2	PD3	PD4	PD5
	(0.037)	(0.083)	(0.122)	(0.151)	(0.169)
$\lambda_1 = (\gamma_1 * \gamma_2)$	−0.122***	−0.236***	−0.311***	−0.362***	−0.393***
	(0.035)	(0.072)	(0.076)	(0.094)	(0.105)
R^2	0.1293	0.177	0.1987	0.2105	0.2193
R^2 Adj	0.1218	0.1699	0.1918	0.2037	0.2125
F-Statistic	17.23***	24.95***	28.77***	30.92***	32.58***
on	(df = 17;	(df = 17;	(df = 17;	(df = 17;	(df = 17;
	1972)	1972)	1972)	1972)	1972)
N. Observations	1991	1991	1991	1991	1991

Note $*p < 0.1$; $**p < 0.05$; $***p < 0.01$

is possible to interpret each sectorial coefficient as the increase of the probability of default concerning the riskiness expressed by the utility sector.

From the results of the empirical analysis, we can affirm that there is any statistical significance for the following sectors: communication; consumer staples; discretionary products; health; and technology.

The utility sector, expressed by the intercept, presents a time-growing coefficient with a confidence interval greater or equal to 99% for four- and five-year default probabilities. A more linear growth trend can be observed for the energetic sector. Each extension of the time horizon leads to an increase in the probability of default. The rationale of the phenomenon could be explained by the intrinsic exposure of the energy sector to sustainability issues e renewable energy sources. The more attention paid since the Paris agreement on climate could generate a more sensitivity of firms belonging to the energetic sector, affecting the probabilities of default observed on the market. This sector presents a confidence interval of 90% except for the one-year PD.

Industrial and material sectors seem to follow the lead defined by the energy sector but with a lower magnitude in charge of their regression coefficients. Even if the absolute value of the coefficients increases as the default likelihood timeframe expands, the contribution to the PD is less remarkable on each time horizon. The confidence interval for both sectors is 90% for each time horizon greater or equal to three years. Even in this model, the F-test evaluated on the multiple null hypotheses on each regressor is rejected for each time extension of the default probabilities: the F-test is remarkably more remarkable than the critical value, with a confidence interval of 99%. The adjusted R-squared grows along with the expansion of the time frame considered to evaluate default probabilities.

λ_1, the coefficient expression of the interaction among time and treatment assumes negative values and a statistical significance of 99% for each PD time extension. These values can be interpreted as the risk mitigation effect affected by belonging to a specific sector, between enterprises that do not implement ESG strategies before the exogenous shock and firms that realize ESG policies after the event represented by the Paris agreement on climate. Even in this case, the regression coefficient increases in absolute values and the time extension considered. This means that the risk mitigation effect is more prominent for the medium-long term than the short term.

4.4.2   Robustness Test

We first checked for the absence of multicollinearity among regressors, and to achieve this goal, we assessed the variance inflation factor (VIF). In this way is possible to affirm that there are no regressors with a VIF superior to 5, the critical value set for this test (Table 4.8).

Furthermore, to verify the absence of heteroskedasticity, we run the Breush-Pagan test for the models presented in the previous section. As a result, we can reject the existence of heteroskedasticity as presented in the Table 4.9.

Table 4.8 Variance inflation factor (VIF)

	ZSC	ENV	SOC	GOV	MKT	LEV	ETA
Model 1 (ENV + SOC + GOV)	1.0204	2.2737	2.0711	1.3635	1.2095	1.0179	1.0532

	ZSC	ESG	MKT	LEV	ETA
Model 2 (ESG)	1.0042	1.1870	1.1789	1.0164	1.0464

Table 4.9 Breush-Pagan test

	BP	df	p-value
Model 1 (ENV + SOC + GOV)	0.0392	10	0.01711
Model 2 (ESG)	0.0723	17	0.02041

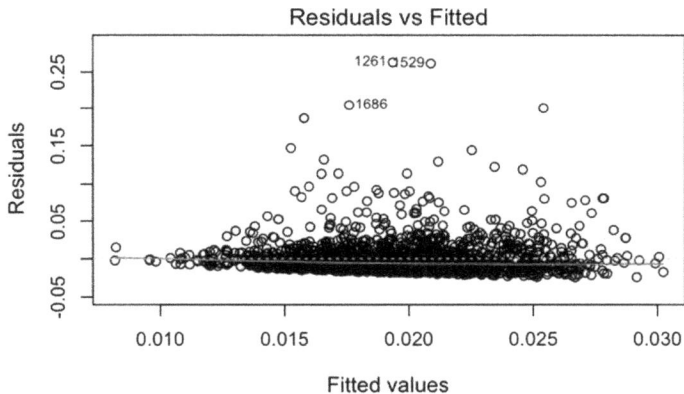

Fig. 4.1   Residual vs. Fitted values and homoskedasticity test (model 2)

It also provides a graphical representation of the absence of heteroskedasticity for the models implemented in the previous section. From the top-left graph, residuals are compared to fitted values, the slope of the red line is approximatively equal to zero, and each observation is distributed randomly (Fig. 4.1).

4.5   Conclusions

In this paper, we have empirically proved the truthfulness of hypothesis 1: environmental improvements produce a more significant risk diversification effect rather than government ones. Furthermore, it is not possible to conclude that enhancements in social score can reduce firms' probabilities of default.

Overall, ESG and environmental regression coefficients follow a u-shaped progression as the time horizon expands. Therefore, developments in environmental performance conduce to a risk mitigation effect more prominent for short-medium term probabilities of default. On the other side, a higher governance score will affect more consistently medium-long-term probabilities of default.

A further contribution is linked to difference-in-difference results: short-medium term default probabilities are sensible to improvements of ESG scores; in fact, the regression coefficient of the interaction among time and treatment, λ_1, manifest a statistical significance of 99%. Due to a negative value in charge of λ_1, it is possible to demonstrate the existence of the risk mitigation raised by ESG score performance developments.

Our overall results reveal that default probabilities are influenced by the sector firms belong to. Each sector we consider is responsible for an increase in the default likelihood; more specifically, the energetic sector experiences the most significant impact due to the intrinsic exposition to sustainability issues. On the other hand, industrial and material sectors present a less consistent contribution to the probability of default. However, for each sector, the magnitude of the coefficient increases as the time horizon expands.

The limits of our study are represented by: (i) the usage of a dataset focused on European listed companies; (ii) the ESG indicators chosen as regressor represent a synthetic evaluation of the range of ESG sub-pillar indicators; (iii) we used a small variety of sectors in our analysis; and (iv) listed firms usually implement more ESG strategies and policies rather than SME companies, these constitute the majority of businesses operating in any country.

Future research lines should analyze the direct impact on the probability of default for a more comprehensive set of ESG performance indicators. It is also necessary to define the most significant subgroup of ESG indicators for the principal sector's firms. In this way, banks can model the adjusting probability of default algorithms more effectively.

REFERENCES

Altman, E.I. Financial Ratios, Discriminant Analysis and the Prediction of Corporate Bankruptcy. The Journal of Finance. 1968, 23, 594–596. https://doi.org/10.1111/j.1540-6261.1968.tb00843.x.

Aslan, A.; Poppe, L.; Posch, P. Are Sustainable Companies More Likely to Default? Evidence from the Dynamics Between Credit and ESG Ratings. Sustainability. 2021, 13, 8568. https://doi.org/10.3390/su13158568.

Avetisyan, E.; Hockerts, K. The Consolidation of the ESG Rating Industry as an Enactment of Institutional Retrogression. Business Strategy and the Environment. 2017, 26, 316–330. https://doi.org/10.1002/bse.1919.

Barth, F.; Hübel, B.; Scholz, H. ESG and Corporate Credit Spreads. Journal of Risk Finance, 2022, 2–4. https://doi.org/10.1108/JRF-03-2021-0045.

Berg, F.; Koelbel, J.F.; Rigobon, R. Aggregate Confusion: The Divergence of ESG Ratings. MIT Sloan School Working Paper. 2019, 5822, 28–33. https://doi.org/10.2139/ssrn.3438533.

Bhattacharya, S.; Sharma, D. Do Environment, Social and Governance Performance Impact Credit Ratings: a Study from India. International Journal of Ethics and Systems. 2018, 35, 479–481. https://doi.org/10.1108/IJOES-09-2018-0130.

Breuer, H.; Fichter, K.; Lüdeke-Freund, F.; Tiemann, I. Sustainability-Oriented Business Model Development: Principles, Criteria, and Tools. International Journal of Entrepreneurial Venturing. 2018, 10, 256–286. https://doi.org/10.1504/IJEV.2018.10013801.

Bruno, M.; Lagasio, V. An Overview of the European Policies on ESG in the Banking Sector. Sustainability. 2021, 13, 12641. https://doi.org/10.3390/su132212641.

Cash, D. Can Credit Rating Agencies Play a Greater Role in Corporate Governance Disclosure? Corporate Governance, 2018, 18, 960–964. https://doi.org/10.1108/CG-04-2018-0150.

Chang, H.Y.; Liang, L.W.; Liu, Y.L. Using Environmental, Social, Governance (ESG) and Financial Indicators to Measure Bank Cost Efficiency in Asia. Sustainability. 2021, 13, 11139. https://doi.org/10.3390/su132011139.

Christensen, D.M.; Serafeim G.; Sikochi A. Why Is Corporate Virtue in the Eye of the Beholder? The Case of ESG Ratings. The Accounting Review. 2021, 34–35. https://doi.org/10.2308/TAR-2019-0506.

De Santis, A.; Di Marzo, G.; Fasano, D.; Marlino, M.; Nigro, B. Pricing Risk Adjusted: il ruolo dei parametri ESG. PE Working Paper. 2020, 20, 40–45. Available at: shorturl.at/lpCY0.

Devalle, A.; Fiandrino, S.; Cantino, V. The Linkage Between ESG Performance and Credit Ratings: A Firm-Level Perspective Analysis. International Journal of Business and Management. 2017, 12, 53–65. https://doi.org/10.5539/ijbm.v12n9p53.

Fama, E.F. Efficient Capital Markets: A Review of Theory and Empirical Work. The Journal of Finance. 1970, 25, 383–417. https://doi.org/10.2307/2325486.

Gibson, R.; Krueger, P.; Schmidt, P.S. ESG Rating Disagreement and Stock Returns. Swiss Finance Institute Research Paper Series. 2021, 19, 25–27. https://doi.org/10.2139/ssrn.3433728.

Gubareva, M. How to Estimate Expected Credit Losses—ECL—for Provisioning Under IFRS 9. Journal of Risk Finance. 2021, 22, 169–190. https://doi.org/10.1108/JRF-05-2020-0094.

Henisz, W.J.; McGlinch, J. ESG, Material Credit Events, and Credit Risk. Journal of Applied Corporate Finance. 2019, 32, 116–117. https://doi.org/10.1111/jacf.12352.

Höck, A.; Klein, C.; Landau, A.; Zwergel B. The Effect of Environmental Sustainability on Credit Risk. Journal of Asset Management, 2020, 21, 90–91. https://doi.org/10.1057/s41260-020-00155-4.

Hübel, B. Do Markets Value ESG Risks in Sovereign Credit Curves? Quarterly Review of Economics and Finance. 2020, 18–23. https://doi.org/10.1016/j.qref.2020.11.003.

Ingo, W. Sense and Nonsense in ESG Ratings. Journal of Law, Finance, and Accounting. 2020, 5, 37–40. https://doi.org/10.1561/108.00000049.

Kiesel, F.; Lücke, F. ESG in credit ratings and the impact on financial markets. Financial Market Institutions & Instruments. 2019, 28, 276–277. https://doi.org/10.1111/fmii.12114.

Kim, S.; Li, Z. Understanding the Impact of ESG Practices. Corporate Finance Sustainability. 2021, 13, 13–14. https://doi.org/10.3390/su13073746.

Liang, H.; Renneboog, L. On the Foundations of Corporate Social Responsibility. The Journal of Finance. 2017, 72, 898–904. https://doi.org/10.2139/ssrn.2360633.

Olmedo, E.E.; Fernández-Izquierdo, M.A.; Ferrero, I.; Rivera-Lirio, J.M.; Muñoz-Torres, M.J. Rating the Raters: Evaluating how ESG Rating Agencies Integrate Sustainability Principles. Sustainability. 2019, 11, 13–14. https://doi.org/10.3390/su11030915.

Sassen, R.; Hinze, A.K.; Hardeck, I. Impact of ESG Factors on Firm risk in Europe. Journal of Business Economics. 2016, 86, 867–904. https://doi.org/10.1007/s11573-016-0819-3.

Stellner, C.; Klein, C., Zwergel, B. Corporate Social Responsibility and Eurozone Corporate Bonds: The Moderating Role of Country Sustainability. Journal of Banking & Finance, 2015, 59, 548. https://doi.org/10.1016/j.jbankfin.2015.04.032.

Stubbs, W.P.R. Lifting the Veil on Environment-Social-Governance Rating Methods. Social Responsibility Journal. 2013, 9, 636–637. https://doi.org/10.1108/SRJ-03-2012-0035.

Wooldridge, J.M.; Imbens G.W. Recent Developments in the Econometrics of Program Evaluation. Journal of Economic Literature. 2009, 47, 5–86. https://doi.org/10.3386/w14251.

Yang, G.; Kang, H.G.; Lee, J.Y.; Bae, K. ESG Scores and the Credit Market. Sustainability. 2020, 12, 2–11. https://doi.org/10.3390/su12083456.

CHAPTER 5

Principles of the Optimal Government Regulation in the Financial Market

Kristaps Freimanis and *Maija Šenfelde*

5.1 INTRODUCTION

Financial market, including banking market, is extremely important for the proper functioning of the economy. The experience of many countries in the world shows that failures in this market could lead to serious social consequences affecting, most probably, every citizen. This situation has pushed governments to act and introduce regulations aimed to prevent crisis arising from failures in the financial market. Over years extent of the regulations has risen significantly, especially after crisis in recent decades.

On the other hand, it is important to promote competition, which as per father of classical economics Adam Smith leads economic system towards equilibrium and is considered as the basic building block of

K. Freimanis (✉) · M. Šenfelde
Riga Technical University, Riga, Latvia
e-mail: kristaps.freimanis_5@rtu.lv

M. Šenfelde
e-mail: maija.senfelde@rtu.lv

S. Carbó-Valverde and P. J. Cuadros Solas (eds.), *New Challenges for the Banking Industry*, Palgrave Macmillan Studies in Banking and Financial Institutions, https://doi.org/10.1007/978-3-031-32931-9_5

modern market economies. Regulation potentially can have adverse effects on the competition thereby it is important to find the balance between the two.

Theoretical concept of regulation is based on the existence of market failures (OECD, 2010; Ajefu, Barde, 2015), which are defined by the deviation from the perfect competition model (Smith, 2002; Walras, 1874; Arrow, Debreu, 1954; McKenzie, 1959; Aumann, 1964; Novshek, Sonnenschein, 1987). In the article, authors have disclosed the review of the literature of the principles of regulation. Literature review covers the period from 1998 till 2022, reviewing 185 sources, from which 30 sources were selected for analysis (disclosed in Table 5.1). Major part of the literature review (53.5%) was journal articles (see Fig. 5.1).

In this review, we have identified 12 principles of the optimal government regulation, including recently highlighted topic of climate-related risks. 68% of sources refer to the following 5 principles: (a) Cost–benefit balanced, (b) Risk based, (c) Consistency and competitive neutrality, (d) High quality, transparent decision-making, and enforcement, (e) International coordination, convergence, and implementation in policy and rulemaking.

5.2   MARKET FAILURES IN THE BANKING MARKET

The perfect competition model as defined by Smith in 1776 (Smith, 2002) and Walras (1874), and further developed by Arrow & Debreu (1954), McKenzie (1959), Aumann (1964) and Novshek & Sonnenschein (1987) sets certain conditions for the market summarized by Healy (2015):

- **Many small price-taking participants**: there are numerous buyers and sellers, none of which can influence the market price substantially, and no single firm or consumer accounts for a large portion of production or purchases.
- **Identical sellers**: suppliers have full access to the same inputs and production technologies as one another.
- **Free entry and exit**: many new firms can enter the market on the very same terms as existing ones if the market is profitable and, similarly, firms can exit the industry without incurring extra costs.
- **Products are identical**: sellers offer the exact same product and buyers are equally willing to buy from any seller.

Table 5.1 Summary table of researchers' conclusions on the principles of regulation

Principles of regulation/ Research articles, other sources	Cost–benefit balanced	Confidentiality	Precaution	Risk based incentives	Sound	Comprehensiveness	Consistency and competitive neutrality	High quality, transparent decision-making, and enforcement	Systematic review	International coordination, convergence, and implementation in policy and rulemaking	Accountability	Management of climate-related risks
Bhattacharya, Boot, Thakor (1998)					X		X					
Freixas, Gabillon (1999)					X							
Wyplosz (2001)			X									
Lockwood (2002)										X		
Crampton (2002)							X					
Dell'Arricia, Marquez (2006)										X		
Llewellyn (2006)	X											
Brunnermeier et al. (2009)					X					X		
Hertog (2010)	X											

(continued)

Table 5.1 (continued)

Principles of regulation/ Research articles, other sources	Cost–benefit balanced	Confidentiality	Precaution	Risk based	Sound incentives	Comprehensiveness	Consistency and competitive neutrality	High quality, transparent decision-making, and enforcement	Systematic review	International coordination, convergence, and implementation in policy and rulemaking	Accountability	Management of climate-related risks
OECD (2010)	X	X	X	X	X	X	X	X	X	X		
BCBS (2012)		X		X	X	X	X			X	X	
Teall (2013)	X					X						
BCBS (2013)				X				X		X		
Ajefu, Barde (2015)	X											
Buck (2015)				X						X		
ESMA (2016)				X								
Coombs (2016)								X				
Mester (2017)				X	X						X	
Kozarević, Polić, Perić (2017)							X					
Panagopoulos, Chatzigagios, Dokas (2018)							X	X				

Principles of regulation/ Research articles, other sources	Cost–benefit balanced	Confidentiality	Precaution	Risk based	Sound incentives	Comprehensiveness	Consistency and competitive neutrality	High quality, transparent decision-making, and enforcement	Systematic review	International coordination, convergence, and implementation in policy and rulemaking	Accountability	Management of climate-related risks
Mnuchin, Phillips (2018)								X	X			
World Bank (2019)				X								
Chester (2020)							X					
BCBS (2021)		X				X			X			
Crisanto, Ehrenraud (2021)	X	X		X						X		
Demekas, Grippa (2021)						X						X
IMF (2021)					X							
Noonan (2021)				X			X					
Groll, Halloran, McAllister (2021)				X				X				
Principles for Good Financial Regulators (n.d)								X				

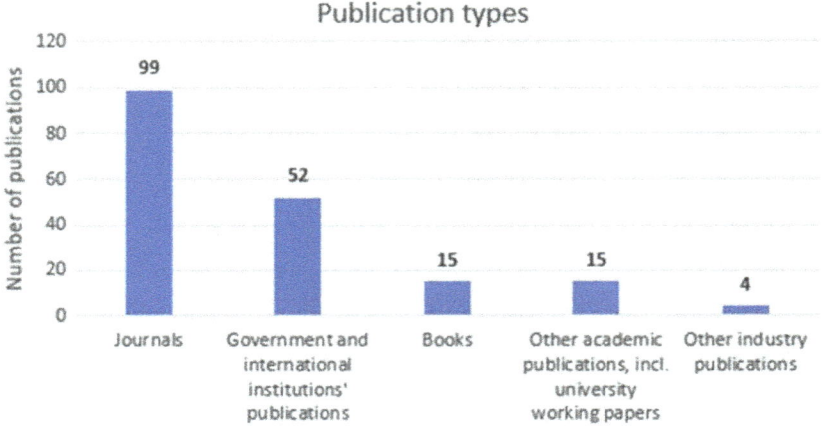

Fig. 5.1 Literature review coverage by publication types

- **Perfect information**: Buyers and sellers are fully informed about the quality of products and prices available in the market.

Considering (a) the specifics of the traditional banking market, (b) the description of conditions of perfect competition in any given market, and (c) OECD's (2010) comments for the expected outcomes of the well-functioning financial market authors have summarized the description of perfect competition in the banking market:

1. Effective and efficient allocation of liquidity and capital.
2. Effective and efficient pooling, management, and transfer of risks accompanied with correct pricing of risk. This aspect covers prudent risk-taking behaviour as well.
3. Sufficient shock resistance with the ability to self-correct.
4. General confidence in the functioning of the financial (banking) market. This aspect covers the condition of "perfect information".

Ajefu & Barde (2015) stresses the importance of consideration of the equity in the discussion of market effectiveness and efficiency pointing to the concepts of fairness and social justice. This could require looking for some trade-offs between economic efficiency and equity.

Market failures have been assessed based on the reference model of the perfect competition. Thereby the deviation from abovementioned conditions is defined as market failure (OECD, 2010; Ajefu, Barde, 2015). There have been several market failures observed in the banking market:

- **Asymmetric information**: the deviation from the condition "perfect information". Those imbalances in information that make it costly if not impossible to perfectly monitor the behaviour or situation of market players. Asymmetric information explains some of the key risks in the financial intermediation process, e.g., credit risk, and accounts for the role of financial institutions in this process. There are two types of asymmetric information: moral hazard and adverse selection (OECD, 2010). Lack of transparency of financial institutions, products, and markets was recognized as one of financial market failures leading to the financial market crisis in 2008 (Kawai, Prasad, 2011). The literature is extensive on adverse selection and moral hazard problems in contractual relationships between lenders and firm agents. Chiappori and Salanié (2000) provide a survey of recent theoretical and empirical studies. Finkelstein and Poterba (2006) present an empirical test of asymmetric information that takes advantages of observable private information to distinguish between adverse selection and moral hazard in the insurance market. Dey and Dunn (2006) outline the literature in credit markets surrounding the concepts of sorting by observed risk and sorting by private information. Other empirical studies include Igawa and Kanatas (1990), Ausubel (1991), Calem and Mester (1995), Ausubel (1999), Edelberg (2004), Davidoff and Welke (2004), and Karlan and Zinman (2006). Einav, Finkelstein, and Cullen (2010) emphasize that the central force that generates inefficiency in asymmetrically informed markets is that firms' marginal costs are increasing in price. Recent papers on this topic are Stroebel (2016), Hertzberg, Liberman and Paravisini (2018) on maturity choice, Indarte (2021) on consumer bankruptcy, and Gupta and Hansman (2022) on mortgages.
- **Negative spillovers**: an externality, which has arisen when the costs of individual actions have not incorporated potential broader social costs. In authors' view, this is the deviation from the condition "perfect information" as the prices do not fully reflect the actual costs and margin. In the financial market negative spillovers often are informational in nature. If confidence in financial products or institutions

evaporate, it can lead to a panic and a rush for the exits (OECD, 2010). Significant part of this failure is systemic risk: one of the most important take-aways from the financial market crisis in 2008 was understanding of interconnectedness of financial institutions and risk-spillovers (Brunnermeier et al., 2009; McSweeney, 2009; Kawai, Prasad, 2011; Grochulski, Morrison, 2014).

- **Market power imbalances**: the deviation from the condition "Many small price-taking participants" when specific market participant can influence the price due to its market share. Market power imbalances can lead to (a) excessive pricing for financial services and products, (b) inefficient allocation of capital, and (c) slower innovation through creation of competing products (OECD, 2010). Bikker and Spierdijk (2009) have structured the determinants of imperfect competition, dividing them into coordinated factors and unilateral factors (one dimension) and demand and supply side factors (second dimension).
- **Market abuse**: the deviation from the condition "perfect information". Due to asymmetric information, some of market participants can be involved in inappropriate practices, e.g., market manipulation of share prices. Market abuse can severely damage general confidence in the financial market leading to even market collapse in worst cases (OECD, 2010). When the financial market crisis in 2008 has been analysed, many researchers refer to the excessive risk taking by financial institutions (Kawai, Prasad, 2011), which, in authors' view, could be interpreted as a market abuse.

Market failures are viewed as a justification for the government to intervene (OECD, 2010; Ajefu, Barde, 2015) to move the market closer to the perfect competition condition. Government consulting institutions (OECD, 2010; Congressional Research Service, 2020) have defined general policy objectives to be achieved, which links to the conditions of the perfect competition in the banking market:

- Confidence in the financial system—point 4,
- Systemic stability (including taxpayer protection against government payouts)—point 3,
- Safety and soundness of financial institutions—point 3,
- Market integrity and transparency—points 2 and 4,

- Market conduct (including ensuring protection against money laundering and similar fraud) and consumer & investor protection—point 4,
- Efficiency (efficiently allocated capital, pricing reflecting costs, expected return appropriately reflecting risks)—points 1 and 2,
- Access to financial services to all worthy clients—point 3.

At the same time, government intervention is associated with certain costs thereby it should be promoted until benefits from the intervention exceeds the costs (OECD, 2010; Hertog, 2010).

5.3   Principles of Regulation

Policy objectives could be achieved by different policy instruments. OECD (2010) is giving an example of what is available to the government for the banking market:

- Surveillance: influence the behaviour and perceptions of market participants thereby deterring misconduct and abuse.
- Moral suasion with market-based solutions: influence the behaviour of market participants thereby introducing sound corporate governance and risk management practices.
- Regulation: key policy instrument setting certain outcomes for market participants in clear, pre-determined fashion.
- Guarantees: guarantee against large-scale losses either from government or market itself (government-imposed requirement to provide guarantees).
- Lending: provision of liquidity or longer-term lending support to market participants.
- Subsidies, grants, and programmes: direct financial support to market participants, e.g., through taxes.
- Government ownership and control: government may establish special government enterprises or take control of existing financial institution in case of financial institution failure.

Regulation is key policy instrument to be used for government intervention in the financial, including banking and market. Authors further have summarized the principles of regulation:

1. Cost–benefit balance: costs should be lower than expected benefits, incl. from minimized market failures (OECD, 2010; Hertog, 2010; Teall, 2013; Ajefu, Barde, 2015). Crisanto & Ehrentraud (2021) comment on the balance seeking in the Big Tech market, which currently becomes more important due to its size. Llewellyn (2006) stresses the importance of proper institutional structure to keep costs as low as possible considering governance risks.

2. Confidentiality: appropriate confidentiality should be ensured due to the concerns of competition, stability of market and its players and security of physical infrastructure (OECD, 2010; BCBS, 2012, 2021). Crisanto, Ehrentraud (2021) comment on the new tendences in Big Tech, which present challenges for competition, data privacy, and cyber security.

3. Precaution: policymakers should proactively anticipate and address emerging risks and problems and not initiate reforms solely in response to the onset of a crisis (OECD, 2010). Wyplosz (2001) stresses the importance of properly assessing risks of liberalized financial systems to avoid absence of critical financial infrastructure in such systems.

4. Risk based: financial regulation should be oriented to the risks in the financial system and give priority to those risks that, due to their nature or impact, have the greatest potential of compromising the achievement of policy objectives or undermine systemic resiliency (Freixas & Gabillon, 1999; OECD, 2010; Buck, 2015; ESMA, 2016; Mester, 2017). Brunnermeier et al. (2009) also emphasize importance of capturing the risk-spillovers from one financial institution to other. BCBS (2012) emphasize the need to develop and maintain a forward-looking assessment of the risk profile of individual banks and banking groups. Current development of Big Tech put challenges to properly identify all the risks associated with developing market (Crisanto, Ehrentraud, 2021). World Bank (2019) documents the importance of defining bank regulatory capital narrowly, as the quality of capital matters in reducing bank risk. Meanwhile even some regulators have warned that too complex regulation poses risks for seeing the real risks building in the financial systems (Noonan, 2021). In separate interviews with the Financial Times, Norway and Denmark's financial supervision chiefs address the issue of too complex regulation

requiring substantial resources to implement them and manage to see the big picture.

5. Sound incentives: financial regulation should seek to align the incentives of participants with policy objectives by adjusting the nature, form, and strength of directive authority, compulsion, and supervision as appropriate, and using other policy instruments where necessary and appropriate (OECD, 2010; BCBS, 2012; IMF, 2021). Mester (2017) stresses that the regulatory framework must recognize that it creates incentives for financial institutions, their customers, and the regulators themselves and that market forces are always at work.

6. Comprehensiveness: financial regulation should ensure that all identified market failures and broader economic and social needs are properly addressed, at a domestic and global level, and involve the full use of all regulatory tools and mechanisms to achieve policy objectives, including through the combination of regulation with other policy instruments (OECD, 2010; BCBS, 2012; Teall, 2013; BCBS, 2021; IMF, 2021).

7. Consistency and competitive neutrality: financial regulation should be applied in a consistent, "functionally equivalent" manner, i.e., neutral from a product, institutional, sectoral, and market perspective so that similar risks are treated equivalently by regulation (Bhattacharya et al., 1998; Crampton, 2002; OECD, 2010; BCBS, 2012; Noonan, 2021; Principles for Good Financial Regulators, n.d). Deviation from this approach in the Australian banking system has been criticized by Chester (2020) arguing that oligopoly in the banking market has resulted in the current pricing power remaining above 40% higher than the average of high-income countries. To this category calls for flexibility are added as well (Kozarević et al., 2017).

8. High quality, transparent decision-making and enforcement (OECD, 2010). Transparent and clear communication is highly appreciated by the market participants. The Institute of Chartered Accountants in England and Wales has published its suggestions for the financial market regulator (Principles for Good Financial Regulators, n.d), where significant focus is dedicated to clear communication and predictability. Simplicity is other perspective of effective regulation element as per BCBS in this respect (2013). Coombs (2016) stresses the importance of theoretical background

of regulation to avoid "sociological hubris". Groll, Halloran and McAllister (2021) developed a general model of the policy-making process in which legislators delegate authority to regulate financial risk at both the firm (micro-level) and systemic levels (macro-level). The model explains changes in U.S. financial regulation leading up to the financial crisis in 2008.

9. Systematic review: this assessment should evaluate whether the regulation achieved its specific objective(s) and did so in a cost-efficient manner, and whether the decision-making process could be improved (OECD, 2010).

10. International coordination, convergence, and implementation in policy and rulemaking: financial regulation should, to the extent possible, be comprehensive and consistent internationally, with effective coordination where relevant and gradual convergence over time insofar as policy objectives are shared (OECD, 2010; BCBS, 2012, 2021; Buck, 2015; Mnuchin, Phillips, 2018). Lock-wood (2002) notes: "The informal conclusions of this literature are that decentralization yields a higher level of surplus than does centralization if (a) inter-regional externalities are small; (b) regions are relatively heterogenous". Dell'Arricia, Marquez (2006) argues in favour of this approach, however, notes that it lowers the level of flexibility. Brunnermeier et al. (2009) stress the importance of international cooperation for capital and liquidity adequacy needed to minimize risks in bailouts.

11. Accountability: the regulatory framework needs to be designed so that institutions, regulators, and policymakers can be held account-able for the responsibilities assigned to them (BCBS, 2012; Mester, 2017; BCBS, 2021).

12. Management of climate-related risks: pressure to adapt financial policies and regulatory frameworks to incorporate climate-based considerations is coming from multiple directions, first and fore-most from growing awareness in the financial industry itself (Demekas, Grippa, 2021).

68% of sources refer to the following 5 principles: (a) Cost–benefit balanced, (b) Risk based, (c) Consistency and competitive neutrality, (d) High quality, transparent decision-making, and enforcement, and (e) International coordination, convergence, and implementation in policy and rulemaking.

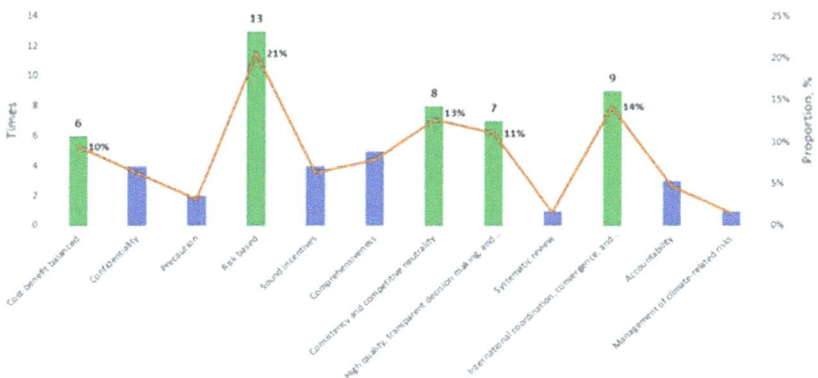

Fig. 5.2 Most important principles of regulation

Many aspects that BCBS (2012) has included in its principles cover surveillance thereby authors have included in the list only those aspects that cover regulation area (Fig. 5.2).

5.4 CONCLUSIONS

In this review, we have identified 12 principles of the optimal government regulation: (a) Cost–benefit balance, (b) Confidentiality, (c) Precaution, (d) Risk based, (e) Sound incentives, (f) Comprehensiveness, (g) Consistency and competitive neutrality, (h) High quality, transparent decision-making and enforcement, (i) Systematic review, (j) International coordination, convergence, and implementation in policy and rulemaking, (k) Accountability, and (l) Management of climate-related risks.

68% of sources refer to the following top 5 principles: (a) Cost–benefit balanced, (b) Risk based, (c) Consistency and competitive neutrality, (d) High quality, transparent decision-making, and enforcement, and (e) International coordination, convergence, and implementation in policy and rulemaking. Those principles are covering the aspects of regulation costs, risk awareness, quality, and regulatory cooperation.

Acknowledgements This work is supported by the European Social Fund [grant number 8.2.2.0/20/I/008] and Riga Technical University [grant number DOK.BUNI/21].

REFERENCES

Ajefu, J. B., Barde, F. (2015). Market efficiency and government intervention revisited: What do recent evidence tell us? *Journal of International Business and Economics*, 3(1), 20–23. https://doi.org/10.15640/jibe.v3n1a3

Arrow, K. J, Debreu, G. (1954). Existence of an equilibrium for a competitive economy. *Econometrica*, 22, 265–290.

Aumann, R. J. (1964). Markets with a continuum of traders. *Econometrica*, 32, 39–50.

Ausubel, L. (1991). The failure of competition in the credit card market. *American Economic Review*, 81 (1), 50–81.

Ausubel, L. (1999). *Adverse selection in the credit card market*. Working Paper, University of Maryland.

BCBS. (2012). Core Principles for Effective Banking Supervision. Basel Committee on Banking Supervision: Bank for International Settlements. Retrieved from: https://www.bis.org/publ/bcbs230.pdf

BCBS. (2013, July). The regulatory framework: balancing risk sensitivity, simplicity, and comparability. Basel Committee on Banking Supervision. Discussion paper. Retrieved from: https://www.bis.org/publ/bcbs258.pdf

BCBS. (2021). Insurance core principles. Basel Committee on Banking Supervision: Bank for International Settlements. Retrieved from: https://www.bis.org/fsi/fsisummaries/icps.pdf

Bhattacharya, S., Boot, A. W. A., Thakor, A. V. (1998). The Economics of Bank Regulation. *Journal of Money, Credit and Banking*, 30(4), 745–770.

Bikker, J. A., Spierdijk, L. (2009). *Measuring and explaining competition in the financial sector*. Tjalling C. Koopmans Research Institute. Discussion Paper Series 09–01. Retrieved from: https://core.ac.uk/download/pdf/6372048.pdf

Brunnermeier, M., Crocket, A., Goodhart, C., Persaud, A. D., Shin, H. (2009). *The fundamental principles of financial regulation*. Geneva, Switzerland: International Centre for Monetary and Banking Studies.

Buck, F. C. (2015). The rents of banking, A public choice approach to bank regulation. Ifo Institute, München. Retrieved from: https://www.ifo.de/DocDL/ifo_Beitraege_z_Wifo_59.pdf

Calem, P. S., Mester, L. (1995). Consumer behavior and the stickiness of credit card interest rates. *American Economic Review*, 85(5), 1327–1336.

Chester, K. (2020). Public policy: The first line of defence. *Economic Analysis and Policy*, 65, 256–261.https://doi.org/10.1016/j.eap.2020.02.003

Chiappori, P. A., Salanié, B. (2000). Testing for asymmetric information in insurance markets. *Journal of Political Economy*, 108(1), 56–78.

Congressional Research Service. (2020). *Who regulates whom: An overview of the U.S. Financial Regulatory Framework*. Washington, D.C. Retrieved from: https://sgp.fas.org/crs/misc/R44918.pdf

Coombs, N. (2016). What is an algorithm? Financial regulation in the era of high-frequency trading. *Economy and Society*, 45(2), 278–302.

Crampton, P. (2002, October 16–17). Striking the right balance between competition and regulation: The key is learning from our mistakes. APEC-OECD Co-operative Initiative on Regulatory Reform: Third Workshop. Jeju Island, Korea.

Crisanto, J. C., Ehrentraud, J. (2021). *The Big Tech Risk in Finance*. International Monetary Fund. Retrieved from: https://www.imf.org/external/pubs/ft/fandd/2021/05/big-tech-fintech-and-financial-regulation-crisanto-ehrentraud.htm

Davidoff, T., Welke, G. M. (2004). *Selection and moral hazard in the US mortgage industry*. Working paper, Haas School of Business, UC Berkeley.

Dell'Arricia, G., Marquez, R. (2006). Competition among regulators and credit market integration. *Journal of Financial Economics*, 79, 401–430.

Demekas, D. G., Grippa, P. (2021). *Financial regulation, climate change, and the transition to a low-carbon economy: A survey of the issues*. International Monetary Fund. https://doi.org/10.5089/9781616356521.001

Dey, S., Dunn, L. (2006). *An empirical investigation of collateral and sorting in the HELOC market*. Working Paper, Bank of Canada.

Edelberg, W. (2004). *Testing for adverse selection and moral hazard in consumer loan markets*. Finance and Economics Discussion Paper Series, Board of Governors of the Federal Reserve System.

Einav, L., Finkelstein, A., Cullen, M. R. (2010). Estimating welfare in insurance markets using variation in prices. *Quarterly Journal of Economics*, 125(3), 877–921.

ESMA. (2016, March). Financial Innovation: Towards a balanced regulatory response. European Securities and Markets Authority. Speech at the London Business School/ Bank of England Conference on: 'How Imminent is the real Fintech Revolution', London, UK. Retrieved from: https://www.esma.europa.eu/sites/default/files/library/2016-345_financial_innovation_towards_a_balanced_regulatory_response_-_speech_by_v._ross_0.pdf

Finkelstein, A., Poterba, J. (2006). *Testing for adverse selection with 'Unused observables'*. Working Paper, MIT and NBER.

Freixas, X., Gabillon, E. (1999, September). Optimal regulation of a fully insured deposit banking system. *Journal of Regulatory Economics*, 16(2), 111–134. Springer.

Grochulski, B., Morrison, W. (2014). *Understanding market failure in the 2007–2008 Crisis*. Economic Brief of Federal Reserve Bank of Richmond, EB14–12. Retrieved from: https://www.richmondfed.org/~/media/richmondfedorg/publications/research/economic_brief/2014/pdf/eb_14-12.pdf

Groll, T., O'Halloran, S., McAllister, G. (2021). Delegation and the regulation of U.S. financial markets. *European Journal of Political Economy*, 70, 1–31.https://doi.org/10.1016/j.ejpoleco.2021.102058

Gupta, A., Hansman, C. (2022). Selection, leverage, and default in the mortgage market. *The Review of Financial Studies*, 35(2), 720–770.https://doi.org/10.1093/rfs/hhab052

Healy, P. (2015). *(Im)perfect competition: Unrealistic economics or useful strategy tool?* Harvard Business School. Retrieved from: https://online.hbs.edu/blog/post/imperfect-competition-unrealistic-economics-or-useful-strategy-tool

Hertog, J. (2010). *Review of economic theories of regulation.* Discussion Paper Series 10–18. Tjalling C. Koopmans Research Institute.

Hertzberg, A., Liberman, A., Paravisini, D. (2018). Screening on loan terms: Evidence from maturity choice in consumer credit. *Review of Financial Studies*, 31(9), 3532–3567.

Igawa, K., Kanatas, G. (1990). Asymmetric information, collateral, and moral hazard. *Journal of Financial and Quantitative Analysis*, 25(4), 469–490.

IMF. (2021). *Financial system soundness.* International Monetary Fund. Retrieved from: https://www.imf.org/en/About/Factsheets/Financial-System-Soundness

Indarte, S. (2021). *Moral Hazard versus liquidity in household bankruptcy.* Working Paper, University of Pennsylvania. Retrieved from: https://haas.berkeley.edu/wp-content/uploads/indarte_bk.pdf

Karlan, D. Zinman, J. (2006). *Observing unobservables: Identifying information asymmetries with a consumer credit field experiment.* Working paper, Yale University.

Kawai, M., Prasad, E. S. (2011). *Financial market regulation and reforms in emerging markets.* Washington, DC: Asian Development Bank Institute and the Brookings Institution.

Kozarević, E., Polić, N., Perić, A. (2017). To liberate or to regulate: Balanced approach to bank-oriented financial system transformation in developing countries. *Banks and Bank Systems*, 12(1), 60–66. https://doi.org/10.21511/bbs.12(1).2017.07

Llewellyn, D. T. (2006). *Institutional structure of financial regulation and supervision: The basic issues.* Washington, DC: World Bank seminar. Retrieved from: http://web.worldbank.org/archive/website01049/WEB/IMAGES/F2FLEMMI.PDF

Lockwood, B. (2002, April). Distributive politics and the costs of centralization. *The Review of Economic Studies*, 69(2), 313–337.

McKenzie, L. W. (1959). On the existence of general equilibrium for a competitive market. *Econometrica*, 27, 54–71.

McSweeney, B. (2009). The roles of financial asset market failure denial and the economic crisis: Reflections on accounting and financial theories and practices. *Accounting, Organizations and Society*, 34, 835–848.

Mester, L. J. (2017). *Guiding principles for financial regulation.* Panel remarks at "The future of global finance: Populism, technology, and regulation" Conference, Columbia University, New York, NY. Retrieved from: https://www.clevelandfed.org/newsroom-and-events/spe eches/sp-20171020-guiding-principles-for-financial-regulation

Mnuchin, S. T., Phillips, C. S. (2018). A financial system that creates economic opportunities. Nonbank Financials, Fintech and Innovation. U.S. Department of the Treasury. Retrieved from: https://home.treasury.gov/sites/default/files/2018-07/A-Financial-System-that-Creates-Economic-Opportunities---Nonbank-Financi....pdf

Noonan, L. (2021, December 23). Europe's over-complex bank rules increase risk, watchdogs warn. *Financial Times.* Retrieved from: https://www.ft.com/content/f520bc35-d84f-4ef5-bfa0-c554a25859fc

Novshek, W., Sonnenschein, H. (1987). General equilibrium with free entry: A synthetic approach to the theory of perfect competition. *Journal of Economic Literature*, 25(3), 1281–1306.

OECD. (2010). Policy framework for effective and efficient financial regulation. *OECD Journal: Financial Market Trends*, 267–321.https://doi.org/10.1787/fmt-2009-5kmn0vkxwng1

Panagopoulos, A. G., Chatzigagios, T., Dokas, I. (2018). The global single and regulated market framework of financial products and the international economic policies: Mathematical approach of the model. *International Journal of Financial Research*, 9(2), 1–22.https://doi.org/10.5430/ijfr.v9n2p1

Principles for Good Financial Regulators. (n.d). London, UK: The Institute of Chartered Accountants in England and Wales. Retrieved from: https://www.icaew.com/technical/financial-services/inspiring-confidence-in-financial-ser vices/principles-for-good-financial-regulators

Smith, A. (2002). *The wealth of nations.* Oxford, England: Bibliomania.com Ltd.

Stroebel, J. (2016). Asymmetric information about collateral values. *Journal of Finance*, 71(3), 1071–1112.

Teall, J. L. (2013). *Financial trading and investing.* Waltham, MA: Elsevier Inc.

Walras, L. (1874). *Elements d'economie politique pure.* Lausanne: L Corbaz.

World Bank. (2019). *Bank regulation and supervision ten years after the global financial crisis.* Policy Research Working Paper. Retrieved from: https://documents1.worldbank.org/curated/en/685851571160819618/pdf/Bank-Regulation-and-Supervision-Ten-Years-after-the-Global-Financial-Crisis.pdf

Wyplosz, C. (2001). How risky is financial liberalization in the developing countries? G-24 Discussion Paper Series United Nations & Center for International Development of Harvard University. Retrieved from: http://unctad.org/en/Docs/pogdsmdpbg24d14.en.pdf

PART II

Sustainability and Green Finance

CHAPTER 6

Firm Pollution and Reputational Risk: Where Do We Stand?

Alexia Ventouri⊙, *Georgios Chortareas, and Fangyuan Kou*

6.1 Introduction

The UN Climate Change Conference presented a goal to restrict the rise of average global temperatures compared to pre-Industrial Revolution standards. Similar concerns in the financial sector led to initiatives such as the launch of the Financial Stability Board (FSB) and Task Force on Climate-Related Financial Disclosures (TCFD), reflecting the eager requirement for more transparent climate-related disclosure in the financial industry. The main goal of such initiatives is to increase disclosure

---

A. Ventouri (✉) · G. Chortareas · F. Kou
King's Business School, King's College London, London, UK
e-mail: alexia.ventouri@kcl.ac.uk

G. Chortareas
e-mail: georgios.chortareas@kcl.ac.uk

F. Kou
e-mail: fangyuan.kou@kcl.ac.uk

S. Carbó-Valverde and P. J. Cuadros Solas (eds.), *New Challenges for the Banking Industry*, Palgrave Macmillan Studies in Banking and Financial Institutions, https://doi.org/10.1007/978-3-031-32931-9_6

transparency, which, in turn, is conjectured to encourage socially responsible behavior from investors and the financial sector in general. Corporate leaders are expected to mitigate polluting practices in their daily operations and contribute to the transition to a net zero-carbon economy. The path to this objective is full of opportunities and challenges, which require collaboration from national, sectoral, and project levels to the global level.

Having a positive reputation is vital for businesses because it can bring a variety of advantages. A good reputation leads to increased customer loyalty because customers tend to stick with a company they perceive as reputable. This can result in repeat business and word-of-mouth recommendations, driving increased sales. Moreover, a company with a good reputation is considered more trustworthy and reliable, enhancing its overall credibility, and making it easier for it to collaborate with other organizations. Such companies also find it easier to secure funding, partnerships, and other resources, because other individuals and organizations are more inclined to want to work with them. Employees of such companies are also more likely to be proud of and satisfied with their work, which leads to higher retention rates and increased productivity. A good reputation also helps the company to be more resilient and to recover from a crisis or negative publicity because their reputation helps to maintain customer trust.

Corporate pollution can have far-reaching and long-lasting consequences, and companies must take steps to minimize their environmental impact and prevent pollution. Even though there is now a growing literature on environmental performance, analyses are typically focusing on its interplay with financial performance (e.g., Chen et al., 2021). Investigating the correlation between corporate pollution and corporate reputational level is of significance for several reasons. Corporate polluting behavior can negatively impact a company's reputation, making it challenging for them to retain customers, employees, and investors. Understanding how corporate pollution impacts a company's reputation allows businesses to make educated decisions on their environmental practices and minimize harm to their reputation. Besides, an in-depth understanding of the association between corporate pollution and reputation aids policymakers and regulators in creating effective policies to tackle corporate pollution. Policies that consider the reputational risks associated with pollution are more likely to encourage companies to minimize their environmental impact. Moreover, corporate reputation is considered a vital intangible asset that can significantly influence its financial conditions in both the short and long run. Understanding the impact of pollution on reputation enables management to weigh the expenses and gains of different environmental policies and make decisions that align with the company's long-term financial objectives. Lastly, in today's society, where environmental consciousness is on the rise and companies are under increasing pressure to operate sustainably and responsibly, understanding the impact of corporate pollution on reputation can enable companies to meet these expectations and avoid reputational risks. Overall, studying the impact of corporate pollution on their reputation can provide valuable insights for businesses, policymakers, regulators, and the broader public in terms of sustainable and responsible corporate behavior.

This chapter considers the relationship between firm pollution and reputational risk for a sample of U.S. firms over 13 years before the COVID-19 pandemic. The data required to construct firm-level pollution measures is drawn from U.S. Environmental Protection Agency (EPA). Our exploratory results illustrate a strong association between corporate emissions and reputation. In particular, firms with higher financial default risk, and poorer corporate governance characteristics, suffer a more severe impact of pollution on reputation. The next section provides a review of the relevant studies; Sect. 3 represents the hypothesis and methodology along with data and empirical analysis; and Sect. 4 concludes.

6.2   What Do We Know?
A Review of the Literature

6.2.1   The Firm and the Environment

6.2.1.1   Interplay Between Environmental and Financial Performance

Several channels exist linking environmental and financial performance. Key issues addressed by the literature include how environmental shocks and climate change affect firm performance, how firms respond to environmental risks, and how the institutional environment (e.g., international agreements) and regulation shape the constraints and incentives faced by firms.

Dechezlepretre et al. (2017) use a global firm-level panel database to consider how energy price divergences impact corporate employment but do not find any evidence of a negative association. Similarly, Engel, Enkvist, and Henderson (2015) reveal that the impacts of climate change risks vary across industries, and those companies that fail to consider these risks are likely to experience negative consequences. Individuals or organizations that can identify the most significant risks, understand their interconnections, and implement suitable measures can start to address the upcoming challenges. Taking effective action can turn risk into a competitive advantage. Yang et al. (2015) suggest that corporate strategic flexibility positively impacts green management efforts. Lee, Min, and Yook (2015) suggest that environmental regulatory legislations encourage environmental investment, which results in the improvement of financial performance. The mandatory requirement to report carbon emissions encourages companies to proactively engage in environmental management practices. Similarly, Yang, Tseng, and Chen (2012) find that stricter environmental regulation induces more corporate environmental innovation. Xie, Yuan, and Huang (2017) examine the impact of regulatory instruments on "green" productivity and their findings back up the "strong" Porter Hypothesis, which proposes that moderate environmental regulation stringency can boost competitiveness. Chao, Laffargue, and Sgro (2012) find that a reduction in pollution inputs reduces the salaries of skilled employees in the traded industry. Berman and Bui (2001) do not find any evidence that air quality policy reduces employment. Besides, Berrone and Gomez-Mejia (2009) argue that regulations slightly affect employment due to the fact that regulated facilities are not in labor-intensive sectors. Moreover, firms with better environmental behavior have lower operation costs, lower employee turnover ratios, and more market opportunities (Berrone and Gomez-Mejia, 2009). It is stated that firms that consider environmental challenges usually face additional costs and financial pressure (Walley and Whitehead, 1994). Besides, some studies argue that there is a detrimental connection between environmental behavior and financial conditions (Sarkis and Cordeiro, 2001; Rassier and Earnhart, 2010). However, another strand of studies indicates that companies which take advantage of environmental opportunities actually have better economic performance (e.g., Griffin and Mahon, 1997; S. L. Hart, 1997; Esty and Porter, 1998; Reinhardt, 1999; Russo and Harrison, 2005; Orsato, 2006; Tang, Hull, and Rothenberg, 2012). Firms with environmental management engagement and prioritizing environmental responsibility can enjoy a competitive advantage (S. L. Hart, 1995) and may be more profitable in long term (e.g., Semenova and

Hassel, 2008). Additionally, certain environmental approaches are advantageous to companies because they are significant in handling relationships with stakeholders (Barnett, 2007). Moreover, Cohn and Deryugina (2018) reveal a negative connection between corporate environmental risk and financial performance. The study by Molina-Azorín et al. (2009) concludes that the literature finding a positive effect of the environment on economic performance predominates. In addition, Levine et al. (2019) suggest that corporate credit situations affect facilities' pollution decisions.

6.2.1.2   Environmental Performance and Financing Cost
A growing body of literature suggests that environmental performance impacts financing sources. Considering the correlation between environmental performance and strategic advantages, investors will find good environmental performance to be appealing. Klassen and McLaughlin (1996) show that environmental record is associated with positive stock market returns. G. Dowell, S. Hart, and Yeung (2000) similarly discover that companies with strict environmental criteria tend to get higher valuations than those that don't. In addition, Bolton and M. Kacperczyk (2021a) find that companies with high $CO2$ pollution earn higher stock returns, indicating that investors seek compensation for their pollution emission risk exposure. Furthermore, Bolton and M. Kacperczyk (2021b) study the influence of carbon disclosure on stock performance and reveal that companies that voluntarily disclose their pollution tend to experience lower stock returns compared to those that do not disclose.

Another line of research explores how companies respond to institutional pressures and environmental disclosure requirements. In recent decades, climate change resulting from global warming has become a tangible issue and a major concern all over the world. As new regulations and policies created in response to climate change mount, the corporate perception of environmental practices changes significantly. The existing literature on corporate debt financing is extensive and focuses particularly on bank loan contracts. According to Cogan (2008), the changing climate and emerging regulations controlling carbon emissions will impact production costs, securities valuations, liabilities, and the allocation of credit. Major banks are starting to take into account the market price for carbon dioxide in their lending and Investment strategies. Nandy and Lodh (2012) empirically investigate and explore the connection between firms' environmental awareness and bank debt. They find that a more environmentally conscious firm receives more favorable terms. Similarly, recent studies show that firms with larger direct emissions face higher loan spreads and stricter non-price terms (e.g., C. Wang and F. Wu, 2018; I.-J. Chen et al., 2021). Houston and Shan (2022) find that banking relationships improve corporate ESG performance. Hasan et al. (2022) state that the financial covenants of high-pollution borrowers of TCFD member banks were strengthened compared to polluting clients of non-TCFD banks, after the establishment of the Task Force on Climate-Related Financial Disclosures (TCFD). Likewise, M. T. Kacperczyk and Peydró (2021) find that polluting firms previously borrowing from banks making carbon-neutrality commitments get less bank debt. Degryse et al. (2021) look into the effect of being environmentally conscious as both a borrower and lender on loan prices and find that companies with green practices can borrow at lower rates, particularly when the lender is also considered "green". Javadi and Masum (2021) study climate-related physical risk and illustrate that companies in locations with higher climate change exposure face higher loan rates. Mueller and Sfrappini (2022) indicate that the effect of climate regulatory risks on loan prices depends on the borrower's region.

6.2.1.3   *Environmental Performance and Corporate Governance*
The area of environmental responsibility and corporate governance has had significant developments in recent decades. Numerous empirical and theoretical studies investigate various firm characteristics such as the composition of the board, corporate governance, leadership, and regulation. In this sub-section, we look into three aspects of the connection between the firm and the environment, i.e., board features and environmental performance, climate change, and financial performance. Cong and Freedman (2011) examine the impact of corporate governance on a firm's environmental practices. They find that good governance is not related to pollution itself but to pollution disclosures (Cong and Freedman, 2011). Besides, Walls, Berrone, and Phan (2012) suggest that smaller, more diverse boards are better at preventing poor environmental outcomes. Similarly, G. Kassinis and Vafeas (2002) find that corporate boards with fewer members perpetrate fewer environmental issues. However, De Villiers, Naiker, and Van Staden (2011) found that firms with a larger number of independent boards and fewer CEO-appointed directors tend to show better environmental behavior. Their study supports the resource dependence theory by showing that environmental practices are improved in companies with active CEOs, boards

with more legal specialists and larger size (De Villiers, Naiker, and Van Staden, 2011).

Some studies on corporate social responsibility (CSR) indicate that CEO characteristics (e.g., gender, duality, personality, education, tenure, salary) influence firms' likelihood of engaging in environmentally friendly behavior. The literature is far yet from reaching a consensus regarding the role of CEO duality on a company's environmental practices. McKendall, Sánchez, and Sicilian (1999) and Berrone, Cruz, et al. (2010) find no link between CEO duality and corporate environmental issues, while Webb (2004) suggests a negative impact of CEO duality on the level of corporate social responsibility. Additionally, Walls, Berrone, and Phan (2012) demonstrate that the highest level of environmental strength is achieved when a company has both CEO duality and a higher number of insider directors.

Much academic research focuses on the divergence in corporate behavior between male and female CEOs. It is suggested that having female leaders in a company has showed to increase its longevity (Weber and Zulehner, 2010), reduce the risk of lawsuits (Adhikari, Agrawal, and Malm, 2019), enhance the accuracy of stock prices information (e.g., Gul, Srinidhi, and Ng, 2011), result in better attendance at board meetings (Adams and Ferreira, 2009), and improve the quality of corporate boards' recommendations (Kim and Starks, 2016). Z. Wang and Yu (2019) reveal that female CEOs tend to be more environmentally conscious, with firms led by female CEOs causing fewer pollution emissions, receiving fewer environmental sanctions, and having more pollution mentioned in their reports.

Another aspect often considered is that of CEO compensation. It is argued that salary is negatively related to corporate reputation (P. A. Stanwick and S. D. Stanwick, 2001) and environmental records (McGuire et al., 2003). Additionally, the bonus is negatively related to the company's social behaviors (Deckop, Merriman and Gupta, 2006) and social responsibilities (Coombs and Gilley, 2005). However, it is also argued that there is a positive connection between long-run CEO incomes and a company's social practices (e.g., Mahoney and Thorne, 2005; Deckop et al., 2006).

The personality of a CEO is also a crucial factor regarding corporate environmental performance. Zhang et al. (2020) investigate the impact of CEO arrogance on a firm's unethical behavior and illustrate that CEO hubris has a positive impact on corporate pollution. Kassinis and

Panayiotou (2006) contend that a CEO's views on the significance of stakeholders in environmental strategy-making impact corporate environmental performance and discover that these views are positively correlated with corporate environmental practices.

6.2.1.4   Corporate Ownership and Environmental Responsibility

How does corporate ownership impact environmental responsibility? Li and Wu (2020) propose that while private companies effectively decrease their negative ESG issues after becoming members of the UNGC, public companies often undertake CSR actions that lack actual effect. Their findings indicate that current CSR initiatives and standardized CSR policy requirements may not necessarily result in improved outcomes for society, and a more targeted policy approach that addresses different types of ownership and industries may be more effective in maximizing ESG benefits. Walls, Berrone, and Phan (2012) study the association between corporate ownership and environmental performance and discover that only shareholder activism and concentration directly affect environmental records. If a company has poor environmental performance, it can anticipate increased investor activism, as poor performance can result in penalties, fines, clean-up costs, and risk exposure. On the other hand, companies with concentrated ownership have limited freedom to implement additional environmentally compliant practices, as these may be perceived as unnecessary expenses (e.g., Walls, Berrone, and Phan, 2012). Shive and Forster (2020) examine corporate governance characteristics and the emissions impact of public and private companies and reveal that private firms tend to emit less and have smaller environmental penalties in some cases compared to public firms. Additionally, Jiang, C. Lin, and P. Lin (2014) demonstrate that state-owned enterprises have more severe pollution issues than both foreign-owned companies and domestic public-listed companies. Akey and Appel (2021) explore the impact of parent liability for subsidiary clean-up expenses on chemical emissions and suggest that greater corporate liability protection results in more pollution by their subsidiaries.

6.2.2   Reputational Risk and Pollution

6.2.2.1   Driving Factors of Corporate Reputation

The rise in reputation-related issues in recent years has sparked increased attention to corporate reputation and the associated risks. Numerous research studies consider the driving factors of corporate reputational risk. Staw and Epstein (2000) posit that firms utilizing well-known management methods were held in high esteem, perceived as being more innovative, and received positive evaluations for management quality. Zyglidopoulos (2005) examines the effect of downsizing on corporate image and notes that downsizing imposes a negative impact on corporate reputation condition. S. Brammer and Pavelin (2006) argue that a firm's reputation could be impacted by multiple factors simultaneously. Their research also reveals that the effect of a firm's social performance on corporate reputation varies between and within sectors, based on the type of social performance. In addition, their findings highlight the importance of aligning the types of social activities with stakeholders' environmental concerns to improve reputation.

Nardella, S. Brammer, and Surdu (2020) reveal that companies that are perceived as having the weakest social responsibility are more likely to face reputational sanctions when accused of being irresponsible. The empirical analysis of Musteen, Datta, and Kemmerer (2010) illustrates an inverted-U relation between the average service years of external board members and a company's reputation. Surprisingly, their results show that a lack of duality in independent leadership structure is negatively related to a company's reputation.

Gardberg (2006) states that the country's institutional framework can impact the creation and expectations of corporate reputation, thus affecting its applicability across borders. Likewise, Gaganis et al. (2020) propose that increased public support for environmentally friendly initiatives leads to a reduction in reputational risks. This could be due to societal beliefs about environmental responsibility putting pressure on business leaders to align their corporate policies with these expectations, resulting in a lower risk of damage to their reputation.

6.2.2.2 Reputational Risk and CSR

The global financial crisis prompted a renewed focus on the connection between social responsibilities and corporate reputation. Integrating both reputation management and sustainability into a company's strategy can offer opportunities to mitigate risk and ensure business resilience, according to Gomez-Trujillo, Velez-Ocampo, and Gonzalez-Perez (2020).

It is argued that corporate sustainability (including economic, social, and environmental aspects) has a positive impact on a firm's reputation (e.g., Pérez-Cornejo et al., 2020). This suggests that pursuing sustainability initiatives can enhance the reputational image (Hult et al., 2018; Irfan et al., 2018). In particular, corporate environmental performance (CEP) positively affects corporate reputation (Arendt and Brettel, 2010; Dögl and Holtbrügge, 2014; Alon and Vidovic, 2015). Similarly, Miles and Covin (2000) discover that good environmental management can lead to a positive reputation. It is also argued that the disclosure of CSR reporting with high quality intensifies the effect of environmental performance on the level of corporate reputation (Pérez-Cornejo et al., 2020).

Furthermore, it is stated that sustainability has a crucial role in shaping reputation, as it can make it more challenging for competitors to copy a company's competitive advantages (e.g., Melo and Garrido-Morgado, 2012). Branco and Rodrigues (2006) claim a company's involvement in CSR and disclosure practices can either enhance or damage its reputation. Likewise, H. Lin et al. (2016) find that irresponsible environmental, social, or economic actions can damage the corporate image. Additionally, it is suggested that companies with a poor reputation may use sustainability initiatives as a way to deceive the public and improve their image, a practice known as greenwashing (Ulke and Schons, 2016; Hult et al., 2018). However, Soleimani, Schneper, and Newburry (2014) do not find any evidence to suggest that there is an interaction effect between CSP on a firm's reputation. In a similar vein, D'Souza, Taghian, and Sullivan-Mort (2013) find that although environmentally friendly practices are important for a company, they do not significantly contribute to its reputation.

Some studies on the connection between corporate sustainability performance and reputation focus on emerging economies. The findings of Rettab, Brik, and Mellahi (2009) and Cambra-Fierro, and Vázquez-Carrasco (2020) reveal that there is a direct association between CSR engagement and a company's image. Likewise, Aguilera-Caracuel and Guerrero-Villegas (2018) study multinational enterprises and argue that corporate socially responsible performance has a positive effect on their reputation.

6.3   ESG-RELATED REPUTATION AND CORPORATE POLLUTION: AN EXPLORATORY ANALYSIS

6.3.1   Hypothesis and Methodology

To examine the association between a company's reputation and its environmental performance, we pursue an exploratory empirical study on the impacts of corporate chemical pollution on reputation. Specifically, we aim to investigate whether firms with higher levels of chemical emissions suffer from greater reputational risk. The association of a corporation with environmental pollution can elicit negative perceptions among stakeholders such as employees, investors, and the public. This can lead to a loss of trust, which harms the company's reputation. Additionally, negative media coverage of corporate pollution can cause significant reputational damage, which can be difficult and costly to repair. Corporate pollution can also result in regulatory fines and penalties, further damaging a company's reputation. In contrast, a company that is seen as an environmental leader that effectively manages its environmental risks can enjoy a positive reputation and increased customer loyalty, employee engagement, and investor confidence. Therefore, we hypothesize that corporate chemical emissions negatively impact a company's public image and increase reputational risk.

$$\text{Reputational Risk}_{i,t} = f\left(\frac{\text{Chemical Emissions}}{\text{Total Assets}_{i,t-1}}, \text{Firm}_{i,t-1}, \mu_t, \varepsilon_{i,t}\right)$$

The dependent variable $Reputational Risk_{i,t}$ refers to the reputational risk rating for firm i in year t; $Chemical Emissions/Total Assets_{i,t-1}$ represents the ratio of the total amount of toxic chemical emissions to total assets for firm i in year t−1; and $Firm_{i,t-1}$ is a vector of control variables for firm i in year t−1 including financial performance captured by ROA, leverage ratio, Tobin's Q, tangibility, and firm size; μ_t accounts for the year fixed effect; and $\varepsilon_{i,t}$ is a random error. The t-statistics are heteroskedastic, and robust standard errors are clustered at the firm level.

As a further test, we investigate the effect of corporate governance on the association between corporate pollution and reputation. Corporate governance plays a crucial role in meeting its legal and regulatory obligations, effectively managing its environmental risks, and making socially responsible decisions. One significant aspect of corporate governance that is associated with environmental performance is board oversight. The board has the responsibility to oversee and guarantee that the company adheres to its environmental obligations. They should regularly review the company's environmental policies and practices, ensuring they align with the company's overall goals. The board should also gain information regarding the company's environmental practices and have the authority to hold management accountable for achieving environmental targets. Another critical aspect of corporate governance that relates to environmental performance is disclosure and transparency. A company should disclose information about its environmental performance, risks, and management, transparently, and accurately. This enables investors, stakeholders, and other interested parties to evaluate the company's environmental performance and make informed decisions. Additionally, a robust corporate culture that values environmental sustainability and ethical behavior is also vital for environmental performance. This can be promoted through appropriate incentives for management, a clear code of conduct, and effective whistleblower mechanisms. In conclusion, the critical role of corporate governance in environmental performance is to ensure that the company is managing its environmental risks responsibly and making decisions that benefit all stakeholders, including the environment. Given this, we anticipate that the negative association between corporate pollution and reputation is intensified under conditions of weaker corporate governance.

We finally turn to the conditional effect of default risk on the pollution-reputation relationship, and we expect that a higher default risk can make this negative relationship more severe. Corporate default risk refers to the possibility that a firm will fail to fulfill its financial obligations, such as making interest payments or repaying debt. When a company is facing default risk, it can exacerbate the negative impact of corporate pollution on its reputation. First, a company facing default risk may be seen as less financially stable and less trustworthy. As a result, stakeholders may be less likely to do business with the company or invest in it. This can cause a decrease in revenue and damage the company's reputation. In addition, a company facing default risk tend to engage in businesses that are environmentally harmful but financially beneficial in the short term. For example, it may prioritize maximizing production or cutting costs over reducing pollution, which can be costly. This can cause further damage to the company's reputation. Furthermore, in case of default, a company may not have the financial capacity to reverse the damage or pay for the consequences of the pollution, which can lead to legal actions and fines and worsen the public perceptions of the company. Therefore, it is reasonable to expect that when a firm is facing default risk the negative impact of corporate pollution on its reputation is exacerbated, which is why it is important for companies to proactively manage both their financial risk and their environmental impact.

6.3.2 Data and Empirical Results

To test the aforementioned specification, we create a US database by combining CEO data from BoardEx, facility toxic chemical releases from the U.S. Environmental Protection Agency (EPA), ESG-related incident rate and reputational risk rating data from RepRisk, and firm financial data from Compustat. An increasing number of studies focus on CSR and ESG reporting. However, a recent study by Berg, Koelbel, and Rigobon (2022) has highlighted the significant differences in ESG ratings provided by six leading ESG rating agencies and the possibility of greenwashing bias in these ratings. Meanwhile, an increasing amount of research focuses on examining the real outcomes of environmental performance, instead of discretionary disclosures. To quantify the environmental performance of the real sectors, policymakers and the academic literature typically utilize the data on CO_2 equivalent (CO2e) emissions and toxic chemical releases, which constitute the most popular databases. According to Greenhouse Gas Protocol, CO2e emissions produced by a company are mainly categorized into three categories: direct emissions from production (scope 1), indirect emissions from consuming purchased electricity, heat, or steam (scope 2), and other indirect emissions due to the production of purchased materials, product usage, waste disposal, and outsourcing activities (scope 3). The latter category of scope 3 emissions is further divided into upstream and downstream indirect emissions. Another widely used proxy of environmental performance is toxic chemical releases provided by the Toxic Release Inventory (TRI) from the U.S. EPA. The U.S. EPA mandates that facilities emitting toxic chemicals exceed a certain limit must report their pollution to the EPA. The emission information is reported through the TRI, which details the amount of chemical releases into the air, water, and ground, the type of chemicals released, the facilities' efforts to reduce these emissions, and the potential health impacts of these releases. In this chapter, we collect toxic chemical emission data, given its broad coverage and fine detail, during our research period from 2007 to 2019. The data sources and description of variables are provided in Table 6.1.

Figure 6.1 and Fig. 6.2 show the change in average chemical emission level, and reputational risk rating over 13 years, respectively. Table 6.2 shows univariate test results on the differences in the average values of the *Reputational Exposure Rating* and firm characteristics for companies with high and low levels of pollution. We split the sample based on the median value of Chemical Emissions/Total Assets. The majority of the differences are statistically significant at the 1% level. Companies with high levels of chemical emissions are prone to receive significantly lower *Reputational Exposure Ratings* (higher reputational exposure) than those with less pollution; they are lower by 0.2218 in the mean test. In terms of firm corporate governance features, high-polluting companies are related to higher profitability (ROA), higher Tobin's Q, lower tangibility, larger firm size, larger board size, a lower percentage of independent board members, and higher CEO total compensation. The signs of the differences are, on balance, consistent with the literature. Figure 6.1 illustrates the change in the sample average chemical emission level over time. Overall, the results show a decreasing pollution release trend. Interestingly, the average reputational risk rating was observed to be falling at the same time (Fig. 6.2) which indicates that the environmental performance of firms is under closer and stricter scrutiny; this is consistent with the increasing public attention and regulation on climate change mitigation.

Furthermore, our evidence shows that, ceteris peritus, firms with lower director age diversity, larger board size, higher CEO compensation, lower board gender ratio, less busy directors, higher board nationality mix, a less staggered board, male CEOs, and CEO duality are related to relative higher reputational rating, implying better reputation management for firms with stronger corporate governance (Fig. 6.3). In contrast, firms with a lower Z-score (higher financial default risk) than the sample median suffer a more severe negative impact of chemical emissions on reputational ratings (Fig. 6.4).

6.4   Conclusions

In this chapter, we discuss contemporary studies on the interactions between environmental and financial performance, environmental performance and financing costs, and environmental performance and corporate governance. We provide a critical analysis of the literature that considers

Table 6.1 Variable definitions

Variable	Definition
Reputational Risk Rating	Reputational risk rating reflects: (i) a company's own ESG-related risk exposure due to risk incidents reported specifically about the company and (ii) the ESG risk that takes into consideration the sector and location of the company's headquarters and states where the company has been exposed to ESG risk incidents. The variable takes a value from 1 to 10, where D = 1 and AAA = 10. Higher values indicate a better reputational rating
Chemical Emissions/Total Assets	The ratio of the total amount of toxic chemicals emitted to the total assets of a firm
ROA	Ratio of earnings before interest, taxes, depreciation, and amortization (EBITDA) to total assets
Leverage	Ratio of long-term debt plus debt in current liabilities to total assets
Tobin's Q	Market value divided by replacement costs
Tangibility	Ratio of net property, plant, and equipment to total assets
Firm Size	Natural logarithm of the total assets in US$ millions
Director Age Diversity	Standard deviation of the ages of directors
CEO Duality	Indicator equals 1 when the CEO also holds the position of chairman of the board
CEO Female	Dummy variable that takes the value of 1 when the CEO is female, and zero otherwise
Board Size	Natural logarithm of the total number of board members at the end of the fiscal year
CEO Compensation	The natural log of total compensation of the CEO
Gender Ratio	The proportion of male directors
Busy Director	A dummy variable for whether a director is busy equals one if a majority of directors hold three or more directorships
Board Nationality Mix	The proportion of directors from different countries
Staggered Board	Indicator equals 1 for a board in which directors are divided into separate classes (typically three) with each class being elected to overlapping terms
Z-score	Altman's Z-score index. Z-score = $1.2 \times$ (working capital/total assets) + $1.4 \times$ (retained earnings/total assets) + $3.3 \times$ (earnings before interest and tax/total assets) + $0.6 \times$ (market value of equity/total liabilities) + $1.0 \times$ (sales/total assets)

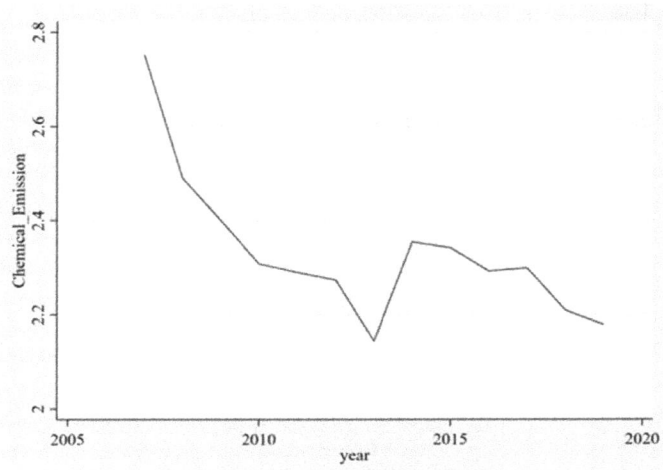

Fig. 6.1   Changes in chemical emissions with time

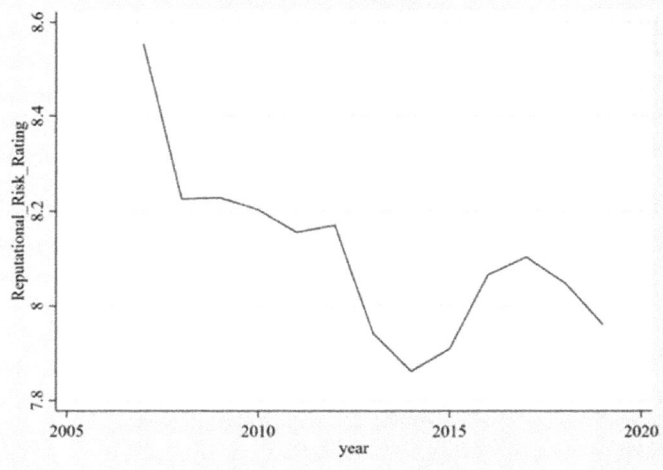

Fig. 6.2   Changes in reputational risk rating with time

Table 6.2 Financial and corporate governance characteristics for firms with high and low chemical emissions

	High chemical emissions/Total assets Group mean	Low chemical emissions/Total assets Group mean	Difference in means	t-statistics
Reputational risk	7.9876	8.2242	−0.2365***	−6.3705
ROA	0.0513	0.0387	0.0126***	6.3989
Leverage	0.2629	0.2662	−0.0032	−0.8065
Tobin's Q	1.8109	1.5500	0.2609***	12.8873
Tangibility	0.2369	0.3925	−0.1557***	−29.8424
Firm size	8.9101	8.3530	0.5571***	14.1291
Staggered board	0.2456	0.3215	−0.0759***	−6.5361
CEO duality	0.4326	0.3576	0.0749***	5.9426
Board independence	82.3659	83.8319	−1.4660***	−5.4406
Board size	2.2901	2.2724	0.0178***	3.2389
CEO total compensation	8000.2681	6176.2726	1823.9955***	14.5752
Female CEO	0.0308	0.0311	−0.0003	−0.0747

This table presents the comparison of means of firm financial and corporate governance characteristics between firms with high and low toxic chemical emissions. We split the sample by the median of Chemical Emissions/Total Assets, which is a measure of the total pounds of toxic chemicals emitted, adjusted for the firm total assets. We use the t-test for difference in means; *, **, and *** denote significance at the 10, 5, and 1% levels, respectively

the links between corporate ownership and environmental responsibility. We also analyze the links between polluting activities and reputational risk, focusing on the driving factors of corporate reputation risk and CSR.

We then provide an exploratory analysis of the link between corporate pollution abatement and reputational risk, considering the experience of U.S. companies. To do so, we develop a distinctive dataset for a sample of U.S. firms operating between 2007 and 2019. Pollution abatement is computed as firm-size standardized annual toxic chemical releases, while reputational risk rating is collected from RepRisk.

Our estimated correlation coefficients reveal evidence of a significant association between firm pollution and reputational rating. Moreover, both the time series of chemical emissions and reputational risk ratings show a downtrend, which suggests a more environmental-friendly approach taken by firms and more prudent reputation scrutiny. We also

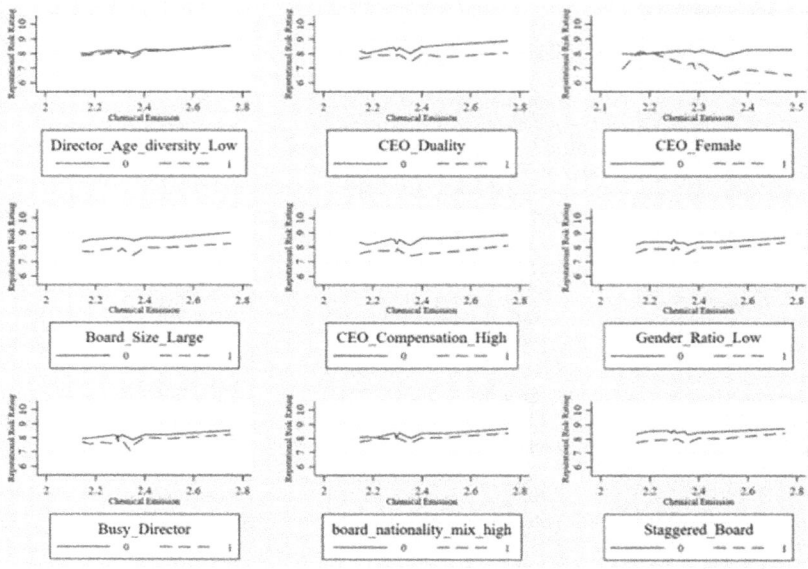

Fig. 6.3 Corporate Governance moderation impact on the relationship between chemical emission and reputational risk

carry out an exploratory analysis of the connection between these variables and corporate governance factors and a measure of the firm-specific risk of insolvency. We find that firms' average reputational risk rating levels are relatively lower for firms with poorer corporate governance and higher financial risk Therefore, corporate pollution can pose a significant risk to a company's reputation, and companies need to take steps to prevent pollution and minimize their environmental impact. This can be achieved through effective corporate governance, risk management, transparency, and communication, investing in sustainable practices, etc.

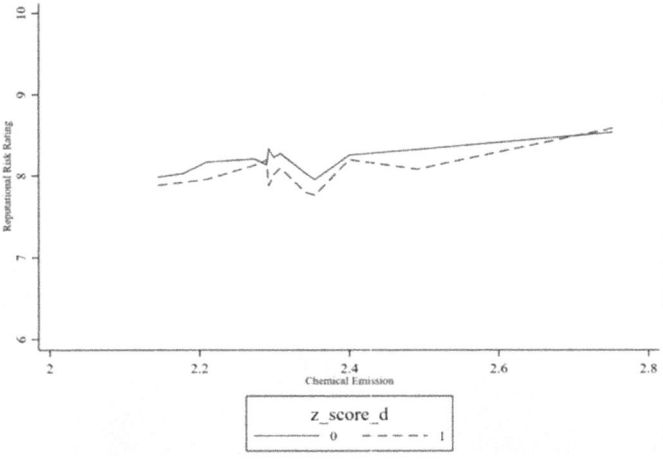

Fig. 6.4 Corporate financial risk moderation impact on the relationship between chemical emission and reputational risk

REFERENCES

Adams, Renée B and Daniel Ferreira (2009). "Women in the boardroom and their impact on governance and performance". *Journal of Financial Economics* 94(2), pp. 291–309.

Adhikari, Binay K, Anup Agrawal, and James Malm (2019). "Do women managers keep firms out of trouble? Evidence from corporate litigation and policies". *Journal of Accounting and Economics* 67(1), pp. 202–225.

Aguilera-Caracuel, Javier and Jaime Guerrero-Villegas (2018). "How corporate social responsibility helps MNEs to improve their reputation. The moderating effects of geographical diversification and operating in developing regions". *Corporate Social Responsibility and Environmental Management* 25(4), pp. 355–372.

Akey, Pat and Ian Appel (2021). "The limits of limited liability: Evidence from industrial pollution". *The Journal of Finance* 76(1), pp. 5–55.

Alon, Anna and Martina Vidovic (2015). "Sustainability performance and assurance: Influence on reputation". *Corporate Reputation Review* 18(4), pp. 337–352.

Arendt, Sebastian and Malte Brettel (2010). "Understanding the influence of corporate social responsibility on corporate identity, image, and firm performance". *Management Decision* 48(10), pp. 1469–1492.

Barnett, Michael L (2007). "Stakeholder influence capacity and the variability of financial returns to corporate social responsibility". *Academy of Management Review* 32(3), pp. 794–816.

Berg, Florian, Julian F Koelbel, and Roberto Rigobon (2022). "Aggregate confusion: The divergence of ESG ratings". *Review of Finance* 26(6), pp. 1315–1344.

Berman, Eli and Linda TM Bui (2001). "Environmental regulation and labor demand: Evidence from the south coast air basin". *Journal of Public Economics* 79(2), pp. 265–295.

Berrone, Pascual, Cristina Cruz, Luis R Gomez-Mejia, and Martin Larraza-Kintana (2010). "Socioemotional wealth and corporate responses to institutional pressures: Do family-controlled firms pollute less?" *Administrative Science Quarterly* 55(1), pp. 82–113.

Berrone, Pascual and Luis R Gomez-Mejia (2009). "Environmental performance and executive compensation: An integrated agency-institutional perspective". *Academy of Management Journal* 52(1), pp. 103–126.

Bolton, Patrick and Marcin Kacperczyk (2021a). "Do investors care about carbon risk?" *Journal of Financial Economics* 142(2), pp. 517–549.

Bolton, Patrick, Marcin Kacperczyk (2021b). "Carbon disclosure and the cost of capital". Available at SSRN: https://ssrn.com/abstract=3755613 or https://doi.org/10.2139/ssrn.3755613

Brammer, Stephen and Stephen Pavelin (2006). "Corporate reputation and social performance: The importance of fit". *Journal of Management Studies* 43(3), pp. 435–455.

Branco, Manuel Castelo and Lúcia Lima Rodrigues (2006). "Corporate social responsibility and resource-based perspectives". *Journal of Business Ethics* 69(2), pp. 111–132.

Chao, Chi-Chur, Jean-Pierre Laffargue, and Pasquale M Sgro (2012). "Environmental control, wage inequality and national welfare in a tourism economy". *International Review of Economics & Finance* 22(1), pp. 201–207.

Chen, I-Ju, Iftekhar Hasan, Chih-Yung Lin, and Tra Ngoc Vy Nguyen (2021). "Do banks value borrowers' environmental record? Evidence from financial contracts". *Journal of Business Ethics* 174(3), pp. 687–713.

Cogan, Douglas G (2008). "Corporate governance and climate change: The banking sector".

Cohn, Jonathan and Tatyana Deryugina (2018). "Firm-level financial resources and environmental spills". *NBER Working Paper 24516*.

Cong, Yu and Martin Freedman (2011). "Corporate governance and environmental performance and disclosures". *Advances in Accounting* 27(2), pp. 223–232.

Coombs, Joseph E and K Matthew Gilley (2005). "Stakeholder management as a predictor of CEO compensation: Main effects and interactions with financial performance". *Strategic Management Journal* 26(9), pp. 827–840.

D'Souza, Clare, Mehdi Taghian, and Gillian Sullivan-Mort (2013). "Environmentally motivated actions influencing perceptions of environmental corporate reputation". *Journal of Strategic Marketing* 21(6), pp. 541–555.

De Villiers, Charl, Vic Naiker, and Chris J Van Staden (2011). "The effect of board characteristics on firm environmental performance". *Journal of Management* 37(6), pp. 1636–1663.

Dechezlepretre, Antoine, Stefania Lovo, Ralf Martin, and Misato Sato (2017). "Does climate change pose a risk to competitiveness? Global firm-level evidence". *Working Paper*.

Deckop JR, KK Merriman, and S Gupta (2006). "The effects of CEO pay structure on corporate social performance". *Journal of Management* 32(3), pp. 329–342.

Degryse, Hans, Roman Goncharenko, Carola Theunisz, and Tamas Vadasz (2021). "When green meets green". *Journal of Corporat Finance forthcoming*, available at SSRN 3724237.

Dögl, Corinna and Dirk Holtbrügge (2014). "Corporate environmental responsibility, employer reputation and employee commitment: An empirical study in developed and emerging economies". *The International Journal of Human Resource Management* 25(12), pp. 1739–1762.

Dowell, Glen, Stuart Hart, and Bernard Yeung (2000). "Do corporate global environmental standards create or destroy market value?" *Management Science* 46980, pp. 1059–1074.

Engel, Hauke, Per-Anders Enkvist, and Kimberly Henderson (2015). "How companies can adapt to climate change". McKinsey. Accessed January 14, 2023. https://www.mckinsey.com/capabilities/sustainability/our-insights/how-companies-can-adapt-to-climate-change.

Esty, Daniel C and Michael E Porter (1998). "Industrial ecology and competitiveness: Strategic implications for the firm". *Journal of Industrial Ecology* 2(1), pp. 35–43.

Flores-Hernández, J Alfredo, Jesús J Cambra-Fierro, and Rosario Vázquez-Carrasco (2020). "Sustainability, brand image, reputation and financial value: Manager perceptions in an emerging economy context". *Sustainable Development* 28(4), pp. 935–945.

Gaganis, Chrysovalantis, Panagiota Papadimiti, Fotios Pasiouras, and Alexia Ventouri (2020). "Informal institutions and corporate reputational exposure: the role of public environmental perceptions". *British Journal of Management* 32(4), pp. 1027–1061.

Gardberg, Naomi A (2006). "Reputatie, reputation, réputation, reputazione, ruf: A cross-cultural qualitative analysis of construct and instrument equivalence". *Corporate Reputation Review* 9(1), pp. 39–61.

Gomez-Trujillo, Ana Maria, Juan Velez-Ocampo, and Maria Alejandra Gonzalez-Perez (2020). "A literature review on the causality between sustainability and corporate reputation". *Management of Environmental Quality: An International Journal* 31(2), pp. 406–430.

Griffin, Jennifer J and John F Mahon (1997). "The corporate social performance and corporate financial performance debate: Twenty-five years of incomparable research". *Business & Society* 36(1), pp. 5–31.

Gul, Ferdinand A, Bin Srinidhi, and Anthony C Ng (2011). "Does board gender diversity improve the informativeness of stock prices?" *Journal of Accounting and Economics* 51(3), pp. 314–338.

Hart, Stuart L (1995). "A natural-resource-based view of the firm". *Academy of Management Review* 20(4), pp. 986–1014.

Hart, Stuart L (1997). "Beyond greening: Strategies for a sustainable world". *Harvard Business Review* 75(1), pp. 66–77.

Hasan, Iftekhar, Haekwon Lee, Buhui Qiu, and Anthony Saunders (2022). "Climate-related disclosure commitment of the lenders, credit rationing, and borrower environmental performance". Available at SSRN: https://ssrn.com/abstract=4150069 or https://doi.org/10.2139/ssrn.4150069

Houston, Joel F and Hongyu Shan (2022). "Corporate ESG profiles and banking relationships". *The Review of Financial Studies* 35(7), pp. 3373–3417.

Hult, G Tomas M, Jeannette A. Mena, Maria Alejandra Gonzalez-Perez, Katarina Lagerström, and Daniel T. Hult (2018). "A ten country-company study of sustainability and product-market performance: Influences of doing good, warm glow, and price fairness". *Journal of Macromarketing* 38(3), pp. 242–261.

Irfan, Muhammad, Mazlan Hassan, and Nasruddin Hassan (2018). "Unravelling the fuzzy effect of economic, social and environmental sustainability on the corporate reputation of public-sector organizations: A case study of Pakistan". *Sustainability* 10(3), p. 769.

Javadi, Siamak and Abdullah-Al Masum (2021). "The impact of climate change on the cost of bank loans". *Journal of Corporate Finance* 69, Article 102019.

Jiang, Liangliang, Chen Lin, and Ping Lin (2014). "The determinants of pollution levels: Firm-level evidence from Chinese manufacturing". *Journal of Comparative Economics* 42(1), pp. 118–142.

Kacperczyk, Marcin T and José-Luis Peydró (2021). "Carbon emissions and the bank-lending channel". *CEPR Discussion Paper No. DP16778*.

Kassinis, George I and Alexia Panayiotou (2006). "Perceptions matter: CEO perceptions and firm environmental performance". *Journal of Corporate Citizenship* 23, pp. 67–80.

Kassinis, George and Nikos Vafeas (2002). "Corporate boards and outside stakeholders as determinants of environmental litigation". *Strategic Management Journal* 23(5), pp. 399–415.

Kim, Daehyun and Laura T Starks (2016). "Gender diversity on corporate boards: Do women contribute unique skills?" *American Economic Review* 106(5), pp. 267–271.

Klassen, Robert D and Curtis P McLaughlin (1996). "The impact of environmental management on firm performance". *Management Science* 42(8), pp. 1199–1214.

Lee, Ki-Hoon, Byung Min, and Keun-Hyo Yook (2015). "The impacts of carbon (CO2) emissions and environmental research and development (R&D) investment on firm performance". *International Journal of Production Economics* 167, pp. 1–11.

Levine, Ross, Chen Lin, Zigan Wang, and Wensi Xie (2019). "Finance and pollution: Do credit conditions affect toxic emissions?" *Working Paper*.

Li, Jun and Di Wu (2020). "Do corporate social responsibility engagements lead to real environmental, social, and governance impact?" *Management Science* 66(6), pp. 2564–2588.

Lin, Han, Saixing Zeng, Liangyan Wang, Hailiang Zou, and Hanyang Ma (2016). "How does environmental irresponsibility impair corporate reputation? A multi-method investigation". *Corporate Social Responsibility and Environmental Management* 23(6), pp. 413–423.

Mahoney LS and L Thorne (2005). "Corporate social responsibility and long-term compensation: Evidence from Canada". *Journal of Business Ethics* 57(3), pp. 241–253.

McGuire, Jean, Sandra Dow, and Kamal Argheyd (2003). "CEO incentives and corporate social performance". *Journal of Business Ethics* 45(4), pp. 341–359.

McKendall, Marie, Carol Sánchez, and Paul Sicilian (1999). "Corporate governance and corporate illegality: The effects of board structure on environmental violations". *The International Journal of Organizational Analysis* 7(3), pp. 201–223.

Melo, Tiago and Alvaro Garrido-Morgado (2012). "Corporate reputation: A combination of social responsibility and industry". *Corporate Social Responsibility and Environmental Management* 19(1), pp. 11–31.

Miles, Morgan P and Jeffrey G Covin (2000). "Environmental marketing: A source of reputational, competitive, and financial advantage". *Journal of Business Ethics* 23(3), pp. 299–311.

Molina-Azorín, José F., Enrique Claver-Cortés, Maria D. López-Gamero, and Juan J. Tarí (2009). "Green management and financial performance: a literature review". *Management Decision* 47(7), pp. 1080–1100.

Mueller, Isabella and Eleonora Sfrappini (2022). "Climate change-related regulatory risks and bank lending". *ECB Working Paper 2670*.

Musteen, Martina, Deepak K Datta, and Benedict Kemmerer (2010). "Corporate reputation: Do board characteristics matter?" *British Journal of Management* 21(2), pp. 498–510.

Nandy, Monomita, and Suman Lodh (2012). "Do banks value the eco-friendliness of firms in their corporate lending decision? Some empirical evidence". *International Review of Financial Analysis* 25, pp. 83–93.

Nardella, Giulio, Stephen Brammer, and Irina Surdu (2020). "Shame on who? The effects of corporate irresponsibility and social performance on organizational reputation". *British Journal of Management* 31(1), pp. 5–23.

Orsato, Renato J (2006). "Competitive environmental strategies: When does it pay to be green?" *California Management Review* 48(2), pp. 127–143.

Pérez-Cornejo, Clara, Esther de Quevedo-Puente, and Juan Bautista Delgado-Garcia (2020). "Reporting as a booster of the corporate social performance effect on corporate reputation". *Corporate Social Responsibility and Environmental Management* 27(3), pp. 1252–1263.

Rassier, Dylan G and Dietrich Earnhart (2010). "Does the porter hypothesis explain expected future financial performance? The effect of clean water regulation on chemical manufacturing firms". *Environmental and Resource Economics* 45(3), pp. 353–377.

Reinhardt, Forest (1999). "Market failure and the environmental policies of firms: Economic rationales for "beyond compliance" behavior". *Journal of Industrial Ecology* 3(1), pp. 9–21.

Rettab, Belaid, Anis Ben Brik, and Kamel Mellahi (2009). "A study of management perceptions of the impact of corporate social responsibility on organisational performance in emerging economies: The case of Dubai". *Journal of Business Ethics* 89(3), pp. 371–390.

Russo, Michael V and Niran S Harrison (2005). "Organizational design and environmental performance: Clues from the electronics industry". *Academy of Management Journal* 48(4), pp. 582–593.

Sarkis, Joseph and James J Cordeiro (2001). "An empirical evaluation of environmental efficiencies and firm performance: Pollution prevention versus end-of-pipe practice". *European Journal of Operational Research* 135(1), pp. 102–113.

Semenova, Natalia and Lars G Hassel (2008). "Financial outcomes of environmental risk and opportunity for US companies". *Sustainable Development* 16(3), pp. 195–212.

Shive, Sophie A and Margaret M Forster (2020). "Corporate governance and pollution externalities of public and private firms". *The Review of Financial Studies* 33(3), pp. 1296–1330.

Soleimani, Abrahim, William D Schneper, and William Newburry (2014). "The impact of stakeholder power on corporate reputation: A cross-country corporate governance perspective". *Organization Science* 25(4), pp. 991–1008.

Stanwick, Peter A and Sarah D Stanwick (2001). "CEO compensation: Does it pay to be green?" *Business Strategy and the Environment* 10(3), pp. 176–182.

Staw, Barry M and Lisa D Epstein (2000). "What bandwagons bring: Effects of popular management techniques on corporate performance, reputation, and CEO pay". *Administrative Science Quarterly* 45(3), pp. 523–556.

Tang, Zhi, Clyde Eirıkur Hull, and Sandra Rothenberg (2012). "How corporate social responsibility engagement strategy moderates the CSR–financial performance relationship". *Journal of Management Studies* 49(7), pp. 1274–1303.

Ulke, Anne-Kathrin and Laura Marie Schons (2016). "CSR as a selling of indulgences: An experimental investigation of customers' perceptions of CSR activities depending on corporate reputation". *Corporate Reputation Review* 19(3), pp. 263–280.

Walley, Noah and Whitehead, Bradley (1994). "It's not easy being green". *Harvard Business Review* 72, pp. 46–52.

Walls, Judith L, Pascual Berrone, and Phillip H Phan (2012). "Corporate governance and environmental performance: Is there really a link?" *Strategic Management Journal* 33(8), pp. 885–913.

Wang, Chong and Feng Wu (2018). "Bank lending in a warming globe: Carbon emission and loan contracting". *Working Paper*.

Wang, Zigan and Luping Yu (2019). "Are firms with female CEOs more environmentally friendly?" Available at SSRN: https://ssrn.com/abstract=335 9180 or https://doi.org/10.2139/ssrn.3359180

Webb, Elizabeth (2004). "An examination of socially responsible firms' board structure". *Journal of Management and Governance* 8(3), pp. 255–277.

Weber, Andrea and Christine Zulehner (2010). "Female hires and the success of start-up firms". *American Economic Review* 100(2), pp. 358–361.

Xie, Rong-hui, Yi-jun Yuan, and Jing-jing Huang (2017). "Different types of environmental regulations and heterogeneous influence on "green" productivity: Evidence from China". *Ecological Economics* 132, pp. 104–112.

Yang, Chih-Hai, Yu-Hsuan Tseng, and Chıang-Ping Chen (2012). "Environmental regulations, induced R&D, and productivity: Evidence from Taiwan's manufacturing industries". *Resource and Energy Economics* 34(4), pp. 514–532.

Yang, Jianjun, Feng Zhang, Xu Jiang, and Wei Sun (2015). "Strategic flexibility, green management, and firm competitiveness in an emerging economy". *Technological Forecasting and Social Change* 101, pp. 347–356.

Zhang, Lu, Shenggang Ren, Xiaohong Chen, Dayuan Li, and Duanjinyu Yin (2020). "CEO hubris and firm pollution: State and market contingencies in a transitional economy". *Journal of Business Ethics* 161(2), pp. 459–478.

Zyglidopoulos, Stelios C (2005). "The impact of downsizing on corporate reputation". *British Journal of Management* 16(3), pp. 253–259.

CHAPTER 7

Is All That Glitters That "Green"? An Empirical Investigation of the Magnitude of Greenwashing in Banking and Its Determinants

Gimede Gigante⬤, *Priscilla Greggio, and Andrea Cerri*

7.1 Introduction

The major private-sector commercial, investment and universal banks have been recognized a key role in the achievement of the most ambitious sustainability-related goals (Berensmann and Lindenberg 2016;

G. Gigante (✉) · P. Greggio · A. Cerri
Bocconi University, Milan, Italy
e-mail: gimede.gigante@unibocconi.it

P. Greggio
e-mail: priscilla.greggio@studbocconi.it

A. Cerri
e-mail: andrea.cerri@unibocconi.it

© The Author(s), under exclusive license to Springer Nature Switzerland AG 2023
S. Carbó-Valverde and P. J. Cuadros Solas (eds.), *New Challenges for the Banking Industry*, Palgrave Macmillan Studies in Banking and Financial Institutions, https://doi.org/10.1007/978-3-031-32931-9_7

145

Migliorelli 2021), since by redirecting the scale and speed of global financial flows they can enable the transition toward a low-carbon future. As a needed response to align to the Paris Agreement goals, as well as to answer the increasing stakeholders' expectations across the environmental, social and governance (ESG) dimensions (Kotsantonis and Bufalari 2019), these institutions have been starting to commit substantial resources to "green" or "sustainable finance" activities (Pinchot and Christianson 2019; Marchant 2020).

However, the lack of a universal definition for "green" and "sustainable finance" gave rise to many different interpretations of what green in financial markets really means. The use of various and often ambiguous terms under the umbrella of "sustainable finance" to describe their pledges makes the interpretation of banks' commitments difficult, and it is impossible to draw comparisons. In addition, despite the sustainable commitment made, these institutions have been massively and constantly financing, without setting specific targets for reduction, fossil fuel companies (Hahn 2021; Rainforest Action Network 2021). Indeed, the nature of banks' public pledges has been recently highly discussed (Pinchot and Christianson 2019; Marchant 2020), such that claims of "greenwashing"—the promotion of misleading environmental performance and practices intended at influencing stakeholders' perceptions (Lyon and Maxwell 2011; Lyon and Montgomery 2015)—have started to arise (Relaño 2011; Berrou et al. 2019; Pinchot and Christianson 2019; Migliorelli 2021; Marchant 2020). The absence of a global governing body auditing the ESG data disclosed by financial institutions, as well as of any mandatory reporting guidelines, contribute to heighten the threat of greenwashing. The issue gains even more relevance considering that, given its role in the transition toward a resilient, sustainable future, the financial system is expected more than other industries to meet its responsibilities to external stakeholders by providing accurate and reliable information on sustainability performance (Breton and Côté 2006).

Despite the relevance of the matter, little effort has been done in studying the phenomenon of greenwashing not only in banking (Khan et al. 2020), but in the entire financial sector. The greater body of academic researches on greenwashing has for long been only focused on understanding its meaning, drivers and determinants for corporates (Belkaoui and Karpik 1989; Cowen et al. 1987, Gray et al. 2001; Delmas and Burbano 2011; Kim and Lyon 2011; Lyon and Montgomery 2013;

Gamerschlag et al. 2011; Marquis et al. 2016; Yu et al. 2020; Ghitti et al. 2020), providing fragmented evidence on the mitigating effects of organizational drivers (i.e., industry, size and profitability), corporate governance and of the geographical location of firms' headquarters. Specifically, firm *size* has been often referred to as a mitigating factor—which hurts greenwashing (Ghitti et al. 2020). On one hand, large firms are more pressured by external stakeholders to adopt greener practices, so they are very active in their Corporate Social Responsibility (CSR) disclosure; on the other hand, the higher reputation at stake limits their incentives to greenwash. The effect of *firms' profitability* on greenwashing is instead more controversial. According to some research, there is a link between companies' profits and the sharing of reliable environmental information (Belkaoui and Karpik 1989; Cowen et al. 1987, Gray et al. 2001; Gamerschlag et al. 2011); others instead conclude that greenwashing is more frequent in profitable organizations because they can better absorb reputational shocks since they have sufficient finances to cover lawsuit expenses or fines (Delmas and Burbano 2011). As an additional firm-level factor, Ghitti et al. (2020) identified the adherence to voluntary reporting initiatives—captured by the compliance to GRI standards—as an indicator of mitigating greenwashing behavior. *External stakeholders' scrutiny* and *public pressure* play a significant role in the disclosure of more reliable environmental and social performance information, as it is well-known by the legitimacy theory (Baldini et al. 2016). According to Lyon and Montgomery (2013), external criticism from environmental activists can inhibit environmental greenwashing activities; the *geographical location* seems to matter as well, as Kim and Lyon (2011) conclude that when companies are headquartered in a place with a higher number of environmental NGO members, they are less likely to greenwash. Finally, Gnyawali (1996) found that the level of economic development measured by countries' GDPs is responsible of influencing environmental sustainability as citizens of advanced economies are more conscious of sustainability issues; it was proven that they demand companies to adopt transparent and environmentally responsible behaviors.

Equivalent studies for the financial sector are very scant (Carnevale and Mazzuca 2014; Carè 2018; Crespi and Migliavacca 2020; La Torre et al. 2020). Finger et al. (2018) explain that this is because banks have some peculiarities, as they operate under a shared regulation that forces them to follow specific accounting and reporting rules. Consequently, researchers tend to exclude banks from multi-sector samples when studying green-washing, as they may bias the research's results (as done by Yu et al. 2020). Moreover, rather than studying greenwashing, the existing literature has mainly focused on understanding the links between Corporate Social Performance (CSP), ESG ratings and/or CSR disclosure, as well as the dynamics between the effects of banks' CSP on Corporate Financial Performance (CFP) (El-Halaby and Hussainey 2015; Khan et al. 2020; Bhasin et al. 2012; Crespi and Migliavacca 2020). By conducting a full review of the determinants of CSP in the financial sector, Crespi and Migliavacca (2020) concluded that firms, country and temporal factors play a role in influencing CSP. However, although the topics of CSP, CSR disclosure and greenwashing are strictly connected, extending these results as if the literature had studied greenwashing has never been empirically proven. What is more, these findings include the "S" and "G"—social and governance factors—and do not isolate financial firms' performance on the "E"—the environment dimension.

This chapter aims at assessing the magnitude of greenwashing in the banking sector and conducting explorative research to understand which factors might influence this behavior. There are two different ways in which this paper contributes to fill the gap in the literature.

Firstly, it differs from previous studies that have quantified green-washing by relying on ESG indexes by proposing an innovative model able to isolate the environmental dimension. Indeed, to compute the level of greenwashing, scholars have commonly relied on two different indexes—the Bloomberg ESG and the Asset4 ESG performance score. The Bloomberg ESG score was used by Tamimi and Sebastianelli (2017) and Yu et al. (2020); however, this measure is only able to capture the quantity of ESG data a firm discloses but it does not communicate anything about its performance (Yu et al. 2020). Other scholars (Ioannou and Serafeim 2012; Cheng et al. 2014; Hartmann and Uhlenbruck 2015; Rees and Rodionova 2015; Del Bosco and Misani 2016) employed the Asset4 ESG performance score available on Reuters, which instead captures companies' ESG performance by using different metrics (Reuters 2017); however, it does not tell anything about the impact that companies just claim to have on the society and environment. Yu et al. (2020) and then Ghitti et al. (2020) proposed a composite measure to capture greenwashing which integrates the two indicators (disclosure and performance) described above. This new methodology represents a step forward; indeed, they quantified greenwashing by considering the difference between a firm's level of disclosure and its relative performance, which is closer to the generally accepted definition of greenwashing provided before. However, it could be stated that this approach presents still some fallacies. Firstly, due to differences in methodology and subjective interpretations of soft data, Doyle (2018) points out that various agencies' ESG ratings can vary substantially, therefore a corporation might be assigned different scores by multiple agencies at the same time. Secondly, the ESG indexes employed to measure greenwashing assign a score to a company also considering social and governance elements (the "S" and "G" in the ESG indexes by Bloomberg and Reuters); instead by definition greenwashing per se is different from sustainable washing (Migliorelli 2021), as the former is only related to the disclosure of misleading environmental practices or claims. In this paper, the model employed aims at isolating the "E" dimension. "Greenwashers" will be therefore referred to as those banks that appear to be very transparent and publish huge amounts of data related to their "green finance" commitment but perform weakly on the environmental aspect. Specifically, their green performance is considered poor when the relative amount devoted to their sustainable finance commitment is lower than their investments in fossil fuel companies.

Secondly, this paper contributes to an increase in the scarcely explored strand of literature that has studied greenwashing in the banking sector. Given the research gap and the lack of clarity of the factors that influence this phenomenon, an explorative research will be performed. To the author's best knowledge, it is the first time that the methodology adopted in this research is used as well as the analysis conducted.

7.2   Research Methodology

7.2.1   Overview

Explorative research has been performed to test whether greenwashing in the banking industry is influenced by firm, country and temporal factors. As previously introduced, these are the determinants that were found to have an influence both on greenwashing in the corporate environment, and on CSP and disclosure in the financial sector, as confirmed by the findings of Crespi and Migliavacca (2020). Indeed, by combining these two strands of literature, the following research questions are asked:

a. to understand whether *firm-level factors* influence greenwashing behavior:

   H1a: The size of a bank has a negative impact on the green-washing score.

   H1b: The involvement of the bank in voluntary disclosing initiatives has a negative impact on the greenwashing score.

b. to understand whether *country-level factors* influence greenwashing behaviors, as they might be affected by major economic and social structures, the following research questions are asked:

   H2a: The higher the economic development of a country where a bank has its headquarters, the lower its greenwashing score.

   H2b: The higher the attention toward sustainability of a country where a bank has its headquarters, the lower its green-washing score.

c. And finally, to test whether the recent regulations and increased attention toward the issues are effective, *time* is tested, leading to the question:

   H3:   There is a significant negative trend in banks' greenwashing scores.

7.2.2   Greenwashing Score

The workable definition of greenwashing provided in the Introduction sets the basis for the computation of the greenwashing score as reported in Eq. (7.1). This score allows assessing the magnitude of a bank's greenwashing activity by quantifying how much a bank discloses—i.e., its transparency—on the green finance commitment it makes, against its actual performance. For this analysis, the green finance commitments considered are defined as "any public pledge that a bank makes to provide a specified quantity of financial services within a certain time frame for the stated purpose of enhancing environmental sustainability and/or supporting low-carbon, climate-resilient development" (Pinchot et al. 2019, p. 3).

$$
\begin{aligned}
\text{Greenwashing score} = &\text{ (A normalized measure representing a bank's} \\
&\text{ Greenness Disclosure score)} \\
&-\text{(A normalized measure representing a bank's} \\
&\text{ Greenness Performance score)} \qquad (7.1)
\end{aligned}
$$

Equation (7.1) was already used by Yu et al. (2020) and Ghitti et al. (2020) in their seminal papers aimed at quantifying greenwashing for corporates; however, there is a substantial difference in the way in which this paper computes both the Greenwashing Disclosure and the Performance scores.

Following the critiques highlighted in the "Introduction" section, it emerges the need to determine a new, transparent approach to source firms' disclosure and performance data which is both able to isolate the environmental dimension and which provides methodological stability. As an attempt to fill the gap, this paper introduces a new model to quantify greenwashing in the banking sector whose basis is represented by the "Framework for Interpreting Private-Sector Bank's Sustainable Finance Commitments" developed by the World Resources Institute in 2019.[1]

The WRI framework was developed by Pinchot et al. (2019) to help stakeholders in giving sense to private banks' active, voluntary green commitments with a simple and clear model. In fact, rather than attempting to examine every feature or attribute of a promise, the authors' goal was to build a model with the fewest feasible indicators that would allow for a meaningful comprehension of the bank pledge's content and context. Following this principle, the WRI framework is based on nine different indicators which are at the same time clustered across three components: Specificity, Accountability—which are qualitative components—and Magnitude—which provides instead a quantitative assessment (Table 7.1). A full description of the components is provided in Tables 7.1, 7.2 and 7.3; for a more complete overview of the overall methodology employed, please refer to the WRI Technical Note.[2]

---

[1] https://www.wri.org/finance/banks-sustainable-finance-commitments/.

[2] https://www.wri.org/research/unpacking-green-targets-framework-interpreting-private-sector-banks-sustainable-finance.

Table 7.1 Description of the three components of the WRI framework

Component	Description
Specificity	It refers to the level of detail that the bank discloses in describing the fundamental parameters of a commitment. Disclosing details about the commitment's thematic focus, financial products and services offered and duration indicates that the commitment is thoughtfully designed for implementation and that the institution is willing to take accountability for the commitment. The greater the degree of specificity, the easier it is for the bank and stakeholders to understand its content and ambition and to track its progress. On the other hand, a statement that uses broad and loosely defined terms may not be backed by a solid implementation plan, despite providing reputational benefit to the bank at the point of announcement
Accountability	It refers to the ability of stakeholders and the bank itself to track and measure progress on the commitment in a way that is rigorous and transparent. The term also refers to the degree of highlevel support and ownership that a commitment enjoys inside a bank, as evidenced by how the commitment is presented to the public
Magnitude	It refers to the quantity of committed resources relative to the bank size and other financing practices of each bank. By itself, the volume of finance in a commitment is not particularly meaningful, especially when comparing the pledges of very large banks or banks of very different sizes. The headline commitment number must be put in context to understand whether it represents a significant push beyond business as usual or is only a small step beyond the status quo. The commitment's size must be compared against the bank's overall size and other business practices

Source Pinchot et al. (2019, p. 4)

The main unit of analysis of the framework is the financial institutions' public available information. The model considers the latest commitments made and adopts an "ex ante" approach since it excludes any assessment of their implementation, but its strength is preserved as it allows to compare bank's commitments at the time of their announcement.

The next subparagraphs define briefly the methodology employed to build the dataset, and how the three components of the framework are used to assess a Greenwashing score.

Table 7.2 Description of the indicators for the Specificity dimension of the WRI framework

A. Specificity		
1. Defines sustainability criteria. The bank clearly defines what is within the scope of sustainable financial services under its commitment	Understanding the scope of the sustainable financial pledge is essential for accountability. If bank staff and stakeholders do not know what the pledge is specifically designated for, they can neither understand the commitment, nor ensure that the bank is allocating resources as promised	Yes/no; detailed description of criteria and/or list of activities, themes and/or sectors
2. Identifies financial services included. The bank discloses the types of financial services (e.g., direct lending, equity finance, fee-based services) counted under the commitment	Transparency about the type of finance offered under the commitment enables stakeholders to understand the types of financing and other services associated with the monetary value of the dollar figure of the commitment (for example, differentiating between direct financing versus indirect support via asset management, advisory services)	Yes/no; description of the types of financial services included
3. Provides specific timeline. The bank specifies a time horizon over which the commitment is to be met, completed with a start date and end date	A time horizon provides an important boundary for commitments, indicating when the activities will take place and the deadline for achieving the target. When comparing multiple commitments, time horizons also help to reveal the magnitude of the commitment by enabling figures to be standardized into dollars per year, using the specific time horizon of each commitment as the denominator	Specific/vague; details about the start and end date of the commitment

Source Pinchot et al. (2019, p. 5)

Table 7.3 Description of the indicators for the Accountability dimension of the WRI framework

B. Accountability

1. Discloses accounting methodology. The bank discloses a methodology for tracking total financing and other services provided under the commitment target. An accounting methodology details the types of businesses, projects and transactions included in the commitment and how the bank counts different financing activities toward the commitment	Because there is no widely accepted accounting methodology for sustainable finance, transparency of the accounting practices for a commitment is essential for clarity and accountability. By explaining its methodology, a bank demonstrates that it is concerned about the sustainability impact of its activity. It also provides stakeholders with insight into the potential impact of the commitment	Yes/no; details about where the methodology is published
2. Includes plans for reporting. The bank has developed and disclosed plans to report progress in terms of the amount of finance provided toward the commitment	By describing the reporting plans, the institution is making a commitment to public accountability and indicating an active intention to meet the targets. Omitting this information may indicate that a bank has either not thought through the implementation process or wants to avoid public accountability, both of which raise doubts about the strength of a commitment	Yes/no; details about what/how the bank will report

B. Accountability

3. Endorsed by CEO/ board chair. The bank's CEO or board chair has publicly supported the commitment in the press release for the pledge or the first annual report following the announcement	An important component of accountability is that an initiative should be integrated across an institution rather than siloed in and confined to a particular business unit, like a sustainability department. One basic indication that the commitment is institution-wide is public endorsement by senior leadership. If leadership does not speak publicly about the commitment, this may suggest that the pledge lacks institutional backing or is not seen as a core part of the institution's strategy	Yes/no; details about who endorsed the commitment

Source Pinchot et al. (2019, p. 5)

7.3   METHODOLOGY

This research's model relies primarily on the dataset already used by Pinchot et al. (2019) in building the WRI framework, as it is made available to the public.[3] Every data and information of the file was reviewed by accessing institutions' sustainability-related pages and by conducting keyword searches on the internet. However, the following adjustments were made for the purpose of this research:

- Different exchange rates were used to convert the sustainable finance commitments from bank's local currencies to dollars and can be found in Table 7.12 of the Appendix.
- Whenever the WRI framework reported a bank's sustainable finance amount which devoted resources to other dimensions than the ones specifically for "green finance", that amount was either decomposed—when possible—to consider only the latter or not considered at all—thus no greenwashing score was computed.
- The WRI analysis considered the sustainable finance commitments made by the world's top 50 private-sector banks, by total assets, from 2016 to 2019. This research extends the assessment at the end of 2020. By conducting keyword searches on the internet and content analysis on the institutions' annual reports, all the banks in the sample were reviewed to see whether new commitments or renewals were made in 2019–2020.
- The WRI analysis considered the sustainable finance commitments made by the world's top 50 private-sector banks by assets. This paper extends instead the original sample to the 60 largest banks by assets. The information for the missing banks were filled for the time frame considered.

7.3.1   Definition of the Greenness Disclosure Score

The first two components of the WRI framework, "Specificity" and "Accountability", were used to determine the banks' Greenness disclosure scores. As they are respectively defined by three indicators each (as illustrated in Tables 7.2 and 7.3), these two components work as synthetic

---

[3] Available at https://www.wri.org/finance/banks-sustainable-finance-commitments/.

indicators—defined as functions of a number of variables, each of which contributes to the quantification of a specific element of a notion whose magnitude must be quantified (Pérez 2016). Each indicator is assessed with Boolean questions—answered with a "Yes" or "No"—therefore, the Boolean data were converted in numerical variables by assigning a score of 1 or 0. Specifically, answers of "Yes" and "Specific" were assigned a score of 1, while "No" or "Vague" answers were given a value of 0. Equal weights of 33.33% were assigned to each indicator for each component to get a % value. To get an overall Greenwashing disclosure score for each institution, an equal weight of 50% for the "Specificity" and "Accountability" dimensions was applied.

7.3.2   Definition of a Greenness Performance Score

The third dimension identified by the WRI framework, "Magnitude", was used to assess effective banks' effective performance on their sustainability commitments, in other words, the Greenness performance score. "Magnitude" is assessed with numerical data. Only two of the original four indicators used by the WRI framework are considered, as the others were considered redundant. As showed in Table 7.3, the bank specific's (a) annualized commitment in sustainable finance and (b) the average annual fossil fuel finance, both relative to the banks' total assets, were taken into consideration. The bank-specific magnitude score will be given by the difference between the % of annualized commitment in sustainable finance and % of average annual fossil fuel finance.

As previously anticipated, the WRI framework works with an ex ante approach. This implies that the performance score cannot be defined as how effectively banks put in place the commitments made. Rather, performance is assessed by considering which is the size of the sustainable finance pledge compared to its brown financing (Weber et al. 2017) for each active year of the commitment. It can be claimed that if its investments in fossil fuel companies are higher than a bank's sustainable commitment, its green performances is really weak and its green commitment should not be taken seriously.

7.3.3   *Computation of the Greenwashing Score*

Before proceeding with the computation of the magnitude of banks' greenwashing, both the identified scores were normalized to the same scale by subtracting the mean and dividing by their standard deviation (Yu et al. 2020). This step was necessary since, as the first boxplots of Fig. 7.1 reports, it can be observed a significant variation across the distributions of disclosure and performance scores. Finally, the greenwashing score was computed as Eq. (7.2) translates in the formula:

$$
\begin{aligned}
\text{Greenwashing score}_{i,t} &= \text{normalized greenness disclosure score}_{i,t} \\
&\quad - \text{normalized greenness performance score}_{i,t} \\
&= \text{normalized}(0.5 * \text{Accountability score} \\
&\quad + 0.5 * \text{Specificity score}) \\
&\quad - \text{normalized Magnitude score} \quad (7.2)
\end{aligned}
$$

Greenwashing is considered to occur when the score takes positive values.

7.4   EMPIRICAL MODEL

The greenwashing score was used as the dependent variable in the following research model, designed to provide empirical evidence of the above-defined research questions:

$$
\begin{aligned}
\text{Greenwashing score}_{i,j,t} &= \beta_0 + \beta_1 * \text{Firm Level Variables}_{i,t} \\
&\quad + \beta_2 * \text{Country Variables}_{j,t} \\
&\quad + \beta_3 * \text{Temporal Variables} + \varepsilon_{i,j,t}
\end{aligned}
$$

That takes more specifically the specification of Eq. (7.3),

$$
\begin{aligned}
\text{Greenwashing score}_{i,j,t} &= \beta_0 + \beta_1 * \text{SIZE}_{i,t} + \beta_2 * \text{V.DISCL}_{i,t} \\
&\quad + \beta_3 * \text{GDP}_{c,t} + \beta_4 \text{COUNTRY.SUST}_{c,t} \\
&\quad + \beta_6 \text{PERIOD} + \beta_7 * \text{ROA}_{i,t} \\
&\quad + \beta_8 * \text{LEVERAGE}_{i,t} + \varepsilon_{i,j,t} \quad (7.3)
\end{aligned}
$$

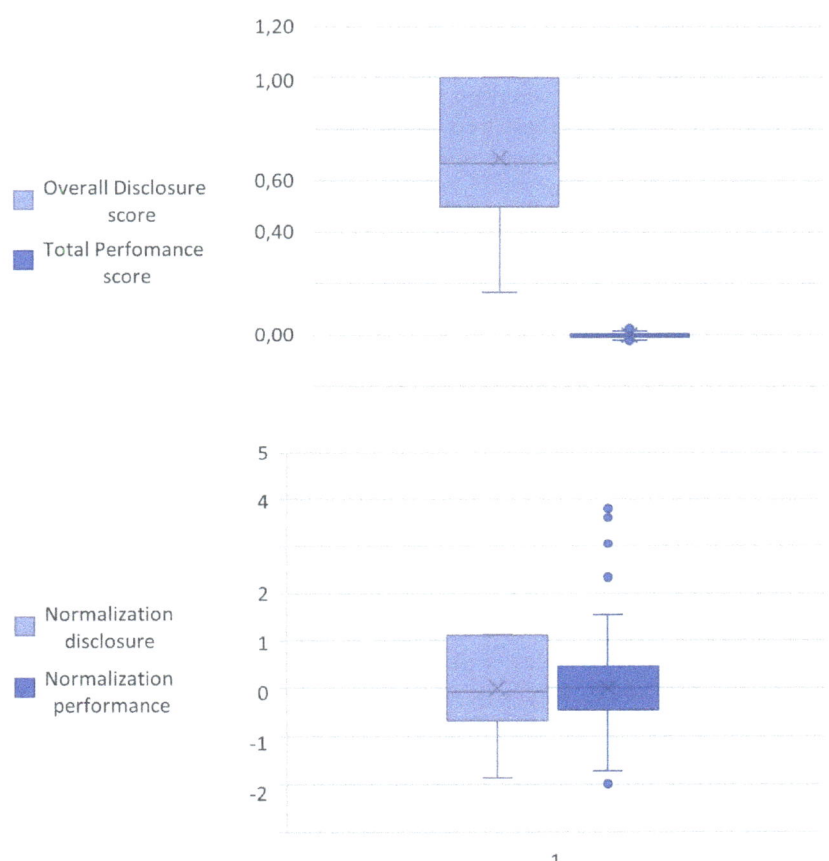

Fig. 7.1 Distribution of the Greenness disclosure score and Greenness performance score

where:

- Greenwashing score$_{i,j,t}$: a greenwashing score which measures the magnitude of greenwashing for a bank i in country j at time t

Firm-level variables include

- $SIZE_{i,t}$ which is measured by the bank's total assets
- $V.DISCL_{i,t}$ which is measured by the number of voluntary disclosure frameworks and guidelines a bank adheres to (over a limited number selected by the author)[4]

Country-level variables include

- $GDP_{j,t}$ which is measured by the GDP of a country j in year t and it measures the country economic development
- COUNTRY.SUST which is an index of the country level of sustainability

Finally, PERIOD measures the temporal factor and indicates the periods ranging from 2016 to 2018 and from 2019 to 2020.

The baseline model employs as firm-level control variables a measure of operating performance, the Return on Asset (ROA), measured as net income over total assets, and Leverage (LEVERAGE), measured as the ratio between total debt over common equity. The reason for incorporating these control variables is that prior literature shows that business variables as profitability, leverage, size and liquidity can influence a firm's environmental greenwashing (Yu et al. 2020). Return on Asset and Leverage were chosen given both the necessity to limit the number of independent variables to include and since they were the most commonly control variables used in the studies reviewed. Refer to Table 7.14 in the Appendix for a complete overview of the variables' definition, the expected sign and their related sources.

Robustness tests are also conducted to better check the results. Specifically, an alternative measure for firm performance was used by substituting ROA with the average Return on Asset for the 5-year period considered (ROA5Y) to check the effect on firm-level factor. Instead, to reflect on the temporal trends, the dummy variable PERIOD was substituted by a categorical variable YEAR. Finally, to assess the overall model, the regression model in (3) is run by lagging all explanatory factors by one year,

---

[4] See the note of Table 7.13 in the Appendix for a detailed determination of the rationale of selection.

with the goal of detecting any dynamic inconsistency and determining whether independent variable values from prior years have influenced greenwashing scores. Given the restricted dataset, checking the robustness of country-level variables by introducing a categorical variable HEAD-QUARTER was not considered meaningful. Therefore, the category of country-level factors has not been checked for robustness.

7.5   SAMPLE

The sample used to test the research's set of hypotheses is made up of the world's 60 largest relevant banks ranked by assets.[5] The rationale for using this limited sample is due to an issue of data constraint on the annual average fossil fuel financing (2016–2020). Indeed, this information was sourced from the 2021 Banking on Climate Chaos dataset[6] published by the Rainforest Action Network and a consortium of partners (Rainforest Action Network 2021) and is only available for the sample identified. Moreover, the Banking on Climate Chaos research considers as relevant for its purpose only the banks with more than $500 million league credit "for economy-wide financing" in 2016–2020. From this original sample all the banks that, in the period 2016–2020, did not make a sustainable finance commitment were excluded. Only 37 banks across the five years are considered in the end; considering the differences in time of when the public pledges were made, this resulted in an overall final international sample made up by 108 observations of banks coming from 14 countries (Table 7.4).

7.6   RESULTS

7.6.1   Descriptive Statistics

Table 7.5 reports descriptive statistics for the explanatory variables used in all the model specifications. Table 7.6 shows instead the correlation between them and the dependent variable. The average magnitude of greenwashing activity for the banks in the sample is 0, with a minimum variable of −5.4751 and a maximum of 3.1113. As Fig. 7.2 shows, it

---

[5] As defined by the S&P Global Market Intelligence ranking, April 2020 (RAN et al., 2021).

[6] Available at https://www.ran.org/bankingonclimatechaos2021/.

Table 7.4 Sample constituents by country and year

Country	2016	2017	2018	2019	2020	Total
Australia	2	3	4	4	4	17
Canada	1	1	2	4	5	13
China	1	1	1	1	1	5
Denmark					1	1
France	2	2	3	3	3	13
Germany					1	1
Italy					2	2
Japan				2	3	5
Netherlands			1	1	1	3
South Korea			1	1	1	3
Spain			1	1	2	4
Switzerland					2	2
UK	2	3	3	4	5	17
US	3	3	5	5	6	22
Total						**108**

Source Author's elaboration

appears how banks that greenwash are nearly perfectly counterbalanced by the presence of firms that present significant negative values. This phenomenon is commonly referred to as "brown-washing", which indicates an understatement of the environmental commitment (Kim and Lyon 2015). However, this term might not totally fit in this case. In fact, given the way in which greenwashing is computed in the paper, it is more likely that the negative scores are driven by the performance and not by the disclosure dimension; that is, these banks have relatively low investments in fossil fuel compared to their sustainable finance commitments.

All the countries in the dataset belong to the list of the 25 most developed nations in the world according to GDP but Denmark that has the minor values for this variable. Finally, the average mean values for the country sustainability scores are high, at slightly more than 78 out of a 100 scale. This supports those theories that consider economic development an important driver of environmental sustainability (Gnyawali 1996).

The correlation matrix of Table 7.7 reports the Pearson correlation coefficients for all variables, which indicate the bivariate relationship between two variables. The results show a significant negative correlation

Table 7.5 Summary statistics

	Greenwashing score (1)	Size (2)	Voluntary disclosure (3)	GDP (4)	Country sustainability score (5)	Period (6)	Leverage (7)	ROA (8)
Min	−5.4751	$411,902 B	0.00	$302,471 B	70.13	0.00	1.508	−0.5788
1st	−1.0933	$709,975 B	0.00	$1638,197 B	75.79	0.00	2.683	0.2351
Median	−0.3086	$1143,243 B	0.66	$2748,275 B	79.15	1.00	3.515	0.5498
Mean	0.0000	$1578,164 B	1.00	$6204,765 B	78.16	0.58	3.935	0.5455
3rd	1.2450	$2079,961 B	1.00	$6785,605 B	80.08	1.00	4.677	0.8570
Max	3.1113	$4832,617 B	1.00	$19,974,534 B	84.85	1.00	10.386	13.6460
NA's					3			

Table 7.6 Correlation matrix of the depended variable and among the explanatory variables

	Greenwashing score (1)	Size (2)	Voluntary disclosure (3)	GDP (4)	Country sustainability score (5)	Period (6)	Leverage (7)	ROA (8)
COUNTRY.SUST	−0.0451	1						
GDP	0.3671****	−0.5357****	1					
LEVERAGE	−0.2953***	−0.0129	−0.0518	1				
ROA	0.2357**	−0.6626***	0.4691****	−0.1289	1			
SIZE	0.2203**	−0.2083*	0.3895*****	0.2084**	0.1906	1		
V.DISCL	−0.0977	0.2581**	−0.3157***	0.0291	−0.3086***	−0.1186	1*	
PERIOD	−0.2161**	−0.1014	−0.0069	0.0285	0.0102	−0.0413	−0.0848	1

Significant codes: ****: 0.001 ; ***: 0.01 ; **: 0.05; *: 0.1

Fig. 7.2 Greenwashing scores across the sample of 109 banks in the sample period 2016–2020 (*Source* Author's elaboration)

between greenwashing scores and the temporal variable PERIOD, while the same is not true for all the firm and country-level variables. More specifically, there is a positive relationship with a bank's size, but this is not significant for voluntary disclosure. Interestingly, GDP is positively and strongly correlated to greenwashing, but the same is not true for countries' sustainability scores. As for the relationships among independent variables, we can see that despite some significant correlation values they are lower than the 0.8 thresholds; therefore, the model appears before being tested already robust to multicollinearity. It is worth pointing out the two stronger negative correlations between GDP and country sustainability scores (at -0.5357) and between the latter and ROA, at -0.6626. We can see that however all the correlations are generally relatively low. As a final note, Outliers and leveraged observations were tested but not omitted, as they were considered an important part of the analysis.

7.6.2 *Multivariate Analysis*

Since the descriptive statistics are derived by either univariate or bivariate analysis, the multivariate analysis was then performed to provide empirical evidence of the research questions. Before running the multivariate regression, seven distinct simple linear regressions for each explanatory variable were tested for homoskedasticity to understand whether log transformations were necessary. All the models' Basic Diagnostic plots

Table 7.7 Baseline model of the OLS regression analysis

	(1)	(2)	(3)
(Intercept)	−23.02905****	−2.611e+01***	−2.380e+01***
	(6.21789)	(8.349e+00)	(8.300e+00)
log(SIZE)	0.85820****	4.751e−01*	4.588e−01*
	(0.22527)	(2.575e−01)	(2.536e−01)
V.DISCL	−0.08751	6.090e−02	6.219e−03
	(0.30676)	(3.109e−01)	(3.073e−01)
GDP		7.396e−14***	7.106e−14***
		(2.652e−14)	(2.615e−14)
COUNTRY.SUST		1.650e−01**	1.464e−01**
		(7.101e−02)	(7.052e−02)
PERIOD			−5.606e−0**
			(2.774e−01)
Control variables			
LEVERAGE	−0.30544****	−2.601e−01***	−2.572e−01***
	(0.08350)	(8.304e−02)	(8.178e−02)
ROA	0.65767*	9.427e−01*	8.692e−01*
	(0.38298)	(4.909e−01)	(4.847e−01)
Adjusted R-squared	0.1956	0.2469	0.2698

All the models are controlled for banks' profitability (ROA) and leverage and are robust to heteroskedasticity. Significance codes: ****: 0.001 ; ***: 0.01 ; **: 0.05; *: 0.1

were examined, and Breusch-Pagan tests were conducted. What emerged is that, for the variable SIZE only, the RvFV plot seemed to confirm the violation of homoskedasticity, although the Breusch-Pagan test did not allow to totally reject this hypothesis. However, to help meet the assumption of constant variance, it was preferred to perform a log trans-formation of the variable, such that model (7.3) took the form of a level-log regression,

$$
\begin{aligned}
\text{Greenwashing score}_{i,j,t} = {} & \beta_0 + \beta_1 * \log(\text{SIZE}_{i,t}) + \beta_2 * \text{V.DISCL}_{i,t} \\
& + \beta3 * \text{GDP}_{j,t} + \beta_4 * \text{COUNTRY.SUST}_{j,t} \\
& + \beta_6 * \text{PERIOD} + \beta_7 * \text{ROA}_{i,t} \\
& + \beta_8 * \text{LEVERAGE}_{i,t} + \varepsilon_{i,j,t} \qquad (7.4)
\end{aligned}
$$

defined as a model with one or more independent variables are log-transformed while the dependent variable stays unchanged.

Table 7.8 Variance inflation factors

Variable	(1)	(2)	(3)
log(SIZE)	1.052123	1.343092	1.344452
V.DISCL	1.104264	1.161145	1.170215
GDP		1.933718	1.939546
COUNTRY.SUST		2.115365	2.151927
PERIOD			1.030076
ROA	1.129508	1.948013	1.959028
LEVERAGE	1.067400	1.098932	1.099277

By finally estimating the re-defined model in (7.4), it was found that greenwashing scores are linearly affected by firm, country and temporal-level factors. Table 7.7 provides the baseline model, where the three groups of explanatory variables have been gradually added.

The three categories of explanatory variables have been gradually added to the model. Since the adjusted R-square increases from model (7.1) to (7.3), it is possible to say that the added predictors contribute significantly to explaining the model variability (Table 7.8).

The results provide evidence of their relevance in affecting greenwashing in the banking sector, although the sign of many factors differs from the existing literature. However, it must be recalled the absence of pure literature on greenwashing in banking; in fact, the hypothesis tested was developed by combining research's results of greenwashing for corporates and corporate social performance (CSP) in the financial industry.

As for the firm-level factors, firm's size (log(SIZE)) seems to be consistently positively related to higher greenwashing scores. At first, this seems to go against both that body of literature that explains how large firms are pressured to limit greenwash given their higher reputation at stake (Ghitti et al. 2020) as well as those studies that consider how size increases the quality of sustainability reporting in banking (Khan et al. 2020; Bhasin et al. 2012). However, this finding could be expected. In fact, the low levels of performance scores are mainly driven by the high investments in fossil fuel companies; as reported by the Rainforest Action Network report (2021), the world's largest banks by assets are exactly the main investors in these industries. The firm's profitability (ROA) and leverage, the control variables for this category, are respectively statistically positively and negatively correlated to greenwashing scores. The result for

ROA goes in the same direction of those studies that, as explained by Delmas and Burbano (2011), claim that more profitable firms can better absorb reputational shocks if they are discovered to be engaged in greenwashing. Moreover, the higher returns which are offered by investment in fossil fuels (Ahlström and Monciardini 2021), contribute to explain why this positive relationship with the dependent variable was found. Instead, the fact that higher indebtedness is associated with lower greenwashing may be explained by the fact that they are exposed to stronger scrutiny from authorities, making banks less likely to make false or inaccurate environmental claims. A negative sign for the variable V.DISCL was originally expected, as taking part in many voluntary disclosing initiatives should indicate the bank's commitment toward a more responsible and sustainable behavior. In line with the institutional theory, more worldwide regulations were expected to deter environmentally detrimental companies from selective disclosure (Marquis et al. 2016). El-Halaby and Hussainey (2015) found in fact that the implementation of accounting standards in Islamic banks was positively correlated with their level of CSR disclosure. However, the variable loses its negativity after country and temporal variables are added. The lack of significance does not allow to make any conclusions, however, this finding rises a question over the efficacy of voluntary reporting guidelines. In general, it is possible to conclude that the firm-level factors have a mixed effect on greenwashing, as H1a is rejected but nothing can be said for H1b.

Country-level factors have a statistically relevant influence on greenwashing as well. The state of economic development of a country (measured through its GDP) is positively related to greenwashing. Prior literature showed contrasting evidence on this aspect. On one hand, some research stated how economic development is a key driver for environmental sustainability, and that citizens of advanced economies drive demand for more transparent, environmentally responsible behavior from businesses (Gnyawali 1996). On the other, mixed evidence in the studies of Chapple and Moon (2005) and Ioannou and Serafeim (2012) let them conclude that economic development cannot fully explain differences in cross-country corporate social performance. The explanation for the positive correlation in this analysis could be explained by the fact that the sample of the model is not random, and all the biggest banks, who are the major responsible for greenwashing, have their headquarters in the most advanced economies. More surprising results concern the positive relationship of greenwashing with COUNTRY.SUST, that in the bivariate analysis was both negatively (but not significantly) correlated with the dependent variable and which was negatively and relevantly related to GDP. This appears as a Simpson's Paradox; however, the positive association between a country's sustainability' score and higher greenwashing level can also be explained by the institutional theory, as external forces and stakeholders' pressure may push banks to make green commitments and disclose more, and also to hide their brown financing. Lastly, it has to be mentioned that the variable COUNTRY.SUST is used as a proxy for sustainability, but the score is based on the country's overall progress toward Sustainable Development Goals (SDGs); therefore, the sustainable environmental dimension is not totally isolated, and results can be misleading. Despite possible limitations, H2 is therefore totally rejected.

Temporal-level factors show a statistically negative relationship with the level of greenwashing scores. More specifically, lower values for greenwashing are observed for the period 2019–2020 compared to the three years 2016–2018. This negative trend goes in the same direction as the increase CSP in the financial industry between 2010 and 2017 found by Crespi and Migliavacca (2020). The low p-value levels confirm that H3 cannot be rejected.

7.6.3   Robustness Tests

To draw stronger inferences between greenwashing scores and firms, country and temporal factors, several robustness checks were performed. Table 7.9 reports the results for a regression in which firm-level variables are tested. The variable ROA of the baseline model was substituted by the five-year average return on assets (ROA5Y), and the three buckets of explanatory variables are added gradually as previously done. As the results appear consistent with the baseline model, there is increasing confidence that the results of H1 have been captured robustly.

The estimates reported in Table 7.10 focus instead on checking the results for the temporal variable. The categorical variable YEAR with values ranging in the timespan 2016–2020 substitutes the dummy PERIOD of the baseline model; we can see that the greenwashing scores tend to be lower than the ones of 2016 in the years 2019 and 2020. These results are not statistically significant but, despite not being "Leamer's robust", they are robust to effect stability (Neumayer and Plümper 2017).

Table 7.9 Robustness checks on firm-level variables

Coefficients	(1)	(2)	(3)
(Intercept)	−22.96598****	−3.340e+0****	−3.114e+01****
	(6.16160)	(8.705e+00)	(8.632e+00)
log(SIZE)	0.84611****	4.752e−01*	4.590e−01*
	(0.22338)	(2.507e−01)	(2.467e−01)
V.DISCL	−0.02381	1.410e−01	8.798e−02
	(0.30681)	(3.044e−0)	(3.005e−01)
GDP		6.842e−14***	6.545e−14**
		(2.592e−1)	(2.554e−14)
COUNTRY.SUST		2.488e−01***	2.308e−01***
		(7.785e−02)	(7.707e−02)
PERIOD			−5.578e−01**
			(2.694e−01)
Control variables			
LEVERAGE	−0.29957****	−2.385e−01***	−2.351e−01***
	(−0.29957)	(8.128e−02)	(7.997e−02)
ROA5Y	0.99742**	2.019e+00***	1.951e+00***
	(0.45120)	(6.636e−01)	(6.535e−01)
Adjusted R-squared	0.21	0.2859	0.3091

All the models are robust to heteroskedasticity. VIF are reported in the Appendix. Significance codes:
****: 0.001 ; ***: 0.01 ; **: 0.05; *: 0.1

The last robustness tests were performed to check the overall esti-mates of the model. Table 7.11 reports the results for a regression model, where firm, country and temporal factors are gradually added, which has a contemporary dependent variable and independent variables lagged by one year. No major differences are found with the baseline model at the firm level, as firm size is still positively associated with greenwashing at a 10% level and the participation in voluntary disclosing initiatives is irrelevant from a statistical point of view. However, country and temporal-level factors change in terms of significance. Indeed, only GDP maintains the same sign and significance of the baseline model; both the country sustainability' scores and the temporal dimension lose their relevance, although robustness for effect stability is preserved. It is also appropriate to remember that many observations were removed to perform this last robustness check. This is since, on one hand, there is the need to drop entirely 2016, as there are no lagged data for 2015, but also because there is no uniformity in the starting date of the sustainable finance

Table 7.10
Robustness checks on
temporal-level variables

Intercept	−2.581e+01***
	(8.549)
log(SIZE)	4.723e−01*
	(2.624e−01)
V.DISCL	1.06e−01
	(3.378e−01)
GDP	7.588e−14***
	(2.702e−14)
COUNTRY.SUST	1.632e−01**
	(7.439e−02)
Year[T.2017]	1.48e−01
	(6.021e−01)
Year[T.2018]	3.68e−02
	(5.727e−01)
Year[T.2019]	−3.48e−02
	(5.494e−01)
Year[T.2020]	−2.68e−01
	(5.340e−01)
LEVERAGE	−2.560e−01***
	(8.444e−02)
ROA	8.18e−01
	(5.497e−01)

The models are robust to heteroskedasticity. VIF are reported in the Appendix. Significance codes: ****: 0.001 ; ***: 0.01 ; **: 0.05; *: 0.1

commitments by all the banks. Given the small sample size of 71 observations, there could be an effect size factor causing the estimates not to be significant (Nayak 2010).

Table 7.11 Robustness checks on the overall model

Coefficients	(1)	(2)	(3)
(Intercept)	−23.7316***	−1.655e+01**	−1.655e+01**
	(7.0406)	(7.620e+00)	(7.629e+00)
log(SIZE)	0.9014****	6.048e−01**	6.090e−01**
	(0.2564)	(2.857e−01)	(2.861e−01)
V.DISCL	0.1025	2.300e−01	2.824e−01
	(0.3350)	(3.348e−0)	(3.399e−01)
GDP		5.513e−14**	5.432e−14**
		(2.676e−14)	(2.680e−14)
COUNTRY.SUST		1.138e−02	1.092e−02
		(1.273e−02)	(1.276e−02)
PERIOD			−3.101e−01
			(3.350e−01)
Control variables			
LEVERAGE	−0.4278****	−4.250e−01****	−4.254e−01****
	(0.1042)	(1.020e−01)	(1.021e−01)
ROA	0.4895	1.274e−01	1.355e−01
	(0.4630)	(5.078e−01)	(5.084e−01)
Adjusted R-squared	0.2435	0.2752	0.2736

All the explanatory variables have been lagged by one year compared to the greenwashing scores. All the models, for which firm, country and temporal variables are progressively added, are robust to heteroskedasticity. VIF are reported in the Appendix. Significance codes: ****: 0.001 ; ***: 0.01 ; **: 0.05; *: 0.1

7.7 Conclusion

This study sets out to assess the magnitude of greenwashing in banking and investigate, through explorative research, whether firms, country and temporal level factors influence banks' greenwashing behavior. To reach these goals, a new methodology to quantify the magnitude of greenwashing by assessing the reliability of banks' green finance commitments was introduced. In this way, it has been possible to build a model which allowed to explore whether the computed greenwashing score was influenced by the factors that the existing literature has identified as relevant mitigating forces. Given the lack of studies for greenwashing in banking, the hypothesis tested are obtained by combining the findings for greenwashing in the corporate environment and the scant literature available for the financial industry, mainly focused on the determinants of corporate social performance and disclosure. The model was tested on a restricted dataset of 108 observations given the current data constraint and tested for robustness. Overall, the empirical results suggest that big, more profitable banks are more likely to engage in greenwashing, especially if they are from more advanced economies. While apparently these findings are contrasting the existing corporate studies which generally state the opposite, how the greenwashing score is computed, and the sample selected, drive the explanation for the obtained results. In fact, as identified by the Rainforest Action Network report (2021), the world's largest banks have the highest investment in fossil fuel companies. On a positive note, the degree of greenwashing has reduced in the last two years of the time period considered.

The findings of this research highlight several implications and especially offer a multitude of points of reflection. The fact that big financial institutions with a systemic role in our economies are accounted as the main ones responsible for greenwashing should worry and put more pressure on regulators to enforce quickly a stricter financial regulation. The need of stringent surveillance by a global governing body to check the reliability of the sustainable data disclosed is also confirmed by the fact that greenwashing does not appear to be influenced by the adherence to voluntary disclosing initiatives. The European Union authorities have already taken concrete positive steps to regulate the sustainable finance market. However, the EU accounts for 10% of the world's greenhouse gases emission (Migliorelli and Dessertine 2019). Only worldwide governance for the battle against climate change can bring the paradigm shift required to achieve environmental goals. On top of the needed stricter and consistent global supervision on sustainability reporting, this paper has highlighted the urgency to stop financing the expansion of fossil fuel companies if banks want to align to the -1.5 °C alignment set in 2015 by the COP21. Banks' sustainable finance commitments and claims of "net-zero by 2050" cannot be taken seriously if they consider them as a license to avoid taking immediate action on their fossil fuel investments.

This study has contributed to the literature on greenwashing by extending for the first time the assessment of its magnitude in a new area, the one of banking, and by employing a new methodology based on the WRI framework. To the authors' best knowledge, it is the first time that such methodology, as well as explorative research, is conducted.

ESG indexes that other studies have employed for their analysis were avoided in favor of a simpler and easier model for different reasons. Indeed, they did not allow to totally isolate the "E" component and they are frequently criticized for being highly subjective. Another reason which explains why introducing a model based on publicly available information could be valuable is to extend the greenwashing assessment also to ethical banks. These institutions are excluded from any rankings as they are private; still, it would be stimulating as future research to assess the magnitude of greenwashing in that sample and compare it to the greenwashing levels of systemic banks. Given the ethical business model, it is highly likely that they do not engage in greenwashing; therefore, they could be set as role models for traditional banks. As the current literature on sustainable banking is very rare (Valls Martínez et al. 2020), additional research able to prove their business model for the achievement of a resilient and transparent financial system is crucial.

The model introduced in this study presents however many limitations which are left to be studied in future research. Specifically, critiques of the validity of the weights used to assess each pillar of the framework, together with solving the issues related to data availability and comparability are encouraged. Given the fact that the effect of new policy takes time to reflect in data, it would be also interesting if the research was repeated in the future to see the effect of the EU Action Plan for Sustainable Growth on greenwashing.

Appendix

See Tables 7.12, 7.13, 7.14, 7.15, and 7.16.

Table 7.12 Exchange rates used in converting Sustainable finance commitments in dollars ($)

Currency	2016	2017	2018	2019	2020	Source
EUR-USD	1.11	1,13	1,18	1,12	1,14	Macrotrends
AUS-USD	0.74	0.77	0.75	0.7	0.69	Macrotrends
YEN-USD	108.69	112.15	110.34	109.01	106.76	Macrotrends
POUND-USD	1.35	1.29	1.33	1.28	1.28	Macrotrends
CANADIAN-USD	0.7553	0.7713	0.7717	0.7538	0.7462	Exchange Rates Uk
DKK-USD	0.14862	0.15191	0.15842	0.14994	0.1532	ofx
KRW-USD	–	–	0.0009	0.0009	0.0008	Exchange Rates Uk
RMB-USD	6.65	6.76	6.63	6.91	6.9	Exchange Rates Uk

Table 7.13 Variable definition

Variable	Definition	Source	Expected Sign
Greenwashing score	Greenwashing score index defined by the difference between the greenness disclosure and performance scores	Author's computation	
Greenness disclosures	Normalized measure of a bank's WRI database and individual sustainable finance commitment banks' websites, annual transparency reports, press releases		
Greenness performance score	Normalized measure of a bank's sustainable finance (S.F) commitment performance, relative to its investment in fossil fuel (F.F.) companies	For S.F. data = individual banks' websites, annual reports, press releases. For F.F. data = Rainforest Action Network.	
Firm-level variables			
Size	Total assets in million of $	FactSet	+
V.DISCL[a]	Dummy variables taking the value of 1 for banks with high voluntary disclosure scores (> = 5), 0 for low voluntary disclosure scores	Individual Banks' websites, Annual reports	−
Country-level variables			
GDP	Annual GDP in million of $. GDP is the sum of gross value added by all resident producers in the economy plus any product taxes and minus any subsidies not included in the value of the products	OECD, Statista (for China for GDP)	−
COUNTRY.SUST	Country sustainability scores interpreted as a % of their achievements toward the SDGs	sdgindex.org	−
Temporal variables			

(continued)

Table 7.13 (continued)

Variable	Definition	Source	Expected Sign
PERIOD	Dummy variables taking the value of 1 for years included in the period 2019–2020, otherwise (2016, 2017 and 2018)		−
YEAR	Categorical variables ranging from 2016 to 2020		−
Control variables			
LEVERAGE	Total debt over common equity	FactSet (Retrieved: 06/06/2021)	−
ROA	Average return on asset	FactSet (Retrieved: 06/06/2021)	±
ROA5Y	Five year average return on asset	FactSet (Retrieved: 06/06/2021)	±

[a]V.DISCL is a variable built by reviewing the most used voluntary reporting standards and sustainable banking initiatives that promote transparent disclosure and selecting the most fit for the purpose. Specifically, seven distinct initiatives were identified: (1) The UNEP FI Principles for Responsible Banking Initiatives, (2) the Carbon Disclosure Project, the (3) Equator Principles, (4) the UN Global Compact, (5) the Green Bond Principles, (6) the Global Reporting Initiatives (GRI) and finally the (6) Taskforce on Climate-Related Financial Disclosure (TCFD). The adherence to these initiatives was checked for each institution i was checked in the timespan 2016–2020. A score of 1 was given if the bank committed to it, 0 otherwise. In total, the score was defined on a scale out of 7

Table 7.14 VIF For robustness checks with ROA5Y

	(1)	(2)	(3)
log(SIZE)	1.053455	1.343092	1.344446
V.DISCL	1.124788	1.173973	1.182545
GDP		1.948397	1.954556
COUNTRY.SUST		2.682301	2.716858
PERIOD			1.026835
ROA5Y	1.151853	2.708000	2.714742
LEVERAGE	1.067770	1.110527	1.110989

Table 7.15 VIF For robustness checks with YEAR

log(SIZE)	1.352423
VS.Cate	1.328792
GDP	1.946785
COUNTRY.SUST	2.250891
YEAR	1.477373
LEVERAGE	1.101777
ROA	2.368366

Table 7.16 VIF For robustness checks with LAGGED explanatory variables

Variable	(1)	(2)	(3)
log(SIZE)	1.075764	1.394604	1.394944
V.DISCL	1.045188	1.089276	1.120406
GDP		1.602871	1.604586
COUNTRY.SUST		1.121013	1.122706
PERIOD			1.035011
ROA	1.064015	1.335689	1.064334
LEVERAGE	1.063992	1.0−64317	1.336088

References

Ahlström, H., Monciardini, D. (2021). The Regulatory Dynamics of Sustainable Finance: Paradoxical Success and Limitations of EU Reforms. *Journal of Business Ethics*. https://doi.org/10.1007/s10551-021-04763-x

Baldini, M., Maso, L., Liberatore, G., Mazzi, F., Terzani, S. (2016). Role of Country- and Firm-Level Determinants in Environmental, Social, and Governance Disclosure. *Journal of Business Ethics, 150*(1), 79–98. https://doi.org/10.1007/s10551-016-3139-1

Belkaoui, A., Karpik, P. (1989). Determinants of the Corporate Decision to Disclose Social Information. *Accounting, Auditing & Accountability Journal, 2*(1). https://doi.org/10.1108/09513578910132240

Berensmann, K., Lindenberg, N. (November, 2016). *Green Finance: Actors, Challenges and Policy Recommendations*. German Development Institute/ Deutsches Institut für Entwicklungspolitik (DIE), Briefing Paper 23/2016, Available at SSRN: https://ssrn.com/abstract=2881922

Berrou, R., Ciampoli, N., Marini, V. (2019). Defining Green Finance: Existing Standards and Main Challenges. In Migliorelli, M. & Dessertine, P. (eds.). *The rise of Green Finance in Europe* (31–51). Palgrave studies in Impact Finance. https://doi.org/10.1007/978-3-030-22510-0_2

Bhasin, M.L., Makarov, R.R., Orazalin, N.S. (2012). Determinants of Voluntary Disclosure in the Banking Sector: An Empirical Study. *International Journal of Contemporary Business Studies* (3), 60–71. Available at SSRN: https://ssrn.com/abstract=2676501

Breton, G., Côté, L. (2006), Profit and the Legitimacy of the Canadian Banking Industry. *Accounting, Auditing & Accountability Journal, 19*(4), 512–539. https://doi.org/10.1108/09513570610679119

Carè, R. (2018). *Sustainable Banking. Issues and Challenges*. 1st ed. Palgrave Pivot. Available at: https://doi.org/10.1007/978-3-319-73389-0

Carnevale, C., Mazzuca, M. (2014). Sustainability Report and Bank Valuation: Evidence from European Stock Markets. *Business Ethics: A European Review, 23*(1), 69–90. https://doi.org/10.1111/beer.12038

Chapple, W., Moon, J. (2005). Corporate Social Responsibility (CSP) in Asia: A Seven-Country Study of CSP Web Site Reporting. *Business & Society, 44*(4), 415–441. https://doi.org/10.1177/0007650305281658

Cheng, B., Ioannou, I., Serafeim, G. (2014). Corporate Social Responsibility and Access to Finance. *Strategic Management Journal, 35*, 1–23. https://doi.org/10.1002/smj.2131

Cowen, S.S., Ferreri, L.B., Parker, L.D. (1987). Determinants of Corporate Social Responsibility Disclosure: An Application of Stakeholder Theory. *Accounting, Organizations and Society, 12*(2), 111–122. https://doi.org/10.1016/0361-3682(87)90001-8

Crespi, F., Migliavacca, M. (2020). The Determinants of ESG Rating in the Financial Industry: The Same Old Story or a Different Tale? *Sustainability, 12*(16), 6398. https://doi.org/10.3390/su12166398

Del Bosco, B., Misani, N. (2016). The Effects of Cross-Listing on the Environmental, Social and Governance Performance of Firms. *Journal of World Business, 51*(6), 977–990. https://doi.org/10.1016/j.jwb.2016.08.002

Delmas, M.A., Burbano, V.C. (2011). The Drivers of Greenwashing. *California Management Review, 54*(1), 64–87. https://doi.org/10.1525/cmr.2011.54.1.64

Doyle, M.T. (2018). *Ratings That Don't Rate: The Subjective World of ESG Ratings Agencies*. American Council for Capital Formation. Available at: https://corpgov.law.harvard.edu/2018/08/07/ratings-that-dont-rate-the-subjective-world-of-esg-ratings-agencies/

El-Halaby, S., Hussainey, K. (2015). The Determinants of Social Accountability Disclosure: Evidence from Islamic Banks Around the World. *International Journal of Business, 20*, 203–223. Available at: https://www.researchgate.net/profile/Sherif-El-Halaby/publication/283522222_The_determinants_of_social_accountability_disclosure_Evidence_from_islamic_banks_around_the_world/links/5af151edaca272bf4255b486/The-determinants-of-social-accountability-disclosure-Evidence-from-islamic-banks-around-the-world.pdf

Finger, M., Gavious, I., Manos, R. (2018). Environmental Risk Management and Financial Performance in the Banking Industry: A Cross-Country Comparison. *Journal of International Financial Markets Institutions and Money, 52*, 240–261. https://doi.org/10.1016/j.intfin.2017.09.019

Gamerschlag, R., Möller, K., Verbeeten, F. (2011). Determinants of Voluntary CSR Disclosure: Empirical Evidence from Germany. *Review of Managerial Science, 5*(2–3), 233–262. https://doi.org/10.1007/s11846-010-0052-3

Ghitti, M., Gianfrate, G., Palma, L. (2020). *The Agency of Greenwashing*. https://doi.org/10.2139/ssrn.3629608

Gnyawali, D.F. (1996). Corporate Social Performance: An International Perspective. *Advances in International Comparative Management, 11*, 251–273.

Gray, R., Javad, M., Power, P.M., Sinclairal, C.D. (2001). Social and Environmental Disclosure and Corporate Characteristics: A Research Note and Extension. *Journal of Business Finance and Accounting, 28*(3), 327–356. https://doi.org/10.1111/1468-5957.00376

Hahn, J. (March 24, 2021). *Many Banks Committing to Climate Goals Are Engaging in Greenwashing*. Sierra. Available at: https://www.sierraclub.org/sierra/many-banks-committing-climate-goals-are-engaging-greenwashing-banking-on-climate-chaos

Hartmann, J., Uhlenbruck, K. (2015). National Institutional Antecedents to Corporate Environmental Performance. *Journal of World Business, 50*, 729–741. https://doi.org/10.1016/j.jwb.2015.02.001

Ioannou, I., Serafeim, G. (2012). What Drives Corporate Social Performance? The Role of Nation-Level Institutions. *Journal of International Business Studies, 43*(9), 834–864. https://doi.org/10.1057/jibs.2012.26

Khan, H.Z., Bose, S., Mollik, A.T., Harun, H. (2020). 'Green Washing' or 'Authentic Effort'? An Empirical Investigation of the Quality of Sustainability Reporting by Banks. *Accounting, Auditing & Accountability Journal.* https://doi.org/10.1108/AAAJ-01-2018-3330

Kim, E.H., Lyon, T.P. (2011). Strategic Environmental Disclosure: Evidence from the DOE's Voluntary Greenhouse Gas Registry. *Journal of Environmental Economics and Management, 61*(3), 311–326. https://doi.org/10.1016/j.jeem.2010.11.001

Kim, E.H., Lyon, T.P. (2015). Greenwash vs. Brownwash: Exaggeration and Undue Modesty in Corporate Sustainability Disclosure. *SSRN Electronic Journal.* https://doi.org/10.2139/ssrn.2546497

Kotsantonis, S., Bufalari, V. (2019). *Do Sustainable Banks Outperform?* Deloitte. https://www2.deloitte.com/content/dam/Deloitte/lu/Documents/financial-services/Banking/lu-do-sustainable-banks-outperform-driving-value-creation-through-ESG-practices-report-digital.pdf

La Torre, M., Leo, S., Panetta, I.C. (2020). Banks and Environmental, Social and Governance Disclosure. Follow the Market or the Authorities? *Corporate Social Responsibility and Environmental Management* (2021), 1–15. https://doi.org/10.1002/csr.2132

Lyon, T.P., Maxwell, J.W. (2011). Greenwash: Corporate Environmental Disclosure Under Threat of Audit. *Journal of Economics and Management Strategy, 20*(1), 3–41. https://doi.org/10.1111/j.1530-9134.2010.00282.x

Lyon, T.P., Montgomery, A.W. (2013). Tweetjacked: The Impact of Social Media on Corporate Greenwash. *Journal of Business Ethics, 118*(4), 747–757. https://doi.org/10.1007/s10551-013-1958-x

Lyon, T.P., Montgomery, A.W. (2015). The Means and End of Greenwashing. *Organization & Environment, 28*(2), 223–249. https://doi.org/10.1177/1086026615575332

Marchant, C. (2020). *Are Banks Really Going Green, or Is It Just....* Environmental Finance, Winter 2020. Available at: https://www.environmental-finance.com/assets/files/magazines/ef-winter-2020.pdf

Marquis, C., Toffel, M.W., Bird, Y. (2016). Scrutiny, Norms and Selective Disclosure: A Global Study of Greenwashing. *Organization Science, 27*(2), 483–504. https://doi.org/10.2139/ssrn.1836472

Migliorelli, M. (2021). What Do We Mean by Sustainable Finance? Assessing Existing Frameworks and Policy Risks. *Sustainability, 13*(2), 975. MDPI AG. https://doi.org/10.3390/su13020975

Migliorelli, M., Dessertine, P. (2019). Green Finance Today: Summary and Concluding Remarks. In Migliorelli, M. & Dessertine, P. (eds.). *The rise of Green Finance in Europe* (263–270). Palgrave studies in Impact Finance. https://doi.org/10.1007/978-3-030-22510-0_2

Nayak, B.K. (2010). Understanding the Relevance of Sample Size Calculation. *Indian Journal of Ophthalmology, 58*(6): 469–470. https://doi.org/10.4103/0301-4738.71673

Neumayer, E., Plümper, T. (2017). *Robustness Tests for Quantitative Research*. Cambridge University Press. https://books.google.it/books?id=BHE2DwAAQBAJ&dq=is+it+ok+if+robustness+checks+same+sign+no+significance&hl=it

Pérez, M.E.S. (2016). *SEBI Index: Measuring the Commitment to the Principles of Social Banking*. Universidad de Extremadura. https://doi.org/10.1016/j.cya.2017.06.015

Pinchot, A., Christianson, G. (October 3, 2019). *How Are Banks Doing on Sustainable Finance Commitments? Not Good Enough*. World Resources Institute. Available at: https://www.wri.org/insights/how-are-banks-doing-sustainable-finance-commitments-not-good-enough

Pinchot, A. Sato, I., Christianson, G., Zhou, L. (2019). *Unpacking Green Targets: A Framework for Interpreting Private-Sector Banks' Sustainable Finance Commitments*. Technical Note. Washington, DC: World Resources Institute. Available online at: https://www.wri.org/research/unpacking-green-targets-framework-interpreting-private-sector-banks-sustainable-finance

Rainforest Action Network. (2021). *Banking on Climate Chaos*. Rainforest Action Network- (RAN)-BankTrack-Indigenous Environmental Network (IEN)-Oil Change International (OCI)-Reclaim Finance-Sierra Club. Available at: https://www.ran.org/bankingonclimatechaos2021/

Rees, W., Rodionova, T. (2015). The Influence of Family Ownership on Corporate Social Responsibility: an International Analysis of Publicly Listed Companies. *Corporate Governance International Review, 23*, 184–202. https://doi.org/10.1111/corg.12086

Relaño, F. (2011). Maximizing Social Return in the Banking Sector. *Corporate Governance, 11*(3), 274-284. https://doi.org/10.1108/14720701111138698

Reuters, T. (2017). *Thomson Reuters ESG Scores*. Available at: https://www.esade.edu/itemsweb/biblioteca/bbdd/inbbdd/archivos/Thomson_Reuters_ESG_Scores.pdf

Tamimi, N., Sebastianelli, R. (2017). Transparency Among S&P 500 Companies: An Analysis of ESG Disclosure Scores. *Management Decision, 55*(8), 1660–1680. https://doi.org/10.1108/MD-01-2017-0018

Valls Martínez, M.D.C., Cruz Rambaud, S., Parra Oller, I.M. (2020). Sustainable and Conventional Banking in Europe. *PLoS ONE, 15*(2), e0229420. https://doi.org/10.1371/journal.pone.0229420

Weber, C., Thomä, J., Dupre, S., Fischer, R., Cummis, C., Patel, S. (2017). *Exploring Metrics to Measure the Climate Progress of Banks*. Washington, DC: World Resources Institute, UNEP Finance Initiative, 2 Degrees Investing Initiative. Available at: https://wedocs.unep.org/bitstream/handle/20.500. 11822/33118/EMMCP.pdf?sequence=1&isAllowed=y

Yu, E.P, Luu, B.V., Chen, C.H. (2020). Greenwashing in Environmental, Social and Governance Disclosures. *Research in International Business and Finance, Elsevier, 52*(C). https://doi.org/10.1016/j.ribaf.2020.101192

Sovereign Green Bonds in Europe: Are They Effective in Supporting the Green Transition?

Giuseppina Chesini

8.1 Introduction

Green bonds refer to debt securities issued to raise capital earmarked to green projects aiming to mitigate the stress of climate risks on public finances while facilitating the transition to greener low carbon economies (Ando et al. 2022).

This research considers how sovereign green bonds could effectively contribute to accelerating the transition to a low carbon economy and address environmental issues. In fact, considering that sovereigns normally issue bonds in order to finance their wide government needs, it is important to understand why they should issue specific green bonds to invest in climate-smart infrastructures, such as renewable energy generation and climate-smart technology research and development.

G. Chesini (✉)
Department of Management, University of Verona, Verona, Italy
e-mail: giusy.chesini@univr.it

S. Carbó-Valverde and P. J. Cuadros Solas (eds.), *New Challenges for the Banking Industry*, Palgrave Macmillan Studies in Banking and Financial Institutions, https://doi.org/10.1007/978-3-031-32931-9_8

Furthermore, it is important to underscore that by issuing green bonds, sovereigns play a role in financial markets, which become a primary vehicle for mitigating and hedging climate risk (Giglio et al. 2021).

In order to comprehend the opportunity provided by the issuance of sovereign green bonds, it is worth mentioning the Paris Agreement under the United Nations Convention on Climate Change and the subsequent commitments of European nations towards mitigating climate change. To this end, the European Union and its Member States submitted their intended nationally determined contributions (NDCs) in March 2015. In December 2020, there was an update setting a binding target of a net domestic reduction of at least 55% in greenhouse gas emissions by 2030 compared to the level of 1990. Related to the Paris Agreement, the Sustainable Development Goals (SDGs) in the 2030 Agenda for Sustainable Development of the United Nations Development Programme impose other commitments, several of which align with the climate-focused commitments of the NDCs (Tolliver et al. 2019).

The Polish government issued the first sovereign green bond at the end of 2016. While green bonds in the private sector have become one of the most prominent innovations in the field of sustainable finance in the last 15 years, issuances at the sovereign level have been relatively recent— triggered by international agreements like the two mentioned above.

All considered, it appears that the main reason for issuing sovereign green bonds is their capacity to support the large-scale investments required to fight climate change without putting extra strains on public finances. In fact, countries are committed to reducing greenhouse gas emissions to levels consistent with the Paris Agreement, and sovereign green bonds can be the perfect financial vehicle to finance environmentally sound and sustainable projects that foster a net-zero emissions economy (The World Bank 2022). Moreover, issuing such bonds can also demonstrate commitment to sustainability as a strong signal to the market, indicating the direction of investments to stakeholders and helping to kickstart private sector green bond issuances.

Another argument for State-issued green bonds is that they allow the distribution of burden for climate change mitigation across generations. In fact, climate change is by definition an intergenerational problem, because greenhouse gases are long-lived, and their impacts will be felt long after the emissions are generated (Sartzetakis 2021).

The issuance of sovereign green bonds could also respond to the need for sovereigns to finance with longer maturities (given the potentially longer horizon of green projects) and maybe at a lower borrowing cost relative to conventional bonds, reflecting what is commonly known as the "greenium". The latter is highly questionable because, in principle, it is difficult to figure out why green bonds should be priced differently than any other bond issued by the same issuer. Furthermore, it is not so easy to argue that these bonds fund projects that otherwise would not have been financed with conventional sovereign bonds (Grzegorczyk and Wolff 2022).

Unfortunately, sovereign green bonds currently present some short-falls: the most relevant is surely the lack of a strict international set of guidelines outlining what constitutes a green bond; this lack of guidance leads to the risk of fund mismanagement, commonly known as greenwashing (Ando et al. 2022). Greenwashing is possible because the issuers, under current regulations, would not receive penalties if their green promises are not kept (Grzegorczyk and Wolff 2022).

Given the significant rise in sovereign green issuances in Europe, particularly in the last two years, it is crucial to examine their characteristics and potential to support countries' efforts to finance the low-carbon transition.

The main research question of this study investigates the possibility of sovereign green bonds contributing to the management of climate risks, accelerating the transition to sustainability and carbon neutrality. Thus, the first research question is formulated as follows:

RQ 1: Are sovereign green bonds effective in supporting the green transition?

A second research question concerns the fact that sovereign issuers have entered the playing field later than other kinds of issuers and, in particular, some eastern European countries seem more committed to these issuances than others. Thus, the second research question is as follows:

RQ 2: What are the motivations that can induce a sovereign to issue green bonds?

A third research question arises from the fact that sovereigns are the latest type of issuers to enter the market when they could have played a role in "greening" the economy even before. Consequently, the third research question explores obstacles to the growth of this market:

RQ 3:   What obstacles exist in the development of a European sovereign green bond market?

A fourth research question concerns the transparency and disclosure of green bonds issued by sovereigns. If issuers are transparent and communicate detailed information concerning their green projects, such as allocation and impact reports, investors can be less concerned about greenwashing. Such transparency also impacts the greenium and supports the development of this financial instrument. Accordingly, the last research question is formulated as follows:

RQ 4:   How does transparency and mandatory reporting impact green projects and green bonds?

The study is organized as follows. After this Introduction, a section reviews the relevant literature concerning green bonds and, in particular, the sovereign green bond market. The following section presents a general discussion of how regulation of green bonds has evolved. Then, the forth section explains the steady increase of European sovereign green bonds while the fifth provides an overview of the data analysis. Finally, the chapter ends with conclusions and implications.

8.2   Literature Review

Issuances of sovereign green bonds represent a very recent phenomenon. Few scholars have studied this phenomenon because of the scarce number of bonds issued and the consequent difficulty in applying quantitative analyses. Most recent studies concentrate on other kinds of issuers (for example, see Apergis et al. 2023) with larger numbers of issuances. The most investigated topic concerns the pricing of green bonds, and in particular, the presence of a greenium between conventional and green bonds.

Thus, it is possible to distinguish between the broader literature considering all types of green bonds and the narrower, more recent stream of research focusing only on green sovereign bonds, including the present study.

Considering the broader literature, no unequivocal conclusions have been reached despite several studies focusing on detecting differences in yields between green bonds and conventional bonds. In fact, the literature results are mixed, depending on the geographical samples and time periods analysed, as well as on the type of issuer and financial market, primary or secondary (Sheng et al. 2021).

Among the numerous studies that have examined premiums in the green bond market, several have discovered that green bonds exhibit the same yields as conventional bonds. Thus, no green bond premium (greenium) does exist. In this regard, Flammer (2021) demonstrates that the-cost-of-capital argument, according to which companies would issue green bonds to benefit from a cheaper source of financing, is inconsistent. She studies the pricing of corporate green bonds in the context of municipal green bonds following the methodology used by Larcher and Watts (2020). Specifically, for each green bond, both the papers above mentioned match an otherwise similar non-green bond by the same issuer. This method ensures that the two bonds are as similar as possible, except for the "greenness". When comparing the yields, Flammer finds no pricing difference between green and non-green bonds in the market. This finding suggests that investors would not invest in green bonds if the returns were not competitive.

Hyun et al. (2019) compare liquidity-adjusted yield premiums of green bonds versus synthetic conventional bonds, finding that, on average, there is no robust and significant yield premium or discount on green bonds. Similarly, Kapraun and Scheins (2019) find no difference in average yields at issuance for green bonds. While they detect the presence of a greenium in the primary and secondary markets, it is negligible on average. In the primary market, they find that the existence and significance of the green premium is high for bonds issued by official entities, such as governments or supra-nationals and for bonds denominated in euro (EUR). They claim that the most important determinant for the existence of a green premium is the perceived "green credibility" of a bond and its issuer. Finally, Lau et al. (2020) indicate that investors remain unwilling to pay for environmental conservation because they perceive that some green bonds may be greenwashed, causing a risk premium that offsets the greenium.

On the contrary, it is possible to assert that investors are willing to pay a premium, i.e. a higher price (accepting a lower yield) over a comparable conventional bond, for investing in environmentally friendly projects, because they appreciate the pursuit of certain environmental goals. In this way, the issuers receive a premium (the so-called greenium) on the cost of issuance. Consequently, pro-environmental investors are willing to forgo some yield to support bonds with environmental or climate benefits.

One of the first papers to confirm the existence of a greenium is the work of Baker et al. (2018). Studying the U.S. corporate and municipal green bond markets, the researchers compare after-tax yields at issue for green bonds to ordinary bonds. They find that green bonds fall about 6-basis points below the yields paid by conventional bonds.

Gianfrate and Peri (2019) study 121 European green bonds issued between 2013 and 2017 by different issuers (mainly corporates, financial institutions and sovereign states); they find that green bonds are more financially convenient to issuers than non-green ones, even if they have to spend more money in order to get the green label. In other words, environmentally-friendly investors accept lower returns as a consequence of stronger demand for these financial products.

Fatica et al. (2021) also study the pricing of green bonds in the primary market, finding a premium for green bonds issued by supranational institutions. They also note that institutions that have declared a commitment to environmental principles (i.e. those subscribing to the United Nations Environment Program Financial Initiative) issued green bonds at a premium, confirming the importance of green credibility.

Finally, it is possible that investors ask for a higher yield when they invest in green bonds because the underlying green projects tend to be innovative, and consequently, riskier. In this case, green bonds provide a higher yield to investors than conventional bonds. A negative premium does exist for the issuers because pro-environmental investors perceive the increased risk and ask for higher returns.

In this regard, Bachelet et al. (2019) find that green bonds issued by private issuers, in comparison with conventional bonds, exhibit higher yields for investors in the presence of relatively lower liquidity and slightly lower volatility. In particular, private issuances of green bonds without third party verification have significantly higher yields for investors and lower liquidity than their privately-verified counterparts. This phenomenon can be attributed to the lack of transparency and information rules that increase informational asymmetries and investors' doubts regarding the "greenness" of their projects. As such, the higher average yields of green bonds issued by private issuers mainly indicate exposure to greenwashing risks, particularly for bonds unverified by third parties. Consequently, if bonds are not green certified, the risk of greenwashing is higher, and investors may require a premium. The private or institutional characteristics of the issuer may also affect the premium in a framework of asymmetric information; usually, an institutional issuer has a stronger reputation and is more likely to be believed to effectively use financial resources for green investments.

Similarly, Karpf and Mandel (2017) analyse the secondary market of U.S. municipal bonds and find that green bonds pay a higher yield to investors than conventional bonds. In particular, green municipal bonds can be considered an increasingly attractive investment, offering a higher premium than conventional bonds for investors wishing to bridge the climate finance gap for climate mitigation and adaptation or other sustainability purposes.

The literature specifically examining sovereign green bonds remains quite limited. The analyses often consider the specific management of public finances and, in general, the methodology applied tends to be more qualitative. However, quantitative analyses are not completely neglected and, for example, Doronzo et al. (2021) use a regression analysis to study a sample of 14 countries around the world and find no evidence of a significant greenium. They assert that the greenium tends to be negative in the primary market but slightly positive (0.5 bps) in the secondary market. The authors present new knowledge by discussing three types of costs associated with sovereign green bond issuance in comparison with conventional sovereign bonds: (1) green bonds require more disclosure and tracking for the use of proceeds; (2) the reputation of the issuer could be damaged if the underlying green project fails or is perceived as greenwashing; and (3) the issuance of green bonds can crowd out that of conventional bonds, resulting in lower liquidity and higher funding costs for both segments.

Analysing only European countries, Grzegorczyk and Wolff (2022) find ten exact matches of green sovereign bonds with conventional bonds and document a systematically lower yield for green sovereign bonds. They explain this finding as a behavioural response of investors who are willing to hold green bonds in their portfolios and are available to receive a lower yield.

The research of Dominguez-Jimenez and Lehmann (2021) also analyses European Union countries, but they focus on sovereign debt and the need to have more transparent and comprehensive information about the climate-related aspects of these countries' public budgets. They claim that greater transparency in this respect would support stability and improve the functioning of green bond markets. In particular, environmentally friendly investors need more information about which expenditures in EU countries' budgets could be labelled green. Importantly, the classification of sustainable activities should no longer be a matter of interpretation.

Ando et al. (2022) discuss the benefits of issuing sovereign green bonds and estimate the sovereign greenium. The methodology adopted is different for Germany because it issues "twin bonds" while other countries do not follow this practice. Germany's greenium oscillates between 2 and 5 basis points. As far as the other countries, the authors distinguish between emerging economies and advanced economies and consider only Euro and USD denominated bonds. The greenium is 3.7 and 30.4 basis points for Euro and USD-denominated bonds, respectively. This difference is attributed to the fact that USD-denominated green bonds are issued by a larger number of emerging countries.

Cheng et al. (2022) focus their research on the hurdles sovereigns face in issuing green bonds. Exploiting the Bank for International Settlement (BIS) sustainable database, they are able to explain the tensions between sovereign green bonds' prescribed use of proceeds and the fungibility requirements of public debt. Furthermore, they describe the leading role assumed by sovereign issuers in promoting best practices in the green bond market. Specifically, the inaugural issuance of a sovereign green bond contributes to increasing the number of green corporate issuances, and in particular, the percentage of corporate issuances with second-party opinions.

Finally, the dynamics of the relationship between sovereign green bonds and country value and risk remain partially unexplored. For this reason, Dell'Atti et al. (2022) investigate the empirical response of the stock and credit default swap (CDS) market to green bond issuance by 10 EU countries during the period from 2016 to 2021. They document that investors regard the issuance of a green bond as a value-enhancing and risk-reducing behaviour for European countries. The issuance of sovereign green bonds provides a signal of the country's involvement in a low-carbon economy by increasing the social and reputational benefits. Thus, the sovereign issuance of green bonds acts as a mitigation mechanism for country risk.

In this context, the present research contributes to increasing the literature on sovereign green bonds in three directions. Firstly, from a regulatory point of view, we point out the lack of recognition system for determining a bond's green status. Secondly, we underscore a lack of homogeneity in the data and in the strategies adopted by sovereigns; in Europe, for example, there are both advanced and emerging economies, and they may have different approaches to financial markets. Thirdly, we offer an updated picture of the fast-growing European sovereign green bond market, providing new insights on the external review process, on allocation and impact reports and on the sustainable development goals (SDGs) specifically pursued by each sovereign issuance.

8.3 The Evolution of Green Bond Regulation

The law has yet to provide a strict definition of green bonds even though an exact delineation of what constitutes a green project would have been important for market operators and market growth. As a result, the financial sector has relied extensively on authoritative guidelines issued by private entities.

In 2014, the International Capital Market Association (ICMA) began to provide guidelines and green project categories (ICMA 2021). The ICMA proposed the Green Bond Principles (GBPs), which have quickly become the most-used references by operators. It is possible to synthetize the GBPs based on four key elements that must be taken into consideration by issuers (OECD 2021; Sartzetakis 2021):

1. a list of ten eligible project categories to ensure that proceeds coming from the issuance are used for green purposes;
2. a process for evaluating and selecting the green projects to be financed, with a recommendation that this process be supplemented by an independent verifier entity;
3. a suggestion that proceeds from bond issuances are credited to a sub-account to track their use and that issuers periodically disclose how the funds have been managed and used, again with external verification; and
4. a reporting framework of amounts allocated to the projects with recommended quantitative performance measures.

The GBPs provide many recommendations but no obligations, which lead to the possibility of misused funds and what is commonly known as greenwashing (Rose 2021).

Similar principles have been issued for self-regulating the green financial industry. For example, the Climate Bonds Initiative (CBI) built its own Climate Bonds Standards (CBSs), providing a sector-specific definition of "green" (Climate Bonds Initiative 2019) in early 2012. This framework is specifically aimed at "climate bonds", which can be categorized as a subset of green bonds. While green bonds are usually issued to raise money for environmental projects, climate bonds more narrowly focus on raising funds for investments in emission reductions or climate change adaptation.

Importantly, the Climate Bond Initiative is also able to provide the issuer with a certification process to enhance the credibility of the bond issuance. Specifically, the Climate Bond Initiative's framework can be summarized in terms of three main constitutive aspects:

- a taxonomy of green investments: the CBSs categorize eligible projects into eight groups: energy, transport, water, buildings, land use and marine resources, industry, waste and pollution control and information communications and technology. Thus, green bonds cover a wide range of environmental activities, some of which could be broader than climate objectives;
- a reporting framework able to confirm the allocation of bond proceeds to eligible projects and the impact of investments through the disclosure of metrics or indicators that reflect their expected or actual impact, both before the issuance and annually after the issuance; and
- a certification process by the CBI with pre-issuance and post-issuance requirements for issuers. This process categorizes projects into automatically compatible, potentially compatible and incompatible projects with a two-degree decarbonization trajectory. A green bond issuer can obtain certification if it pays fees to one of the verifier organizations and the latter confirms that the CBSs are met.

As described for the ICMA's Green Bond Principles, CBI's Climate Bond Standards are the result of a private initiative, and compliance by bond issuers remains voluntary.

In summary, private soft-law frameworks, including the two mentioned above, have played a key role in green bond issuances. However, the diversity of green bond definitions and the lack of standardized rules for certification reduce the transparency of the green bond market (Mosionek-Schweda and Szmelter 2019). Consequently, this fast-growing market in the European Union is not yet well regulated and harmonized and this inconsistency may curb additional growth in issuances, even in the sovereign sector.

In this context, in December 2019, the European Commission launched the European Green Deal, with the goal of promoting and facilitating the transition to a climate-friendly, competitive and inclusive economy, while pursuing the growth of the economy itself. In particular, the Commission intended to propose a European climate law that would permit the EU to become climate neutral by 2050. The main idea was to transform the challenge of climate change into an opportunity, boosting the efficient use of resources and further decoupling resource use from economic growth. To reach this ambitious goal, a comprehensive mix of legislative and non-legislative measures has been scheduled and progressively implemented (Claeys et al. 2019).

According to this ambitious strategy, the European Union adopted the Sustainable Finance Disclosure Regulation (SFDR) in November 2019 and the Regulation on the establishment of a framework to facilitate sustainable investment (better known as the EU Taxonomy Regulation) in June 2020. The former aims to increase transparency in the market for sustainable investment products and prevent greenwashing. The latter develops a taxonomy for sustainable investments permitting the EU Commission to create the first standardized criteria for climate-friendly economic activities. The main goal is to inform all stakeholders of investments that avoid greenhouse gas emissions and can thus be categorized as sustainable (CBI 2022).

In January 2020, the Commission announced the European Green Deal Investment Plan to establish an EU Green Bond Standard (EU GBS). In July 2021, the European Commission presented a proposal for a Regulation of European Green Bonds (European Commission 2021). The proposal is based on the recommendations of the Technical Expert Group (TEG) on Sustainable Finance, published in June 2019 and updated in a subsequent March report (TEG 2020). The EU GBS is a set of voluntary standards aiming to help scale up and support the environmental ambitions of the green bond market. The fundamental intention is to impose tougher sustainability requirements on issuers when they raise funds in order to protect investors from greenwashing (European Commission 2021).

The EU GBS applies to any kind of green bond issuer and can be synthetized in four key requirements:

- taxonomy alignment: the funds raised by the bond should be allocated fully to projects that are aligned with the EU Taxonomy Regulation, which sets six environmental objectives, specifically climate change mitigation, climate change adaptation, sustainable use and protection of water and marine resources, transition to a circular economy, pollution prevention and control and protection and restoration of biodiversity and ecosystems.
- transparency: full transparency on how the bond proceeds are allocated through detailed reporting requirements.
- external review: all European green bonds must be checked by an external reviewer to ensure compliance with the Regulation and taxonomy alignment of the funded projects.
- registration and supervision of the external reviewers by the European Securities Markets Authority (ESMA).

In May 2022, the Economic and Monetary Affairs Committee (ECON) of the European Parliament adopted its negotiation position on the Regulation of European green bonds (European Parliament 2022). The new text has introduced numerous amendments to the Commission's proposal, seeking to better regulate the entire green bond market rather than simply establishing the European Green Bond label. The amendments include increasing disclosure requirements and extending the scope of the EU GBS to all issuers of bonds labelled as environmentally sustainable and even to issuers of sustainability-linked bonds. The ECON Report further provides for increased liability and sanctions in case of non-compliance; more generally, it attempts to better align the EU GBS with already-enacted EU sustainability legislation.

Among the most relevant innovations introduced by the proposal is the role of ESMA, which will have to establish a registration system and a supervisory framework for external reviewers. This provision will ensure the quality of reviewers' services and the reliability of their reviews, thus protecting investors and ensuring market integrity. The registered external reviewers would ensure compliance with the EU GBS Regulations, particularly the alignment of the funded projects with the EU taxonomy. The supervisory task of ESMA would allow it to investigate complaints, impose fines and, if necessary, withdraw registration.

Sovereign issuers are different in many aspects from the other issuers and the proposal contemplates some flexibility for them. In particular, state auditors and external reviewers mandated by a sovereign can be exempted from the registration system managed by ESMA (see art. 11 of the EU proposal).

At the moment, there are different views on the more controversial provisions of the draft text. For example, there is contention around making the regulation of European green bonds voluntarily or mandatory, fully aligned with green Taxonomy or more flexible; in addition, there is a grandfathering issue in the event of a change in the EU Taxonomy Technical Screening Criteria (TSC) after bond issuance. With the grandfathering issuers can have the possibility to make use of pre-existing criteria, for example, for five more years (Spinaci 2022).

The European Central Bank (ECB) has recommended that the EU GBS become mandatory for newly-issued green bonds within a reasonable time period; moreover, it has favoured the full grandfathering, arguing it would give certainty for bond issuers and investors while supporting full alignment with the Taxonomy regulation (ECB 2021). Other commentators believe that the EU GBS may not become effective for some time, but in the end, it will be conducive to a new asset class in global capital markets, which will reduce greenwashing (Lehmann 2021).

In conclusion, when the EU GBS comes into effect, greenwashing and the possibility for issuers to misrepresent the environmental benefits of various types of debt-securities should be minimized and the effectiveness of green bonds in supporting the green transition maximized. The EU GBS aims to improve and standardize green definitions while enhancing transparency and the credibility of external reviewers. This process is crucial for the further development of the green financial market, particularly the sovereign green bond market.

8.4   The Rise of Sovereign Green Bond Issuances

The green sovereign bond segment has only existed since the end of 2016. Sovereign issuers have not been present in this market segment mainly due to tensions between the use of proceeds specifically earmarked to green bonds and the fungibility requirements of financial resources (Doronzo et al. 2021).

The fungibility of fiscal revenues is one of the main principles of public financial management, and it poses a challenge for many potential sovereign issuers of green bonds; such issuers cannot legally commit themselves to using the proceeds of the bond for a specifically green purpose. Even if this restriction does not apply to all sovereigns (Dominguez-Jimenez and Lehmann 2021), public budgets are subject to frequent changes, and thus potentially to uses other than those envisaged for the proceeds of an existing green bond (Cheng et al. 2022). Consequently, the existing framework for most sovereign green bonds does not guarantee that new green investments will be made using the bond proceeds; often, the funds are used to refinance past expenditures. Some sovereigns have tried to address this issue by committing some proportion—for example, at least fifty per cent—of the proceeds for same-year expenditures, or for a combination of current and future expenditures (Cheng et al. 2022).

As Table 8.1 illustrates, in Europe, sixteen countries have issued 41 green debt securities of different maturities and outstanding amounts up to the end of 2022. The maturity range is between three and thirty years, with the exception of a recent green Austrian T-bill with a four-month maturity (see Appendix).

The largest number of sovereign green debt securities, 25 out of 41, is EUR denominated. The other currencies used are the Hungarian forint (HUF), the Swedish krona (SEK), the Japanese Yen (JPN), the Chinese Renminbi (CNY), the Great British Pound (GBP), the Swiss Franc (CHF) and the Danish Krone (DKK).

Table 8.1 European green bond issued (mil. EUR)

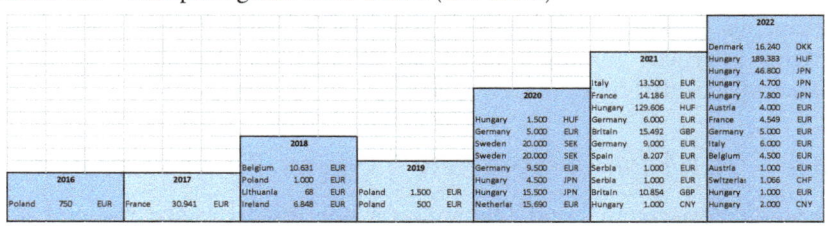

Source Author's elaboration from Bloomberg database

At the end of 2016, building on the momentum of the Paris Agreement adopted in 2015, Poland became the first issuer of sovereign green bonds followed by France in 2017 (Tsonkova 2019). Many other sovereigns have issued green bonds since then. Developed countries compose the majority of issuances while emerging countries (Poland, Hungary, Lithuania and Serbia) together present a considerable number of issuances (Ando et al. 2022). In terms of the number of issuances, Poland, a pioneer in this market, issued four green bonds between 2016 and 2019. Starting in 2020, the sovereign green market has shown rapid growth, and two other sovereigns have issued a larger number of bonds than other countries: Germany with five green bonds and Hungary with eleven green bonds.

Germany and Hungary present different economic characteristics of course. Developed economies and emerging markets tend to approach financial markets differently owing to multiple factors, such as inherent risks, different levels of liquidity and depth of financial markets. For example, on average, emerging markets have been issuing sustainable debt at much higher coupons and shorter tenors in comparison with advanced economies. This divergence is also reflected in the weaker credit ratings for emerging markets' bonds (Goel et al. 2022). Consequently, even if both Germany and Hungary have issued more green bonds than other European sovereigns, they have done so by pursuing different strategies.

Germany has been somewhat of a latecomer in tapping into the potential of green sovereign bonds, contrasting with its reputation as an energy transition pioneer. It has been issuing "twin bonds" since September 2020. The approach of "twin bonds" consists of issuing a conventional bond and a green bond that share the same maturity date and coupon. The main difference is that the use of proceeds from the green bond is earmarked to green projects (Federal Ministry of Finance 2020). There are, however, other differences: the green bond's issuance volume is generally smaller, and the issuance date is later than the related conventional bond. The German government launched twin bonds in an attempt to attract investors into the sustainable finance market without disadvantaging them with respect to other investors. The twin bond concept allows investors to swap conventional German government bonds with green bonds that are launched in parallel. The concept aims to make the still-marginalized green bond market more attractive by allowing investors, especially larger institutional investors, to switch to the conventional market if deemed necessary for liquidity purposes (CBI 2021).

Furthermore, through the issuance of twin bonds, Germany's strategy aims to establish the yields of green federal securities as the reference for the Euro green finance market. As of the end of 2022, five twin bonds are on the market with maturity dates in 2025, 2027, 2030, 2031 and 2050. Coupons are zero for all bonds except the last one issued in 2022, which presents a coupon of 1.3%. Doronzo et al. (2021) note that, in German twin bonds, the greenium is consistently positive and does not seem to react much to large uncertainty shocks, such as the Russian invasion of Ukraine in February 2022.

The second party consultant for the German green bonds is Institutional Shareholder Services (ISS), which is majority owned by Deutsche Bourse Group. The company evaluated the green bonds regarding their use of proceeds, their processes for project evaluation and selection and their management of proceeds and reporting, certifying that everything was in line with the ICMA's GBPs and assigning a positive evaluation.

As for Hungary, following the UN Climate Agreement in Paris (December 2015), the nation has proven to be particularly sensitive to international requirements seeking to address climate change. In 2016, it became the first country in Europe to ratify legislation to support the Paris Agreement and broke with its traditional European Visegrad Group allies: Poland, the Czech Republic and Slovakia. In the past, these countries tended to stick together in resisting measures that would price out the dirtiest fossil fuel. However, Hungary was not as coal-reliant as some of its central and eastern European neighbours.

In 2018, the rising costs of EU carbon prices after years of lagging motivated Hungary towards a climate strategy aiming to reduce carbon emissions by replacing fossil fuels, improving energy efficiency, developing a green economy and adding forests. Consequently, in June 2020, Hungary began to issue green bonds after having set a climate neutrality goal for 2050 in a law signalling support for the net zero emission strategy (Government Debt Management Agency of Hungary 2020). Hungary has issued sovereign green bonds with maturity dates of 2024, 2027, 2029, 2031, 2032, 2035 and 2051. The bulk of funds raised with the first issuance has been earmarked to run, maintain and upgrade the Hungarian railway system. As Table 8.3 illustrates, the second party consultant for the Hungarian green bond issuances is CICERO, the Norwegian Climate Research Institute (CICERO 2020). The latter rated the first Hungarian bond "medium green" based on its intended purposes, meaning that it avoids locking in fossil-fuel technologies but is not fully consistent with the goals of the Paris Agreement. CICERO focused on environmental credibility and did not consider other aspects characterizing this country, such as the high level of corruption. In fact, according to CICERO, investors should do their own due diligence on corruption risk.

In December 2021, Hungary received permission from the Bank of China to issue the first green sovereign Panda bond denominated in Chinese yuan. Moreover, at the beginning of 2022, Hungary became the first foreign sovereign issuer to enter the yen green bond market. At the end of 2022, Hungary had issued one green bond in EUR, three in HUF, two in CNY and five in YEN. The strategy pursued by the Hungarian government is oriented towards expanding its international scope in financial markets while implementing wide and overreaching climate, energy and environmental policies to transition the country to a low carbon and environmentally friendly economy (Government Debt Management Agency of Hungary 2020).

If we consider not only the number of issuances, but also the funds raised, the ranking of the European sovereigns appears different. As Fig. 8.1 illustrates, France is the larger issuer in terms of funds raised through green bonds, followed by Germany. France issued its first sovereign bond in January 2017, following Poland, which preceded it by only one month. It has started playing the role of leader in this market with a substantial issuance serving as testimony and proof of the authoritative role played in 2015 when France was the host and convenor of the historic Paris Agreement. Clearly, the first French sovereign bond raised Paris's sustainable finance profile among European countries and worldwide (CBI 2018).

The French Treasury commissioned Vigeo SASV (see Table 8.2) to provide an independent opinion on the sustainability credentials and management of the Green OAT. Since 2019, Vigeo has been part of Moody's ESG Solutions, a business unit of Moody's Corporation that serves the growing global demand for ESG and climate insights. Vigeo attributed the highest level of assurance on the sustainability of the green OAT at the time of issuance.

In sum, issuances of sovereign green bonds have involved many European countries, with both advanced and emerging economies. All of the countries have to comply with the Sustainability Development Goals

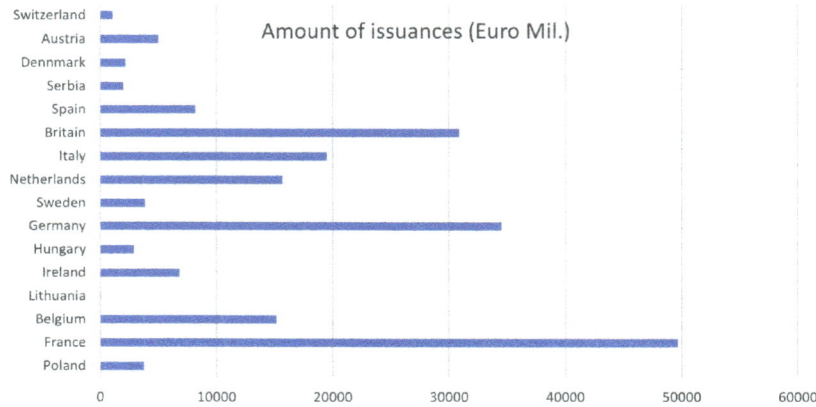

Fig. 8.1 Amount of issuances in European countries (*Source* author's elaboration from Bloomberg database)

Table 8.2 External reviewers, reports and UN sustainable goals

	ISIN	External reviewer / 2nd Party Consultant	Allocation report	Impact report	1	2	3	4	5	6	7	8	9	10	11	12	13	14	15	16	17
1	XS1536786939	Sustainalytics BV	N	N							x						x		x		
2	FR0013234333	Vigeo SASV	Y	Y							x		x		x	x	x	x	x		
3	BE0000346592	Sustainalytics BV	N	Y							x				x	x	x		x		
4	XS1766612872	Sustainalytics BV	Y	Y							x						x		x		
5	LT0000610305	-	N	N													x		x		
6	XB00BF2KQ242	Sustainalytics BV	N	Y			x	x			x	x			x						
7	XS1858534528	Sustainalytics BV	Y	Y							x								x		
8	XS1960361720	Sustainalytics BV	Y	Y							x								x		
9	XS2181686639	CICERO Senter for Klimaforskni	N	Y						x	x								x		x
10	DE0001030716	ISS-oekom	Y	Y	x		x				x	x	x		x	x	x	x	x		x
11	IT0005436004	Vigeo SASV	Y	Y						x	x		x		x	x	x	x	x		
12	FR0014002JM6	Vigeo SASV	Y	Y							x		x		x	x	x	x	x		
13	HU0000404991	CICERO Senter for Klimaforskni	N	N						x	x				x		x		x		
14	DE0001030724	ISS Corporate Solutions	Y	N							x				x		x		x		
15	GB00BM8Z2521	Vigeo SASV	N	N			x				x		x		x	x	x	x	x		
16	DE0001030732	ISS Corporate Solutions	N	N							x				x		x		x		
17	ES0000012J07	Vigeo SASV	Y	Y							x		x		x	x	x	x	x		
18	XS2388561677	ISS-oekom	N	N				x			x		x		x	x	x	x	x		
19	XS2388558889	ISS-oekom	N	N				x			x		x		x	x	x	x	x		
20	GB00BM8Z2V59	Vigeo SASV	Y	N			x				x		x		x	x	x	x	x		
21	DK0009824375	CICERO Senter for Klimaforskni	N	N							x		x		x		x		x		
22	CND100040ZFJ7	Lianhe Equator Environmental I	N	N							x						x		x		
23	HU0000405835	CICERO Senter for Klimaforskni	N	N						x	x				x		x		x		
24	JP534800BN26	CICERO Senter for Klimaforskni	N	N							x				x		x		x		
25	JP534800DN24	CICERO Senter for Klimaforskni	N	N							x				x		x		x		
26	JP534800CN25	CICERO Senter for Klimaforskni	N	N							x				x		x				
27	AT0000A2YBG4	ISS-oekom	N	N				x			x		x		x	x	x	x	x		
28	FR00140DAGJH0	Vigeo SASV	N	N							x		x		x	x	x	x	x		
29	DE0001030740	ISS-oekom	N	N	x		x				x	x	x		x	x	x	x	x		
30	IT0005508590	Vigeo SASV	N	N						x	x				x	x	x	x	x		
31	BE0000356650	Moody's Corp	N	N							x		x		x		x		x		
32	BBG01BVNFXP8	ISS-oekom	N	N				x			x				x		x		x		x
33	CHO440081567	ISS-oekom	N	N							x				x		x		x		
34	XS2226974413	CICERO Senter for Klimaforskni	N	N			x	x			x	x			x		x		x		
35	XS2226974504	CICERO Senter for Klimaforskni	Y	Y			x	x		x	x	x	x		x	x	x		x		
36	DE0001030708	ISS Corporate Solutions	Y	Y	x		x				x		x		x	x	x		x		
37	JP534800DU91	CICERO Senter for Klimaforskni	N	N						x	x				x		x		x		
38	JP534800CL92	CICERO Senter for Klimaforskni	N	N						x	x				x		x		x		
39	NL0013552060	Sustainalytics BV	Y	Y							x						x		x		
40	XS2358594391	CICERO Senter for Klimaforskni	N	N							x				x		x		x		
41	CND1000WTB0	CICERO Senter for Klimaforskni	N	N						x	x				x		x		x		

Source Author's elaboration from Bloomberg database

Table 8.3 UN sustainability goals more mentioned in the sovereign issuances of green bonds

Sustainable Development Goals (SDGs)	No. of mentions
7. Ensure access to affordable, reliable, sustainable and modern energy for all	38 issuances out of 41
11. Make cities and human settlements inclusive, safe, resilient and sustainable	34 issuances out of 41
13. Take urgent action to combat climate change and its impact	38 issuances out of 41
15. Protect, restore and promote sustainable use of terrestrial ecosystems, sustainably manage forests, combat desertification and halt and reverse land degradation and halt biodiversity loss	36 issuances out of 41

Source Author's elaboration from Bloomberg database

(SDGs) and the ambitious requirements established in the Paris Agreement. The benefits in tackling the challenge of climate change that both types of countries derive from green bond issuances are considerable. Besides the signalling of their international commitments, emerging countries can certainly obtain even greater benefits in terms of the involvement of new international investors, improvement of ratings and consequent lowering of funding costs (The World Bank 2022).

8.4.1   Data Analysis on Disclosure, Transparency and Reporting

We compiled a data set of sovereign green bonds from Bloomberg's fixed income database in order to answer to the issues of this paper. The data set covers the green sovereign bonds, as identified by Bloomberg, issued since December 2016 until the end of 2022. The dataset is composed of 41 European sovereign bonds and includes quantitative and qualitative data concerning bond financial characteristics and the environmental aspects of each issuance.

Bloomberg defines green bonds as "fixed income instruments for which the proceeds will be applied towards projects or activities that promote climate change mitigation or adaptation, or other environmental sustainability purposes". Moreover, all green bonds apply proceeds to market-accepted green activities, which are mostly consistent with the green bond principles (GBPs) formulated by the International Capital Market Association (ICMA). These principles currently dominate the market standards for the issuances examined, constituting the de facto global standard.

In the qualitative analysis for each bond we have collected data on the second party opinions by external reviewers, on the availability of allocation and impact reports via the Bloomberg database and on the UN sustainable goals specifically declared to be pursued with the green projects. These are the three relevant aspects of transparency in using proceeds that promote investors' confidence in green investments while easing their concerns about the possibility of greenwashing.

As far as the external reviewers, they represent an effective market-based solution to reduce information asymmetries between issuers and investors and constitute an important determinant of the effectiveness of green bonds (Flammer 2019). They provide the bond with a certification based on third-party evaluation of compliance mainly to the ICMA's GBPs. They also provide assurance that the eligible projects address climate change. Several scholars (Fatica et al. 2021; Bachelet et al. 2019; Hyun et al. 2019) have pointed out that certified bonds benefit from a larger premium for issuers compared to self-labelled green securities. The external reviewers can provide investors with three primary services: (1) a second party opinion on the green bond framework, (2) a revision of the allocation report and (3) a review of the impact report and its related methodologies.

As previously mentioned, the GBPs simply recommend a third-party external review, while the EU GBS will require it and establish a supervisory framework for external reviewers. In our dataset, aside from the Lithuanian bond, all of the others have received an external review before issuance. It must be noted that, differing from the others, the Hungarian bond issued in Chinese Renminbi (CNY) has a Chinese consulting organization, Lianhe Equator Environmental Impact Assessment, as an external reviewer.

As we can see in Table 8.2, omitting the two exceptions already mentioned, there are only six second party verifiers consulted by the issuers: CICERO (13 issuances), Vigeo SASV (8 issuances), Sustainalytics BV (7 issuances), ISS oekom (7 issuances), ISS Corporate Solutions (3 issuances) and Moody's Corp (1 issuance). Absent from Table 8.3, it must be mentioned that the sovereign bond issued by The Netherlands has two external reviewers; in addition to Sustainalytics, it also includes the Climate Bond Initiative (CBI). As previously detailed, the latter has its own Climate Bonds Taxonomy, which covers eight sectors and provides related screening criteria. In comparison, the EU Taxonomy, and therefore the EU GBS, covers a broader range of objectives than the climate ones (for example, water use and protection, biodiversity and circular economy). The external review requirements of CBI are quite similar to those of the EU GBS, but external reviewers must be pre-approved by CBI instead of being authorized by ESMA.

As for the allocation report and the impact report, in Table 8.2, Y (yes) means that, in the Bloomberg database, post-issuance reports are available for each green bond, while N (no) indicates that there is no availability. Both reports provide investors with a strong level of assurance that green bonds achieve environmental benefits. As the table illustrates, few sovereign bonds to date have presented an allocation report and an impact report post-issuance in the Bloomberg database, fundamentally because they were only recommended in the ICMA's GBPs. As Bolton et al. (2022) affirm, sovereigns that have issued green bonds have generally not set separate accounts in which the proceeds can be placed and earmarked for specific green expenditures due to public finance constraints. Consequently, in the beginning, many sovereign green bonds were deliberatively opaque in how the borrowed money would be spent. However, from a deeper analysis of the Bloomberg database, it emerges that nearly all bonds present a green bond framework and a second party opinion concerning the framework. The allocation and impact report is not included at the moment of issuance, and sometimes, they are publicized two or three years after issuance. So "N" means that initially they were not available in the database but in certain cases they have been added later on, in particular in 2022, following the progress in the European regulation.

It is worth noting that, in the EU GBS, the publication of a framework document (a "fact sheet" for the EU GBS) before issuance has become mandatory. In particular, the issuers first report on their commitment to align with the standard. Then, they report annually on the allocation of proceeds, and finally, they report on the aggregate environmental impact. These disclosures undergo thorough pre-issuance and post-issuance reviews by external reviewers (Spinaci 2022). As a consequence, nearly all of the sovereigns have prepared allocation and impact reports in their 2022 issuances and sometimes have even prepared such reports for previous issuances.

In effect, this study only includes green sovereign bonds, and external review, allocation and impact reporting are most common for green bonds issued by sovereigns. Conversely, Cheng et al. (2022) report that as many as a fifth of corporate green bonds are simply self-labelled as green by the issuer.

Aside from compliance with the Paris Climate Agreement, sovereigns, as the other kind of issuers, have to advance specific environmental policy targets included in the UN Sustainable Development Goals (SDGs). Table 8.2 indicates that each bond issuer has declared which of the seventeen SDGs is specifically pursued by its issuance. Of course, in several bonds, it is possible to observe a large number of goals declared. Such declarations might not be positive because they may indicate uncertainty about the real "green" investments. In fact, the UN SDGs have a broad scope, aiming to achieve a better and more sustainable future for all, addressing not only climate change and environmental degradation but also poverty, inequality, peace and justice. Meanwhile, green bonds, by definition, should focus predominantly on the first two goals.

Looking at the entire dataset, thirty-eight issuances predictably pursue UN goals 7 and 13, thirty-six issuances pursue number 15 and thirty-four issuances pursue goal 11, as synthetized in Table 8.3.

The most recent report of the United Nations (2022) indicates that the current pace of progress is insufficient to achieve goal number 7 by 2030, which involves improvements in energy efficiency to reduce greenhouse gas emissions. Concerning goal number 11, the population living in cities is increasing, accounting for more than 70% of global greenhouse gas emissions. Consequently, urban development must be planned and managed properly in order to reduce emissions and generate inclusive prosperity. As far as climate action in goal number 13, the United Nations reports that the world is facing many catastrophes, such as heatwaves, droughts and floods; in response, countries are articulating climate action plans to cut emissions and adapt to climate impacts through nationally determined contributions (NDCs). At the moment, the NDCs are insufficient to meet the 1.5 °C target limit warming. Finally, concerning goal number 15, the United Nations has signalled that bio-diversity has been largely neglected in public spending, and various opportunities have been lost. Even though many countries are sustainably managing their forests, protecting sites critical to biodiversity, and enacting national conservation legislation, much remains to be accomplished. Definitely, there is a huge demand for financial resources to be found in the capital markets and green bonds are surely part of the solution to the necessity of achieving the SDGs.

Summarizing, sovereigns and all the other economic operators around the world are expected to invest more in mitigating and adapting to climate change. Green bonds can play an increasingly important role in financing assets needed for the low-carbon transition. In particular, when they are issued by the sovereigns, they represent a financial tool that, beyond offering specific funds for large green public investments, tend to induce other private operators to enter the market. In addition, such actions offer the possibility of distributing the burden of climate action across generations.

8.5 CONCLUSIONS

This research presents an overview of the recent development of the European sovereign green bond market discussing how such bonds could effectively contribute to the challenge of climate change. This work also describes existing barriers for green bonds' further development. This research contributes to the literature because the market is still in its infancy, and there exist few studies concerning European sovereign green bonds.

Even though the market remains small, the European sovereign green bond market has increased steadfastly in the last few years. This growth signals countries' commitment to environmental issues and the necessity to allocate funds specifically to green projects to face the challenge of climate change. Countries have set ambitious goals to reduce greenhouse gas emissions and adapt to the adverse consequences of climate change. In 2015, they signed and adopted the Paris Agreement and designed ambitious nationally determined contributions (NDCs) in order to implement adaptation and mitigation actions. The NDCs require substantial funding and are part of an even more significant financial need to meet the United Nations Sustainable Development Goals (SDGs). Sovereigns are now calling for more credible policies that support a low carbon transition, and green bond issuance can represent an effective complement to other actions that have to be implemented.

Among the benefits of sovereign green bond issuances, it is worth underscoring their role as a benchmark in domestic debt markets. Government issuance of green bonds will be instrumental in financing large infrastructure projects, which in turn will help create a pipeline of projects for the private sector to invest in. In essence, sovereign issuers can serve as a model for other types of issuers.

Moreover, sovereign green bond issues have always been oversubscribed to because of the growing ESG investor clientele demanding more ESG assets; the supply of green bonds is not keeping up with the demand. Of course, demand dynamics vary according to the prevailing economic and geo-political backdrop as well as the size and maturity of different securities. For example, the first French issuance of green bonds presented a demand eight times higher than the supply.

The presence of emerging economies among issuers necessitates an exploration of their motivations for entering this market. It emerges that green bonds tend to be issued with a long maturity, so the refinancing risk is lower, and the benefits may be larger for emerging countries that have less stable demand for extra-long maturities. In addition to signalling their commitment to sustainability goals, emerging economies can diversify their investor base and achieve better pricing. The case of Hungary, with its issuances in the Chinese and Japanese financial markets, illustrates this phenomenon quite well. On the other side, Serbia achieved the lowest annual coupon rate in its history with its first issuance of green bonds.

Two main obstacles previously have prevented European countries from paving the way in issuing green bonds. First, most sovereign debt legal frameworks do not allow the earmarking of proceeds to specific green projects because of fungibility requirements. In fact, unlike sovereign conventional bonds whose proceeds can be used for general purposes, the proceeds from green bonds need to finance green projects, "tying the hands" of the issuer. Second, there is no uniform green bond standard within the EU, which can prevent growth in the green bond market.

The new European Green Bond Standard (EU GBS) aims to ensure that European issuers can benefit from green financing and that investors can find the green investments they seek with a reduced risk of greenwashing. The EU GBS should help to improve the integrity of the green bond market in general. Initially, European States began issuing green bonds simply to signal their commitment to climate change mitigation. The entry into force of the EU GBS will mean that States, and all other kinds of issuers, will no longer be able to benefit from simply sending a signal—they will have to take action to actually implement green projects, under the penalty of sanctions.

As several scholars have unveiled, issuers' and projects' green credibility is crucial for market development and achievement of the so-called greenium. With the coming into effect of the EU GBS, the credibility of issuers will be amplified by the initial registration and stronger supervision of external reviewers by the ESMA. The latter will be able to investigate complaints, impose fines and, if necessary, withdraw the registration of external reviewers, ultimately improving the transparency and credibility of the green bond market.

APPENDIX

See Table 8.4.

REFERENCES

Ando S., Fu C., Roch F. and Wiridinata, U., 2022. Sovereign Climate Debt Instruments: An Overview of the Green and Catastrophe Bond Markets. IMF Staff Climate Note 2022/004.

Apergis N., Chesini G. and Poufinas, T., 2023. The Yields of Green Bank Bonds. Are Banks Perceived as Trustworthy in the Green Financial Markets? Routledge (in printing).

Bachelet M.J., Becchetti L. and Manfredonia, S., 2019. The Green Bonds Premium Puzzle: The Role of Issuer Characteristics and Third-Party Verification. Sustainability, 11(4): 1098. https://doi.org/10.3390/su11041098

Baker M., Bergstresser D., Serafeim G. and Wurgler, J., 2018. Financing the Response to Climate Change: The Pricing and Ownership of U.S. Green Bond. National Bureau of Economic Research.

Bolton P., Buchhit L., Gulati M., Panizza U., Weder di Mauro B. and Zettelmeyer, J., 2022. Climate and Debt. Geneva Reports on the World Economy. CEPR Press, September.

Cheng G., Ehlers T. and Packer, F., 2022. Sovereigns and Sustainable Bonds: Challenges and New Options. BIS Quarterly Review, September.

CICERO, 2020. Hungary Green Bond Second Opinion, May 25.

Claeys G., Tagliapietra S. and G. Zachmann, 2019. How to Make the European Green Deal Work. Bruegel Policy Contribution, N° 13.

Climate Bond Initiative (CBI), 2018. Sovereign Green Bonds Briefing, March.

Climate Bond Initiative (CBI), 2019. Growing Green Bond Markets: The Development of Taxonomies to Identify Green Assets, March.

Table 8.4 List of sovereign green bonds

	ISIN	Issuer
1	XS1536786939	Republic of Poland
2	FR0013234333	France (Govt of)
3	BE0000346552	Belgium Kingdom
4	XS1766612672	Republic of Poland
5	LT0000610305	Lithuania Government Bond
6	IE00BFZRQ242	Ireland Government Bond
7	XS1958534528	Republic of Poland
8	XS1960361720	Republic of Poland
9	XS2181689659	Hungary
10	DE0001030716	Bundesobligation
11	IT0005438004	Buoni Poliennali Del Tes
12	FR0014002JM6	France (Govt of)
13	HU0000404991	Hungary Government Bond
14	DE0001030724	Bundesrepub. Deutschland
15	GB00BM8Z2521	United Kingdom Gilt
16	DE0001030732	Bundesrepub. Deutschland
17	ES0000012J07	Bonos Y Oblig Del Estado
18	XS2388561677	Republic of Serbia
19	XS2388558889	Republic of Serbia
20	GB00BM8Z2V59	United Kingdom Gilt
21	DK0009924375	Kingdom of Denmark
22	CND10004QFJ7	Hungary
23	HU0000405535	Hungary Government Bond
24	JP534800BN26	Hungary
25	JP534800DN24	Hungary
26	JP534800CN25	Hungary
27	AT0000A2Y8G4	Republic of Austria
28	FR001400AQH0	France (Govt of)
29	DE0001030740	Bundesobligation
30	IT0005508590	Buoni Poliennali Del Tes
31	BE0000356650	Belgium Kingdom
32	BBG019VNFXP8	Austrian T-Bill
33	CH0440081567	Switzerland
34	XS2226974413	Kingdom of Sweden
35	XS2226974504	Kingdom of Sweden
36	DE0001030708	Bundesrepub. Deutschland
37	JP534800DL91	Hungary
38	JP534800CL92	Hungary
39	NL0013552060	Netherlands Government
40	XS2558594391	H ungary
41	CND1000WTB0	Hungary

Climate Bond Initiative (CBI), 2021. Sovereign Green, Social and Sustainability Bond Survey, January.

Climate Bond Initiative (CBI), 2022. Global Green Taxonomy Development, Alignment, and Implementation, February.

Dell'Atti S., Di Tommaso C. and Pacelli V., 2022. Sovereign Green Bond and Country Value and Risk: Evidence from European Union Countries. Journal of International Financial Management Account, 33: 505–521.

Dominguez-Jimenez M. and Lehmann A., 2021. Accounting for Climate Policies in Europe's Sovereign Debt Market. Bruegel Policy Contribution, N° 10.

Doronzo R., Siracusa V. and Antonelli S., 2021. Green Bonds: The Sovereign Issuers' Perspective, Banca d'Italia, March.

ECB, 2021. Opinion of the European Central Bank of 5 November 2021 on a Proposal for a Regulation on European Green Bonds (CON/2021/30).

European Commission, 2021. Proposal for a Regulation of the European Parliament and of the Council on European Green Bonds. Bruxelles, July 6.

European Parliament, 2022. Report on the Proposal for a Regulation of the European Parliament and of the Council on European Green Bonds COM (2021)0391—C9-0311/2021–2021/0191(COD).

EU Technical Group on Sustainable Finance, 2020. TEG Proposal for an EU Green Bond Standard, March.

Fatica S., Panzica R. and Rancan, M., 2021. The Pricing of Green Bonds: Are Financial Institutions Special? Journal of Financial Stability, 54: 100873.

Federal Ministry of Finance, 2020. Green Bond Framework. August 24.

Flammer C., 2019. Green Bonds: Effectiveness and Implications for Public Policy. NBER Working Paper Series, 25950.

Flammer C., 2021. Corporate Green Bonds. Journal of Financial Economics, 142.

Gianfrate G. and Peri M., 2019. The Green Advantage: Exploring the Convenience of Issuing Green Bonds. Journal of Cleaner Production: 127–135.

Giglio S., Kelly B. and Stroebel J., 2021. Climate Finance. Annual Review of Financial Economics, 13: 15–36.

Goel R., Gautam D. and Natalucci F., 2022. Sustainable Finance in Emerging Markets: Evolution, Challenges, and Policy Priorities. IMF WP/22/182.

Government Debt Management Agency of Hungary ("ÁKK"), 2020. Green Bond Framework.

Grzegorczyk M. and Wolff G., 2022. Greeniums in Sovereign Bond Markets, Working Paper 17/2022, Bruegel.

ICMA, 2021. Green Bond Principles. Voluntary Process Guidelines for Issuing Green Bonds. June

Hyun S., Donghyun P. and Shu T., 2019. The Price of Going Green: The Role of Greenness in Green Bond Markets. Accounting and Finance, 60(1): 73–95. https://doi.org/10.1111/acfi.12515

Kapraun, J. and Scheins C., 2019. (In)-Credibly Green: Which Bonds Trade at a Green Bond Premium? Working Paper. Frankfurt: Goethe Universität Frankfurt.

Karpf, A. and Mandel A., 2017. Does It Pay to Be Green? A Comparative Study of the Yield Term Structure of Green and Brown Bonds in the US Municipal Bonds Market. Université Panthéon-Sorbonne Paris 1, February 25.

Larcher D.F. and Watts E.M., 2020. Where's the Greenium? Journal of Accounting and Economics, 69(2–3): 101312.

Lau P., Sze A., Wan W. and Wong A., 2020. The Economics of the Greenium: How Much Is the World to Pay to Save the Earth? Hong Kong Institute for Monetary and Financial Research.

Lehmann A., 2021. The EU Green Bond Standard: Sensible Implementation Could Define a New Asset Class. Bruegel Blog, July12.

Mosionek-Schweda M. and Szmelter M., 2019. Sovereign Green Bond Market— A Comparative Analysis. Hulkó, G. and Vybíral, R. (Eds.), European Financial Law in Times of Crisis of the European Union. Budapest.

OECD, 2021. Financial Markets and Climate Transition Opportunities, Challenges and Policy Implications.

Rose P., 2021. Debt for Climate: Green Bonds and Other Instruments. Research on Climate Finance and Investment Law. Edward Elgar.

Sartzetakis E.S., 2021. Green Bonds as an Instrument to Finance Low Carbon Transition. Economic Change and Restructuring, 54.

Sheng Q., Zheng X. and Zhong N., 2021. Financing for Sustainability: Empirical Analysis of Green Bond Premium and Issuer Heterogeneity. Natural Hazards, 107(3).

Spinaci S., 2022. European Green Bonds. A Standard for Europe, Open to the World. European Parliamentary Research Service, January.

Technical Expert Group on Sustainable Finance (TEG), 2020. Usability Guide for the EU Green Bond Standard, March.

The World Bank, 2022. Sovereign Green, Social and Sustainability Bonds: Unlocking the Potential for Emerging Markets and Developing Economies, October.

Tolliver C., Keeley A.R. and Managi S., 2019. Green Bonds for the Paris Agreement and Sustainable Development Goals. Environmental Research Letter, 14: 064009.

Tsonkova V.D., 2019. The Sovereign Green Bonds Market in the European Union: Analysis and Good Practices. Knowledge–International Journal, 30.

United Nations, 2022. The Sustainable Development Goals Report. Department of Economic and Social Affairs (DESA).

CHAPTER 9

The Impact of ESG Score and Controversy on Stock Performance

Paola Brighi[iD], *Antonio Carlo Francesco Della Bina*[iD],
and Valeria Venturelli[iD]

9.1 Introduction

A vast literature investigates how the environmental, social, and governance (hereafter ESG) factors affect both, together and separately, the value and risk of firms. To our knowledge, only a few research introduce the ESG controversies to explain a firm's market value (Aouadi and Marsat 2018), to explore financial portfolios performance (Dorfleitner et al., 2020), and to understand which are their determinants in the financial and banking sectors (Neitzert and Petras 2021; Shakil et al. 2021).

P. Brighi · A. C. F. Della Bina (✉)
Department of Management, University of Bologna, Bologna, Italy
e-mail: antonio.dellabina@unibo.it

P. Brighi
e-mail: paola.brighi@unibo.it

S. Carbó-Valverde and P. J. Cuadros Solas (eds.), *New Challenges for the Banking Industry*, Palgrave Macmillan Studies in Banking and Financial Institutions, https://doi.org/10.1007/978-3-031-32931-9_9

The recent international debate among institutions and regulators on the importance of ESG investments for the transition towards global sustainable development (see among others: OECD 2020; World Economic Forum 2021; EBA 2021) contributes generating two effects: i) on the one hand, firms increase their ESG investments contributing to improving their ESG scoring; and ii) on the other, one citizens become more active in starting public or private ESG controversies with economic and reputational costs for firms.

Specifically, based on an extensive international sample of an average of 7,175 companies over the 2002–2018 span, the present chapter explores how on one side the value and risk of firms depend on the ESG scoring and, on the other, how the ESG controversies may negatively affect their market and financial performance.

To the best of our knowledge, this study is one of the first attempt to offer a comprehensive framework that specifies theoretical and empirical connections between ESG controversies and market/risk levels at the international level, both for financial and non-financial firms. In this paper, we argue that firms may assume ESG responsibility to generate spillover benefits to the worldwide community and to achieve their own strategic goals.

The remainder of the paper is organized as follows. The second section summarizes the existing literature and presents arguments for the two tested hypotheses. Section three discusses the data and methodology. In section four, we present the results. The last section concludes.

P. Brighi · V. Venturelli
CEFIN—Centro Studi Banca e Finanza, Modena, Italy
e-mail: valeria.venturelli@unimore.it

V. Venturelli
Department of Economics Marco Biagi, University of Modena and Reggio Emilia, Modena, Italy

9.2   Literature Review
and Hypotheses Development

From an empirical point of view, a vast literature investigates the relationship between corporate financial performance and ESG scores for a specific country or at the international level (Aouadi and Marsat 2018; Buallay et al. 2021) concentrating more, with some relevant exceptions (Buallay 2020; Shakil et al. 2021), on non-financial companies. The evidence appears controversial with sometimes a positive impact of ESG efforts and CSR strategies on company performance; based on more than 100 studies, Dam and Scholtens (2015) conclude that there is a positive association between social and financial performance and that little evidence exists of a negative association (Hillman and Keim 2001; Brammer et al. 2006; Bird et al. 2007; Crisóstomo et al. 2011; Kim et al. 2018; Nirino et al. 2019; Albuquerque et al. 2019; Forgione et al. 2020); and some more studies show mixed results (Shakil et al. 2021).

In terms of the relationship between firm risk-taking and ESG scores, most of the empirical evidence on ESG activities and firm risk related to the non-financial sector produces mixed results (Mishra and Modi 2013; Lin et al. 2014; Chen et al. 2018; Cholleta and Sandwidi 2018). Higher ESG investment can enhance a company's reputation, suggesting that higher ESG scores lead to fewer financial risks (Luo and Bhattacharya 2006). Sassen et al. (2016) conclude that higher ESG investments decrease total and idiosyncratic risk. Differently, only a few papers show a positive relationship or a weakly negative relationship between ESG investment and risk (Menz 2010; Goss and Roberts 2011; Di Tommaso and Thornton 2020).

Based on the above considerations, we expect that the following hypothesis holds:

HP.1: *ESG practices positively impact on firm's financial performance & risk.*

Differently, only a few papers have analysed the effects of ESG controversies in terms of performance and risk effects. Controversy can be defined as a dispute or scandal that involves a firm in actions or incidents that can adversely impact its stakeholders as well as the environment. Such negative events often give rise to negative publicity and pose a severe reputational risk to the firm. According to the literature, scandals and controversies have the potential to negatively impact on company's reputation and as a consequence to generate a negative effect on company performance (Walsh et al. 2009).

From an empirical point of view, Aouadi and Marsat (2018) show that negative market news about the firm destroys reputation, which results in lower market value and increase in risk. In a similar vein, Derrien et al. (2021) show that, following the occurrence of negative ESG incidents, financial analysts revise downward their earnings forecasts which generates a subsequent negative impact in stock price and market value of the firms. Li et al. (2019) suggest that in case of disputes and controversies; a company establishes new CSR strategies to bring the relationship with stakeholders back to the pre-controversy level. In terms of investors' behaviour, negative ESG events seem generate significant negative market reactions (Ho et al. 2020; Scholtens and Witteveen 2021; Serafeim and Yoon 2022; Wong et. al. 2022). Based on the above considerations, we propose the following hypothesis:

HP.2: *Corporate controversies negatively impact firm's financial performance & risk.*

9.3   DATA AND METHODOLOGY

9.3.1   Data

We obtained accounting and financial data on listed companies with ESG coverage between 1 January 2002 and 31 December 2018 from Thomson Reuters (now Refinitiv). We only consider firms included in the ASSET4 universe directory as of the end of 2018. Our final sample consists of 7,175 firms from 47 countries resulting in 57,316 firm-year observations. Data for ESG scores and ESG controversies are from the same source. Refinitiv provides a score for 10 categories that contribute to generating the three ESG pillar scores environmental, social, and corporate governance.[1] The three pillar scores are then aggregated to obtain the overall Refinitiv ESG score. ESG controversies are environmental, social, or corporate governance evidence of misconduct collected by Refinitiv

---

[1] For a detailed explanation on the data process and scores calculation methodology see: Refinitiv (2021), Environmental, social, and governance (ESG) scores from Refinitiv, https://www.refinitiv.com/en/sustainable-finance/esg-scores.

based on publicly reported information. Refinitiv ESG controversies are counted for 23 different indicators classified into 7 sub-categories related to one of the 3 ESG pillars. Based on the number of controversies in sectors and countries an overall ESG Controversies score is usually also provided by Refinitiv for the specific firm covered. This score is a percentile ranking also benchmarked on the respective industry groups. Finally, an ESG Combined score (hereafter ESGC score) that incorporates both the ESG score and the ESG Controversies score in a unique and diversified measure of ESG performance is included in the analysis.[2] At the end of the data collection process, we identify 27,952 ESG controversies relating to 3,231 firms worldwide (45% of the total) involving 11,017 firm-year observations (19.22% of the total) over the 2002–2018 sample period.

9.3.2   *Variables Definition*

9.3.2.1   *Dependent Variables*
To measure firm value, we use the Market-to-Book (M/B) ratio, computed as the market capitalization of firm i at the end of 31 December of the fiscal year t divided by the book value of equity. Idiosyncratic risk (Merton 1987; Ang et al. 2006 and 2009; Lin et al. 2014) is obtained as the annualized standard deviation of the residuals of the Fama–French five-factor asset pricing model using previous year monthly excess returns (Fama and French 2015, 2017):

$$r_{i,t} - r_{f,t} = \alpha_i + b_i\left(r_{m,t} - r_{f,t}\right) + s_i SMB_t + h_i HML_t$$
$$+ r_i RMW_t + c_i CMA_t + \varepsilon_{i,t} \tag{9.2}$$

In Eq. (9.2), $r_{m,t}$ - $r_{f,t}$ is the excess return on a regional (including firms listed in a developed or emerging market) value weighted market portfolio minus the United States one month T-bill rate; SMB_t is the return on a regional diversified portfolio of small stocks minus the return on a regional diversified portfolio of big stocks; HML_t is the difference between the returns on regional diversified portfolios of high and

---

[2] Environmental controversies include resource use issues, social controversies deal with a firm's misbehaviors connected to the community, human rights, product responsibility, and workforce topics and corporate governance controversies involve management compensation and conflicts with shareholders negative news.

low book-to-market (B/M) stocks; RMW_t is the difference between the returns on regional diversified portfolios of stocks with robust and weak profitability; and CMA_t is the difference between the returns on regional diversified portfolios of low and high investment stocks, which Fama and French define conservative and aggressive.[3] For each firm, we first run separate OLS regressions by using monthly data and replicate the estimation of Eq. (9.2) for every year of the sample. We then obtain the corresponding firm-month residuals and compute the annualized standard deviation of the residuals as $\sigma(\epsilon_{i,t}) \times \sqrt{n}$, where n represents the number of finite months of trading in the year. Total risk is computed as the annualized standard deviation of daily returns of firm i over year t: $\sigma(r_{i,t}) \times \sqrt{n}$ where n represents the actual number of trading days in the year.

9.3.2.2   ESG, Controversy and Control Variables

ESG pillar scores evaluate a company's relative environmental, social, and corporate governance "*performance*, *commitment*, and *effectiveness*" (Refinitiv 2021). Each pillar score, as well as the overall ESG score, varies between 0 and 100. We adopt the convention of converting the final values of the scores into decimal points to simplify the interpretation of the estimated coefficients in our regression models. We replicate the same procedure used for the ESG scores also for the ESGC score. Refinitiv also records if a firm experienced a controversy during the fiscal year and the number of negative news related to environmental, social, and governance topics. To take into account the existence of a potential effect generated by a controversial event, we consider a dummy variable that takes the value of 1 if a firm faced at least a controversy in a given year and 0 otherwise. The value of the ESG Controversies score is expressed on a reverse decimal basis for a more convenient interpretation of the negative events that can affect a specific firm. By using such a transformation, the fewer controversies the firms face, the lower their score is. To control for firms' characteristics, we add the following variables: *ROA* is the ratio of net income over total assets; *Age* is the natural logarithm of the difference between the year of incorporation and the year of observation; *Size* is the natural logarithm of total assets; *Leverage* is the ratio of total liabilities

[3] Data for ($R_{m,t}$ - $R_{f,t}$), SMB_t, HML_t, RMW_t, CMA_t, and the US one month T-bill rate used for the regional five-factor model are from Kenneth French's website: https://mba.tuck.dartmouth.edu/pages/faculty/ken.french/data_library.html.

over total assets; *Capex* is the ratio of capital expenditures to total assets; and *Asset growth* is relative variation of total asset between year t and t-1. We further control for country characteristics by adding *GDP growth* as the relative variation of the national GDP between years t and t-1. We describe the variables in Table 9.1. All variables used in the models, except for the ESG scores and dummy variables, are winsorized at the 1% and 99% levels and expressed in US dollars.

Table 9.1 Variable definitions

Market-based Characteristics	
Market-to-Book	Market to book ratio computed as market capitalization on December 31st of the fiscal year divided by the book value of equity. Negative values are excluded. *Source*: Refinitiv Worldscope
Total risk	Annualized standard deviation in current year t of daily stock returns for firm i. *Source*: Refinitiv Datastream
Idiosyncratic risk	Annualized standard deviation of Fama–French 5-factor model's residuals in current year t using monthly excess returns for firm i. *Source*: Refinitiv Datastream and Kenneth R. French Data library (http://mba.tuck.dartmouth.edu/pages/faculty/ken.french/data_library.html)
ESG & Controversies Characteristics	
ESG Score	The overall company ESG score measures the company's performance on environmental, social and corporate governance pillars. *Source*: Refinitiv ESG
Environmental Score	The weighted average relative rating of a company based on the reported environmental information and the resulting three environmental category scores. *Source*: Refinitiv ESG
Social Score	The weighted average relative rating of a company based on the reported social information and the resulting four social category scores. *Source*: Refinitiv ESG
Governance Score	The weighted average relative rating of a company based on the reported governance information and the resulting three governance category scores. *Source*: Refinitiv ESG
ESG Controversies Score	ESG controversies category score measures a company's exposure to environmental, social and governance controversies and negative events reflected in global media. *Source*: Refinitiv ESG

(continued)

Table 9.1   (continued)

Market-based Characteristics	
ESGC Score	The overall company combined ESG score (ESG score net of ESG controversies). *Source*: Refinitiv ESG
Controversy	Dummy variable equal to 1 if firm i is involved in a recent ESG controversy; 0 otherwise. *Source*: Refinitiv ESG
Firm and Country Characteristics	
ROA	Return on assets ratio computed as the net income divided by the total assets. *Source*: Refinitiv Worldscope
Age	Natural logarithm of the current age of firm i in year t of observation. Current age is computed as the difference between the firm's i year of incorporation and year t. *Source*: Refinitiv Worldscope and Bureau van Dijk
Size	Natural logarithm of total assets. *Source*: Refinitiv Worldscope
Leverage	Ratio computed as total liabilities divided by total assets. *Source*: Refinitiv Worldscope
Capex	Ratio computed as capital expenditures divided by total assets. *Source*: Refinitiv Worldscope
Asset Growth	Ratio computed as the difference of total assets at year t and t-1 divided by total assets at year t-1. *Source*: Refinitiv Worldscope
GDP Growth	Annual percentage growth rate of GDP at market prices based on constant local currency. Aggregates are based on constant 2010 US dollars. *Source*: World Bank national accounts data

9.3.3   Methodology

Following the existing research, we first consider the effect of ESG scores only. Subsequently, we include the impact of controversies on market-based performance and risk measures. To this end, we estimate two distinct econometric models. The first one presents the direct effect of ESG scores only, whereas the second model tests for the existence of a negative relationship between our dependent variable and ESG controversy. The two models can be described by the following equations, in which $y = $ [market to book ratio, total risk, and idiosyncratic risk] are the dependent variables:

$$y_{i,t} = \alpha_{i,t} + \beta_1 ESG\ Score_{i,t} + \sum_{k=1}^{7} \varphi_k X'_{i,t}$$

$$+ \sum_{t=2002}^{2018} \delta_t Year_t + \sum_{i=1}^{7175} \delta_i Firm_i + \sum_{c=1}^{47} \delta_c Country_c + \varepsilon_{i,t} \qquad (9.3)$$

$$y_{i,t} = \alpha_{i,t} + \beta_1 Controversy_{i,t} + \sum_{k=1}^{7} \varphi_k X'_{i,t}$$

$$+ \sum_{t=2002}^{2018} \delta_t Year_t + \sum_{i=1}^{7175} \delta_i Firm_i + \sum_{c=1}^{47} \delta_c Country_c + \varepsilon_{i,t} \qquad (9.4)$$

where i represents the individual firm observation belonging to the sample ($i = 1, 2, 3, ..., 7175$); t indicates time ($t = 2002, ..., 2018$); β represents the parameters to be estimated; and X' is a vector of control variables that includes firm and country characteristics based on findings in the prior literature. Both constant and error terms are included in the model.

The multivariate panel models also incorporate firm, year, and country fixed effects. Standard errors are clustered by firm, and the regressions are estimated separately for value and risk measures.

The effect of the overall ESG score on firm's value, idiosyncratic, and total risk is estimated in model (3) by using *ESG Score*$_{i,t}$; the firm's i ESG score expressed on a percent basis. In model (4), the likely negative impact of controversies on firm's i value and risk at time t is measured by the dummy variable *Controversy*$_{i,t}$. In order to evaluate, if the individual factors that make up the general controversy and ESG score (environmental, social, and governance) can differently impact our dependent variables (performance/risk), in models 3 we substitute the ESG aggregated score with the ones associated to each individual pillar (i.e.: environmental, social and governance) and in models 4 we also use the ESG Controversies score and ESGC score alternatively.

9.4   Empirical Results

9.4.1   *Descriptive Statistics*

Table 9.2 shows the descriptive statistics of our sample. Market-to-Book ratio has a mean (median) value of 2.95 (1.90) with a high degree of dispersion given by a 3.40 standard deviation. Idiosyncratic risk is, on average equal to 0.19, with yearly values between 0.04 and 0.71. Concerning the ESG scores, the mean value of the overall ESG score

Table 9.2 Descriptive statistics

	N	mean	median	sd	min	max	skewness	kurtosis
Market-to-Book	56,181	2.950	1.896	3.402	0.305	23.325	3.601	18.944
Total risk	57,316	0.367	0.319	0.182	0.134	1.136	1.736	6.739
Idiosyncratic risk	57,063	0.192	0.161	0.120	0.042	0.713	1.860	7.352
ESG Score	57,316	0.399	0.372	0.207	0.000	0.954	0.384	2.273
ESGC Score	56,628	0.385	0.364	0.194	0.000	0.940	0.363	2.347
Environmental Score	57,307	0.303	0.235	0.286	0.000	0.991	0.551	2.002
Social Score	57,316	0.394	0.362	0.235	0.000	0.992	0.405	2.296
Governance Score	57,316	0.481	0.481	0.227	0.002	0.996	0.013	2.054
ESG Controversies Score	56,511	0.913	1.000	0.212	0.000	1.000	−2.617	8.723
ROA	57,316	0.055	0.051	0.110	−0.472	0.380	−1.194	9.689
Age	57,316	3.250	3.258	0.974	0.000	4.990	−0.512	3.138
Size	57,316	15.521	15.428	1.736	11.325	20.329	0.238	3.169
Leverage	57,316	0.574	0.574	0.233	0.054	1.151	−0.022	2.520
Capex	57,316	0.047	0.032	0.050	0.000	0.275	2.085	8.326
Asset Growth	57,316	0.104	0.053	0.289	−0.399	1.849	3.220	18.047
GDP Growth	57,316	0.022	0.022	0.022	−0.043	0.106	0.022	0.022

(ESGC score) is almost exactly equal to 0.40 (0.39), with a standard deviation of approximately 20% (19%). Of the three pillars, the Governance score has the highest mean value (0.48), followed by the Social score (0.39) and the Environment score (0.30). The ESG Controversies score is relatively low in magnitude equal to 0.08. Yearly average ROA is 5.50% with a maximum of 38.00% and a minimum of −47.20%. Firms' average age (expressed in levels) is 38,7 years (median 27 years). The average firm's size (expressed in terms of total assets) varies from 7.76 million of US dollars to 356 billion of US dollars, with a mean value of 24.5 billion (median of 5,1 billion). Financial and non-financial liabilities account on average for 57% of total assets with a standard deviation of 23.3%. Firms in the sample exhibit a yearly average rate of capital expenditures equal to 4.7% (median 3.2%) and a positive tendency to increase the value of total assets with a mean (median) annual growth rate of 10.4% (5.3%). At a country level, the yearly average growth of GDP ranges from −4.3% to 10.6% with a mean value of 2.2%.

Table 9.3 highlights the pairwise correlations between firm financial variables (Part A) and between the ESG scores (Part B). Except for the high correlation between total and idiosyncratic risk, there is no evidence that explanatory variables are highly correlated. The correlation matrix suggests that the market-to-book ratio is positively associated with profitability, leverage, capital expenditures, asset, and GDP growth, but is negatively related to age and firm size. The risk-dependent variables (idiosyncratic and total) are negatively linked to the set of independent variables, except for capital expenditures, and asset growth. As expected, the correlations between the overall ESG score, the individual pillar scores, and the ESGC score are positive and statistically significant. Not surprisingly, the correlation between the ESG Controversies score and the other scores is negative. The distribution of our sample firms across countries, geographical regions, industries, and years is presented in Appendix A. Table 9.9 of the appendix shows that the United States has the largest number of firms (2,876), followed by Australia (496), United Kingdom (475), Japan (467), Canada (401), and China (300). The smallest number of firms included in the sample belongs to Portugal and Qatar (14), Egypt (12), Czech Republic and Pakistan (5), and Hungary (4), respectively. Panel B highlights that North America (3,277), Asia–Pacific (2,009), and Europe (1,387) account for the large majority of firms and the number of firms with non-missing observations located in developed countries is much higher than in emerging countries (5,871 and 1,304, respectively). Financials, Industrials, and Consumer Cyclicals industries have the highest numbers of firms covered and firm-year observations, accounting together for nearly 50% of the overall sample as shown in Table 9.11. The number of firm-year observations increases steadily during the sample period reaching its peaks in 2017 and 2018. In appendix B, we shed further light on the distribution of ESG controversies. The vast majority of negative news is related to the social category (25,419 controversies or 90.9%). Governance and Environmental controversies account for the remaining 6.6% and 2.5%, respectively. Controversies are more likely to occur in North America, Europe, and in the Asia–Pacific region and for firms located in developed countries, mimicking the distribution of firm-year observations. Financials, Consumer Cyclicals and Industrials firms seem to be more affected by controversies. Not surprisingly, for the Basic Materials, Energy, and Utilities industries the number of controversies related to environmental issues is higher than in the corporate governance category.

9.4.2   Research Findings

Table 9.4 reports the effect of ESG scores (Hp.1) on market-based performance and risk measures. The results associated with the first hypothesis on market-to-book ratio, idiosyncratic risk and total risk are reported from columns (1) to (12). The results of columns (1), (5), and (9) confirm that ESG score positively affects market-to-book ratio ($\beta_1 = 0.7044$; $p < 0.01$) and decreases idiosyncratic and total risk ($\beta_1 = -0.0254$, $p < 0.01$ and $\beta_1 = -0.0328$, $p < 0.01$, respectively) confirming hypothesis 1.[4] In the remaining columns of Table 9.3, we replicate the empirical analysis at the individual pillar level (E, S, and G). The evidence underlines that the individual pillar score positively and significantly affect market value, while decreasing idiosyncratic and total risk. The highest impact for the social pillar can be found in all specifications. The results for the control variables are in line with our expectations, thus confirming the prevalent literature except for a less significant impact on idiosyncratic risk found for Age and Asset Growth variables.

The role of controversies is analysed in Table 9.5. ESG adverse events (Hp. 2) negatively and significantly impact market value ($\beta_1 = -0.1423$; $p < 0.01$): in the presence of controversy, the market performance is lower of about 4.79%. In terms of risk (columns 4 and 7), controversy increases idiosyncratic ($\beta_1 = 0.0068$; $p < 0.01$) and total risk ($\beta_1 = 0.0102$; $p < 0.01$) by 3.55% and 2.79%, respectively.[5] In all cases, we confirm a

---

[4] One standard deviation increases in the overall ESG score expressed on a percent basis significantly increases market-to-book ratio by 0.7044 (20,70% of the corresponding standard deviation in the market-value variable) and significantly decreases idiosyncratic risk and total risk by—0.0254 and—0.0328 (21,16% and 18,02% of the corresponding standard deviations in the idiosyncratic and stock volatility variables).

[5] The marginal mean values of market-to-book ratio, idiosyncratic risk and total risk in the presence of controversies (Dummy Controversy = 1) and in the absence of controversies (Dummy Controversy = 0) in models (1), (4) and (7) are: 2.8262 and 2.9685; 0.1975 and 0.1908; 0.3753 and 0.3651, respectively.

Table 9.3 Correlation coefficients

Part A Variables

	(1)	(2)	(3)	(4)	(5)	(6)	(7)	(8)	(9)	(10)
(1) Market-to-Book	1									
(2) Idiosyncratic risk	0.0121 [0.00]***	1								
(3) Total risk	-0.0435 [0.00]***	0.7463 [0.00]***	1							
(4) ROA	0.1854 [0.00]***	-0.3062 [0.00]***	-0.3504 [0.00]***	1						
(5) Age	-0.0808 [0.00]***	-0.1408 [0.00]***	-0.1433 [0.00]***	0.0714 [0.00]***	1					
(6) Size	-0.2442 [0.00]***	-0.3185 [0.00]***	-0.2548 [0.00]***	0.0445 [0.00]***	0.1754 [0.00]***	1				
(7) Leverage	0.0844 [0.00]***	-0.0725 [0.00]***	-0.049 [0.00]***	-0.1529 [0.00]***	0.0545 [0.00]***	0.4607 [0.00]***	1			
(8) Capex	0.0345 [0.00]***	0.1031 [0.00]***	0.1151 [0.00]***	0.0299 [0.00]***	-0.0787 [0.00]***	-0.1805 [0.00]***	-0.1827 [0.00]***	1		
(9) Asset Growth	0.1142 [0.00]***	0.0255 [0.00]***	0.0158 [0.00]***	0.0835 [0.00]***	-0.1448 [0.00]***	-0.0587 [0.00]***	-0.0801 [0.00]***	0.0698 [0.00]***	1	
(10) GDP Growth	0.0711 [0.00]***	-0.0751 [0.00]***	-0.1932 [0.00]***	0.0731 [0.00]***	-0.0843 [0.00]***	0.0007 [0.86]	-0.0368 [0.00]***	0.0269 [0.00]***	0.1023 [0.00]***	1

(continued)

Table 9.3 (continued)

Part B ESG Scores

	(1)	(2)	(3)	(4)	(5)	(6)
(1) ESG Score	1					
(2) ESG Combined Score	0.9632 [0.00]***	1				
(3) ESG Controversies Score	-0.2674 [0.00]***	-0.0594 [0.00]***	1			
(4) ESG Environmental Score	0.8507 [0.00]***	0.8166 [0.00]***	-0.2303 [0.00]***	1		
(5) ESG Social Score	0.8948 [0.00]***	0.8585 [0.00]***	-0.2529 [0.00]***	0.7115 [0.00]***	1	
(6) ESG Governance Score	0.7077 [0.00]***	0.6849 [0.00]***	-0.1793 [0.00]***	0.4269 [0.00]***	0.4414 [0.00]***	1

p values in brackets. *** p < 0.01, ** p > 0.05, * p < 0.1

Table 9.4 ESG scores effect on value and risk

Variables	(1) Market-to-Book	(2)	(3)	(4)	(5) Idiosyncratic risk	(6)	(7)	(8)	(9) Total risk	(10)	(11)	(12)
ESG_Score	0.7044 (4.62)***				−0.0254 (−4.71)***				−0.0328 (−4.16)***			
ESG_ENV Score		0.3057 (2.90)***				−0.0124 (−3.35)***				−0.0128 (−2.33)**		
ESG_SOC Score			0.4193 (3.51)***				−0.0132 (−3.09)***				−0.0224 (−3.68)***	
ESG_GOV Score				0.2092 (2.26)**				−0.0119 (−3.62)***				−0.0134 (−2.97)***
ROA	6.0260 (19.56)***	6.0501 (19.54)***	6.0524 (19.54)***	6.0336 (19.55)***	−0.1801 (−16.01)***	−0.1788 (−15.91)***	−0.1790 (−15.92)***	−0.1801 (−16.01)***	−0.3070 (−20.80)***	−0.3065 (−20.78)***	−0.3066 (−20.78)***	−0.3070 (−20.82)***
Age	−0.2816 (−3.48)***	−0.2756 (−3.40)***	−0.2737 (−3.38)***	−0.2773 (−3.44)***	−0.0015 (−0.57)	−0.0017 (−0.64)	−0.0180 (−0.66)	−0.0016 (−0.60)	−0.0070 (−1.88)*	−0.0074 (−1.98)**	−0.0074 (−1.97)**	−0.0072 (−1.91)*
Size	−1.2469 (−20.83)***	−1.2321 (−20.56)***	−1.2316 (−20.72)***	−1.2293 (−20.63)***	−0.0234 (−12.74)***	−0.0238 (−12.89)***	−0.0239 (−13.02)***	−0.0238 (−12.97)***	−0.0304 (−12.03)***	−0.0312 (−12.24)***	−0.0310 (−12.26)***	−0.0310 (−12.30)***
Leverage	9.1498 (27.56)***	9.1658 (27.51)***	9.1687 (27.52)***	9.1521 (27.52)***	0.0775 (10.49)***	0.0778 (10.50)***	0.0779 (10.52)***	0.0775 (10.48)***	0.1090 (10.90)***	0.1082 (10.79)***	0.1081 (10.80)***	0.1090 (10.89)***
Capex	3.5626 (8.20)***	3.6008 (8.23)***	3.5655 (8.16)***	3.5774 (8.22)***	−0.1502 (−7.11)***	−0.1509 (−7.11)***	−0.1491 (−7.04)***	−0.1504 (−7.12)***	−0.2122 (−8.22)***	−0.2103 (−8.11)***	−0.2099 (−8.11)***	−0.2126 (−8.23)***
Asset Growth	0.2285	0.2246	0.2203	0.2237	−0.0011	−0.007	−0.0005	−0.0010	−0.0082	−0.0074	−0.0073	−0.0080
GDP Growth	0.0846 (4.60)***	0.0851 (4.50)***	0.0846 (4.41)***	0.0839 (4.51)***	−0.0029 (−0.49)	−0.0029 (−0.31)	−0.0029 (−0.23)	−0.0029 (−0.45)	−0.0064 (−3.37)***	−0.0064 (−3.06)***	−0.0064 (−3.02)***	−0.0064 (−3.31)***

(continued)

Table 9.4 (continued)

Variables	(1) Market-to-Book	(2)	(3)	(4)	(5) Idiosyncratic risk	(6)	(7)	(8)	(9) Total risk	(10)	(11)	(12)
Constant	(9.82)***	(9.84)***	(9.79)***	(9.74)***	(−6.52)***	(−6.57)***	(−6.53)***	(−6.45)***	(−10.53)***	(−10.56)***	(−10.54)***	(−10.47)***
	17.1778	17.1064	17.0207	17.0713	0.5460	0.5470	0.5501	0.5489	0.8481	0.8530	0.8547	0.8525
	(19.19)***	(18.97)***	(19.00)***	(19.09)***	(19.01)***	(18.94)***	(19.10)***	(19.08)***	(22.03)***	(21.98)***	(22.12)***	(22.11)***
Firm-fixed effect	YES	YES	YES	YES	YES	YES	YES	YES	YES	YES	YES	YES
Year-fixed effect	YES	YES	YES	YES	YES	YES	YES	YES	YES	YES	YES	YES
Country-fixed effect	YES	YES	YES	YES	YES	YES	YES	YES	YES	YES	YES	YES
Observations	56,645	56,510	56,519	56,645	57,138	57,006	57,015	57,138	57,446	57,312	57,321	57,446
N. Firms	7,114	7,095	7,096	7,114	7,127	7,109	7,110	7,127	7,193	7,175	7,176	7,193
R-squared	0.768	0.768	0.768	0.767	0.553	0.553	0.552	0.553	0.742	0.742	0.742	0.742
Adj. R-squared	0.734	0.734	0.734	0.734	0.488	0.488	0.488	0.488	0.705	0.705	0.705	0.705

Robust t-statistics in parentheses. *** $p<0.01$, ** $p<0.05$, * $p<0.1$

direct and negative significant relationship between corporate controversies and financial performance and risk.[6] We further extend the analysis by using the ESG Controversies score and the ESGC score to evaluate the impact of controversies. As expected, a better ESG Controversies score (i.e., lower impact of negative ESG events) and higher ESGC score significantly improve the market-to-book ratio and decrease idiosyncratic and total risk.

In the following tables, we evaluate if the ESG scores and controversies change in relation to the country stage of development, to the firm sector and to different measures of dependent variables. The control variables will be skipped from Table 9.6 to ensure greater readability since the expected signs are always confirmed.[7]

Results from Table 9.6, signal that the positive effects on market-to-book (increase) and on risk (decrease) generated by higher ESG overall and individual pillar scores are more evident for firms located in developed countries than in emerging one (Part A.1 and Part A.2). For firms' sectors (Table 9.6—Part B.1 and B.2), the results suggest that the effect of overall ESG score is confirmed for both financials and non-financials firms with a more pronounced impact of the environmental and social effects for non-financials firms and governance effect for financials firms.

In Table 9.7, we replicate the analysis of Table 9.5 at a country- and firm-level. Results from emerging/developed countries (Part A.1 and Part A.2) highlight that the negative effect of controversies impacts market-to-book and risk for developed countries and only idiosyncratic and total risk for emerging countries. However, the magnitude of coefficients is almost double for emerging countries, indicating a more substantial effect of adverse ESG events. Controversies impact more widely financial firms (Part B.1 and Part B.2). For all dependent variables (M/B, idiosyncratic, total and systematic risk), the negative effect of adverse ESG events (Controversy dummy) appears statistically significant and higher in magnitude than for non-financial firms.

---

[6] In not-tabulated results, we found that firms with a recent controversy have a current (past) average ESG score of 0.5245 (0.5097) and firms with no controversies have a current (past) average ESG score of 0.3689 (0.3648).

[7] Results are available upon request to the authors.

Table 9.5 Controversies effect on value and risk

Variables	(1) Market-to-Book	(2)	(3)	(4) Idiosyncratic risk	(5)	(6)	(7) Total risk	(8)	(9)
Controversy	−0.1423			0.0068			0.0102		
	(−4.92)***			(5.71)***			(6.72)***		
ESG Controversies Score		0.2947			−0.0135			−0.0230	
		(5.12)***			(−5.82)***			(−7.22)***	
ESG Combined Score			0.7622			−0.0289			−0.0400
			(5.62)***			(−6.07)***			(−5.77)***
ROA	6.0270	6.0238	6.0103	−0.1776	−0.1774	−0.1794	−0.3047	−0.3041	−0.3060
	(19.47)***	(19.48)***	(19.54)***	(−15.81)***	(−15.80)***	(−15.95)***	(−20.66)***	(−20.67)***	(−20.75)***
Age	−0.2664	−0.2672	−0.2836	−0.0020	−0.0020	−0.0014	−0.0078	−0.0078	−0.0068
	(−3.29)***	(−3.30)***	(−3.51)***	(−0.76)	(−0.75)	(−0.53)	(−2.08)**	(−2.09)**	(−1.84)*
Size	−1.2141	−1.2169	−1.2488	−0.0246	−0.0245	−0.0233	−0.0320	−0.0318	−0.0301
	(−20.44)***	(−20.50)***	(−21.01)***	(−13.33)***	(−13.27)***	(−12.67)***	(−12.63)***	(−12.58)***	(−11.92)***
Leverage	9.1712	9.1764	9.1569	0.0777	0.0775	0.0774	0.1079	0.1076	0.1087
	(27.51)***	(27.52)***	(27.57)***	(10.50)***	(10.49)***	(10.47)***	(10.79)***	(10.78)***	(10.89)***
Capex	3.5721	3.5615	3.5612	−0.1491	−0.1486	−0.1501	−0.2101	−0.2091	−0.2120
	(8.18)***	(8.15)***	(8.19)***	(−7.04)***	(−7.01)***	(−7.10)***	(−8.12)***	(−8.08)***	(−8.22)***
Asset Growth	0.2141	0.2143	0.2282	−0.0002	−0.0002	−0.0011	−0.0069	−0.0069	−0.0082

Variables	(1) Market-to-Book	(2)	(3)	(4) Idiosyncratic risk	(5)	(6)	(7) Total risk	(8)	(9)
	(4.30)***	(4.30)***	(4.60)***	(−0.10)	(−0.11)	(−0.49)	(−2.84)***	(−2.84)***	(−3.39)***
GDP Growth	0.0838	0.0840	0.0845	−0.0029	−0.0029	−0.0029	−0.0064	−0.0064	−0.0064
	(9.71)***	(9.72)***	(9.82)***	(−6.46)***	(−6.47)***	(−6.52)***	(−10.48)***	(−10.48)***	(−10.53)***
Constant	16.9204	16.9612	17.1981	0.5543	0.5524	0.5451	0.8613	0.8586	0.8463
	(18.86)***	(18.93)***	(19.26)***	(19.23)***	(19.17)***	(18.98)***	(22.28)***	(22.25)***	(21.99)***
Firm-fixed effect	YES	YES	YES	YES	YES	YES	YES	YES	YES
Year-fixed effect	YES	YES	YES	YES	YES	YES	YES	YES	YES
Country-fixed effect	YES	YES	YES	YES	YES	YES	YES	YES	YES
Observations	56,519	56,519	56,645	57,015	57,015	57,138	57,321	57,321	57,446
N. Firms	7,096	7,096	7,114	7,110	7,110	7,127	7,176	7,176	7,193
R-squared	0.768	0.768	0.768	0.553	0.553	0.553	0.742	0.742	0.742
Adj. R-squared	0.734	0.734	0.734	0.488	0.488	0.488	0.705	0.705	0.705

Robust t-statistics in parentheses. *** $p<0.01$, ** $p<0.05$, * $p<0.1$

Table 9.6 ESG score effect on value and risk for different sub-samples

Part A.1—Developed Countries

Variables	(1)	(2)	(3)	(4)	(5)	(6)	(7)	(8)	(9)	(10)	(11)	(12)
	Market-to-Book				*Idiosyncratic risk*				*Total risk*			
ESG_Score	0.8450 (5.00)***				-0.0233 (-4.01)***				-0.0334 (-3.92)***			
ESG_ENV Score		0.4040 (3.47)***				-0.0109 (-2.79)***				-0.0154 (-2.62)***		
ESG_SOC Score			0.5230 (3.92)***				-0.0101 (-2.20)**				-0.0225 (-3.46)***	
ESG_GOV Score				0.2129 (2.10)**				-0.0122 (-3.47)***				-0.0114 (-2.38)**
(control variables omitted)												
Firm-fixed effect	YES	YES	YES	YES	YES	YES	YES	YES	YES	YES	YES	YES
Year-fixed effect	YES	YES	YES	YES	YES	YES	YES	YES	YES	YES	YES	YES
Country-fixed effect	YES	YES	YES	YES	YES	YES	YES	YES	YES	YES	YES	YES
Observations	47,990	47,862	47,871	47,990	48,537	48,410	48,419	48,537	48,784	48,655	48,664	48,784
N. Firms	5,806	5,788	5,789	5,806	5,837	5,819	5,820	5,837	5,889	5,871	5,872	5,889
R-squared	0.755	0.755	0.755	0.755	0.567	0.567	0.567	0.567	0.746	0.746	0.746	0.746
Adj. R-squared	0.721	0.721	0.721	0.721	0.507	0.507	0.507	0.507	0.711	0.711	0.711	0.711

Part A.2—Emerging Countries

Variables	(1)	(2)	(3)	(4)	(5)	(6)	(7)	(8)	(9)	(10)	(11)	(12)
	Market-to-Book				*Idiosyncratic risk*				*Total risk*			
ESG_Score	0.1299				−0.0391				−0.0437			
	(0.41)				(−2.56)**				(−2.13)**			
ESG_ENV Score		−0.0409				−0.0237				−0.0070		
		(−0.19)				(−2.05)**				(−0.42)		
ESG_SOC Score			0.0380				−0.0318				−0.0332	
			(0.16)				(−2.72)***				(−2.09)**	
ESG_GOV Score				0.1162				−0.0086				−0.0270
				(0.56)				(−0.90)				(−2.07)**
(control variables omitted)												
Firm-fixed effect	YES	YES	YES	YES	YES	YES	YES	YES	YES	YES	YES	YES
Year-fixed effect	YES	YES	YES	YES	YES	YES	YES	YES	YES	YES	YES	YES
Country-fixed effect	YES	YES	YES	YES	YES	YES	YES	YES	YES	YES	YES	YES
Observations	8,655	8,648	8,648	8,655	8,601	8,596	8,596	8,601	8,662	8,657	8,657	8,662
N. Firms	1,308	1,307	1,307	1,308	1,290	1,290	1,290	1,290	1,304	1,304	1,304	1,304
R-squared	0.852	0.852	0.852	0.852	0.458	0.458	0.458	0.458	0.726	0.726	0.726	0.726
Adj. R-squared	0.824	0.824	0.824	0.824	0.358	0.358	0.359	0.358	0.675	0.675	0.675	0.675

(continued)

Table 9.6 (continued)

Part B.1—Financial Firms

Variables	(1) Market-to-Book	(2)	(3)	(4)	(5) Idiosyncratic risk	(6)	(7)	(8)	(9) Total risk	(10)	(11)	(12)
ESG_Score	0.6262 (3.51)***				-0.0283 (-2.25)**				-0.0446 (-2.17)**			
ESG_ENV Score		0.3085 (2.59)***				-0.0119 (-1.52)				-0.0116 (-0.95)		
ESG_SOC Score			0.1154 (0.90)				-0.0158 (-1.49)				-0.0256 (-1.56)	
ESG_GOV Score				0.2957 (2.92)***				-0.0144 (-1.88)*				-0.0210 (-1.73)*
(control variables omitted)												
Firm-fixed effect	YES	YES	YES	YES	YES	YES	YES	YES	YES	YES	YES	YES
Year-fixed effect	YES	YES	YES	YES	YES	YES	YES	YES	YES	YES	YES	YES
Country-fixed effect	YES	YES	YES	YES	YES	YES	YES	YES	YES	YES	YES	YES
Observations	12,080	12,048	12,057	12,080	11,974	11,943	11,952	11,974	12,059	12,027	12,036	12,059
N. Firms	1,555	1,551	1,552	1,555	1,535	1,531	1,532	1,535	1,555	1,551	1,552	1,555
R-squared	0.794	0.794	0.794	0.794	0.519	0.519	0.518	0.519	0.730	0.730	0.729	0.730
Adj. R-squared	0.762	0.762	0.762	0.762	0.444	0.444	0.444	0.444	0.688	0.687	0.687	0.688

Part B.2—Non-Financial Firms

Variables	(1) Market-to-Book	(2)	(3)	(4)	(5) Idiosyncratic risk	(6)	(7)	(8)	(9) Total risk	(10)	(11)	(12)
ESG_Score	0.6429				-0.0224				-0.0248			
	(3.42)***				(-3.80)***				(-3.12)***			
ESG_ENV Score		0.2588				-0.0112				-0.0100		
		(1.94)*				(-2.71)***				(-1.73)*		
ESG_SOC Score			0.4184				-0.0114				-0.0196	
			(2.91)***				(-2.49)**				(-3.18)***	
ESG_GOV Score				0.1790				-0.0111				-0.0118
				(1.58)				(-3.06)***				(-2.56)**
(control variables omitted)												
Firm-fixed effect	YES	YES	YES	YES	YES	YES	YES	YES	YES	YES	YES	YES
Year-fixed effect	YES	YES	YES	YES	YES	YES	YES	YES	YES	YES	YES	YES
Country-fixed effect	YES	YES	YES	YES	YES	YES	YES	YES	YES	YES	YES	YES
Observations	44,565	44,462	44,462	44,565	45,164	45,063	45,063	45,164	45,387	45,285	45,285	45,387
N. Firms	5,559	5,544	5,544	5,559	5,592	5,578	5,578	5,592	5,638	5,624	5,624	5,638
R-squared	0.760	0.760	0.760	0.760	0.552	0.552	0.552	0.552	0.753	0.753	0.753	0.753
Adj. R-squared	0.726	0.726	0.726	0.725	0.488	0.487	0.487	0.488	0.717	0.717	0.717	0.717

Table 9.7 Controversies effect on value and risk for different sub-samples

Part A.1—Developed Countries

Variables	(1)	(2)	(3)	(4)	(5)	(6)	(7)	(8)	(9)
	Market-to-Book			Idiosyncratic risk			Total risk		
Controversy	-0.1538			0.0060			0.0087		
	(-4.76)***			(4.73)***			(5.38)***		
ESG Controversies Score		0.3103			-0.0117			-0.0197	
		(4.94)***			(-4.77)***			(-5.78)***	
ESG Combined Score			0.9129			-0.0255			-0.0381
			(6.10)***			(-5.02)***			(-5.09)***
(control variables omitted)									
Firm-fixed effect	YES	YES	YES	YES	YES	YES	YES	YES	YES
Year-fixed effect	YES	YES	YES	YES	YES	YES	YES	YES	YES
Country-fixed effect	YES	YES	YES	YES	YES	YES	YES	YES	YES
Observations	47,871	47,871	47,990	48,419	48,419	48,537	48,664	48,664	48,784
N. Firms	5,789	5,789	5,806	5,820	5,820	5,837	5,872	5,872	5,889
R-squared	0.755	0.755	0.755	0.567	0.567	0.567	0.746	0.746	0.746
Adj. R-squared	0.721	0.721	0.721	0.507	0.507	0.507	0.711	0.711	0.711

Part A.2—Emerging Countries

Variables	(1) Market-to-Book	(2)	(3)	(4) Idiosyncratic risk	(5)	(6)	(7) Total risk	(8)	(9)
Controversy	0.0229 (0.46)			0.0108 (3.23)***			0.0155 (3.81)***		
ESG Controversies Score		−0.0005 (−0.00)			−0.0245 (−3.50)***			−0.0399 (−4.72)***	
ESG Combined Score			0.0240 (0.08)			−0.0488 (−3.56)***			−0.0600 (−3.28)***
(control variables omitted)									
Firm-fixed effect	YES	YES	YES	YES	YES	YES	YES	YES	YES
Year-fixed effect	YES	YES	YES	YES	YES	YES	YES	YES	YES
Country-fixed effect	YES	YES	YES	YES	YES	YES	YES	YES	YES
Observations	8,648	8,648	8,655	8,596	8,596	8,601	8,657	8,657	8,662
N. Firms	1,307	1,307	1,308	1,290	1,290	1,290	1,304	1,304	1,304
R-squared	0.852	0.852	0.852	0.458	0.459	0.459	0.726	0.727	0.726
Adj. R-squared	0.824	0.824	0.824	0.359	0.359	0.359	0.676	0.676	0.676

(continued)

Table 9.7 (continued)

Part B.1—Financial Firms

Variables	(1) Market-to-Book	(2)	(3)	(4) Idiosyncratic risk	(5)	(6)	(7) Total risk	(8)	(9)
Controversy	-0.1731 (-4.74)***			0.0097 (3.31)***			0.0178 (4.14)***		
ESG Controversies Score		0.3249 (4.75)***			-0.0309 (-4.60)***			-0.0525 (-5.10)***	
ESG Combined Score			0.7376 (4.65)***			-0.0335 (-2.94)***			-0.0549 (-2.94)***
(control variables omitted)									
Firm-fixed effect	YES	YES	YES	YES	YES	YES	YES	YES	YES
Year-fixed effect	YES	YES	YES	YES	YES	YES	YES	YES	YES
Country-fixed effect	YES	YES	YES	YES	YES	YES	YES	YES	YES
Observations	12,057	12,057	12,080	11,952	11,952	11,974	12,036	12,036	12,059
N. Firms	1,552	1,552	1,555	1,532	1,532	1,535	1,552	1,552	1,555
R-squared	0.794	0.794	0.794	0.519	0.520	0.519	0.730	0.731	0.730
Adj. R-squared	0.762	0.762	0.762	0.444	0.446	0.445	0.688	0.689	0.688

Part B.2—Non-Financial Firms

Variables	(1) Market-to-Book	(2) Market-to-Book	(3) Market-to-Book	(4) Idiosyncratic risk	(5) Idiosyncratic risk	(6) Idiosyncratic risk	(7) Total risk	(8) Total risk	(9) Total risk
Controversy	−0.1281 (−3.78)***			0.0061 (4.72)***			0.0085 (5.45)***		
ESG Controversies Score		0.2703 (4.08)***			−0.0106 (−4.38)***			−0.0185 (−5.84)***	
ESG Combined Score			0.6775 (4.08)***			−0.0262 (−5.06)***			−0.0330 (−4.75)***
(*control variables omitted*)									
Firm-fixed effect	YES	YES	YES	YES	YES	YES	YES	YES	YES
Year-fixed effect	YES	YES	YES	YES	YES	YES	YES	YES	YES
Country-fixed effect	YES	YES	YES	YES	YES	YES	YES	YES	YES
Observations	8,648	8,648	8,655	8,596	8,596	8,601	8,657	8,657	8,662
N. Firms	1,307	1,307	1,308	1,290	1,290	1,290	1,304	1,304	1,304
R-squared	0.852	0.852	0.852	0.458	0.459	0.459	0.726	0.727	0.726
Adj. R-squared	0.824	0.824	0.824	0.359	0.359	0.359	0.676	0.676	0.676

Robust t-statistics in parentheses. *** $p<0.01$, ** $p<0.05$, * $p<0.1$

9.4.3   Robustness Checks

We also use different specifications of the dependent variables in models (3) and (4) and test for the robustness of our main results (Table 9.8). First, we substitute the market-to-book ratio with Tobin's Q as a measure of market-based performance indicator. Tobin's Q is measured as the ratio of (total assets—book value of shareholder's equity + market capitalization) to total assets. Second, we also consider two alternative measures of idiosyncratic risk. In place of the regional diversified Fama and French five-factor model, we use the regional Fama–French-Carhart four factor model (Fama and French 1993; Carhart 1997) and a global version of the previous regional five-factor model used in capital asset pricing model in Eq. (1):

$$r_{i,t} - r_{f,t} = \alpha_i + b_i \left(r_{m,t} - r_{f,t} \right) + s_i SMB_t + h_i HML_t \\ + r_i WML_t + \varepsilon_{i,t} \tag{9.5}$$

where, WML_t is the return on a regional diversified (including firms listed in a developed or emerging market) portfolio of winners stocks minus the return on a regional diversified portfolio of losers stocks.

Finally, we also use the Altman's Z-score (Altman 1968) as a measure of firm's probability of default closely linked to idiosyncratic risk. Based on both accounting and market indicators, higher values of the score indicate lower probability of financial distress or default:

$$Altman's \ Z \ = 1.2 \times \frac{WC}{TA_i} + 1.4 \times \frac{RE}{TA} + 3.3 \times \frac{EBIT}{TA} \\ + 0.999 \times \frac{Sales}{TA} + 0.6 \times \frac{MV}{TL} \tag{9.6}$$

where, WC = working capital, TA = total assets, $EBIT$ = earnings before interest and taxes, RE = retained earnings, MV = market capitalization, TL = total liabilities, PE = preferred equity, and MI = minority interest. All accounting and marked based variables are from Refinitiv Worldscope. Our results are quite satisfactory (Table 9.8) confirming the main evidence in Table 9.4 and 9.5 and supporting the positive relation between ESG scores and the measures of market performance and risk as well as the overall negative impact of ESG negative events.

Table 9.8 Alternative measures of value and risk

Part A—ESG Effect

Variables	(1) Tobin's Q	(2)	(3)	(4)	(5) Idiosyncratic risk (4FF Regional)	(6)	(7)	(8)
ESG_Score	0.2648 (5.44)***				−0.0289 (−4.97)***			
ESG_ENV Score		0.1412 (4.17)***				−0.0116 (−2.95)***		
ESG_SOC Score			0.1802 (4.53)***				−0.0157 (−3.45)***	
ESG_GOV Score				0.0513 (1.75)*				−0.0141 (−3.99)***
(control variables omitted)								
Firm-fixed effect	YES	YES	YES	YES	YES	YES	YES	YES
Year-fixed effect	YES	YES	YES	YES	YES	YES	YES	YES
Country-fixed effect	YES	YES	YES	YES	YES	YES	YES	YES
Observations	56,622	56,487	56,496	56,622	57,181	57,048	57,057	57,181
N. Firms	7,111	7,092	7,093	7,111	7,137	7,119	7,120	7,137
R-squared	0.814	0.814	0.815	0.814	0.566	0.566	0.566	0.566
Adj. R-squared	0.787	0.788	0.788	0.787	0.503	0.503	0.503	0.503

(continued)

Table 9.8 (continued)

Variables	(9)	(10)	(11)	(12)	(13)	(14)	(15)	(16)
	Idiosyncratic risk (5FF Global)				Altman's z-score			
ESG_Score	-0.0255 (-4.53)***				0.7596 (3.58)***			
ESG_ENV Score		-0.0119 (-3.08)***				0.4540 (3.26)***		
ESG_SOC Score			-0.0148 (-3.39)***				0.5845 (3.42)***	
ESG_GOV Score				-0.0103 (-3.04)***				0.1330 (1.05)
(control variables omitted)								
Firm-fixed effect	YES	YES	YES	YES	YES	YES	YES	YES
Year-fixed effect	YES	YES	YES	YES	YES	YES	YES	YES
Country-fixed effect	YES	YES	YES	YES	YES	YES	YES	YES
Observations	57,117	56,895	56,994	57,117	57,808	57,673	57,682	57,808
N. Firms	7,124	7,105	7,107	7,124	7,217	7,198	7,199	7,217
R-squared	0.545	0.545	0.545	0.545	0.772	0.772	0.772	0.773
Adj. R-squared	0.479	0.479	0.479	0.479	0.739	0.740	0.740	0.740

Part B—Controversies Effect

Variables	(1) Tobin's Q	(2)	(3)	(4) Idiosyncratic risk (4FF Regional)	(5)	(6)
Controversy	−0.0464 (−5.47)***			0.0077 (6.07)***		
ESG Controversies Score		0.1065 (6.64)***			−0.0170 (−6.82)***	
ESG Combined Score			0.3000 (7.08)***			−0.0358 (−6.94)***
(control variables omitted)						
Firm-fixed effect	YES	YES	YES	YES	YES	YES
Year-fixed effect	YES	YES	YES	YES	YES	YES
Country-fixed effect	YES	YES	YES	YES	YES	YES
Observations	56,496	56,496	56,622	57,057	57,057	57,181
N. Firms	7,093	7,093	7,111	7,120	7,120	7,137
R-squared	0.814	0.7814	0.814	0.565	0.566	0.566
Adj. R-squared	0.787	0.787	0.787	0.503	0.503	0.503

(continued)

Table 9.8 (continued)

Variables	(7)	(8)	(9)	(10)	(11)	(12)
	Idiosyncratic risk (5FF Global)			Altman's z-score		
Controversy	0.0067 (5.61)***			−0.0625 (−1.81)*		
ESG Controversies Score		−0.0157 (−6.50)***			0.1529 (2.17)**	
ESG Combined Score			−0.0312 (−6.22)***			0.8642 (4.28)***
(*control variables omitted*)						
Firm-fixed effect	YES	YES	YES	YES	YES	YES
Year-fixed effect	YES	YES	YES	YES	YES	YES
Country-fixed effect	YES	YES	YES	YES	YES	YES
Observations	56,994	56,994	57,177	57,659	57,659	57,785
N. Firms	7,107	7,107	7,124	7,196	7,196	7,214
R-squared	0.545	0.545	0.545	0.754	0.754	0.754
Adj. R-squared	0.479	0.478	0.478	0.713	0.713	0.713

9.5   Conclusion

This work offers a comprehensive framework that specifies theoretical and empirical connections between ESG controversies and measures of market performance and risk at the international level for financial and non-financial firms. In this chapter, we argue that firms may assume ESG responsibility not only to generate spillover benefits to the worldwide community but also to achieve their own strategic goals.

The results of our analysis point out that [1] higher ESG performance significantly increases market value while decreasing idiosyncratic and total risk. The results hold at a general level as well as at an individual pillar level. Empirical results confirm that these beneficial effects are weaker for the systematic risk except for the social score. Turning to the role of controversies the results confirm that [2] adverse ESG events decrease the market-to-book ratio and significantly increase risk (idiosyncratic and total). Moreover, at the general ESG score level this research shows that [3] controversies generate negative effects in performance and risk measures.

The investigation of the effect of investment in ESG summarized by the ESG scores and the presence of negative effects produced by the ESG controversies suggest that controlling for ESG is important not only from a macro sustainability point of view but also from the individual firm perspective.

Appendix A: Sample Description

See Table 9.9–9.14

Table 9.9 Country distribution

Country	# of Firms	# of Firm-Year Obs	% of total firms	% of total Firm-Year obs	avg Firm-Year Obs
Argentina	32	93	0.45	0.16	2.91
Australia	496	3,642	6.91	6.35	7.34
Austria	22	250	0.31	0.44	11.36
Belgium	35	417	0.49	0.73	11.91
Brazil	102	793	1.42	1.38	7.77
Canada	401	3,426	5.59	5.98	8.54
Chile	41	269	0.57	0.47	6.56
China	300	1,352	4.18	2.36	4.51
Colombia	23	131	0.32	0.23	5.70
Czech Republic	5	47	0.07	0.08	9.40
Denmark	31	385	0.43	0.67	12.42
Egypt	12	98	0.17	0.17	8.17
Finland	31	399	0.43	0.70	12.87
France	128	1,475	1.78	2.57	11.52
Germany	131	1,265	1.83	2.21	9.66
Greece	27	285	0.38	0.50	10.56
Hong Kong	215	1,873	3.00	3.27	8.71
Hungary	4	41	0.06	0.07	10.25
India	110	855	1.53	1.49	7.77
Indonesia	40	303	0.56	0.53	7.58
Ireland	18	205	0.25	0.36	11.39
Italy	76	724	1.06	1.26	9.53
Japan	467	5,900	6.51	10.29	12.63
Malaysia	59	476	0.82	0.83	8.07
Mexico	46	314	0.64	0.55	6.83
Netherlands	55	551	0.77	0.96	10.02
New Zealand	58	320	0.81	0.56	5.52
Norway	33	362	0.46	0.63	10.97
Pakistan	5	10	0.07	0.02	2.00
Peru	29	97	0.40	0.17	3.34
Philippines	27	217	0.38	0.38	8.04
Poland	36	285	0.50	0.50	7.92
Portugal	14	161	0.20	0.28	11.50
Qatar	14	80	0.20	0.14	5.71

(continued)

Table 9.9   (continued)

Country	# of Firms	# of Firm-Year Obs	% of total firms	% of total Firm-Year obs	avg Firm-Year Obs
Russian Federation	38	362	0.53	0.63	9.53
Saudi Arabia	15	99	0.21	0.17	6.60
Singapore	56	665	0.78	1.16	11.88
South Africa	143	1,059	1.99	1.85	7.41
South Korea	135	1,035	1.88	1.81	7.67
Spain	64	681	0.89	1.19	10.64
Sweden	80	850	1.11	1.48	10.63
Switzerland	82	902	1.14	1.57	11.00
Thailand	41	299	0.57	0.52	7.29
Turkey	31	262	0.43	0.46	8.45
United Arab Emirates	16	79	0.22	0.14	4.94
United Kingdom	475	4,880	6.62	8.51	10.27
United States	2,876	19,042	40.08	33.22	6.62
Total	7,175	57,316	100	100	7.99

Table 9.10   Region distribution

Region	# of Firms	# of Firm-Year Obs	% of total firms	% of total Firm-Year obs	avg Firm-Year Obs
Africa	143	1,059	1.99	1.85	7.41
Asia–Pacific	2,009	16,947	28.00	29.57	8.44
Central/South America	273	1,697	3.80	2.96	6.22
Europe	1,385	14,527	19.30	25.35	10.49
Middle East	88	618	1.23	1.08	7.02
North America	3,277	22,468	45.67	39.20	6.86
Developed	*5,871*	*48,660*	*81.83*	*84.90*	*8.29*
Emerging	*1,304*	*8,656*	*18.17*	*15.10*	*6.64*
Total	7,175	57,316	100	100	7.99

Table 9.11 Industry distribution

Industry	# of Firms	# of Firm-Year Obs	% of total firms	% of total Firm-Year obs	avg Firm-Year Obs
Basic Materials	696	6,083	9.70	10.61	8.74
Consumer Cyclicals	992	8,457	13.83	14.76	8.53
Consumer Non-Cyclicals	469	4,037	6.54	7.04	8.61
Energy	507	4,196	7.07	7.32	8.28
Financials	1,551	12,033	21.62	20.99	7.76
Healthcare	635	3,919	8.85	6.84	6.17
Industrials	1,057	9,139	14.73	15.94	8.65
Other	134	560	1.87	0.98	4.18
Technology	670	4,763	9.34	8.31	7.11
Telecommunication Services	170	1,509	2.37	2.63	8.88
Utilities	294	2,620	4.10	4.57	8.91
Total	7,175	5,7316	100	100	7.99

Table 9.12 Year distribution

Year	# of Firm-Year Obs	% of total Firm-Year obs
2002	851	1.48
2003	867	1.51
2004	1,615	2.82
2005	2,026	3.53
2006	2,065	3.60
2007	2,247	3.92
2008	2,703	4.72
2009	3,104	5.42
2010	3,604	6.29
2011	3,733	6.51
2012	3,832	6.69
2013	3,942	6.88
2014	4,066	7.09
2015	4,846	8.45
2016	5,713	9.97
2017	6,240	10.89
2018	5,862	10.23
Total	57,316	100

APPENDIX B: CONTROVERSIES DISTRIBUTION

Table 9.13 Controversy types by region distribution

Region	Number of controversies			
	Environment	Social	Governance	Total
Africa	4	310	10	324
Asia–Pacific	104	4,043	239	4,386
Central/South America	39	393	42	474
Europe	239	7,837	514	8,590
Middle East	1	79	4	84
North America	299	12,757	1,038	14,094
Developed	*587*	*23,010*	*1,713*	25,310
Emerging	*99*	*2,409*	*134*	2,642
Total	686	25,419	1,847	27,952

Table 9.14 Controversy types by industry distribution

Industry	Number of controversies			
	Environment	Social	Governance	Total
Basic Materials	166	1,885	106	2,157
Consumer Cyclicals	107	3,925	236	4,268
Consumer Non-Cyclicals	17	2,289	116	2,422
Energy	261	1,753	151	2,165
Financials	5	4,723	497	5,225
Healthcare	13	2,386	172	2,571
Industrials	31	3,274	209	3,514
Other	0	155	24	179
Technology	1	3,076	231	3,308
Telecommunication	0	1,176	59	1,235
Utilities	85	777	46	908
Total	686	25,419	1,847	27,952

250   P. BRIGHI ET AL.

REFERENCES

Albuquerque, R., Koskinen, Y., & Zhang, C. (2019). Corporate social responsibility and firm risk: Theory and empirical evidence. Management Science, 65(10): 4451–4469.

Altman, E.I. (1968). Financial ratios, discriminant analysis and the prediction of corporate bankruptcy. Journal of Finance, 23: 589– 609.

Ang, A., Hodrick, R.J., Xing, Y., & Zhang, X. (2006). The cross-section of volatility and expected returns. Journal of Finance, 61(1): 259–299.

Ang, A., Hodrick, R.J., Xing, Y., & Zhang, X., (2009). High idiosyncratic volatility and low returns: International and further us evidence. Journal of Financial Economics, 91(1): 1–23.

Aouadi, A., & Marsat, S. (2018). Do ESG controversies matter for firm value? Evidence from international data. Journal of Business Ethics, 151(4): 1027–1047.

Bird, R., Hall, A.D., Momentè, F., & Reggiani, F. (2007). What corporate social responsibility activities are valued by the market? Journal of Business Ethics, 76(2): 189–206.

Brammer, S., Brooks, C., & Pavelin, S. (2006). Corporate social performance and stock returns: UK evidence from disaggregate measures. Financial Management, 35(3): 97–116.

Buallay, A.M, (2020). Sustainability reporting and bank's performance: Comparison between developed and developing countries. World Review of Entrepreneurship, Management and Sustainable Development, 16(2): 187–203.

Buallay, A.M., Al Marri, M., Nasrallah, N., Hamdan, A., Barone, E. & Zureigat, Q. (2021). Sustainability reporting in banking and financial services sector: A regional analysis, Journal of Sustainable Finance and Investment.

Carhart, M., (1997). On persistence in mutual fund performance. Journal of Finance, 52(1): 57–82.

Chen, R., Hung, S-W., & Lee, C.-H. (2018). Corporate social responsibility and firm idiosyncratic risk in different market states. Corporate Social Responsibility and Environmental Management, 25(4): 642–658.

Cholleta, P., & Sandwidi, B. (2018). CSR engagement and financial risk: A virtuous circle? International evidence. Global Finance Journal, 38: 65–81.

Crisóstomo, V.L., Freire, F.D., & de Vasconcellos, F. C. (2011). Corporate social responsibility, firm value and financial performance in Brazil. Social Responsibility Journal, 7(2): 295-309.

Dam, L., & Scholtens, B. (2015). Towards a theory of responsible investing: On the economic foundations of corporate social responsibility. Resource and Energy Economics, 41: 103-121.

Derrien, F., Krueger, P., Landier, A., & Tianhao, Y. (2021). ESG news, future cash flows, and firm value. Swiss Finance Institute Research Paper No. 21–84, available at SSRN. https://doi.org/10.2139/ssrn.3903274

Di Tommaso, C., & Thornton, J. (2020). Do ESG scores effect bank risk taking and value? Evidence from European banks. Corporate Social Responsibility and Environmental Management, 27 (5): 2286-2298.

Dorfleitner, G., Kreuzer, C., & Sparrer, C. (2020). ESG controversies and controversial ESG: About silent saints and small sinners. Journal of Asset Management, 21: 393–412.

EBA. (2021). Report on management and supervision of ESG risks for credit institutions and investment firms, EBA/REP/2021/18.

Fama, E., & French, K. (1993). Common risk factors in the returns on stocks and bonds. Journal of Financial Economics 33(1): 3–56.

Fama, E., & French, K. (2015). A five-factor asset pricing model. Journal of Financial Economics, 116(1): 1-22.

Fama, E., & French, K. (2017). International tests of a five-factor asset-pricing Model. Journal of Financial Economics, 123(3): 441-463.

Forgione, A.F., Laguir, I., & Stagliànò, R. (2020). Effect of corporate social responsibility scores on bank efficiency: The moderating role of institutional context. Corporate Social Responsibility and Environmental Management, 27 (5): 2094-2106.

Goss, A., & Roberts, G.S. (2011). The impact of corporate social responsibility on the cost of bank loans. Journal of Banking and Finance, 35: 1794–1810.

Hillman, A.J., & Keim, G.D. (2001). Shareholder value, stakeholder management, and social issues: What's the bottom line? Strategic Management Journal, 22(2): 125-139.

Ho, C., Nguyen, T.H., & Vu, V.H. (2020). Do environmental and social risks affect corporate financial policies? Working paper, available at SSRN.https://doi.org/10.2139/ssrn.3601616

Kim, K.H., Kim, M., & Qian, C. (2018). Effects of corporate social responsibility on corporate financial performance: a competitive-action perspective. Journal of Management. 44 (3): 1097–1118.

Li, J., Haider, Z., Jin, X., & Yuan, W. (2019). Corporate controversy, social responsibility and market performance: International evidence. Journal of International Financial Markets, Institutions & Money, 60: 1–18.

Lin, Y.-M., Chao, C.-F., & Liu, C.-L., (2014). Transparency, idiosyncratic risk, and convertible bonds. European Journal of Finance. 20 (1): 80–103.

Luo, X., & Bhattacharya, C.B. (2006). Corporate social responsibility, customer satisfaction, and market value. Journal of Marketing, 70(4): 1–18.

Menz, K.M. (2010). Corporate social responsibility: Is it rewarded by the corporate bond market? A critical note. Journal of Business Ethics, 96: 117–134.

Merton, R.C., (1987). A simple model of capital market equilibrium with incomplete information. Journal of Finance, 42(3): 483–510.

Mishra, S., & Modi, S.B. (2013). Positive and negative corporate social responsibility, financial leverage, and idiosyncratic risk. Journal of Business Ethics, 117(2): 431–448.

Neitzert, F., & Petras, M. (2021). Corporate social responsibility and bank risk. Journal of Business Economics, open access.

Nirino, N., Miglietta, N., & Salvi, A. (2019). The impact of corporate social responsibility on firms' financial performance, evidence from the food and beverage industry. British Food Journal, 122(1): 1–13.

OECD, (2020). OECD Business & Finance Outlook 2020: Sustainable and resilient finance. OECD Publishing, Paris.

Refinitiv, (2021). Environmental, social and governance (ESG) scores from Refinitiv

Sassen, R., Hinze, A.K, & Hardeck, I. (2016). Impact of ESG factors on firm risk in Europe. Journal of Business Economics, 86: 867–904.

Scholtens, B., & Witteveen, E. (2021). Shocks, stocks and ratings: The financial community response to global environmental and health controversies. Global Environmental Change, 68: 1–9.

Serafeim, G., & Yoon, A. (2022). Which corporate ESG news does the market react to? Financial Analysts Journal, 78(1): 59–78.

Shakil, M.H., Tasnia, M., & Mostafiz, M.I. (2021). Board gender diversity and environmental, social and governance performance of US banks: Moderating role of environmental, social and corporate governance controversies. International Journal of Bank Marketing, 39(4): 661–677.

Walsh, G., Mitchell, V.W., Jackson, P.R., & Beatty, S.E. (2009). Examining the antecedents and consequences of corporate reputation: A customer perspective. British Journal of Management, 20(2): 187–203.

Wong, J.B., & Zhang, Q. (2022). Stock market reactions to adverse ESG disclosure via media channels. The British Accounting Review, 54(1): 101045.

World Economic Forum. (2021). The global risks report 2021, 16th Edition.

PART III

Innovation

CHAPTER 10

The Digitalization of the European Banking Industry: Some Evidence

Santiago Carbó-Valverde, Pedro J. Cuadros-Solas⃝,
Cristina Gonnella, and Francisco Rodríguez-Fernández

10.1 INTRODUCTION

During the last decades, but especially since the COVID-19 pandemic, a digitalization wave has been taking place in most societies. Consumers and companies have started to use the digital channel to interact with their peers but also to conduct different economic activities. As a result of this digitalization wave, most industries have undergone an intense process of

S. Carbó-Valverde
University of Valencia, Valencia, Spain
e-mail: Santiago.Carbo@uv.es

S. Carbó-Valverde · P. J. Cuadros-Solas · F. Rodríguez-Fernández
Funcas, Madrid, Spain

P. J. Cuadros-Solas (✉)
CUNEF Universidad, Madrid, Spain
e-mail: pedro.cuadros@cunef.edu

digital transformation to meet the new expectations of their customers. This digital journey is especially intense for the banking industry (Carletti et al. 2021). Historically, banks have been used to deal with the adoption of technological innovations (e.g., phone banking, ATMs, online banking, or mobile banking). However, unlike what happened in the past, nowadays several new technologies have all emerged at the same time (e.g., cloud computing, blockchain, artificial intelligence, biometrics, and/or big data). Ongoing changes are more fundamental than the previous ones. All these technologies have their own potential to be considered, separately, disruptive for the banking industry (Boot et al. 2021). The need of adopting all of them to meet the customers' expectations results in a challenge for the banking industry. Consequently, over the last years the technological efforts of banks, measured by their expenses on information technology (IT),[1] have become more relevant than they have ever been. Especially, as banks have also felt the pressure of competing with digitally born companies such as FinTech firms, neobanks, or BigTech companies (Stulz 2019; Vives 2019).

As prior studies have underlined, examining the digital journey of banks is relevant since digitalization is important for banks because it can help them to improve their efficiency and reduce costs (Casolaro and Gobbi 2007), improve their performance (Chowdhury 2003; Kozak 2005) and their customers' experience (Cuadros-Solas 2019; Carbó Valverde et al. 2020; Xue, et al. 2011; Ciciretti et al. 2009). In this sense,

---

[1] The terms "expense" and "investment" are used interchangeably throughout the manuscript. The accounting standards consider all the economic resources employed for technological purposes as an expense. Specifically, they are part of the total operating expenses. However, from an economic point of view these IT expenses could be considered as an investment as they lead to growth. While accountants treat IT spending as an expense rather than as an investment, though there is continuous debate over whether this is the correct classification, the accounting distinction between an investment and an expense is not relevant for our purposes. As Beccalli (2007) states, the term "investment" does not assume any accounting qualification.

C. Gonnella
University of Pisa, Pisa, Italy
e-mail: cristina.gonnella@phd.unipi.it

F. Rodríguez-Fernández
University of Granada, Granada, Spain
e-mail: franrod@ugr.es

the effect of technology is beyond profitability, being a digital bank eases the design of new products with lower costs (Doran et al. 2022). By going digital, banks can provide more convenient, faster, and personalized financial services (DeYoung et al. 2007; Hernando and Nieto 2007). Moreover, high-IT banks can also expand their base of customers (Modi et al. 2022). Furthermore, the effect of technology in the banking industry seems to be especially positive in crisis times—during the Global Financial Crisis (Pierri and Timmer, 2022) and the COVID-19 pandemic (Branzoli et al. 2021).

Using a representative sample of the European banking industry, this investigation aims to provide empirical evidence on how banks have gone digital by examining the evolution of the annual technological expenses. Furthermore, this study also examines what are the main banks' determinants of dedicating resources to IT-related expenses. By doing so, we aim to characterize the type of banks that consistently spend large amounts of their budgets on technology. Finally, this research also aims to analyze to what extent banks are concerned about the implementation of new digital bank technologies—artificial intelligence, blockchain, cloud computing, biometrics, and big data. Overall, this study aims to contribute to the growing literature on the technological transformation of the banking industry by documenting the technological transformation of the European banking industry as well as by depicting the profile of those high-IT banks.

Methodologically, instead of measuring the digitalization of the banking industry based on the adoption of specific technologies (e.g., ATMs, PCs per employee, or online banking), as a growing literature (Aldasoro et al. 2022; Dadoukis et al. 2021; Koetter and Noth, 2013; Kwon et al. 2023; Martín-Oliver and Salas-Fumás, 2011; Modi et al. 2022), we rely on measures based on banks' IT expenses. By doing so, we could provide a reliable quantitative measure of the degree of banks' digitalization. In particular, we compute three different ratios to provide a broader view of the degree of the banks' IT expenditure: (i) IT expenses over total operating expenses, (ii) IT expenses over total operating income, and (iii) IT expenses over total assets.

Using a sample of 33 European banks from 2017 to 2021, we document that during our sample period, the total volume of banks' IT expenses has increased by 14.54%. The ratio of IT expenses to total operating expenses and the ratio of IT expenses to total operating income have increased by 1.02 percentage points (+10.34%) and 0.95 percentage points (+15.82%), respectively. We also find that the IT expenses per employee have increased, on average, by more than 2,100€ and that the ratio of IT expenses over total staff expenses has increased by 4 percentage points (+21.04%). Around 67% of the increase in banks' IT expenses between 2017 and 2021 has taken place after the pandemic. Regarding the evolution of IT expenses compared to staff expenses, we find that IT expenses per employee increased significantly since the outbreak of the pandemic—by 10.67% in 2020 compared to the previous year. Similarly, we also find that *IT expenses* over total *Staff expenses* increased by 4 percentage points (+21.03%) from 2017 to 2021.

Regarding the determinants of spending on technology, the chapter also documents that banks that are less capitalized, riskier, more profitable, less efficient, and those that exhibit a lower growth of total assets spend a larger amount of their resources on IT. This result suggests that there are some key features of banks that are associated with being involved in a technological transformation. Finally, examining banks' annual reports, we find that banks disclose information about new banking technologies—big data, artificial intelligence, blockchain, cloud computing, and biometrics. In particular, 78% of the surveyed banks report information on big data and 72% on cloud computing. These results suggest that banks are concerned about the implementation of new digital bank technologies.

The rest of the chapter is organized as follows. Section 10.2 presents the related literature and discusses the impact of the technological transformation of the banking industry. Section 10.3 describes the data and the methodology used. Section 10.4 provides the main empirical results on the evolution and determinants of banks' IT expenses. Section 10.5 discusses what are the new banking technologies and shows to what extent banks are concerned about them. Finally, Sect. 10.6 concludes.

10.2   Literature Review: Banking Digitalization

Digitalization is important for banks because it can help them improve their efficiency, reduce costs, offer new products, and improve customer experience (Cuadros-Solas 2019; Carbó Valverde et al. 2020; Xue et al. 2011; Ciciretti et al. 2009).

Economic theory underlines the first impact of digitalization concerning the banks' profitability. Mainly as an enabling factor of cost reduction for transactions, production, and delivery of services, and an enabling for the standardization of processes (Cuadros-Solas 2019). Indeed, digitalization can help banks to streamline and automate many of their processes, such as account opening, loan applications, and risk management. This can reduce the time and resources needed to complete these tasks, allowing banks to operate more efficiently. Furthermore, digitalization can also help banks to reduce their operating costs by automating manual processes and reducing the need for physical infrastructure, such as branches and paper documents. Casolaro and Gobbi (2007) reveal that Italian banks' investment in IT augments short-term profitability by reducing costs. Additionally, Kozak (2005) underlined the positive relationship for a US sample of banks by studying the effects of IT investment on banks' profitability. Moreover, for the Asia–Pacific region, Chowdhury (2003) shows that technological investments for capital and labor upgrading have a statistically significant positive effect on banks' productivity and profitability.

Furthermore, digitalization can also help banks define new revenue streams (DeYoung et al. 2007; Hernando and Nieto, 2007). Indeed, as shown by the context of COVID-19 pandemic, digitalization helped banks to develop products and services, such as mobile payments, peer-to-peer lending, and wealth management, and to reach customers through digital channels. It also gains the banks to better serve their customers and to adapt to changing market conditions (Ciciretti et al. 2009). Doran et al. (2022) analyze the relationship that previous investments in IT had on the prudential performance of banks during the coronavirus crisis. In their study, the authors conclude that investments in IT have an effect beyond profitability, as they help to design new products with lower costs, which undoubtedly helped during the confinement. Additionally, Pierri and Timmer's (2022) empirical evidence indicates a crucial role of IT adoption in strengthening a bank's resilience during a crisis. The authors' loan-level analysis shows that high-IT banks originated mortgages with better performance, indicating better borrower screening. They show that high-IT adopters experienced a significantly smaller increase in NPLs on their balance sheets and provided more credit to the economy during the crisis.

Other important positive effects of the process of bank digitalization have been recognized referring to customer satisfaction, with the consequence on customer loyalty, and augmentation of the affected transactions (Xue et al. 2011). Carbó Valverde et al. (2020) point out that there are other positive effects that lead to the design of better and cheaper products and the provision of more efficient services. In this sense, digitalization can allow banks to offer customers a more convenient, faster, and personalized service (DeYoung et al. 2007; Hernando and Nieto 2007). For example, through online banking, mobile apps, and chatbots, customers can access their accounts, make transactions, and get assistance at any time and from any location.

From the point of view of the impacts of banks' digitalization on the other economic actors, Carbó-Valverde et al. (2020) show that banks' investment in technology affect the process of consumers' digitalization, as consumers perceive that digital channels are safe, convenient, and of high quality. Also, Campbell and Frei (2010) underline a positive relationship between banks' implementation and consumers' utilization of online banking. Furthermore, customers' digitalization, as noted by DeYoung et al. (2007), He (2015), Hernando and Nieto (2007), seems to impact banks' performance positively.

A study published by the Monetary and Economic Policy Department of the Basel International Bank for Settlements (BIS), Ahnert et al. (2021) shows that investments in technology have a positive effect on granting credit to start-ups due to better screening results, resulting in job creation. Finally, Branzoli et al. (2021) state that investments in technology positively affected the financing of individuals and businesses in the months following the pandemic, when direct contact and attendance at bank counters were non-existent. For these authors, the IT investment contributed to better profiling of credit risk and favored granting loans to customers who requested them in an uncertain environment. Furthermore, IT investments may also improve the access to credit of less well-off households given that technologies could improve banks' ability to manage risk. As Modi et al. (2022) find, IT banks are more likely to receive applications from lower-income applicants and also more likely to accept them. This underlines the crucial role of IT in favoring credit access for low-income borrowers.

Some studies search for the motivations behind banks' digitalization adoptions. Hernández-Murillo et al. (2010) show that the adoption of online and mobile banking could be in part due to the digitalization of competitors. The evolution of digitalization in the banking industry has been driven by a combination of technological advances and changing customer preferences. In the early days of digital banking, many banks offered simple online services such as the ability to check account balances and make basic transactions. In the following years, banks began to introduce more advanced features such as mobile banking apps and personalized financial management tools. More recently, the rise of FinTech companies has also played a role in the evolution of digital banking (Modi et al. 2022). As noted by Modi et al. (2022), which relies on administrative data to study determinants and implications of US banks' Information Technology (IT) investments, large and small banks had similar IT expenses a decade ago. However today, large banks sharply increased their spending in IT due to their exposure to FinTech leaders' competition. These fintech companies have often been at the forefront of innovation, using new technologies such as artificial intelligence, blockchain, and biometrics to offer customers new and improved services. Overall, the evolution of digitalization in banking has led to the development of a wide range of digital banking tools and services, including mobile banking apps, online account management, digital payments, and more. These tools and services have made it easier for customers to access their accounts, make transactions, and manage their finances from any location (Arnaudo et al. 2022).

This process of digitalization for banks is not without concerns. For this reason, it is important for banks to address the concerns in order to ensure that the digitalization of the banking industry is beneficial for both banks and the economic systems. Despite the flows of positive effects, researchers highlight the "paradox of productivity" (formulated for the first time by Robert Solow), suggesting digital transformation does not translate itself into productivity and, thus, the profitability of banks. Indeed, as Berger (2003) states, several difficulties in estimating the linkage between IT investments and productivity growth do not ensure a positive relationship. Building on this paradox, several empirical studies developed before 2000 collected data, not finding a positive relationship between digitalization and profitability (Cuadros-Solas 2019). For instance, Markus and Soh (1993), studying the impact of IT expenses on profitability in the 1980s, found that IT investments do not translate to higher profits for small banks. Beccalli (2007), focusing on a sample of EU banks from 1995–2000, found a heterogeneous effect of technology: outsourcing technologies (offered by third parties) have positive effects on profitability, however, hardware and software acquisition impact negatively on profitability. Borello et al. (2022) suggest that no relationship exists between IT investments and efficiency, but more efficient banks are more technological. This strange paradox undoubtedly reflects the difficulty of empirically measuring the degree of technologization of a bank and its impact on efficiency while simultaneously leaving open the possibility that other factors favor its performance. However, although there is no concordant and universal evidence confirming the positive effect of banks' IT investments on their profitability, studies that have examined in particular the impact of some specific IT banks' internal investments such as ATMs (Haynes and Thompson 2000) or interbank-payment system SWIFT (Scott et al. 2017) show their positive effect on productivity and long-term bank profitability.

There are other concerns that banks need to consider for the digitalization process. Some open debates involve the possibility that digitalization acted as a complement (Xue et al. 2011; Campbell and Frey 2009; Ciciretti et al. 2009) or a substitute (Bonaccorsi di Patti et al. 2004; Carmignani et al. 2020; Galardo et al. 2021) to the physical branches; the banks' ability to deal with cyber-attacks and data breaches (Aldasoro et al. 2022) and to ensure financial inclusion (Julião et al. 2023).

Building on the consideration above, the chapter considers to what extent banks, compete in a digital post-pandemic context, are adopting or concerned about the implementation of new digital bank technologies in the European context, considering specific IT investments (such as artificial intelligence, blockchain, cloud computing, biometrics, and big data).

10.3   METHODOLOGY

10.3.1   Measuring the Digitalization of the Banking Industry

As prior studies have underlined, it is difficult to measure the degree of digitization of a financial institution. Several measures have been used over the last years to quantify the digital transformation of the banking industry. On the one hand, some papers have relied on the measures used by seminal studies on the digitalization of non-financial companies to measure the adoption of IT in the banking industry. Typically, those studies focused on non-financial companies (see among others, Beaudry et al. 2010; Bloom et al. 2012; Bresnahan et al. 2002; Brynjolfsson and Hitt 2003) used the ratio of PCs per employee within each bank as the main measure of bank-level IT adoption. In most cases, this data was retrieved from survey data collected by some data providers.[2] Following these studies, some papers have used the same measures applied to the banking industry (Ahnert et al. 2021; Kwan et al. 2021; Pierri and Timmer 2022). The main advantage of using this measure is that it is simple, based only on hardware availability, and tends to be a strong predictor of other measures of IT adoption such as the IT budget or the adoption of new banking technologies.[3] However, this measure is retrieved from survey data from U.S. banks, it is difficult to extrapolate to other jurisdictions. Moreover, as Modi et al. (2022) argue, marketing survey data can sometimes be plagued by errors and opaque imputations. Furthermore, the banking industry seems to have left behind a first wave of technological innovation, where using PCs meant being at the technological forefront. Nowadays, almost of the banks' employees work with their own PC. On the other hand, other studies have tried to measure digitalization by examining the adoption of specific technologies (e.g., ATMs, online banking, or Mortgage Electronic Registration System) (Hannan and McDowell 1987; Hernández-Murillo et al. 2010; Lewellen and Williams 2021). While these measures could reflect to what extent a bank is digitalized, they are referred to the implementation of very specific technologies, so they are not able to provide a full picture of the digital transformation of the bank.

To circumvent the disadvantages of the abovementioned measures, a growing literature has become to employ new measures based on the banks' IT expenses (Aldasoro et al. 2022; Dadoukis et al. 2021; Koetter and Noth 2013; Kwon et al. 2023; Martín-Oliver and Salas-Fumás 2011; Modi et al. 2022). These technological investments are reported in banks' income statements.[4] One of the advantages of using

---

[2] Most of the studies have used the one collected by the marketing intelligence company Aberdeen (previously known as Harte Hanks). This company provides this information for over 3,2 million establishments in the United States.

[3] For example, Timmer et al. (2021) show that the correlation between the IT budget and the number of computers as a share of employees was 0.65 in 2016. Moreover, using data from 2016, they also show that there is also a positive correlation between PCs per Employee and the probability of adoption of cloud computing.

[4] Banks tend to disclose this information as part of "Other administrative expenses". Together with the technology-related expenses, banks also report information on expenses related to advertising, marketing and communication, consulting, professional services, and administrative and logistic services. To ensure that we are capturing the total IT expenses, following Kovner et al. (2014) and Modi et al. (2022), we classify an expense line as

this measure is that it provides a more global picture of the degree of digitalization of the IT budget typically includes several IT-related expenses (e.g., acquisition of hardware and software, outsourcing of IT services to external providers, shared service center and information transmission expenditures, or building and maintaining enterprise-wide systems, among others). Moreover, by using data extracted from banks' annual reports, we ensure that this data is likely to be of much higher quality because of the legal obligation and resources involved in these documents. Furthermore, these documents are revised by the national supervisors and by external audit companies. However, this measure also has some drawbacks. Unfortunately, banks are not specifically required to report their IT expenses when disclosing their operating expenses (non-interest expenses). In any case, a larger number of banks are disclosing this information as being transparent in engaging in a digitalization transformation is becoming crucial in a digital competitive environment. Using U.S. data, Modi et al. (2022) show that the percentage of banks reporting IT-related expenses has increased over time.

10.3.2   Sample and Data

Our final sample covers 33 European banks from 12 countries over the period 2017–2021. In 2021, these banks account for 14.4 trillion euros (87% of the European GDP and 50.1% of the total European banks' assets). Bank-level information comes from the ORBIS Bank Focus Database (Bureau Van Dijk). Table 10.1 reports the list of banks included in our sample.

To provide an accurate measurement of the digitalization of the banking industry, we have computed three different ratios with the aim of providing a broader view of the degree of the banks' IT expenditure. As De Haan, (2021) underline, using different ratios is better than relying just on a single one. Each of the ratios provides a different insight into

"IT expense" if its description contains any IT-related keyword such as "IT expenses", "Technology and systems", "Technology spend", "Technology and system costs", and/or "IT services".

Table 10.1 Sample

Bank	Country	Average Total Assets (2017–2021) €m
Abanca	Spain	61,712.09 €
ABN AMRO Group NV	Belgium	311,739.00 €
Banco Cooperativo Español	Spain	692,899.80 €
Banco de Sabadell SA	Spain	13,481.88 €
Banco Santander SA	Spain	231,026.85 €
Bankinter	Spain	1,506,071.20 €
Bayerische Landesbank	Germany	87,080.55 €
BBVA SA	Spain	236,698.60 €
Belfius Banque SA	Belgium	176,941.16 €
CaixaBank SA	Spain	458,530.40 €
Commerzbank AG	Germany	471,598.00 €
Cooperative Rabobank UA	The Netherlands	493,249.20 €
Deutsche Bank AG	Germany	1,353,959.00 €
DNB Bank Group	Norway	256,149.34 €
DZ Bank AG	Germany	561,102.80 €
Erste Group Bank	Austria	257,593.20 €
Ibercaja	Spain	55,653.38 €
ING Groep NV	The Netherlands	744,455.60 €
Intesa Sanpaolo SpA	Italy	894,567.60 €
Jyske Bank	Denmark	633,379.00 €
Kutxabank	Spain	60,996.95 €
Landesbank Baden-Wurttemberg	Germany	258,865.60 €
Lloyds Banking Group Plc	United Kingdom	840,278.80 €
Norddeutsche Landesbank	Germany	139,659.00 €
Nordea Bank Group	Finland	562,076.20 €
OP Financial Group	Finland	151,768.00 €
Raiffesen Bank International	Austria	157,104.17 €
Skandinaviska Enskilda Banken Group	Sweden	279,369.01 €
Societe Generale SA	France	1,120,162.80 €
Svenska Handelsbanken Group	Sweden	293,466.87 €
Swedbank Group	Sweden	237,279.75 €
Unicaja Banco	Spain	70,327.59 €
Unicredit SpA	Italy	874,547.14 €

Source Authors' elaboration and Bank Focus

the banks' technological expenditure. Then, we calculate the following ratios:

- $\frac{IT\,Expenses}{Operating\,expenses}$: This ratio shows the percentage of operating expenses that each bank decides to deploy on technology. Then, it indicates how much a bank spends on technology for each monetary unit spent on the total expenses directly related to its normal business operations.
- $\frac{IT\,Expenses}{Operating\,income}$: This ratio shows the percentage of operating income that each bank decides to deploy on technology. This ratio indicates how much a bank must spend on technology to generate each monetary unit of income.
- $\frac{IT\,Expenses}{Total\,assets}$: This ratio indicates how much a bank spends on technology related to its size.

10.3.3   Methodology

With the aim of examining the main drivers of banks' IT expenses, we consider the following regression:

$$
\begin{aligned}
IT\ expenses\ (\%)_{i,t} = {} & \beta_0 + \beta_1 Size_{i,t-1} + \beta_2 Capital\ Ratio_{i,t-1} \\
& + \beta_3 Asset\ Quality_{i,t-1} + \beta_4 NIM_{i,t-1} \\
& + \beta_5 ROA_{i,t-1} + \beta_6 Efficiency\ ratio_{i,t-1} \\
& + \beta_7 Liquidity_{i,t-1} + \beta_8 Growth\ TA_{i,t-1} \\
& + \beta_9 Staff\ exp.\ per\ employee_{i,t-1} + \mu_i \\
& + \lambda_t + \varepsilon_{it} +
\end{aligned}
$$

where i and t refer to the country and year, respectively. We regress our three measures for banks' IT expenses on the main banks' features. By including these variables, we aim to characterize the type of bank that is more likely to spend a larger amount on technology. This set of financial ratios accounts for the different characteristics of the banks: size, liquidity, performance, efficiency, and capital adequacy.

As is standard in the literature, *Size* is defined as the natural logarithm of a bank's total assets. The *Capital Ratio* is computed as the ratio of total equity to total assets. This ratio is used as a proxy for the level of bank risk aversion or capitalization. A variable reflecting banks' asset quality is employed to account for credit risk. In this sense, we account for this level of risk using the ratio of impaired loans to total equity assuming that banks face higher levels of risk at larger volumes of impaired loans.

We also include two variables that reflect bank performance. *NIM* is the net interest margin, which is computed as the ratio of net interest income to average earning assets, and *ROA* is the net return on assets. We measure banks' management *efficiency* using the cost-to-income ratio (Cost-to-income). A large value would mean that the bank is more inefficient as it needs more to incur more costs to generate profits. *Liquidity* is measured using the ratio of liquid assets to total deposits and borrowings. We also consider the growth of bank total assets (*Growth TA*) as the annual growth of total bank assets. Finally, since banks could be using technology to replace human labor, we also include the total *Staff expenses per employee*. In the regression, all these variables are lagged by one period to reduce potential endogeneity concerns.

μ_i is a set of country dummy variables used to control for characteristics specific to each country that persist over time. The inclusion of these variables allows us to capture unobserved country-invariant effects. λ_t is a set of year dummy variables that captures country-invariant heterogeneity due to time. $\varepsilon_{i,t}$ is a white-noise error term. Standard errors are clustered at the bank level. Table 10.2 provides the summary statistics for all the variables.

Table 10.2 Summary statistics

	mean	p50	sd	min	max	N
Dependent variables						
IT exp /operating expenses	10.48	8.95	5.52	2.14	27.47	165
IT exp / operating income	6.60	5.51	3.98	1.16	21.76	165
IT exp /assets	0.13	0.11	0.06	0.01	0.37	165
Explanatory variables						
Size	26.52	26.53	1.13	23.00	28.25	165
Capital ratio	6.05	5.80	1.34	2.15	10.08	165
Asset quality	28.91	23.82	23.67	0.29	189.73	165
NIM	1.37	1.21	0.58	0.46	3.06	165
ROA	0.44	0.44	0.34	−1.51	1.31	165
Efficiency ratio	61.19	61.72	13.29	26.44	109.20	165
Liquidity	24.87	22.82	10.65	3.77	58.88	165
Growth TA	4.38	3.11	10.84	−47.86	76.29	165
Staff expenses per employee	98,550.12	90,594.77	29,989.75	36,359.96	165,915.90	165

Source Authors' elaboration

10.4   DIGITALIZATION
OF THE BANKING INDUSTRY: 2017–2021

10.4.1   *Evolution of IT Expenses in the European Banking Industry*

To examine to what extent there has been a growth in the intensity of using technology in the European banking industry, we have conducted some descriptive analyses regarding the evolution, current situation, and future of digitalization in the European banking industry.

Figure 10.1 plots the annual volume of IT expenses of our sample of European banks from 2017 to 2021. As could be observed, the total volume of IT expenses has increased in the sample years (2017–2021). In 2017, these IT expenses amounted to 18.9 billion euros. In 2021, these same banks spent 3.21 billion more to reach a total amount of 21.65 billion euros. Specifically, banks' IT expenses have increased by 14.54% from 2017 to 2021.

Additionally, Fig. 10.2 plots the evolution of the ratio of IT expenses to total operating expenses and the ratio of IT expenses to total operating income. Over the sample period, on average, the ratio of IT expenses to total operating expenses has increased by 1.02 percentage points (+10.34%). Similarly, the ratio of IT expenses to total operating income has experienced a growth of 0.95 percentage points (+15.82%). As could be seen, our analysis of the trend of IT expenses as a share of operating

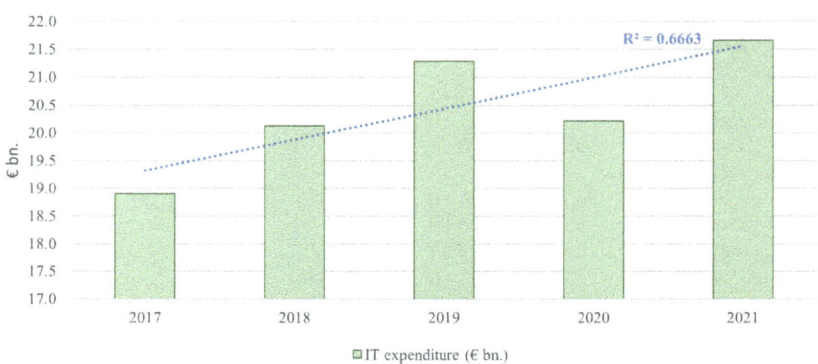

Fig. 10.1   Evolution of total IT expenses (2017–2021) (*Source* Authors' elaboration based on a sample of 33 European banks from 12 countries over the period 2017–2021)

income, and as a share of operating costs is homogeneous: an increase of the ratio of around 1% during our observation period. In 2021, European banks spent almost 11% of their budget on technology while four years before they allocated 9.9% of their resources to technology. In recent years, the trend toward digital transformation has accelerated, leading to an increase in banks' IT spending. This trend, measured through several indicators, showing an increase in IT expenditure in recent years, seems to reflect both the attention of European supervisory authorities to the issue of digitalization and the need to find alternative ways of implementing business strategies that the COVID-19 pandemic has raised.

This increase could also be explained by the measures that regulators and supervisors put in place to boost the digital transformation of the industry. In the European banking sector, the European Banking Authority (EBA) has promoted the digitalization of the banking industry by developing regulatory guidelines and technical standards. For example, in 2016, the EBA issued guidelines on the security of internet payments, which set out requirements for banks to ensure the security of online transactions. In 2018, the EBA also issued guidelines on using cloud services in the banking sector, which guided how banks can use cloud services securely and efficiently (EBA 2017). In addition to regulatory guidelines, the EBA has also been promoting IT and digitalization through its work on innovation, including establishing its Innovation

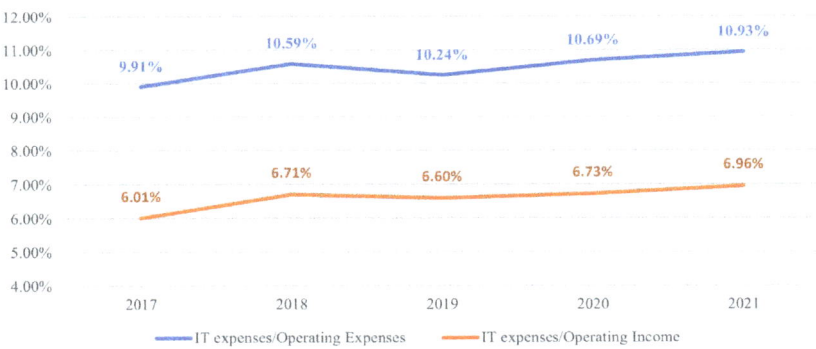

Fig. 10.2 Evolution of IT expenses ratios (2017–2021) (*Source* Authors' elaboration based on a sample of 33 European banks from 12 countries over the period 2017–2021)

Hub in 2018. The Innovation Hub provides a platform for banks and fintech firms to test their innovative ideas in a regulatory sandbox environment to foster innovation in the EU banking sector (EBA 2018). Overall, the EBA has been playing a pivotal role in promoting the concept of IT and digitalization in the European banking sector, and its efforts will likely have a significant impact in the future.

As illustrated in Fig. 10.1, while the EBA's focus may have influenced decisions to increase IT investments (see for the year 2019), the restrictions of COVID-19 may have accelerated the digital transformation process. Indeed, as we could see in Fig. 2, in 2020, the first year in which the effects of the pandemic are noticeable, the IT expenses/ Operating Expenses ratio and IT expenses/Operating Income registered an increase. In the post-pandemic context (at the end of 2021), the IT expenses over total operating expenses were 6.72% higher than they were before the pandemic (in 2019). In a similar vein, the IT expenses over total operating income were 5.40% higher than they were before the pandemic (in 2019). Around 67% of the increase in banks', IT expenses between 2017 and 2021 has taken place after the pandemic. These findings reveal the relevance that the COVID-19 pandemic had in fostering the digital transformation of banks.

This trend is likely to continue in the future as technology continues to evolve and banks look to adopt new technologies to improve their operations, streamline processes, and enhance their customer experience, driven by the need to modernize and compete in a rapidly changing technological landscape. As a result, IT has become and will be a critical component of most businesses. Banks are investing more in IT to ensure that their technology infrastructure is up-to-date and capable of meeting their needs.

Based on the trend in IT expenditure in the years analyzed, we can anticipate, barring various contextual factors that could reverse the trend, an increase of approximately more than 10.000 bn € in IT expenditure from 2022 to 2040. Furthermore, also in terms of trends of IT expenses/ Operating Expenses ratio and terms of IT expenses/Operating Income, results suggest that banks will be continued to be concerned about the implementation of new digital bank technologies in the next years. Particularly, in 2040 the IT expenses could reach 14.87% of the total operating expenses and 10.58% of the total operating income.

10.4.2   Determinants of IT Expenses in the Banking Industry

Table 10.3 provides the results for the regressions on banks' IT expenses. Column 1 reports the results for the regression on the ratio of IT expenses over total assets, while Columns 2 and 3 present the results for the regressions on the ratios of IT expenses over operating expenses and income, respectively. Overall, this table shows that the banks that spend a larger amount on IT are those banks that are less capitalized, riskier (as they have a larger volume of impaired loans with respect to their equity), more profitable, less efficient, and those that exhibit a lower growth of total assets. In any case, these results also show that the analysis is likely to differ according to the measure used.

When focusing on the ratio of IT expenses to total operating expenses, which is the standard ratio used in the literature, it seems that larger banks do not seem to spend a higher fraction of their budget on technology. In this sense, going digital does not seem to be correlated with being a large bank. All banks, regardless of their size, are facing the pressure of transforming their business model by being more technological. It can also be observed that those banks less capitalized are likely to spend more on IT. This result could suggest that holding large volumes of capital, which is costly, could hinder the technological transformation of banks. Moreover, we also observe that more profitable banks—characterized by having a large ROA—spend a higher percentage of their operating expenses on technology. While the coefficient is positive, we do not find a statistically significant correlation when examining the NIM. So, it seems that those banks that can be more profitable because they could generate more income through fees and commissions are the ones that spend more on IT. Furthermore, we also observe that banks' efficiency is a driver of IT expenses. Those banks that need to incur larger costs to generate income (more inefficient) are those that tend to spend more resources on technology.

Overall, these results suggest that there are some key features of banks that are associated with being more or less involved in the technological transformation.

10.4.3   Staff Expenses vs IT Expenses

Both *Staff* and *IT expenses* are essential components of a bank's budget, and the optimal allocation of resources between these two categories

Table 10.3   Determinants of IT expenses in the banking industry

Variables	(1) IT expenses / assets	(2) IT expenses / operating expenses	(3) IT expenses / operating income
$Size_{t-1}$	−0.052**	−0.585	−0.305
	(0.021)	(2.042)	(1.012)
Capital ratio$_{t-1}$	−0.021**	−1.572**	−0.815
	(0.008)	(0.594)	(0.522)
Asset quality$_{t-1}$	−0.001**	−0.013	−0.013***
	(7.96e-05)	(0.008)	(0.004)
NIM_{t-1}	0.019	0.017	1.239
	(0.019)	(1.198)	(1.472)
ROA_{t-1}	0.035**	3.293***	0.951
	(0.013)	(1.013)	(0.912)
Efficiency ratio$_{t-1}$	0.001**	0.073***	−0.024
	(0.0003)	(0.024)	(0.025)
Liquidity$_{t-1}$	−0.0004	−0.036	−0.005
	(0.0003)	(0.027)	(0.025)
Growth TA$_{t-1}$	−0.0006**	−0.037	−0.0312*
	(0.0003)	(0.025)	(0.0184)
Staff expenses per employee$_{t-1}$	−5.14e-07**	−2.54e-05	-2.01e-05
	(2.14e-07)	(2.34e-05)	(1.50e-05)
Observations	132	132	132
Number of Banks	33	33	33
Clustered Std	Bank	Bank	Bank
Bank Fixed Effects	Yes	Yes	Yes
Time Fixed Effects	Yes	Yes	Yes
R-squared	0.280	0.273	0.179

Notes (1) N = 132. 2) $p < 0.1$, * $p < 0.05$, ** $p < 0.01$, *** $p < 0.001$

depends on various factors, including the bank's size, business strategy, and technology requirements. *Staff expenses* refer to the costs associated with hiring and employing employees, such as salaries, benefits, training, and recruitment. *IT expenses* refer to the costs of acquiring, maintaining, and upgrading technology and information systems, including hardware, software, and technical support. *Staff expenses* are a significant portion of a bank's operating costs, as employees are the main drivers of its operations and customer service. *IT expenses* are also a high cost for banks, as technology plays a crucial role in banking operations and is essential for providing efficient and secure services to customers.

The simultaneous analysis of the trends of these two typologies of expenses allows us to have a first understanding of the phenomena of technology usage in replacing human labor in the banking sector. Information technology has replaced some aspects of human labor in the banking industry. However, it has also created new job opportunities in technology development, cyber security, and data analysis. As a result, while IT has replaced some human labor in banks, the role of human employees remains essential and continues to evolve. For this open debate on using IT in substituting or complementing human labor, we analyze the IT expenses/staff expenses ratio and the IT expenses for an employee from 2017 to 2021. In this sense, if technology has become more relevant since the pandemic, the potential replacement of human labor for technology should be observed especially after the pandemic.

Table 10.4 shows that before the COVID-19 pandemic (from 2017 to 2019), the IT expenses per employee almost remained unchanged at around 21,600€ per employee. Since the outbreak of the pandemic, we observe a significant increase in IT expenses per employee. Particularly, the analysis shows that IT expenses per employee increased in 2020 by 10.67% compared to the previous year. This finding reveals the impact of the pandemic on accelerating the digital transformation of banks. Overall, considering the entire period, we find that the IT expenses per employee have increased, on average, by more than 2,100€. Looking at the ratio of *IT expenses* over total *Staff expenses* (Table 10.4), it has increased by 4 percentage points (+21.03%) during the sample period.

The results emerging from this further analysis on the ratio of IT expenditure to staff expenditure again underline how embedded banks are in the digitization process. However, they also raise the need to investigate in future research whether this digitization is handled ethically

Table 10.4 Evolution of Staff expenses and IT expenses

Year	IT expenses/Staff expenses	IT expenses per employee
2017	19.51%	21,592.17 €
2018	21.30%	21,565.27 €
2019	22.62%	21,644.19 €
2020	22.94%	23,952.68 €
2021	23.61%	23,778.93 €

Source Authors' elaboration and Bank Focus

especially considering human and community needs. The replacement of human labor with IT in the banking sector raises social concerns at the micro level regarding job loss and income inequality and, thus, to the macro level for communities. The recent acceleration of digital transformation has triggered a debate on "ethical digitalization" concerning the impact of advanced technologies on the human factor and society (EC 2021).

Automating specific tasks could result in job loss for some employees, particularly in data management, account management, and loan processing. This could lead to high levels of unemployment. Furthermore, replacing human labor with IT may increase banks' profits. However, it can also lead to a widening income gap between highly skilled workers who benefit from the new technology and low-skilled workers who are displaced by automation. Finally, we have to consider that banks' digital transformation, if not ethically managed, could also negatively impact communities that are heavily dependent on the banking industry for employment, leading to increased poverty, crime, and social unrest.

10.5   New Banking Technologies

10.5.1   *Toward a New Technological Era in Banking*

In order to compete with new digital competitors such as neobanks, FinTech firms, or Big Technological companies, banks have started to implement several innovative technologies. These "new" technologies are known as the "new banking technologies". In this sense, prior reports (e.g., Deloitte 2020; Ernst and Young 2018; McKinsey 2020) point to five technologies that are considered to have the largest potential to transform the provision of financial services. These new banking technologies are being employed in some key areas of banks' business models: strengthening the competitive position of the banks as new competitors emerge, improving the (digital) customer experience to attract new (digital) customers, and improving bank efficiency by reducing their operational costs. While these technologies could be employed for several purposes, these five technologies are commonly used in the following areas:

- *Big Data*: This technology that allows banks to analyze, process, and extract information from extremely complex and large datasets is mainly used to customize financial services, as a risk management tool, and prevent and detect fraud. For example, credit scorings relying on algorithms used this technology to evaluate the risk of banks' customers.
- *Artificial Intelligence*: This technology enables the use of expert systems, machine learning, natural language processors, and advanced algorithms to analyze texts and identify feelings and other information from unstructured data. Nowadays, it is used for automated decision-making processes, to enhance the consumer experience (e.g., chatbot), to deal with regulatory compliance, or to discover investment opportunities for customers (e.g., using robo-advisors).
- *Blockchain*: This technology structures data and information in a chain of blocks with the aim of creating a single, consensual, and distributed registry network with several nodes. Apart from being used to issue digital currencies (e.g., Bitcoin or Ethereum), blockchain is also used in the banking industry. For example, it is used for cross-border payments, to issue corporate debt, or to automatize back-office processes.
- *Cloud computing*: This new banking technology allows the delivery of computing services—including servers, storage, databases, networking, software, analytics, and intelligence—over a public or private network. It is largely used for data management. It would be crucial if banking is moving to a platform-based ecosystem.
- *Biometrics*: This technology allows the automatic identification of a person based on his/her physiological or behavioral characteristics to grant him/her access to systems, devices, or data. It is used to authenticate customers ease the digital onboarding of new customers or segment customers into different groups. It is key to help the adoption of digital banking through smartphones.

10.5.2   Relevance of the New Banking Technologies in the European Banking Industry

Finally, looking at the banks' annual reports, we count the number of times the words related to new digital bank technologies—artificial intelligence/AI, big data, biometrics, blockchain, and cloud computing appear in each bank's 2021 annual report. We consider the Annual Report as the central document for gathering information because "it discloses the most important actions, operations, and facts involving the company's activity" (Bernini et al. 2021). Consistent with Mention (2011), we assume that the degree of the disclosure can represent the banks' commitment to a specific topic such as digitalization. This is consistent with the fundamental concept of content analysis (Krippendorff 1980), according to which "the extent of reporting demonstrates the significance of the disclosed issue" (Bernini et al. 2021). Thus, we collect the number of words from annual reports to reveal the bank's efforts in developing a specific IT technology (artificial intelligence/AI, big data, biometrics, blockchain, and cloud computing).

After collecting all words from annual reports, we find that 78% of the surveyed banks report information on big data and 72% on cloud computing (Table 10.5). These results show the great attention on big data and cloud computing as the main new digital bank technologies. These technologies have become increasingly important for the banking sector in recent years. In this sense, the use of big data and cloud computing in the banking sector has several benefits. Banks can use big data to better understand customer behavior and preferences, which can be used to offer personalized services and products. Cloud computing enables banks to automate many processes, reducing manual effort and increasing efficiency. Overall, big data and cloud computing are transforming the banking sector by enabling organizations to process and analyze large amounts of data more efficiently and in real-time. This not only improves customer experiences and makes better-informed decisions but also, by analyzing large amounts of data, banks can identify and mitigate potential risks such as fraud, more effectively.

Furthermore, more than 50% of surveyed banks report, in their annual reports, information on artificial intelligence (Table 10.5), and it represents the second most reported topic in general (115 times reported in all examined banks' annual reports with an average of 3.59 on the total of IT technology's word selected).

Table 10.5 Disclosure of new banking technologies (in 2021)

	% banks reporting	# technology reported	Avg. # technology reported
Artificial Intelligence	66	115	3.59
Big Data	78	99	3.00
Biometrics	50	41	1.28
Blockchain	44	39	1.22
Cloud Computing	72	162	4.91

Source: Authors' elaboration and Banks' annual reports

10.6   CONCLUSIONS

While technology has become more important for the banking industry, the technological change in the banking industry is accelerating. Some of the latest technological developments have the capacity of changing the way traditional financial intermediation activity could be performed. Banks have responded to this technological challenge by being proactive in the adoption of technological innovations. This study aims to contribute to the growing literature on the technological transformation of the banking industry by documenting the technological transformation of the European banking industry, as well as, by depicting the profile of those high-IT banks. In doing so, we rely on measures based on banks' IT expenses. In particular, we compute three different ratios with the aim of providing a broader view of the degree of the banks' IT expenditure: (i) IT expenses over total operating expenses, (ii) IT expenses over total operating income, and (iii) IT expenses over total assets.

Our results show that during the period 2017–2021, the European banking industry has largely increased the magnitude of its IT expenses. The ratio of IT expenses over total operating expenses and the ratio of IT expenses over total operating income have increased by 1.02 basis points (+10.34%) and 0.95 basis points (+15.82%), respectively. A significant fraction of this increase has taken place after the COVID-19 pandemic, which confirms that the pandemic has accelerated the digital transformation of the European banking industry. Moreover, we also observe that IT expenses have been gaining relevance compared to Staff expenses. The ratio of *IT expenses* over total *Staff expenses* increased by 4 percentage points (+21.03%) from 2017 to 2021. The chapter also reveals that becoming a high-IT bank is associated with some key banking features. In particular, we provide evidence that less capitalized, riskier, more profitable, and less efficient, and those that exhibit a lower growth of total assets dedicate more resources to IT.

These findings may have some relevant implications for the incumbent banking industry. In this sense, the growth of IT expenses in the European banking industry reveals that these banks are more prepared to compete in a digital ecosystem. However, this study could not evaluate whether the current technological effort of European banks is enough to compete with other digital players (FinTech, neobanks, or BigTech) and also if the banks concerned in digital transformation also took into account ethical implications of IT technologies on human workforce and the society (EC 2021). Regardless of the industry considered, being adapted to a digital competitive environment is not an easy task. Increasing the resources dedicated to IT could not be easily done for those banks that have a legacy. In any case, what is always crucial is being committed to facing a technological revolution by trying to lead it instead of fighting for postponing it. In this case, it seems that the European banking industry has opted for being the protagonist of the digital transformation rather than being a mere spectator.

References

Ahnert, T., Doerr, S., Pierri, N., and Timmer, Y. (2021). Does IT help? Information technology in banking and entrepreneurship. *IMF Working Papers*, (214), 1. https://doi.org/10.5089/9781513591803.001

Aldasoro, I., Gambacorta, L., Giudici, P., and Leach, T. (2022). The drivers of cyber risk. Journal of Financial Stability, 60 (May 2021): 100989.

Arnaudo, D., Del Prete, S., Demma, C., Manile, M., Orame, A., Pagnini, M., ... and Soggia, G. (2022). The digital trasformation in the Italian banking sector. *Bank of Italy Occasional Paper*, (682).

Beaudry, P., Doms, M., and Lewis, E. (2010). Should the personal computer be considered a technological revolution? Evidence from U.S. metropolitan areas. Journal of Political Economy, 118(5): 988–1036.

Beccalli, E. (2007). Does IT investment improve bank performance? Evidence from Europe. Journal of banking and finance, 31(7): 2205–2230.

Berger, A. N. (2003). The Economic Effects of Technological Progress: Evidence from the Banking Industry. Journal of Money, Credit, and Banking, 35(2), 141–176. https://doi.org/10.1353/mcb.2003.0009

Bernini, F., Ferretti, P., and Angelini, A. (2021). The digitalization-reputation link: A multiple case-study on Italian banking groups. Meditari Accountancy Research, 30(4): 1210–1240.

Bloom, N., Sadun, R., and Van Reenen, J. (2012). Americans do it better: US multinationals and the productivity miracle. American Economic Review, 102(1): 167–201.

Bonaccorsi di Patti, E., Gobbi, G., and Mistrulli, P. E. (2004). *The interaction between face-to-face and electronic delivery: the case of the Italian banking industry* (No. 508). Bank of Italy, Economic Research and International Relations Area.

Boot, A., Hoffmann, P., Laeven, L., and Ratnovski, L. (2021). Fintech: what's old, what's new? Journal of Financial Stability, 53.

Borello, G., Pampurini, F., and Quaranta, A. G. (2022). Can High-tech investments improve banking efficiency? Journal of Financial Management, Markets and Institutions, 10(01): 2250003.

Branzoli, N., Rainone, E., and Supino, I. (2021). The role of banks' technology adoption in credit markets during the pandemic. *Available at SSRN 3878254*.

Bresnahan, T. F., Brynjolfsson, E., and Hitt, L. M. (2002). Information technology, workplace organization, and the demand for skilled labor: Firm-level evidence. The Quarterly Journal of Economics, February.

Brynjolfsson, E., and Hitt, L. M. (2003). Computing productivity: Firm-level evidence. Review of Economics and Statistics, 85(4): 793–808.

Campbell, D., and Frei, F. (2010). Cost structure, customer profitability, and retention implications of self-service distribution channels: Evidence from customer behavior in an online banking channel. Management Science, 56(1): 4–24.

Carbó-Valverde, S., Cuadros-Solas, P. J., Rodríguez-Fernández, F. (2020). The effect of banks' IT investments on the digitalization of their customers. Global Policy, 11: 9–17.

Carletti, E., Claessens, S., and Vives, X. (2021). *The Bank Business Model in the Post-Covid-19 World*.

Carmignani, A., Manile, M., Orame, A., and Pagnini, M. (2020). Servizi bancari online e dinamica degli sportelli bancari (Online Banking Services and Branch Networks). *Bank of Italy Occasional Paper*, (543).

Casolaro, L., and Gobbi, G. (2007). Information technology and productivity changes in the banking industry. Economic Notes, 36(1): 43–76.

Chowdhury, A. (2003). Information technology and productivity payoff in the banking industry: Evidence from the emerging markets. Journal of International Development, 15(6): 693.

Ciciretti, R., Hasan, I., and Zazzara, C. (2009). Do internet activities add value? Evidence from the traditional banks. Journal of financial services research, 35(1): 81–98.

Cuadros-Solas, P. J. (2019). La nueva tecnología bancaria: Aplicaciones, adopción e impacto en banca. Papeles De Economía Española, (162): 126–175.

Dadoukis, A., Fiaschetti, M., and Fusi, G. (2021). IT adoption and bank performance during the Covid-19 pandemic. Economics Letters, 204: 109904.

De Haan, J. (2021). Low IT spending by banks: Reason for concern? *Working Paper, June.*

DeYoung, R., Lang, W. W., and Nolle, D. L. (2007). How the Internet affects output and performance at community banks. Journal of Banking and Finance, 31(4): 1033–1060.

Deloitte. (2020). *2021 banking and capital markets outlook.*

Doran, N. M., Bădîrcea, R. M., and Manta, A. G. (2022). Digitization and financial performance of banking sectors facing COVID-19 challenges in central and Eastern European countries. *Electronics*, 11(21), 3483.

Ernst and Young. (2018). Global Banking Outlook 2018. *Ernst & Young Global Limited*, 1–19.

European Banking Authority—EBA (2017). Final report recommendations on outsourcing to cloud service providers.

European Banking Authority—EBA (2018). Report-FinTech: Regulatory sandboxes and innovation hubs.

Europena Commission—EC (2021). Industry 5.0. Towards a sustainable, human-centric and resilient European industry.

Galardo, M., Garrì, I., Mistrulli, P. E., and Revelli, D. (2021). The geography of banking: Evidence from branch closings. Economic Notes, 50(1): e12177.

Hannan, T. H., and McDowell, J. M. (1987). Rival precedence and the dynamics of technology adoption: An empirical analysis. Economica, 54(214): 155–171.

Haynes, M., and Thompson, S. (2000). The productivity impact of IT deployment: An empirical evaluation of ATM introduction. Oxford Bulletin of Economics and Statistics, 62(5): 607–619.

He, Z. (2015). Rivalry Market Structure and Innovation: The Case of Mobile Banking. Review of Industrial Organization. *47*(2), 219–242. https://doi.org/10.1007/s11151-015-9466-z

Hernández-Murillo, R., Llobet, G., and Fuentes, R. (2010). Strategic online banking adoption. Journal of Banking and Finance, 34(7): 1650–1663.

Hernando, I., and Nieto, M. J. (2007). Is the Internet delivery channel changing banks performance? The case of Spanish banks. Journal of Banking and Finance, 31(4): 1083–1099

Julião, J., Ayllon, T., and Gaspar, M. (2023). Financial inclusion through digital banking: The case of Peru. In *International Conference Innovation in Engineering* (pp. 294–304). Springer, Cham.

Koetter, M., and Noth, F. (2013). IT use, productivity, and market power in banking. Journal of Financial Stability, 9(4): 695–704.

Kovner, A., Vickery, J., and Zhou, L. (2014). Do Big Banks Have Lower Operating Costs? Economic Policy Review, 20(2), 1–27.

Kozak, S. (2005). The role of information technology in the profit and cost efficiency improvements of the banking sector. Journal of Academy of Business and Economics, 5(2).

Krippendorff, K. (1980), Content analysis: An introduction to its methodology, Sage Publications, Beverly Hills.

Kwan, A., Lin, C., Pursiainen, V., and Tai, M. (2021). Stress testing banks' digital capabilities: Evidence from the COVID-19 Pandemic. SSRN Electronic Journal.

Kwon, K. Y., Molyneux, P., Pancotto, L., and Reghezza, A. (2023). Banks and FinTech Acquisitions. In Journal of Financial Services Research (Issue December 2022). Springer US.

Lewellen, S., and Williams, E. (2021). Did technology contribute to the housing boom? Evidence from MERS. Journal of Financial Economics, 141(3): 1244–1261. https://doi.org/10.1016/j.jfineco.2021.04.002

Markus, M. L. and Soh, W. L. C. (1993). Banking on information technology: converting IT spending into firm performance. En M. A. Banker, R. Kaufmann, R. J. Mahood (eds.), Strategic information technology management: perspectives on organizational growth and competitive advantage, pp. 375–403. Harrisburg, PA.: Idea Group Publishing

Martín-Oliver, A., and Salas-Fumás, V. (2011). IT investment and intangibles: Evidence from banks. Review of Income and Wealth, 57(3): 513–535.

McKinsey. (2020). Next-gen technology transformation in financial services. April.

Mention, A.L. (2011), "Exploring voluntary reporting of intellectual capital in the banking sector", Journal of Management Control, 22(3): 279–309.

Modi, K., Pierri, N., and Timmer, Y. (2022). The Anatomy of Banks' IT investments: Drivers and implications. Working Paper.

Pierri, N., and Timmer, Y. (2022). The importance of technology in banking during a crisis. Journal of Monetary Economics, 128: 88–104.

Scott, S. V., Van Reenen, J., and Zachariadis, M. (2017). The long-term effect of digital innovation on bank performance: An empirical study of SWIFT adoption in financial services. Research Policy, 46(5): 984–1004.

Stulz, R. M. (2019). FinTech, BigTech, and the future of banks. Journal of Applied Corporate Finance, 31(4): 86–97.

Vives, X. (2019). Digital disruption in banking industry. Annual Review of Financial Economics, 11: 243–272.

Xue, M., Hitt, L. M., and Chen, P. Y. (2011). Determinants and outcomes of internet banking adoption. Management Science, 57(2): 291–307.

CHAPTER 11

The Relation Between Patent Pledgeability and Credit Rationing

Aineas Mallios, Ted Lindblom, and Stefan Sjögren

11.1 INTRODUCTION

Empirical evidence shows that today's knowledge-based economy is characterized by firms that invest more in intangible assets than in tangible assets (Eisfeldt and Papanikolaou 2014; Kahle and Stulz 2017). The increasing importance of intangibles to produce goods and services has implications for firms' asset structure and financing. For example, banks may not be a suitable source of finance for such innovative firms because of the lack of tangible collateral (Petersen and Rajan 1994). An increase

A. Mallios (✉) · T. Lindblom · S. Sjögren
School of Business, Economics and Law, University of Gothenburg,
Gothenburg, Sweden
e-mail: aineas.mallios@handels.gu.se

T. Lindblom
e-mail: ted.lindblom@handels.gu.se

S. Sjögren
e-mail: stefan.sjogren@handels.gu.se

© The Author(s), under exclusive license to Springer Nature   283
Switzerland AG 2023
S. Carbó-Valverde and P. J. Cuadros Solas (eds.), *New Challenges for the Banking Industry*, Palgrave Macmillan Studies in Banking and Financial Institutions, https://doi.org/10.1007/978-3-031-32931-9_11

in low-tangibility assets in the firms' asset structure would then lead to less debt financing implying forgone potential tax shield benefits for the firms and higher cost of capital.

However, the possibility for debt financing would increase if the firms may instead offer their patents as bank collateral (e.g., Neumyer 2008; Hall and Lerner 2010; Fischer and Ringler 2014). For example, Loumioti (2012) finds that using intangible assets as collateral increases loan size by 18%. Chava et al. (2017) show that highly cited patents help innovative firms to secure more debt financing (see, also, Chava et al. 2013). Bracht (2017) provides evidence that small and young firms in Sweden secure bank loans by using patents as collateral. More specifically, they find that five-year-old or younger firms with no more than 50 employees are among the firms with the highest number of pledged patents in Sweden. This is particularly true for firms operating in the technical fields of medical technology and civil engineering. Mann (2018) finds that 38% of US patenting firms had patent-backed loans in 2013 or earlier and 16% of the patents registered in USA have been pledged in return for receiving capital (e.g., see Loumioti 2012). Bracht and Czarnitzki (2022) show that patent pledging significantly increases debt financing, i.e., Dutch and Swedish patent pledging firms have on average 34% and 20% more debt than a matched sample of non-pledging firms, respectively.

On the one hand, the use of patents as bank collateral is problematic since patent valuation is challenging and there exists no established secondary market where patents could be traded. As both patent valuation and liquidation is difficult, financial intermediaries like banks tend to restrict the use of patents as collateral (see Fischer and Ringler 2014; Hochberg et al. 2014). On the other hand, financial institutions with expertise in assessing intangible assets may solve this information asymmetry problem and supply credit to firms active in the market of ideas (cf. Gans and Stern 2010). We find that not all banks in our sample accept patent collaterals to provide credit, i.e., more specialized banks seem to lend more to these types of firms. The emergence of an efficient patent-backed loan market is determined by several factors, such as the patent act, the enforcement of intellectual property, the quality of patents, the characteristics of the borrower, and the rights of creditors to collateral (e.g., Harhoff et al. 2003).

We present a theoretical model of the effectiveness of intangible assets as securities used for collateralization. This may also minimize the credit rationing problem among innovative firms that lack tangible assets. More specifically, credit rationing occurs when a financial institution or interme-diary, such as a bank, refuses to supply credit to a borrower (firm), even at a higher lending rate than that posted by lenders (Jaffe and Russell 1976; Stiglitz and Weiss 1981; Bester and Hellwig 1987; Calomiris and Kahn 1991). Credit rationing is an equilibrium outcome determined by the information asymmetry between the lender and the borrower (see Jaffe and Russell 1976). In this context, the bank, although being a profit-maximizing agent, rations credit and therefore creates unsatisfied credit demand at the lending rate posted by itself. Apart from other market imperfections, credit rationing might appear because of imperfect information in loan markets (Stiglitz and Weiss 1981), bank's insufficient capital (Holmström and Tirole 1997), bank's capital requirements (Basel Accord), and other criteria for extending credit imposed by regulators (Greenbaum et al. 2016).

Banks are financial institutions heavily regulated by supervisory author-ities. Today's banks have to comply with an ever-increasing number of regulations directly or indirectly restricting their lending capacity. Further, the provision of capital to finance innovation may arise in response to unobservable factors that affect the bank-firm relation. For example, the Basel Accord from the late 1980s is central in the regulatory frame-work and has been revised frequently over the years, particularly in the wake of the 2007–2009 financial crisis. The objective of regulators is to strengthen the soundness of the banking system by ensuring that banks are sufficiently liquid and solid setting aside equity capital to meet finan-cial obligations and other needs. In the Basel Accord, loans to innovative firm's investments in R&D are classified with a high-risk weight requiring the bank to set aside additional equity capital when (if-ever) extending credits to such firms.

One way to mitigate rationing is by increasing collateral requirements as a mechanism to increase the borrower's liability in the event of default (e.g., Besanko and Thakor 1987; Shleifer and Vishny 1992). This reduces the risk undertaken by the lender and may facilitate financing (e.g., Tirole 2005). However, the increase in intangible assets is associated with chal-lenges in the valuation process of patenting firms. The high levels of risk and the uncertainty about future cash flows of intangible assets make it difficult for patenting firms to secure debt financing for realizing an optimal capital structure and thereby minimizing their weighted average cost of capital. Hence, the low tangibility of firms' assets implies a higher opportunity cost of capital, which could also result in less investment in R&D (Amable et al. 2010).

Prior patent literature shows that patents can be, and to some extent are, used as loan collateral to facilitate debt financing (e.g., Loumioti 2012; Mann 2018; Bracht and Czarnitzki 2022). We argue that considering the increasing strategic importance and value of intangibles (Ocean Tomo 2015), valuable patents can be used by banks to separate between good and bad borrowers in need for capital. Such patents can also be used as loan collateral which reduces the level of information asymmetry in the loan market and facilitates bank lending. Patent-backed loans can be used as a contracting mechanism to decrease credit rationing and potentially prevent an under-investment problem caused by too high funding costs after tax.

We contribute to the patent literature by providing a theoretical foundation showing how the information asymmetry (adverse selection problem) between borrowing firms and banks can be solved offering intangible collateral—patent pledging—in addition to tangible collateral. We also try to find empirical evidence that pledged patents have a higher collateral value than other patents and can increase the supply of credit among innovative firms in the Swedish market for loans. We follow the standard approach in the literature matching a treatment group of patent pledging firms with a control group of non-pledging firms based on observable firm characteristics that the bank can use but that does not reveal the individual firm's likelihood of success from future investment in R&D. We apply the propensity score matching (PSM) model to match the treatment with the control group.

Using a simple ordinary least square regression (OLS), we find that patent pledging has a positive relationship with the change in investments in R&D, however this is not statistically significant.[1] In theory, banks can use pledged patents to separate between "good" borrowers and "bad" borrowers, which may increase the availability of capital and decrease credit rationing for innovative firms that lack tangible assets. More specifically, firms able to signal their credit quality by pledging valuable patent portfolios could secure more debt financing and invest more in R&D

---

[1] Note that the number of Swedish firms that have pledged at least one patent to receive debt financing is very small and thus the standard small sample size problems may apply, i.e., problems of reproducibility, false negatives, and reliability (see Wooldridge 2015).

than other firms. This will increase the leverage of firms in the period after patent pledging, which may also imply the emergence of a secondary-type market for ideas based on the characteristics of the patents and collateral types. However, the empirical evidence based on a sample of Swedish patent pledging firms is weak, implying that it is difficult for young firms to secure more debt financing through patent collateralization. Patent valuation and liquidation are difficult, and most banks do not have the knowledge to do so, thus they do not accept patents as collateral (see Fischer and Ringler 2014). The indication of a secondary-type market for ideas is very weak.

This chapter proceeds as follows. Section 11.2 reviews the existing empirical record of patents and patenting firms in Sweden. Section 11.3 presents a model of patent collateralization that may decrease credit rationing. Section 11.4 describes the data and tries to provide empirical evidence for our theoretical propositions. Section 11.5 overviews the main findings and concludes.

11.2   Patents and Patenting Firms in Sweden

Sweden is a highly innovative country with strong intellectual property rights and many start-ups or young patenting firms with at least one patent that can be used as loan collateral. For instance, one may use the number of patents filed by a firm to measure how innovative a firm is implying that the aggregate number of patents filed by Swedish firms can be used as an indicator of Sweden's innovation level (e.g., Griliches 1990). Additionally, the number of patent citations is in general used as a proxy for the quality or risk of patent collateral (Hall et al. 2001).

Bracht (2017) studies patent characteristics that matter for collateralization and provides detailed descriptive statistics of pledged patents and patenting firms in Sweden. The number of pledged patents in Sweden is approximately 600 patents owned by 217 Swedish firms. Overall, the number of patents has been increasing from 1980 until 2007. It then decreased sharply between 2008 and 2010 because of the financial crisis, which led to a drastic decline in the supply of new bank loans (cf. Ivashina and Scharfstein 2010). During this period and for some more years, there was little or no demand for collaterals. Only in the years following 2015, the use of patents as collateral started increasing again in Sweden (see Bracht 2017, Fig. 2), a trend observed also in the US market since 2010 (Mann 2018).

Bracht (2017) focuses only on patents being filed at the Swedish Patent and Registration Office (PRV) during the 1980–2015 period, whereas any missing information for specific patents is complemented using patent data from the database of the European Patent Office (EPO) named PATSTAT.[2] Moreover, the SERRANO database is used to gather additional accounting data for the sample firms, particularly with respect to the patent pledging firms. By matching the patent level data with additional firm level characteristics, Bracht (2017) finds several interesting patterns.

Specifically, the pledged patents on average have a young age, i.e., within a period of five to ten years after the filing date (see, also, Serrano 2006, 2010). Additionally, patents belonging to the same family, i.e., patents in various jurisdictions protecting the same invention, seem to have been pledged significantly more and before the occurrence of collateralization (see, also, Van Zeebroeck 2011). Furthermore, patented innovations related to the same technology, which are protected in various jurisdictions, tend to have a higher value for financing use (e.g., Putnam 1997). This implies that the more firms within an industry that are patenting in the same field, the higher the likelihood of patents being traded and, hence, patents with a higher liquidity.

Also of interest, usually small patent portfolios are pledged to secure credit and most loan applicants have used pledged patents only once. Clearly, patents that have been traded before can be more easily used as collateral as a prior market for their value is already established (Serrano 2006, 2010). The former result indicates the difficulty of accessing the bank loan market through collateralized patents, and that probably only young and small firms rely on such an instrument to access capital, i.e., more than 80% of the firms have less than 50 employees. These new high-risk ventures lack tangible assets and need capital to expand, why they are the ones most affected by capital restrictions (Brown et al. 2009; Hall and Lerner 2010). Consequently, they are more willing to incur higher interest rates for getting bank loans and to pledge intangible assets to overcome capital restrictions.

In a more recent study, Bracht and Czarnitzki (2022) use a sample including information on pledged patents in the Netherlands and Sweden

---

[2] PRV contains patent pledging information, i.e., the date of the patent being pledged, the number of patents pledged per firm, the pledging Swedish firm, and the holders of the pledged patents, which can be matched with other data sources using the unique patent number.

for the periods 1994–2018 and 1997–2018, respectively. They find that although very few firms choose to pledge patents to access capital, patent pledging has increased debt financing significantly, i.e., by 34% more for Dutch firms and about 20% more for Swedish firms, implying that collateralized patents may help firms to access more debt. They did also find that the increase in debt was delayed by an on average of three years after patents have been pledged. Notably, although Swedish pledging firms being larger in terms of employees and total assets than Dutch pledging firms, it seems that the latter can increase their debt level more by pledging patents.

11.3   Patent Collateralization for Receiving Debt Financing

11.3.1   Theoretical Framework

It is evident that, over the years, the largest firms by market capitalization have increased their reliance on intangible assets and decreased their investment in tangible assets, such as property, plant, and equipment (Steijvers and Voordeckers 2009; Eisfeldt and Papanikolaou 2014; Kahle and Stulz 2017). The continuous increasing proportion of intangible assets as compared to tangible asset for S&P 500 companies from 17% (1975) to 84% (2015) (Ocean Tomo 2015) re-positions the significance of lending through patent-backed debt in the economic literature. We focus only on the use of patents as loan collateral because patenting reflects a stronger tangibility property of intellectual property than other assets do. Patent portfolios often represent firm's most valuable assets and as such enable these firms to pledge these assets to increase the availability of debt financing and potentially increase firm's return on investment.

Innovative firms that do not have valuable tangible assets are usually unable to secure debt financing, which in turn may raise their cost of capital (e.g., Brown et al. 2009; Hall and Lerner 2010; Harhoff 2011; Czarnitzki and Hottenrott 2011; Hall and Harhoff 2012). For many of these firms, bank lending may be the only option. This financing problem is commonly referred to as credit rationing, i.e., unsatisfied credit demand even at sufficiently high lending rates posted by banks (Jaffe and Russell 1976; Stiglitz and Weiss 1981; Bester and Hellwig 1987). To overcome these capital restrictions, firms may pledge their intangible assets to secure capital to invest in innovation.

However, patent valuation is very uncertain since patents derive their value from future cash flows that can be very risky and highly uncertain. Hence, investments in R&D are difficult to value and to be transferred to the creditors (like banks) in the case of default. In addition, an increase of investments in R&D will affect expenses and result in a higher firm leverage in accounting (book) values, which may increase the likelihood of distress and bankruptcy (Kahle and Stulz 2017). Moreover, patents are seldom valuable and cannot always be used as collateral (e.g., Gambardella et al. 2006; Harhoff 2011).

The collateralization of patentable investment in R&D, i.e., patent-backed loans, can be used to overcome firms' capital restrictions and minimize information asymmetries between debt providers and borrowers (e.g., Hall and Lerner 2010; Bracht 2017; Mann 2018). In this context, the ownership of the patent collateral is transferred to the lender to be liquidated. One of the main features of collaterals is the liquidation value of the pledged asset (Shleifer and Vishny 1992; Diamond and Rajan 2001). Patents of higher quality and liquidation value may result in more debt financing, because of higher collateral value (Chava et al. 2017; Farre-Mensa et al. 2020). Clearly, there are also other credit features of the borrower that may influence debt financing through the quality of the pledged assets (i.e., firm's historical background, profitability, leverage, market share, and future growth opportunities).

In addition, patent pledgeability also reveals information about the project and the firm's probability of default. This aligns borrowing firms' incentives to those of the lender, which can in turn reduce the adverse selection problem or the risk of the lender investing in an unprofitable project. The borrower does also incur the risk of losing the patented technology under an adverse scenario and, thus, has more incentives to perform or behave. This reduces the moral hazard problem or the risk of bearing high financial risk. Overall, patent pledgeability reduces the level of information asymmetry between the counterparties and may in that way affect debt financing, i.e., more debt financing implies less credit rationing for innovative firms. On the one hand, firms with weak patent portfolios, and thereby low-quality collateral, need to offer more collateral to increase the availability of credit. This also applies to firms with more credit constraints and lower profitability (e.g., Bracht 2017; Bracht and Czarnitzki 2022). On the other hand, firms with valuable patents, and thereby high-quality collateral, may overcome a potential credit rationing problem and secure more debt financing to better loan pricing terms.

Last, patent collateralization and debt financing affect the leverage of firms. Highly levered firms have a higher likelihood of financial distress or default than other firms, why a highly levered firm may need to pledge more collateral in order to gain capital (Kahle and Stulz 2017). However, empirical evidence shows that innovative firms, which lack tangible assets but have projects that require investment in R&D, are less levered than less innovative firms (Hall and Lerner 2010). Leverage is an indicative measure of firm's ability to repay its debt with respect to the likelihood of default. It can be measured using the debt-to-equity ratio or the debt-to-total-assets ratio, which are financial risk measures of the firm based on accounting data. Considering that patent-backed debt may be more risky than debt secured by tangible collateral, banks, and other lenders require pledged patents as additional collateral to extend credit to borrowing firms with few tangible assets in place (Loumioti 2012). Hence, debt covered by fixed assets and patents may be preferable to other forms of collateralized debt.

11.3.2   The Model

Consider an innovative firm (a borrower) with an idea or project that requires an investment $I > 0$ to be undertaken. The borrower may either be of a good type, i.e., having a probability of success p or of a bad type, i.e., having a probability of success q, where $1 \geq p > q \geq 0$.[3] The idea or project may either succeed and yield an income or rent equal to $R > 0$, or fail and yield no income. In the case of success, both parties share the income R, i.e., R_b for the borrower and R_l for the lender in terms of interest payments with respect to the share of loans and, thus, the debt to equity financing of the investment. Assume that the banks are competitive and know the project types, which have both a positive NPV. If the project is good, then the bank solves $pR_l^G = I$, which is equivalent to $R_l^G = I/p$. The utility of the borrower with a good idea can then be shown to be $U_b^G = pR_b^G = p(R - R_l^G) = p(R - I/p) = pR - I$. The same analysis can be used to derive the utility of the bad borrower. More specifically, for a bad project the bank solves $qR_l^B = I \leftrightarrow R_l^B = I/q$. This

---

[3] This model is a refinement of Holmström and Tirole (1997)'s model, which is also developed to describe numerous credit rationing situations in Tirole (2005).

results to $U_b^B = qR_b^B = q(R - R_l^B) = q(R - I/q) = qR - I$. It is evident that $U_b^G > U_b^B$, meaning that good projects or ideas receive more surplus.

Suppose that the bank knows the proportion of good firms or borrowers in the market, i.e., α, then the average probability of success is $m = \alpha p + (1 - \alpha)q$. Consequently, the net expected return from a project is $mR - I$. Let $pR - I > qR - I > 0$, then it is optimal that both types obtain debt and equity financing. Particularly, the bank will choose R_l such that $mR_l = I$ and since $p > m > q$, then $m(R - R_l) = mR - I > 0$. This implies that both types of borrowers will get financed according to the same contract (pooling equilibrium). It can also be shown that $U_b^G = p(R - R_l) = pR - p(I/m) < pR - I$ and $U_b^B = q(R - R_l) = pR - q(I/m) > qR - I$. This result suggests that although the good type subsidizes the bad type of borrowers, market efficiency is achieved.

Let $pR - I > 0 > qR - I$, then the equilibrium is determined from the value of parameter α. In particular, as α approaches zero, the average probability of success m approaches q and thus $mR - I \to qR - I < 0$. Similarly, as α approaches 1, the average probability of success m approaches p and thus $mR - I \to pR - I > 0$. These results imply that there exists α^* such that $mR - I \geq 0$ for $1 \geq \alpha \geq \alpha^*$ and $mR - I < 0$ for $\alpha^* > \alpha \geq 0$. In this context, if $1 \geq \alpha \geq \alpha^*$ then both types get funded, whereas if $\alpha^* > \alpha > 0$ then no borrower receives debt financing. The abovementioned equilibrium outcomes are both inefficient in terms of aggregate surplus.

Let us now introduce collateral and analyze whether pledging collateral may help a good borrower to differentiate itself from a bad borrower. First, let $\tilde{V} \equiv qR - I < pR - I \equiv V$ and assume symmetric information, where $R_l^G = I/p$ and $R_l^B = I/q$. This implies $U_b^G = p(R - R_l^G) = V$ and $U_b^B = q(R - R_l^B) = \tilde{V}$. These relationships under asymmetric information will change since $R_l^G = R_l^B = R_l = I/m$. Evidently, $U_b^G < V$, whereas $U_b^B > \tilde{V}$, meaning that the good borrower is worst off while the bad borrower is better off than his corresponding situations under symmetric information. Second, let the borrower pledge an intangible asset like a patent worth C as collateral, i.e., such that the collateral is valued according to the borrower and aims to facilitate the borrower to secure financing to undertake the investment in the idea or project described above. The lender, however, being more efficient in assessing intangible property values the borrower's patent βC for $0 < \beta < 1$, i.e., the lender values the collateral at a discounted price. The problem that the good borrower should now solve is:

$$\max_{\{R_b, C\}} [p R_b - (1 - p)C] \tag{11.1}$$

s.t

$$q R_b - (1 - q)C \leq \tilde{V} \tag{11.2}$$

$$p(R - R_b) + (1 - p)\beta C \geq I \tag{11.3}$$

where Eq. 11.3 is the individual rationality condition and thus should be binding at the optimum. Equation 11.2 should also be binding since it ensures that the bad type does not mimic the good type. The solution of the optimization problem is equal to

$$C^* = \frac{I}{1 + q(1 - p)\left(\frac{1-\beta}{p-q}\right)} \tag{11.4}$$

This results to an optimal income for the borrower equal to

$$R_b^* = R - \left[\frac{(1-q) - \beta(1-p)}{p(1-q) - \beta q(1-p)}\right] I > R_b^G \tag{11.5}$$

Equation 11.5 implies that it is in the interest of the good type of borrower to offer patents as collateral. It can also be shown that the good type of borrower prefers using patents as collateral to separate from the bad type if and only if $p R_b^* - (1 - p)C^* \geq p(R - I/m)$, which is equivalent to $(p/m - 1)I > (1 - p)(1 - \beta)C^*$. This result also suggests that pledging collateral is costly to both types, because of the loss of value if the collateral is transferred to the lender in case of trouble. However, the cost of collateral is lower for the good type than for the bad type, because the good type has a lower probability of failure (i.e., $p > q$). This is why a good type of borrower prefers to pledge patents as collateral to separate itself from a bad type. In this case, the lender also benefits from the signaling value of patents since adverse selection is reduced. Patent pledgeability can in fact be used as a contracting device to mitigate the rationing problem of credit demand being unsatisfied in the market for bank loans.[4]

We have shown that pledging patents have a higher collateral value than other patents and can also facilitate bank lending. This may reduce credit rationing among innovative firms competing in bank loan markets. We also try to provide empirical evidence of the theoretical propositions by exploring cross-sectional differences in securing debt financing between patent pledging firms and non-pledging firms, and how this relates to credit rationing. We find a positive relationship between patent pledging and investments in R&D, implying an increased supply of credit in loan markets. However, the results are not statistically significant, and thus further empirical analysis and a larger sample of patent pledging firms are needed to study this issue.

11.4   DATA AND EMPIRICAL ANALYSIS

11.4.1   Data

We focus on the Swedish patent market, specifically to patents filed by Swedish firms at the Swedish Intellectual Property Office (PRV) and the European Patent Office (EPO). We use three different data sources to construct a database used to test the theoretical propositions established from the analysis.

The information about our patent data comes from the PRV, which also provides information about all Swedish patents pledged in Sweden. This source contains data on the date the pledge was granted, the applicant at the time of pledge, the pledge holder, and the institution type of the pledge holder. All pledged patents owned by entities other than Swedish firms have been excluded from the sample. Also, all patents filed by Swedish firms to patent authorities other than Sweden and the EPO have been excluded from the sample. These data also include the patent identifier number and are matched with data from the Patlink and the SERRANO database to match patent information and accounting, financial information on the patenting firms.

---

[4] We can also show that a contingent pledge dominates the non-contingent pledge, i.e., transferring the ownership of the pledged patent only in case of failure is superior, in terms of lower collateral requirements, to transferring the patent regardless of the outcome of the project (see Tirole 2005).

Patlink includes all patents belonging to Swedish firms from 1990 to 2018, where the patent data are extracted from PATSTAT, the EPO's patent database containing patent data from all developed and emerging economies, and the firms' organization numbers are extracted from the SERRANO database. The SERRANO database has information on the historical accounting data extracted from the yearly financial statements of all patenting Swedish firms. More specifically, SERRANO is a controlled and quality assured database, which is aimed for research purposes since it contains information on all Swedish firms (public and private). These data source includes a unique firm identifier number (organization number) for Swedish firms determined by the Swedish Tax Office (Skatteverket), which is used to match the historical firm level data to the patent level data and identify the patent pledging firms. The unbalanced data panel stretches for the period 1998–2019. Table 11.1 reports the descriptive statistics for the final sample of Swedish firms used in the analysis.

11.4.2   The Research Design

The data on patents include in total 1055 pledged patents at 436 different occasions. This means that many firms often pledge more than one patent. We are able to match only 423 pledged patents to the Patlink database that includes organization number and the unique patent application number. In a next step, we merge these 432 pledged patents with the SERRANO data. This results in 152 unique firm year observations of firms with at least on pledged patent. We construct a propensity score matching (PSM) on the 152 firm year observations with the total set of companies in the SERRANO database (over 1 million firm year observations). The variables used for matching are the firms' total assets, net sales, tangible assets, intangible assets, and the ratio of intangible assets over total assets. The latter variable controls for firms' reliance on intellectual capital. This is a normalization of the total collateral value available for a firm (collateral capacity) compared to a firm's total value. This results in 145 untreated firm year observation that matched with the 152 treated firms. Hence, 7 observations are matched twice with the group of firms with pledged patents, resulting in a final total sample of 304 firm year observations.

To test our theoretical prediction that "good" borrowers use patents as collateral to receive debt financing, which is very costly for "bad" borrowers to mimic, we use the group of 304 treated and untreated

Table 11.1 Descriptive statistics of key variables

Variable	Patent pledging firms					Non-pledging firms				
	N	Min	Mean	Max	SD	N	Min	Mean	Max	SD
Change in inv R&D	440	−33,690	969.5	55,067	9810	133	−41,283	−744.47	5775	4374
Change in inv R&D (%)	52	−1	1.7948	76	10.8	33	−1	−0.282	0.656	0.404
Cut	152	0	0.1842	1	0.389	145	0	0.158	1	0.366
Leverage	152	−0.0149	0.8055	25.33	2.038	144	0	1.28	71.6	6.143
Pledged pat	152	1	1	1	0	145	0	0	0	0
Log net sales	132	0.6931	10.05	17.62	3.588	122	1.946	9.73	17.89	3.225
EBIT per tang ass	119	−137.82	−8.33	103.06	33.638	28,5	−2.30	8.77	13.05	2.15

Table 11.1 reports the descriptive statistics on the Swedish firms used in the analysis. Specifically, Table 11.1 reports the following summary statistics for the patent pledging and non-pledging firms: the number of observations, mean, standard deviation, and the minimum and maximum values per variable in the sample

firm year observations. The choice of variables follows the reasoning in Bushee (1998), investigating how institutional investors affect a firm's R&D activity. Specifically, we estimate the following model:

$$
\begin{aligned}
\text{Change in inv R\&D (\%)} = {} & \text{Leverage} + \text{Leverage} \times \text{Pledged pat} \\
& + \text{Pleadged pat} + \text{Log net sales (\%)} \\
& + \text{EBIT per tang ass} + \varepsilon,
\end{aligned}
$$

where the dependent variable is a firm's percentage change in investments in R&D the year after pledging a patent as collateral ((Inv R&D$_{t+1}$ − Inv R&D$_t$)/Inv R&D$_{t+1}$), and the main independent variable is firms' leverage ((Total assets$_t$ − Equity$_t$)/Total assets$_t$). The capital expenditure in R&D measures investments that aim at gaining new scientific or technical knowledge. Firms with a recognized patent portfolio (with high patent quality, with high number of granted patents, or with a strong patent family size) and with new high-quality patents recently filed should, ceteris paribus, be less capital constrained and, hence, more leveraged. We argue that considering the objective of pledging patents as collateral, more leverage implies more investment in R&D. Hence, we expect to find differences in the investments in R&D between pledging firms and other firms.

We assign the dummy pledged patent (Pledged pat) as 1 if the firm year observation includes a pledged patent. We argue that patents can be used by banks to separate between "good" and "bad" borrowers, i.e., pledged patents signal a higher collateral and patent value. An interaction term between the leverage and the pledged patent dummy is used to find the effect of increased debt and patent collateralization. Established firms may have debt capacity to cover future investment needs. The interaction term will isolate if it is pledged patents that initiate the R&D investments. We claim that patent pledging facilitates financing for firms with investment opportunities which in turn implies more investment in R&D. Firms with less investment opportunities will to a higher degree secure financing for other reasons than R&D activity. The control variables are firms' logarithm of net sales (Log net sales) and the ratio of earnings before income and tax (EBIT) over the tangible assets of the firms (EBIT per tang ass).

In an alternative model, we test if a cut (Cut) in capital expenditures in R&D (Bushee 1998) is related to our independent variables. This dummy takes the value of 1 if the capital expenditures in R&D are less than the previous year and is a proxy for a firm's realized investment opportunities.

A cut in R&D investments may be considered a stronger signal on "bad" prospects. Firms having patents of high-quality, high stand-alone value, and that may be realized into positive investment opportunities, will take on investment in R&D to a higher degree compared to firms not being able to pledge their patents. For example, EBIT scaled by tangible assets is a proxy for lack of funds available for investment in future growth and should be negatively related to a cut in capital expenditures in R&D.

11.5   RESULTS AND CONCLUSION

In this chapter, we analyze whether banks can use patents to separate between "good" and "bad" borrowers to infer to the relationship between patent pledging and bank lending. Prior literature shows that patents can be used to support innovative firms in securing debt loans and overcome financial constraints (Hall and Lerner 2010; Hirshleifer et al. 2012; Hsu et al. 2015). More specifically, we argue that patenting firms may secure more debt financing and better borrowing terms than non-patenting firms. This is because patents can be used as collateral to secure credit for investments in R&D and reduce the adverse selection problem. This also implies that pledged patents may have a higher quality and collateral value than patents filed but not accepted for collateralization. We also argue that patent pledging may mitigate credit rationing, i.e., induce banks and other lending institutions to provide capital to innovative firms, and scale-up investment in innovation. This may drive more firms to use patents for collateralization and undertake risky projects.

Accounting practices should also reflect to incorporate the increasing importance of the value of intangibles for firms and their use to access capital markets. Our theoretical model shows that banks can rely on patents to separate between "good" and "bad" borrowers (i.e., the signaling value of patents) and also that pledging patents leads to increased debt financing. In fact, the objective of patent collateralization is to raise capital with an aim to invest more in R&D, thus we suggest that patent pledging can increase the supply of bank loans and mitigate the credit rating problem faced by young firms that lack tangible assets. A reduced credit rationing effect may lead to more investment in innovation and more growth.

Using a sample of Swedish firms, we expect to find significant differences in the investments in R&D between patent pledging firms and non-pledging firms. However, there is only weak empirical evidence that in fact banks use patents to screen borrowers. Table 11.2 presents the results from our baseline model testing the main hypothesis, whether there are cross-sectional differences in bank lending between patent pledging firms and non-pledging firms. We find a positive relationship between patent pledging and the change in investments in R&D; however, this is not statistically significant. This result does not alter even when we use the cut (Cut) in capital expenditures in R&D (Bushee 1998) as our dependent variable, or when we try different refinements of the dependent variable and control variables.[5] However, in the latter model leverage is statistically significant at the 1% level, implying that more leverage leads firms to invest more in R&D, i.e., to not cut capital expenditure in R&D.

Table 11.2 The relationship between patent pledging and investments in R&D

Variable	(1) Change in inv R&D (%)	(2) Change in inv R&D (%)	(3) Cut	(4) Cut
Leverage	−0.1140072	0.561606	−0.0024745***	−0.0075544
	(0.2208)	(0.5717)	(0.0007)	(0.9620)
Leverage × Pledged pat	1.855499	8.867843	0.0014403	0.0315448
	(2.2421)	(7.3615)	(0.0074)	(0.1533116)
Pledged pat	0.7744995	−3.070459	−0.0116808	−0.0116808
	(1.1840)	(2.9161)	(0.1164)	(0.1163)
Log net sales		−0.2834224		−0.0014303
		(0.3274)		(0.0073)
EBIT per tang ass		0.0135191		0.0000181
		(0.0139)		(0.0002)
Constant	−0.2160637	2.469651	0.01628904***	0.2177292**
	(0.1717)	(3.0867)	(0.3132)	(0.1063)
Observations	84	74	296	227

Table 11.2 reports the results from regressions with Change in inv R&D (%) and Cut as dependent variables. Column 1 reports the results of the baseline model, while Column 2 also includes the control variables Log net sales and EBIT per tangible assets. Column 3 reports the results of the model with Cut as the dependent variable following Bushee (1998). In Column 4, we amend the latter model with the standard control variables. The standard errors are robust. ***, **, and * indicate significance at the 1, 5, and 10% level, respectively

[5] The latter results are untabulated and available upon request.

In general, banks do not issue loans to innovative firms based on patent collateral. This may occur due to several reasons. First, the number of pledging firms in Sweden is very small because mostly young and small firms rely on patent collateralization to receive debt financing. Second, most banks do not have the necessary expertise to value patents and their liquidity, and thus restrict bank financing. Third, the objective of patent collateralization is to invest in new high-risk projects, and banks are not willing to accept this risk shifting even at higher lending rates than those posted by themselves. Patent-backed debt may be riskier than standard collateralized debt, and thus banks and other lenders require pledged patents in addition to tangible collateral to extend credit. However, these borrowing firms have few tangible assets in place and thus are unable to secure debt financing (Loumioti 2012). Taken together, these arguments imply that there exists no secondary-type market where patents could be traded (cf. Andersson and Tell 2018).

Venture capital-backed patents might also matter for collateralization given the certification and signaling role of the VCs as intermediaries. It should be noted that we do not consider firms that in the past have shown inefficient investments in R&D, which will very likely affect firms' ability to secure debt financing. Clearly, the opposite is true for successful firms. Moreover, we do not have data on the amount of loans raised using patent collateral. This may provide information about patent valuation and the patent characteristics that drive bank's loan granting behavior. Finally, it would have been interesting to increase the sample size to include other innovative countries and to replicate this analysis to other intangible assets, such as copyrights. However, unlike patents that are sold or transferred regularly in bankruptcy proceedings, other intangible assets are not that liquid to act upon. Establishing an online platform or market to trade intangible property would enhance their liquidity being an interesting development in the evolution of intellectual property literature.

REFERENCES

Amable, B., Chatelain, J. and Ralf, K. 2010. Patents as collateral. *Journal of Economic Dynamics and Control* 34 (6), 1092–1104.

Andersson, D. and Tell, F. 2018. The market for patents in Sweden: Past and present. *Stockholm Intellectual Property Law Review* 1 (2), 6–17.

Besanko, D. and Thakor, A. 1987. Collateral and rationing: Sorting equilibria in monopolistic and competitive credit markets. *International Economic Review* 28 (3), 671–689.

Bester, H. and Hellwig, M. 1987. Moral hazard and equilibrium credit rationing: An overview of the issues. *Agency theory, information, and incentives*. 135–166.

Bracht, F. 2017. Patents as loan collateral in Sweden: An empirical analysis of what patent characteristics matter for collateralization.

Bracht, F. and Czarnitzki, D. 2022. Patent collateral and access to debt. ZEW - Centre for European Economic Research Discussion Paper No. 22-033. Available at: https://ssrn.com/abstract=4217986.

Brown, J, Fazzari, S. and Petersen, B. 2009. Financing innovation and growth: Cash flow, external equity, and the 1990s R&D boom. *The Journal of Finance* 64 (1), 151–185.

Bushee, B. 1998. The influence of institutional investors on myopic R&D investment behavior. *The Accounting Review* 73 (3), 305–333.

Calomiris, C. and Kahn, C. 1991. The role of demandable debt in structuring optimal banking arrangements. *The American Economic Review* 81 (3), 497–513.

Chava, S., Nanda, V. and Xiao, S. 2017. Lending to innovative firms. *The Review of Corporate Finance Studies* 6 (2), 234–289.

Chava, S., Oettl, A., Subramanian, A. and Subramanian, K. 2013. Banking deregulation and innovation. *Journal of Financial Economics* 109 (3), 759–774.

Czarnitzki, D. and Hottenrott, H. 2011. R&D investment and financing constraints of small and medium-sized firms. *Small Business Economics* 36 (1), 65–83.

Diamond, D. and Rajan, R. 2001. Liquidity risk, liquidity creation, and financial fragility: A theory of banking. *Journal of Political Economy* 109 (2), 287–327.

Eisfeldt, A. and Papanikolaou, D. 2014. The value and ownership of intangible capital. *The American Economic Review* 104 (5), 189–194.

Farre-Mensa, J., Hegde, D. and Ljungqvist, A. 2020. What is a patent worth? Evidence from the US patent "Lottery". *The Journal of Finance* 75 (2), 639–682.

Fischer, T. and Ringler, P. 2014. What patents are used as collateral? An empirical analysis of patent reassignment data. *Journal of Business Venturing* 29 (5), 633–650.

Gambardella, A., Harhoff, D. and Verspagen, B. 2006. The value of patents. Paper presented at the EPIP Conference. Munich, Germany.

Gans, J. and Stern, S. 2010. Is there a market for ideas? *Industrial and Corporate Change* 19 (3), 805–837.

Greenbaum, S., Thakor, A. and Boot, A. 2016. *Contemporary financial intermediation*. Academic Press.

Griliches, Z. 1990. Patent statistics as economic indicators: A survey. *Journal of Economic Literature* 28 (4), 1661–1707.

Hall, B. and Harhoff, D. 2012. Recent research on the economics of patents. *Annual Review of Economics* 4 (1), 541–565.

Hall, B. and Lerner, J. 2010. The financing of R&D and innovation. In *Handbook of the Economics of Innovation* 1, 609–639. North-Holland.

Hall, B., Jaffe, A. and Trajtenberg, M. 2001. The NBER patent citation data file: Lessons, insights and methodological tools. NBER Working Paper.

Harhoff, D. 2011. The role of patents and licenses in securing external finance for innovation. *Handbook of Research on Innovation and Entrepreneurship* 55.

Harhoff, D., Scherer, F. and Vopel, K. 2003. Citations, family size, opposition and the value of patent rights. *Research Policy* 32 (8), 1343–1363.

Hirshleifer, D., Hsu, P. and Li, D. 2012. Innovative efficiency and stock returns. *Journal of Financial Economics* 107 (3), 632–654.

Hochberg, Y., Serrano, C. and Ziedonis, R. 2014. Patent collateral, investor commitment, and the market for venture lending. NBER Working Paper.

Holmström, B. and Tirole, J. 1997. Financial intermediation, loanable funds, and the real sector. *The Quarterly Journal of Economics* 112 (3), 663–691.

Hsu, P., Lee, H., Liu, A. and Zhang, Z. 2015. Corporate innovation, default risk, and bond pricing. *Journal of Corporate Finance* 35, 329–344.

Ivashina, V. and Scharfstein, D. 2010. Bank lending during the financial crisis of 2008. *Journal of Financial Economics* 97 (3), 319–338.

Jaffe, D. and Russell, T. 1976. Imperfect information, uncertainty, and credit rationing. *The Quarterly Journal of Economics* 90 (4), 651–666.

Kahle, K. and Stulz, R. 2017. Is the US public corporation in trouble? *The Journal of Economic Perspectives* 31 (3), 67–88.

Loumioti, M. 2012. The use of intangible assets as loan collateral. Working paper. The University of Texas at Dallas.

Mann, W. 2018. Creditor rights and innovation: Evidence from patent collateral. *Journal of Financial Economics* 130 (1), 25–47.

Neumyer, D. 2008. Future of using intellectual property and intangible assets as collateral. *The Secured Lender* 64 (1), 42–48.

Ocean Tomo. 2015. The intangible asset market value. Ocean Tomo LLC. Available at: https://www.oceantomo.com/insights/ocean-tomo-releases-2015-annual-study-of-intangible-asset-market-value/.

Petersen, M. and Rajan, R. 1994. The benefits of lending relationships: Evidence from small business data. *The Journal of Finance* 49 (1), 3–37.

Putnam, J. 1997. *The value of international patent rights.* Yale University.

Serrano, C. 2006. *The market for intellectual property: Evidence from the transfer of patents.* University of Minnesota. PhD Thesis.

Serrano, C. 2010. The dynamics of the transfer and renewal of patents. *The RAND Journal of Economics* 41 (4), 686–708.

Shleifer, A. and Vishny, R. 1992. Liquidation values and debt capacity: A market equilibrium approach. *The Journal of Finance* 47 (4), 1343–1366.

Steijvers, T. and Voordeckers, W. 2009. Collateral and credit rationing: A review of recent empirical studies as a guide for future research. *Journal of Economic Surveys* 23 (5), 924–946.

Stiglitz, J. and Weiss, A. 1981. Credit rationing in markets with imperfect information. *The Economic Review* 71 (3), 393–410.

Tirole, J. 2005. *The theory of corporate finance*. Princeton University Press. Princeton and Oxford.

Van Zeebroeck, N. 2011. The puzzle of patent value indicators. *Economics of Innovation and New Technology* 20 (1), 33–62.

Wooldridge, J. 2015. *Introductory econometrics: A modern approach*. Cengage learning.

CHAPTER 12

Increasing the Predictive Power of Financial Distress models—The Case of the New Alert System Proposed by the Italian Nccaae

Federico Beltrame, *Giulio Velliscig*, *Gianni Zorzi*,
and Maurizio Polato

12.1   Introduction

The outbreak of the COVID-19 pandemic brought financial distress prediction methods under the spotlight for a close scrutiny as traditional predictive frameworks may poorly perform facing the volatile and evolving pandemic and economic scenario.

This question gains in relevance as the pandemic poses a serious threat to the resilience of small and medium-sized enterprises (SMEs) which represent the backbone of the European economy. SMEs are

F. Beltrame · G. Velliscig · M. Polato
University of Udine, Udine, Italy
e-mail: federico.beltrame@uniud.it

G. Velliscig
e-mail: giulio.velliscig@uniud.it

S. Carbó-Valverde and P. J. Cuadros Solas (eds.), *New Challenges for the Banking Industry*, Palgrave Macmillan Studies in Banking and Financial Institutions, https://doi.org/10.1007/978-3-031-32931-9_12

indeed prevalent in those sectors which have been hardest hit by the pandemic such as retail, hospitality, food services, entertainment services and construction activities (Albaz et al. 2020).

On the one hand, the decrease in consumer spending has negatively affected SME's profitability whereas, on the other hand, the disruption of the supply chain has caused shortages of the raw materials, goods and parts that are essential for SMEs to produce their goods and services.

In addition, the bank-based financing of SMEs, together with the loose monetary policy and regulatory forbearance further complicate the picture by raising the specter of zombie firms.

The undermined SMEs' resilience and the pandemic's evolution resume therefore the need for a revision of financial distress prediction methods better suited to navigate the pandemic.

This paper develops and tests an alternative measure to the alert system elaborated by the NCCAAE which combines the benefits of the Z-score's multivariate discriminant model with the background employed to develop the NCCAAE' predictors.

The Legislative Decree n.14 of 01/12/2019 introduced in the Italian national law the new Code of Business Crisis and Insolvency (CBCI) which will enter into force starting from 1st September 2021. The new Code represents a major overhaul of the Italian Bankruptcy Law as it grounds on a prevention and recovery framework which should prevent a firm to incur into insolvency. In this regard, the main difference with the previous legislative framework consists with an approach designed to preserve the know-how, the expertise and the level of employment related to an ailing firm instead of simply removing it from the economic fabric. This purpose clearly emerges from the introduction of a set of tools aimed to monitor the viability of a firm in order to pre-empt distress conditions and, in such cases, promptly employ recovery measures in order to avoid reaching insolvency conditions. These tools, disciplined by Art.1 of the CBCI, are required to be elaborated every three years, and in

M. Polato
e-mail: maurizio.polato@uniud.it

G. Zorzi (✉)
Ca' Foscari University, Venice, Italy
e-mail: gianni.zorzi@unive.it

accordance with the sectors identified by the Italian national institute of statistics, by the NCCAAE. This set of tools concurs with the logics above descripted to create the structure of the alert system which, accordingly, scrutinizes a firm's viability following a sequential approach that checks for the violation of each tool's threshold following a hierarchy based on their relevance in terms of distress prediction.

The first tool required to be examined is net equity which, if negative or below the minimum legal threshold, represents a reasonable indication of crisis. If positive, instead, the system requires the analysis of another tool, the Debt Service Coverage Ratio (DSCR), namely a measure of dynamic debt repayment. If this tool does not provide an indication of crisis, then the alert system requires the joint consideration of the following five sector ratios: the interest expenses to revenue ratio; the net equity to total debt ratio; the cash-flow to total assets ratio; the current assets to current liabilities ratio; and the pension and tax debts to total assets ratio. The sector ratios provide a reasonable indication of crisis only if all of them violate their specific thresholds conjunctly. In addition, the CBCI recognizes as crisis indicators two further tools: the reiterated and significative delays in payments and the lack of viability perspectives due to causes different from probable insolvencies.

We, thus, aim to empirically test the financial distress predictive accuracy of the alert system so defined and further compare it to the well-established and widely known Z-score model. In addition, on the basis of the results, we further elaborate and evaluate the revised versions of both approaches, which consist with an alignment of the Z-score to the current socio-economic conditions and an alternative version of the NCCAAE's alert system based on the multivariate discriminant analysis' premises.

We, therefore, contribute to the literature that studies the financial distress prediction developments by contaminating two different approaches to develop a unique predictor.

For the analysis, we use a casual sample of 83 Italian SMEs so distributed: 43 viable firms and 43 non-viable firms. We collected annual firm financial data form the AIDA (Bureau Van Dijk) database over the period 2015–2019.

We, thus, provide an initial analysis of the ex-post application of the alert system designed by the Italian NCCAAE and of the Z-score model to our sample. We break down the analysis by year and tool, or classification output, depending on whether we are considering the alert system or the Z-score, respectively. Further information is provided as regards the timing of the indication of crisis of both approaches. Finally, the confusion matrices of each approach are used to compare the results. Then, we elaborate two multivariate discriminant functions using both the ratios employed to construct the Z-score and the sector ratios developed by the NCCAAE. We, therefore, obtain a modern version of the Z-score and a NCCAE's version of the Z-score. The former is thus compared with its baseline specification by mean of the confusion matrices. Similarly, we compare the NCCAE's version of the Z-score with its previous examined specifications and then we embed it into the alert system framework to obtain the new measure whose financial distress prediction accuracy is finally assessed and compared to its baseline specification.

The first stage of analysis points out contrasting results. Regarding the sample of non-viable firms, the Z-score has a higher accuracy compared to the alert system as the former has correctly identified the financial distress of 41 out of 43 firms in the year before bankruptcy whereas the latter has correctly identified only 33 out of 43. The Z-score model overperforms the alert system also as regards the rapidity of the intervention as the average time between the first signal of distress and actual bankruptcy is 2 years and 4 months for the Z-score whereas 1 year and 6 months for the alert system. Regarding the sample of viable firms, instead, the alert system overperformed the Z-score as the former inaccurately classified as non-viable an average of 15 out of 43 firms per tool in the five years considered whereas the latter classified as non-viable an annual average of 35 out of 43 firms.

The second stage of the analysis, instead, points out an enhanced financial distress predictive accuracy of both the revised Z-score and alert system. Moreover, the NCCAE's version of the Z-score overperforms both the traditional and updated versions of the Z-score correctly classifying 78 out of 86 firms. Finally, when the NCCAE's version of the Z-score is integrated in the new alert system, the resulting measure emerges as best predictor correctly classifying 80 out of 86 firms.

These results have relevant implications for policymakers, managers, investors and creditors. We indeed provided an alternative measure to the alert system developed by the NCCAAE which, combining the benefits of the Z-score's multivariate discriminant function with the background employed to develop the NCCAAE' sector ratios, overperformed its original version and also the famous Z-score, both in its original and enhanced version. As a result, our analysis points out the limits of the alert system as designed by the NCCAAE and suggests an alternative and better performing measure which may be used also by third-party bodies to predict financial distress alternatively to traditional and widely used methods like the Z-score.

The paper is organized as follows: Sect. 12.2 reviews the relevant literature; Sect. 12.3 describes the sample selection strategy and the sample; Sect. 12.4 presents the methodology employed; Sect. 12.5 presents and discusses the results; and Sect. 12.6 concludes.

12.2   Literature Review

Literature does not provide for a univocal and consistently shared definition of financial distress. The decline of a firm's health is indeed a dynamic ongoing process which develops across different stages ranging from early-stage symptoms to bankruptcy (Sun et al. 2014). The financial distress that an enterprise experiences broadly refers to the difficulties in fulfilling certain obligations which generally are related to liquidity or capital issues (Carminchael 1972; Foster 1986; Doumpos and Zopounidis 1999). If not properly addressed, these difficulties may degenerate into the most severe stage of distress, namely bankruptcy, which literature explores under different perspectives: (i) business failure, which refers to the situation when an enterprise is not able to pay the outstanding debt after liquidation; (ii) legal bankruptcy, when an enterprise or its creditors requires a court to initiate a bankruptcy proceeding; (iii) technical bankruptcy, identifies the situation in which an enterprise cannot fulfill the contract on schedule to repay principal and interest; (iv) accounting bankruptcy, when an enterprises' book net assets are negative (Ross et al. 1999). In general, two frameworks are adopted to disentangle the concept of financial distress: the theoretical and the empirical framework. The former considers the intensity of financial distress to identify different degrees of it which range from mere symptoms, such as cash-flow difficulties, to the more severe bankruptcy. The empirical framework instead leads scholars focusing on single criteria in order to clearly identify financial difficulty.

The prediction of a firm's financial distress is core in the decision-making process of several actors such as managers, investors and creditors. Moreover, financial distress prediction is crucial in providing an early warning which should trigger the prompt deployment of recovery strategies aimed at preserving the enterprise from failure. As a result, different contributions have been provided by researchers to the development of financial distress prediction methods which can be generally classified in: (i) pure single classifier methods; (ii) hybrid single classifier methods; (iii) ensemble methods; (iv) dynamic modeling methods; and (v) group decision-making methods.

In detail, pure single classifier methods are divided into: (i) statistical single classifier methods and (ii) artificial intelligence single classifier methods.

Statistical single classifier methods include the single variable analysis, the multivariate discriminant analysis and logit models. The seminal work of Beaver (1966) entitled "Financial Ratios as Predictors of Failure" used the single variable analysis to study the ability of accounting data, i.e., a set of 30 financial ratios, to predict bankruptcy considering a sample of 79 firms over the period 1954–1964. This method allowed to compare the score of a financial ratio of a given firm with that of a benchmark ratio so to discriminate between failed and non-failed firms. Two years later, Altman (1968) employs the multivariate discriminant analysis to predict bankruptcy. Specifically, he developed the Z-score model which is a multivariate linear discriminant function with five financial ratios: working capital to total assets, retained earnings to total assets, earnings before interest and taxes to total assets, market value of equity to total liabilities and sales to total assets. The purpose of discriminant analysis is indeed that of generating a linear combination of variables which best discriminates between failed and non-failed firms. After gaining importance as reliable measure for predicting bankruptcy, the Z-score developed into more refined versions of the original model. The second version of the Z-score is the Z'-score (Altman 1983) which simply replaces the market value of equity with its book value in the fourth ratio so to allow for the prediction of bankruptcy also for non-listed firms which cannot rely on market data. Nevertheless, the fifth ratio, namely sales to total assets, might have caused an industry effect if the sample would have included industries different from manufacturing. From this observation takes shape the third version of the Z-score, namely the Z''-score (Altman 1995), which rules out the ratio of sales to total assets therefore removing the industry effect and allowing for different sectors to be included into the analysis. This model is still in use for predicting bankruptcies both by scholars and practitioners across different sectors and countries (Shaher et al. 2012; Altman et al. 2013, 2017; Chieng 2013; Malik et al. 2016;

Januri et al. 2017; Babatunde et al. 2017; AlAli 2018; AlManaseer and Al-Oshaibat 2018). The logit linear probability model employs the logistic function to make the dependent variable of financial distress probability totally continuous so to fit linear regression analysis and overcome the limits of the multivariate discriminant analysis (Ohlson 1980).

Artificial intelligence single classifier methods include among others: neural networks (Tam 1991; Tam and Kiang 1992); support vector machines (Wang et al. 2005); evolution algorithms (Varetto 1998; Shin and Lee 2002; Kim and Han 2003); case-based reasoning (Li et al. 2011; Li and Sun 2008; 2009, 2010; Borrajo et al. 2011); rough set (Dimitras et al. 1999; McKee, 2000); decision tree including RSP, CART and See 5.0 (Frydman et al. 1985; McKee and Greenstein 2000; Gepp et al. 2010; Li et al. 2010). In general, artificial intelligence methods differ from statistical methods as they are not constrained by statistical assumptions and can fit more complex data sets.

Hybrid single classifier methods, instead, harness the combined use of different techniques to predict financial distress. The most common forms consist with integrating neural networks, support vector machines and case-based reasoning with other techniques.

Regarding ensemble methods, an ensemble system is able to harness each base classifier's unique information for classification. Classifier ensemble, which is also known as combination of multiple classifiers, has proven performing better as regards financial distress prediction. The seminal work on ensemble has been performed by Bates and Granger (1969) whereas the first application to financial distress prediction is to be attributed to Jo and Han (1996).

Dynamic modeling methods use incremental sample data to update financial distress prediction models as times goes on (Sun and Li 2011; Sun et al. 2011, 2013). Depending on whether the sample data that flows in the model is collected from different companies or from different time points of a certain company, the dynamic model is named lateral or longitudinal, respectively. These methods focus on the adaptability of financial distress prediction models to internal and external environmental changes for an enterprise.

Group decision-making methods integrate non-financial information and the expertise of key actors related to the firms to support quantitative financial distress prediction methods.

12.3   Sample Selection Strategy and Description

The sample selection procedure starts with the identification of non-viable firms. From AIDA (Bureau Van Dijk) database, we create this group setting criteria regarding: the legal form, the legal status, the start of the insolvency proceedings, the sector and the availability of balance sheet data for each year of the sample period.

We require the legal form of the firm to be either limited liability company or sole shareholder limited liability company. This criterium matches the characteristics of the Italian socio-economic fabric which mostly consists with small and medium enterprises that adopt the above-mentioned legal forms. We, therefore, ruled out joint stock companies, sole shareholder joint stock companies and limited joint stock partnerships as well as partnerships and sole proprietorships due to the fact that the former are not representative of the Italian business environment whereas the latter are not required to publish the balance sheet therefore the AIDA database does not provide any data for them.

We require the legal status to be bankrupt and rule out every other status involved with recovery proceedings. The existence of the insolvency proceeding has been checked using the creditor's portal of Fallco platform granted by Zucchetti Group.

We require the insolvency proceeding to be started between 1st January 2020 and 30th November 2020.

In order to allow for the application of the sector ratios elaborated by the NCCAAE, our sector criteria include all the sectors classified in the 2007 Ateco codes but the following ones: letter K "Financial and Insurance activities", letter L "Real estate activities", letter O "Public administration and defense, compulsory social insurance", letter T "Activities of households as employers of domestic personnel, production of undifferentiated goods and services for own use of households", letter U "Activities of extraterritorial organizations and bodies".

Finally, we require data availability for each year of the time-period, namely 2015 to 2019.

This procedure resulted in 527 Italian firms. Then, we manually refined the sample ruling out those firms which does not have the financial data necessary to calculate the parameters of both the Z-score and the alert system. At the end of this procedure, the sample counted 322 firms. Then, we have organized firms in descending order according to the total assets as per 2019 accounting value. Thus, we selected the first 43 firms to constitute our sample of non-viable firms.

In order to create the sample of viable firms, we select for each non-viable firm a viable peer comparable in terms of size (i.e., total assets as per 2019 accounting value) and Ateco sector. Regarding the other criteria, the legal form and the availability of balance sheet data follow those set out for the sample of non-viable firms but the legal status in this case is active.

Table 12.1 shows the sector distribution of our sample according to the ISTAT's 2007 Ateco codes. Our sample results characterized by wide sector heterogeneity as it consists with 22 different sectors. The most prevalent sectors are: (i) "manufacture of products in metal" (13,95%); (ii) "wholesale trade" (11,63%); and, at the same level, (iii) "special-ized construction works", "furniture manufacturing" and "restaurant business" (6,98%).

12.4 METHODOLOGY

The analysis develops along two stages: the former compares the appli-cation of the NCCAAE's alert system and the Altman's Z-score to our sample whereas the latter consists in the elaboration of two alternative and refined measures whose financial distress predictive accuracy is assessed to draw conclusions on the most accurate financial distress predictor.

The first stage consists in two steps which describe the implementation and presentation of the results of the NCCAAE's alert system and the Z-score model, respectively.

The first step consists in applying the alert system, as developed by the NCCAAE, to our sample of firms. Of the set of tools elaborated by the NCCAAE, we ruled out the DSCR because of its previsional nature which impedes its calculation using balance sheet data. Therefore, the tools examined by this analysis consist only with the net equity and the five sector ratios. In addition, it is worth to notice that we calculate the pension and tax debts to total assets ratio net of debts already expired in previous business years and not reported in the following balance sheets due to the unavailability of values. We, therefore, strictly follow the approach as designed by the NCCAAE applying to the firms of our sample the net equity tool first, and in case of positive value, further checking for the joint violation of the sector ratios. The objective of the analysis is to evaluate the financial distress predictive accuracy of the alert system by

Table 12.1 Sample's firms according to their relative 2007 Ateco code

2007 Ateco codes	No. of firms	No. of firms (%)
Food industries	2	2.33
Textile industries	4	4.65
Manufacture of other non-metallic mineral products	2	2.33
Metallurgy	2	2.33
Manufacture of products in metal	12	13.95
Manufacture of electrical equipment	2	2.33
Manufacture of nca machinery and equipment	2	2.33
Furniture manufacturing	6	6.98
Other manufacturing industries	2	2.33
Construction of buildings	4	4.65
Specialized construction works	6	6.98
Wholesale and retail trade and repair of motor vehicles and motorcycles	4	4.65
Wholesale trade	10	11.63
Retail trade	4	4.65
Land transport and pipeline transport	4	4.65
Restaurant business	6	6.98
Software production, software production, IT consulting and related activities	2	2.33
Business management and management consulting activities	2	2.33
Activities of architectural and engineering firms; technical testing and analysis	4	4.65
Advertising and market research	2	2.33
Creative, artistic and entertainment activities	2	2.33
Repair of computers of goods for personal and home use	2	2.33
Total	86	100.00

controlling the number of firms correctly classified after its implementation. As we know the legal status a priori, it is indeed possible to observe the wrong indications of crisis in both sub-samples of viable and non-viable firms. Such wrong indications emerge as Type I and Type II errors, namely the case of judging a firm insolvent when it is viable and the opposite, respectively. As a result, our evaluation of the alert system would be higher the less errors the system produces. Results are thus presented distinguishing between viable and non-viable firms and considering each year of the time-period and each tool of the alert system. Results about the timing of the indication of crisis conclude the reporting.

The second step consists in applying the Z-score to our sample of firms. In particular, we apply the Z'-score (Altman, 1983) to firms belonging to the manufacturing sector, namely those firms conducting an activity listed in the Section C of the 2007 Ateco codes, and the Z"-score (Altman, 1995) to the remaining firms.

As introduced in the literature review section, the Z'-score is a multivariate linear discriminant function of five financial ratios so defined:

$$Z' = 0,717X1 + 0,847X2 + 3,107X3 + 0,420X4 + 0,998X5 \quad (12.1)$$

where: X1 is the ratio of working capital to total assets; X2 is the ratio of retained earnings to total assets; X3 is the ratio of earnings before interest and taxes to total assets; X4 is the ratio of book value of equity to total liabilities; and X5 is the ratio of sales to total assets. According to Z'-score, a firm is considered viable for values greater than 2.99 whereas the same firm is considered non-viable for values lower than 1.23. The intermediate values between these two extremes represent the so called grey area which signal uncertainty regarding the viability of the firm. With respect to the original formulation of the Z-score, this version replaces the ratio of market value of equity to total liabilities with the ratio of book value of equity to total liabilities so to also fit those manufacturing firms, on which the original Z-score has been designed, that are not listed.

In a similar vein, the Z"-score further refine the model ruling out the variable X5 which regards the ratio of sales to total assets because of its sensitivity to the firm-specific sector. As a result, the model addresses possible concerns stemming from the sectorial bias. The refined model is as follow:

$$Z'' = 3,25 + 6,56X1 + 3,26X2 + 6,72X3 + 1,05X4 \quad (12.2)$$

where the variables X1, X2, X3 and X4 resembles those of the Z'-score. In addition, as can be noted, this formulation differs from the previous one as regards the weights assigned to each variable, which maximize the medium values of Z among viable and non-viable firms and minimize the within-group variability, and the presence of a constant of 3.25 in order to standardize the Z"-score for values equal or lower than 0. Regarding its specific thresholds, a firm is considered viable for values greater than 6.25 whereas the same firm is considered non-viable for values lower than 4.75. The "grey area" consists, in this case, of those values ranging from 4.75 to

6.25. As a result, we test the financial distress predictive accuracy of the Z-score and present the results coherently with those of the NCCAAs alert system so to provide a consistent framework for the comparison between the two measures.

Finally, the confusion matrices of each approach are used to compare the results.

The second stage consists in two steps which describe the elaboration, application and presentation of the results of the refined version of the Z-score and the NCCAAE's alert system, respectively.

The first step consists in elaborating a new version of the Z-score, which we call Z*-score, aligned with the current socio-economic situation. To this purpose, we use DTREG, a software of predictive modeling to calculate the new coefficients for our model and the cut-off points which enables the classification of firms between viable, non-viable and uncertain (i.e., belonging to the grey area). The software requires the definition of a dependent variable, which in our case is binary and assumes value 1 if the firm is non-viable and 0 otherwise, and a set of independent variables which we retrieve from the Z''-score. The values of the variables refer to the 2018 business year. The software provides, thus, information regarding the accuracy of the model so defined bringing out the Type I and Type II errors and the coefficients to weigh each variable. The resulting Z*-score model is as follows:

$$Z^* = -0,108X1 + 3,291X2 + 6,987X3 - 0,142X4 \tag{12.3}$$

where: X1 is the ratio of working capital to total assets; X2 is the ratio of retained earnings to total assets; X3 is the ratio of earnings before interest and taxes to total assets; and X4 is the ratio of book value of equity to total liabilities. Then, we calculate the new Z*-scores using 2018 accounting data and relate each error to its relative score. The grey area is therefore the interval delimited by the lowest score associated with type I errors and the highest score associated with type II errors. According to the new thresholds, a firm is considered viable for values greater than 0.286 whereas the same firm is considered non-viable for values lower than 0.227. Thus, so defined, we use the new model to calculate the Z*-scores using 2019 accounting data and present the results in form of distribution of firms according to their classification as viable, non-viable and uncertain. Finally, we use the confusion matrices to compare the financial distress predictive accuracy of the new Z*-score to that of the classic Z-scores employed in the first stage.

The second step consists in elaborating a different version of the NCCAAE's alert system with the purpose of combining the NCCAAE's expertise underlying the choice of the predictors with the simplicity, immediacy and synthesis of the Z-score model. Similarly, to the approach deployed in the first step, we use the DTREG software to identify the cut-off points and the coefficients for the new Z-score model which we call Z**-score. The software requires as input a dependent variable, which we model as binary variable assuming value 1 if the firm is non-viable and 0 otherwise, and a set of independent variables, which we retrieve from the five sector ratios elaborated by the NCCAAE. The values of the variables refer to the 2018 business year. The software provides, thus, information regarding the accuracy of the model so defined bringing out the Type I and Type II errors and the coefficients to weigh each variable. The resulting Z**-score model is as follows:

$$Z^{**} = 1,72 + 0,013709X1 + 0,002998X2 - 0,000036X3$$
$$+ 0,041849X4 - 0,045367X5 \tag{12.4}$$

where: X1 is the interest expenses to revenue ratio; X2 is the net equity to total debt ratio; X3 is the cash-flow to total assets ratio; X4 is the current assets to current liabilities ratio; and X5 is the pension and tax debts to total assets ratio. Then, we calculate the new Z**-scores using 2018 accounting data and relate each error to its relative score. The grey area is therefore the interval delimited by the lowest score associated with type I errors and the highest score associated with type II errors. According to the new thresholds, a firm is considered viable for values greater than 1.476 whereas the same firm is considered non-viable for values lower than 1.146. Thus, so defined, we use the new model to calculate the Z**-scores using 2019 accounting data. We present the results in the form of distribution of firms according to their classification as viable, non-viable and uncertain. In addition, we provide the confusion matrix with respect to the other previous specifications of the Z-score examined. We, therefore, design the new alert system which requires the joint interpretation of two measures: the net equity value and the Z**-score. Thus, we develop an interpretative framework that attributes to each combination of both measures' values an alert level which permits us to consider them jointly and assess the predictive accuracy of the new alert system. Therefore, we provide the results of the new alert system according to the interpretative framework and along its confusion matrix with respect to that of its baseline model.

12.5   RESULTS

As regards the first step of the first stage of our analysis, we present the results of the application of the NCCAAE's alert system to our sample of firms.

Table 12.2 reports, for each tool and each year of analysis, the number of non-viable firms for which the specific tool has violated (in red) or not (in green) its relative thresholds. Regarding the net equity, the tool performs good in 2019 indicating as non-viable 33 out of 43 firms in 2019. However, the tool gradually loses its predictive power as time distances from the start of the insolvency proceedings till identifying only one non-viable firm in 2015. Regarding sector ratios, results point out the good performance of the cash-flow to total assets ratio and the pension and tax debts to total assets ratio. In addition, it is worth to notice that, focusing on the results of the net equity to total debt ratio, firms do not suffer from structural issues as signaled firms are always lower than non-signaled firms.

Table 12.3 reports for each tool and each year of analysis, the number of viable firms for which the specific tool has violated (in red) or not (in green) its relative thresholds. The net equity tool only indicates two firms from 2015 to 2016 and one firm from 2017 to 2019 which provide and indication of crisis. Regarding the sector ratios, the cash-flow to total assets ratio and the pension and tax debts to total assets ratio poorly performed as well as the current assets to current liabilities ratio.

Finally, Table 12.4 reports, per each year, the number of viable and non-viable firms which have provided an indication of crisis according to the alert system. As can be noted, the 38,37% of the entire sample have provided an indication of crisis the year before the start of the insolvency proceedings. On the other hand, only one firm has provided an indication of crisis in the 5th year before bankruptcy. As a result, the accuracy of the model decreases the higher the period analyzed.

As regards the second step of the first stage of our analysis, we present the results of the application of the Z-score to our sample of firms. The logic behind the presentation of the results resembles that used in the first step to ease the comparison.

Table 12.2 Non-viable firms according to the compliance or violation of NCCAAE tools' thresholds—Detail per years

Years	Negative value of net equity		The interest expenses to revenue ratio		The net equity to total debt ratio		The current assets to current liabilities ratio		The cash-flow to total assets ratio		The pension and tax debts to total assets ratio	
2019	10	33	5	5	7	3	4	6	1	9	1	9
2018	32	11	16	16	18	14	20	12	5	27	8	24
2017	37	6	23	14	30	5	25	10	11	24	13	22
2016	41	2	25	16	34	7	41	10	16	25	17	24
2015	42	1	23	19	34	8	31	11	15	27	19	23

Table 12.3 Viable firms according to the compliance or violation of NCCAAE tools' thresholds—Detail per years

Years	Negative value of net equity		The interest expenses to revenue ratio		The net equity to total debt ratio		The current assets to current liabilities ratio		The cash-flow to total assets ratio		The pension and tax debts to total assets ratio	
2019	1	42	6	36	5	37	9	33	13	29	7	35
2018	1	42	2	40	2	40	8	34	8	34	6	36
2017	1	42	5	37	2	40	6	36	8	34	5	37
2016	2	41	6	35	5	36	9	32	9	32	10	31
2015	2	41	8	33	8	33	11	30	13	28	12	29

Table 12.4 Non-viable firms signaled by the alert system—Detail per time series

Time	t_{-1}	t_{-1} (%)	t_{-2}	t_{-2} (%)	t_{-3}	t_{-3} (%)	t_{-4}	t_{-4} (%)	t_{-5}	t_{-5} (%)
No. of non-viable firms	33	38.3	15	17.44	4	4.65	2	2.33	1	1.16
Average (years)	1.60									

Table 12.5 reports, for each year, the number of viable and non-viable firms distributed according to the Z-score thresholds which divide firms in viable, non-viable and uncertain. In 2019, Z-scores identify as non-viable 57 out of 86 firms, almost the 66,28% of the entire sample. As opposite, Z-scores identify as viable only 9 firms which all belong to the viable sample. The number of non-viable firms correctly classified has a fluctuating trend until 2017 and then steadily increase whereas, as expected, the number of non-viable firms wrongly classified as viable decreases. Regarding viable firms, it is interesting to notice that, despite the higher presence among non-viable and uncertain classifications, their number does not change substantially across time, especially as regards viable firms signaled as non-viable which maintain an almost constant trend throughout time. A possible explanation stems from the fact that 9 out of 20 of the viable firms signaled as non-viable in 2015 have been established in 2013. Due to their recent constitution, the losses, which emerge from the initial material costs beared to start the business, do not permit to retain earnings therefore their net equity value results low and so the Z-score values which provide an indication of crisis.

Table 12.5 Sample's firms according to the Z-scoreclassification

		Non-viable	Uncertain	Viable	Total
	Non-viable	41	2	0	43
2019	Viable	16	18	9	43
	Total	57	20	9	86
	Non-viable	34	7	2	43
2018	Viable	16	18	9	43
	Total	50	25	11	86
	Non-viable	27	12	4	43
2017	Viable	18	17	8	43
	Total	45	29	12	86
	Non-viable	28	10	5	43
2016	Viable	18	17	8	43
	Total	46	27	13	86
	Non-viable	26	13	4	43
2015	Viable	20	17	6	43
	Total	46	30	10	86

Table 12.6 reports, for each year, the number of non-viable firms which has a constant status of non-viable according to the Z-score category in the following years. The trend is stable from 2015 to 2017 and then sharply increases from 2017 to 2019 suggesting that crisis stems from the perpetuated overlook of a negative physiological situation.

The analysis conducted over the financial distress predictive accuracy of the alert system and the Z-score are now compared to draw conclusions about the pros and cons of each approach.

Table 12.7 provides a summary of the financial distress predictive accuracy of the two approaches. In detail, the table reports, per each year, the number and relative percentage of the viable and non-viable firms signaled by the alert system and the Z-score model. The Z-score model outperformed the alert system as regards the financial distress predictive accuracy

Table 12.6 Non-viable firms signaled by the Z-score—Detail per time series

Time	t_{-1}	t_{-1} (%)	t_{-2}	t_{-2} (%)	t_{-3}	t_{-3} (%)	t_{-4}	t_{-4} (%)	t_{-5}	t_{-5} (%)
No. of non-viable firms	41	47.67%	25	29.07	14	16.28	13	15.12	12	13.95
Average (years)	2.33									

of the non-viable firms along all the period considered. In this regard, the distance between the two performance is greater in the period 2015–2017 but shrinks approaching the start of the insolvency proceedings which suggests that the net equity tool of the alert system may be good predictor in the short terms but loses efficacy for longer time periods.

However, it is interesting to notice the steady and high number of viable firms classified as non-viable due to their poor Z-score. Thus, we decided to delve into the drivers of such low Z-scores. The scrutiny of the balance sheets of these firms brought out the negative values of working capital, or irrelevant with respect to the total assets, which highlight a severe financial disequilibrium because of firms may not be able to fulfill obligations due to a lack of liquid assets. Another driver is represented by the operating income, measured as difference between income and production costs. It results, indeed, that the income is mostly absorbed by the costs related to the personnel and the purchase of raw materials. Finally, also the ratio of net equity to total debts concurs to lower the Z-score as net equity values are way lower than total debt values signaling a situation of undercapitalization.

With the purpose of providing a more detailed comparison, Table 12.8 reports, for each year and tool of the alert system, the summary statistics relative to viable and non-viable firms. The values of each statistic measure significantly differ between viable and non-viable firms suggesting a good accuracy of the alert system in discerning between viable and non-viable

Table 12.7 Sample's firms as classified by the alert system and the Z-score model

Year	Firms signaled by the alert system		Percentage of firms signaled by the alert system (*)		Firms signaled by the Z-score		Percentage of firms signaled by the Z-score (*)	
	Non-viable	Viable	Non-viable (%)	Viable (%)	Non-viable	Viable	Non-viable (%)	Viable (%)
2019	33	1	38.37	1.16	41	16	47.67	18.60
2018	15	1	17.44	1.16	34	16	39.53	18.60
2017	6	1	6.98	1.16	27	18	31.40	20.93
2016	2	2	2.33	2.33	28	18	32.56	20.93
2015	2	2	2.33	2.33	26	20	30.23	23.26

(*) The percentage is given by the ratio of the annual number of signaled firms to the total number of firms.

firms. Moreover, the accuracy increases as approaching the start of the insolvency proceedings as the average and median values of each tool keep exceeding the NCCAAE's thresholds for non-viable firms and instead remain below the thresholds for viable firms.

In a similar vein, Table 12.9 reports, for each year, the summary statistics of the Z-score relative to viable and non-viable firms. Also in this case, the average and median values of the Z-score decrease, with respect to non-viable firms, as approaching the start of the insolvency proceedings therefore suggesting the higher accuracy of the model in predicting financial distress the closer the point of no return. Regarding viable firms, the average and median values relative to the Z-score are higher but we cannot draw solid conclusions because of the employment of two different versions of the Z-score which have different thresholds.

Finally, Table 12.10 shows the 2019 confusion matrices of the alert system and the Z-score model. The table reports the combination between the effective and the predicted status of viable and non-viable firms so to highlight the type I and type II errors which allow for the comparison between the financial distress predictive accuracy of each approach. The Z-score model outperformed the alert system as regards the financial distress predictive accuracy of non-viable firms with a result of 41 out of 43 compared to the 33 out of 43 of the latter (10 type II errors). It is worth to specify that the alert systems indication of crisis stem all from the violation of the net equity tool as the joint violation of all sector ratios is instead a rare case. However, the alert system over-performed the Z-score model as regards the financial distress predictive accuracy of the sample of viable firms. The alert system, indeed, correctly classifies 42 out of 43 viable firms whereas the Z-score model correctly classifies only 9 firms causing therefore 34 type I errors.

Overall, the alert system correctly classifies 75 out of 86 firms therefore outperforming in general terms the Z-score model which correctly classifies only 50 out of 86 firms.

Due to the lack of consistency in the performance of both approaches, we proceed with the second stage of this analysis which consists with presenting the results of the application of the refined version of both the Z-score and the alert system to our sample of firms. We start presenting the results of the implementation of the Z*-score. Table 12.11 reports, for year 2019, the number of viable and non-viable firms distributed according to the Z*-score thresholds which divide firms in viable, non-viable and uncertain. From the results, it clearly emerges that the Z*-score

Table 12.8 Summary statistics of the alert system

		Net equity value		The interest expenses to revenue ratio		The net equity to total debt ratio		The current assets to current liabilities ratio		The cash-flow to total assets ratio		The pension and tax debts to total assets ratio	
		Non-viable firms	Viable firms	Non-viable firms	Viable firms	Non-viable firms	Viable firms	Non-viable firms	Viable firms	Non-viable firms	Viable firms	Non-viable firms	Viable firms
2019	Mean	-1,610,824	1,443,151	4.58	1.19	-24.02	74.05	63.75	167.62	-35.67	2.32	34.48	4.45
	Median	-560,359	461,769	2.69	0.35	-25.29	26.64	64.66	121.56	-32.29	2.86	25.26	2.28
	Std. Dev	n.d	3,257,436	5.20	2.05	32.02	97.34	33.38	129.17	28.21	7.76	28.85	6.87
	Minimum	-11,491,159	-41,568	0.22	0.00	-88.29	1.64	3.26	38.16	-109.33	-17.79	0.46	0.01
	Maximum	6,991,962	19,222,520	22.83	11.96	49.43	404.26	151.52	563.43	4.31	22.09	115.05	34.52
2018	Mean	121,280	1,276,058	3.75	1.05	22.69	72.51	108.30	385.25	-7.61	4.63	17.91	4.41
	Median	116,225	407,143	1.96	0.42	12.90	29.85	114.23	127.28	-3.28	3.09	13.11	2.00
	Std. Dev	n.d	n.d	6.99	1.47	26.92	116.95	45.87	1519.62	14.65	6.97	15.79	7.03
	Minimum	-5,815,932	638	0.26	0.00	0.19	0.74	27.25	26.00	-77.62	-11.12	0.41	0.00
	Maximum	8,794,774	15,543,834	40.67	7.22	93.85	634.17	245.12	9976.03	3.22	20.22	63.80	36.73
2017	Mean	707,137	1,115,143	2.44	1.15	26.45	64.11	112.21	365.29	-2.29	5.45	11.82	3.59
	Median	464,809	362,608	2.06	0.49	18.70	26.41	108.54	118.64	-0.72	4.41	9.08	1.46
	Std. Dev	n.d	n.d	2.04	1.86	26.47	119.25	41.19	1429.50	7.18	7.21	9.86	6.84
	Minimum	-1,873,322	8,737	0.17	0.00	-1.21	1.34	12.49	24.68	-38.01	-11.98	0.18	0.01
	Maximum	3,453,948	14,052,352	9.44	10.86	112.40	730.45	235.72	9374.26	6.17	23.39	39.07	35.17
2016	Mean	816,068	963,634	3.19	1.26	25.89	57.51	112.72	295.57	-1.69	4.47	11.68	3.46
	Median	482,598	285,417	2.03	0.81	17.26	23.21	109.22	115.14	0.04	3.19	7.49	1.57
	Std. Dev	n.d	n.d	3.03	1.52	27.04	96.92	37.69	677.76	5.51	7.51	11.31	5.30
	Minimum	-269,324	-92,842	0.23	0.00	0.57	1.41	14.91	24.03	-17.48	-13.26	0.40	0.00
	Maximum	3,641,091	10,639,041	13.71	6.91	119.07	582.31	194.26	3815.76	5.56	24.55	57.66	28.34
2015	Mean	803,355	765,938	3.37	1.43	25.75	52.30	110.04	172.64	-0.93	4.37	9.79	6.36

	Net equity value		The interest expenses to revenue ratio		The net equity to total debt ratio		The current assets to current liabilities ratio		The cash-flow to total assets ratio		The pension and tax debts to total assets ratio	
	Non-viable firms	Viable firms	Non-viable firms	Viable firms	Non-viable firms	Viable firms	Non-viable firms	Viable firms	Non-viable firms	Viable firms	Non-viable firms	Viable firms
Median	470,590	216,615	2.49	0.79	14.95	23.13	106.17	118.32	0.10	2.28	7.73	2.22
Std. Dev	n.d	n.d	4.23	1.77	32.29	92.01	36.94	168.49	5.17	8.76	10.00	10.86
Minimum	−255,308	36	0.24	0.00	0.64	1.52	17.92	14.39	−18.69	−10.13	0.09	0.00
Maximum	4,778,372	7,991,233	26.35	8.00	164.42	563.63	205.07	849.91	7.24	39.68	55.46	46.11

Table 12.9   Summary statistics of the Z-score

Year	Firm status	Mean	Median	Std. Dev	Minimum	Maximum
2019	Non-viable firms	−1.73	−1.52	4.00	−14.32	5.76
	Viable firms	4.04	3.48	2.81	0.69	10.84
2018	Non-viable firms	1.74	1.13	2.73	−3.99	8.78
	Viable firms	3.88	2.99	2.81	−0.29	10.75
2017	Non-viable firms	2.64	1.83	2.33	−1.17	8.52
	Viable firms	3.85	3.56	2.66	−0.69	12.28
2016	Non-viable firms	2.90	2.19	2.18	−0.30	7.83
	Viable firms	3.77	3.24	2.97	−2.65	11.74
2015	Non-viable firms	2.92	2.83	2.20	−0.58	8.69
	Viable firms	4.13	3.05	4.15	−0.37	24.21

Table 12.10   Confusion matrixes of the alert system and the Z-score model

		Alert system's predicted status				Z-score's predicted status	
		Non-viable	Viable			Non-viable	Viable
Actual status	Non-viable firms	33	10	Actual status	Non-viable firms	41	2
	Viable firms	1	42		Viable firms	34	9

outperformed its traditional version wrongly classifying only 11 out of 86 firms against the 36 out of 86 of the latter. A detailed comparison between the Z^*-score and its traditional version, employed in the first stage of the analysis, is provided by Table 12 which shows the confusion matrix of the two approaches. The Z^*-score correctly classifies 75 over 86 firms therefore equaling the performance of the baseline alert system. However, it is worth to recommend the use of the Z^*-score only to limited companies as its employment for partnerships could bias the results regarding the firm predicted status due to their different economic and patrimonial structure.

Finally, we present the results of the application of the Z^{**}-score and the overall new alert system to our sample of firms. The logic underlying the functioning of the new alert system entails the joint interpretation of two variables: the net equity value and the Z^{**}-score. With the purpose

Table 12.11 Sample's firms as classified by the Z*-score

Year	Firm Status	Non-viable	Uncertain	Viable	Total
2019	Non-viable firms	39	0	4	43
	Viable firms	5	2	36	43
Total		44	2	40	86

Table 12.12 Confusion matrices comparing the Z*-score to the Z-score

		Z*-score's predicted status					Z-score's predicted status	
		Non-viable	Viable				Non-viable	Viable
Actual status	Non-viable firms	39	4		Actual status	Non-viable firms	41	2
	Viable firms	7	36			Viable firms	34	9

of providing a synthetic description of the new alert system, table 12.13 reports, for each combination resulting for the joint read of the two variables, a specific alert level with a brief description of the associated firm' status. Table 12.14 reports, for year 2019, the number of viable and non-viable firms distributed according to the Z**-score thresholds which divide firms in viable, non-viable and uncertain. From the results, it emerges that the Z**-score correctly predicts the financial distress of 78 out of 86 firms, namely the 90.69% of the entire sample. Thus, the Z**-score already overperforms all the specifications employed so far, as presented in Table 12.15. We then present the results of the new alert system which jointly considers the net equity value and the Z**-score. Table 12.16 reports, for each level of alert identified by the joint read of the net equity value and the Z**-score, the number of viable and non-viable firms identified by the new alert system. The results point out the new alert system as the best financial distress predictor as it correctly identifies as non-viable 41 out of 43 firms and as viable 39 out of 43 (namely the sum of the firms included in the low and medium/low alert levels). Thus, the new alert system outperformed the original version correctly

Table 12.13 Z**-scores' alert levels and description

Net equity tool	Z**-Score	Level of alert	Description
Negative, namely below the minimum legal threshold	Non-viable	High	Certain crisis status due to severe losses and serious liquidity and structural difficulties.
Negative, namely below the minimum legal threshold	Uncertain	Medium-High	High probability of insolvency due to high leverage and/or temporary liquidity difficulties which jeopardize the fulfillment of financial obligations
Negative, namely below the minimum legal threshold	Viable	Medium	Significant probability of insolvency due to structural and assets disequilibria
Positive	Non-viable	Medium	Moderated probability of insolvency due to financial and economic fragilities
Positive	Uncertain	Medium-Low	Low probability of insolvency given the great assets equilibrium
Positive	Viable	Low	Very low probability of insolvency given the solid assets and economic equilibria and the ability of timely fulfilling financial obligations

classifying 80 out of 86 firms against the 75 out of 86 firms of the latter as presented by the confusion matrices of the two approaches in Table 12.17.

12.6   Conclusions

The study develops an alternative measure to the alert system elaborated by the NCCAAE which combines the benefits of the Z-score's multivariate discriminant model with the background employed to develop the NCCAAE' predictors.

Table 12.14 Sample's firms as classified by the Z**-score

Year	Firm Status	Non-viable	Uncertain	Viable	Total
2019	Non-viable firms	40	2	1	43
	Viable firms	3	2	38	43
Total		43	4	39	86

Table 12.15 Confusion matrices comparing all the specifications of the Z-score

		Z*-score's predicted status					Z-score's predicted status	
		Non-viable	Viable				Non-viable	Viable
Actual status	Non-viable firms	39	4	Actual status	Non-viable firms		41	2
	Viable firms	7	36		Viable firms		34	9
Actual status	Non-viable firms	40	3					
	Viable firms	5	38					

Table 12.16 Sample's frims as classified by the new alert system – Year 2019

Net Equity Index Value	Z**-Score	Alert level	No. Of Non-viable firms	No. Of Viable firms
Negative, namely below the minimum legal threshold	Non-viable	High	32	0
Negative, namely below the minimum legal threshold	Uncertain	Medium/High	1	0
Negative, namely below the minimum legal threshold	Viable	Medium	0	1
Positive	Non-viable	Medium	8	3
Positive	Uncertain	Medium/Low	1	2
Positive	Viable	Low	1	37
Total			43	43

The study consists of an initial comparison exercise between the financial distress predictive accuracy of the NCCAAE's alert system with respect to that of the traditional Z-score over the period 2015–2019. The emerging results are then used to refine and reassess both measures as the

Table 12.17 Confusion matrixes of the specifications of the alert system

| | | New Alert System's predicted status | | | | | Alert system's predicted status | |
		Non-viable	Viable				Non-viable	Viable
Actual status	Non-viable firms	41	2	Actual status	Non-viable firms	33	10
	Viable firms	4	39		Viable firms	1	42

traditional Z-score is aligned to the current socio-economic conditions whereas the alert system is integrated with a Z-score calculated using its predictors as inputs.

Initially, our analysis highlights the limits of the alert system as designed by the NCCAAE.

First of all, it should be noted that the notion of crisis used by the alert system is that indicated in the new Code of Business Crisis and Insolvency, it is to say "the inadequacy of current liquid funds and prospective cash flows to regularly meet existing and expected obligations over a period of six months". Such a short time horizon was probably chosen to increase the reliability of the system of indicators. Furthermore, the NCCAAE itself specified that the model has been set up in such a way as to minimize the number of "false positives", that is, those companies whose insolvency is expected but that they will not incur in the time span examined and admit the possibility of a greater number of "false negatives", or companies whose crisis is not diagnosed but will become insolvent.

The disclaimers listed above are indicative of the NCCAAE awareness that the alert measures can have significant repercussions on a large number of companies and so that the alert thresholds have to lead to pointing out only those companies that appear to be very close to insolvency. It seems almost superfluous to say that an alert signal is useful only when it actually manages to identify the first hints of a business crisis.

From this point of view, our empirical results were not surprising as we found some problems in the alert system in predicting the financial distress of non-viable firms.

In detail, the alert system detected only 33 out of 43 non-viable firms, therefore committing 10 type II errors. The Z-score, instead, showed a better accuracy predicting the financial distress of 41 out of 43 non-viable firms. As regards viable firms, the alert system outperformed the

Z-score model by correctly predicting the viable status of 42 against 9 firms. Regarding timing, the Z-score has an average of two years and four months between the first signal and the effective bankruptcy of a firm against the one year and six months of the alert system.

The above-mentioned considerations clarify the logical and practical limits of the NCCAAE's alert system.

We, therefore, developed the enhanced version of both approaches which consists of aligning the traditional Z-score to the current socio-economic situation and compensate the limits of the alert system with the complementarities expressed by the Z-score. The revised Z-score outperformed its traditional version fixing its poor financial distress predictive accuracy as regards viable firms. However, the Z-score employed as part of the renewed alert system already overperformed the revised version as regards the financial distress predictive accuracy of both non-viable (40 out of 43 against 39 out of 43) and viable firms (38 out of 43 against 36 out of 43). In addition, when integrated into the alert system framework, it permits the resulting new alert system to significantly improve its performance. In detail, the new alert system improves the financial distress predictive accuracy of non-viable firms with respect to its baseline version (41 out of 43 against 33 out of 43) while slightly decreased its accuracy as regards viable firms (39 out of 43 against 42 out of 43). Overall, the new alert system emerges as best measure employed in this study by correctly classifying 80 out of 86 firms.

In conclusion, our finding may have important policy implications since it points out the limits of the alert system as designed by the NCCAAE and suggests an alternative and better performing measure which may be used by third-party bodies to predict financial distress.

The range of these implications is significant given the hampered resilience of SMEs, which play a crucial role played for the European economy, in particular that of Italy, and the uncertain future caused by the pandemic.

Traditional predictive frameworks, indeed, may prove inadequate to address the upcoming and volatile economic scenario and need, therefore, a new design able to capture the peculiarities of the pandemic implications for SMEs' resilience.

Loose regulatory and policy action further complicate the picture by raising the specter of zombie firms and laying down the conditions for government funding to be vanished in the "wrong hands".

A suitable predictive framework is therefore of utter importance and our study contributes in this vein by developing a financial distress prediction method that may help navigating the new scenario posed by the pandemic.

Much more work has however to be done; it is clear, in fact, that every backward-looking test completely loses its meaning considering the new pandemic economic scenario that companies will have to face.

REFERENCES

AlAli, M. S. (2018). The application of Altman's Z-Score model in determining the financial soundness of healthcare companies listed in Kuwait Stock Exchange. *International Journal of Economic Papers, 3*(1), 1–5.

Al-Manaseer, S. R., Al-Oshaibat, S. D. (2018). Validity of Altman Z-Score model to predict financial failure: Evidence from Jordan. *International Journal of Economics and Finance, 10*(8), 181–189.

Albaz, A., Mansour, T., Rida, T. Schubert, J. (2020). Setting up small and medium-size enterprises for restart and recovery. https://www.mckinsey.com/industries/public-and-social-sector/our-insights/setting-up-small-and-medium-size-enterprises-for-restart-and-recovery

Altman, E. I., Iwanicz-Drozdowska, M., Laitinen, E. K., Suvas, A. (2017). Financial distress prediction in an international context: A review and empirical analysis of Altman's Z-Score model. *Journal of International Financial Management and Accounting, 27*, 131–171.

Altman, E., Danovi, A., Falini, A. (2013). Z-Score models' application to Italian companies subject to extraordinary administration. *Journal of Applied Finance, 23*(1), 128–137.

Altman, E., Hartzell, J., Peck, M. (1995). *A Scoring System for Emerging Market Corporate Bodns*. NY: Salomon Brothers High.

Altman, EI. (1968). Financial ratios, discriminant analysis and the prediction of corporate bankruptcy. *The Journal of Finance, 23*(4), 589–609.

Altman, EI. (1983). *Corporate Financial Distress*. NY: John Wiley & Sons.

Babatunde, A. A., Akeju, J. B., Malomo, E. (2017). The effectiveness of Altman's Z-Score in predicting bankruptcy of quoted manufacturing companies in Nigeria. *European Journal of Business, Economics and Accountancy, 5*(5), 74–83.

Bates, J.M., Granger, C.W.J. (1969). The combination of forecasts. *Operational Research Quarterly, 20*, 451–68.

Beaver, W. (1966). Financial ratios as predictors of failure. *Journal of Accounting Research, 4*, 71–111.

Borrajo, M., Baruque, B., Corchado, E., Bajo, J., Corchado, J. (2011). Hybrid neural intelligent system to predict business failure in small-to-medium-size enterprises. *International Journal of Neural Systems, 21*(4), 277–296.

Carminchael, D.R. (1972). The auditor's reporting obligation. The meaning and implementation of the fourth standard of reporting. *Auditing Research Monograph* (1). NY: AICPA.

Chieng, J.R. (2013). Verifying the Validity of Altman's Z Score as a Predictor of Bank Failures in the case of the Eurozone. http://norma.ncirl.ie/865/1/jasminechieng.pdf.

Dimitras, A.I., Slowinski, R., Susmaga, R. (1999). Business failure prediction using rough sets. *European Journal of Operational Research 114*, 263–280.

Doumpos, M., Zopounidis, C. (1999). A multinational discrimination method for the prediction of financial distress: the case of Greece. *Multinational Finance Journal 3*(2), 71–101.

Foster, G. (1986). *Financial Statement Analysis*. NJ: Prentice Hall.

Frydman, H., Altman, E.I., Kao, D. (1985). Introducing recursive partitioning for financial classification: the case of financial distress. *The Journal of Finance, 40*, 269–291

Gepp, A., Kumar, K., Bhattacharya, S. (2010). Business failure prediction using decision trees. *Journal of Forecasting, 29*(6), 536–555.

Januri, Sari, E.N., Diyanti, A. (2017). The analysis of the bankruptcy potential comparative by Altman Z-Score, Springate and Zmijewski methods at cement companies listed in Indonesia Stock Exchange. *IOSR Journal of Business and Management, 19*(10), 80–87.

Jo, H., Han, I. (1996). Integration of case-based forecasting, neural network, and discriminant analysis for bankruptcy prediction. *Expert Systems with Applications, 11*, 415–422.

Kim, M.-J., Han, I. (2003). The discovery of experts' decision rules from qualitative bankruptcy data using genetic algorithms. *Expert Systems with Applications, 25*, 637–646.

Li, H., Adeli, H., Sun, J., Han, J. (2011). Hybridizing principles of TOPSIS with case-based reasoning for business failure prediction. *Computers & Operations Research, 38*(2), 409–419.

Li, H., Sun, J. (2008). Ranking-order case-based reasoning for financial distress prediction. *Knowledge-Based Systems, 21*(8), 868–878.

Li, H., Sun, J. (2009). Hybridizing principles of the Electre method with case-based reasoning for data mining: Electre-CBR-I and Electre-CBR-II. *European Journal of Operational Research, 197*(1), 214–224.

Li, H., Sun, J. (2010). Business failure prediction using hybrid2 case-based reasoning. Computers & Operations Research, 37(1), 137–151.

Li, H., Sun, J., Wu, J. (2010). Predicting business failure using classification and regression tree: an empirical comparison with popular classical statistical methods and top classification mining methods. *Expert Systems with Applications, 37*(8), 5895–5904.

Malik, M. S., Awais, M., Timsal, A., Hayat, F. (2016). Z-Score Model: Analysis and Implication on Textile Sector of Pakistan. *International Journal of Academic Research, 4*(2), 140-158.

McKee, T.E. (2000). Developing a bankruptcy prediction model via rough sets theory. *Intelligent Systems in Accounting Finance & Management, 9*(3), 159-173.

McKee, T.E., Greenstein, M. (2000). Predicting bankruptcy using recursive partitioning and a realistically proportioned data set. *Journal of Forecasting, 19*, 219–230.

Ohlson, J.A. (1980). Financial ratios and probabilistic prediction of bankruptcy. *Journal of Accounting Research 18*, 109–131.

Ross, S.A., Westerfield, R.W., Jaffe, J.F. (1999). *Corporate Finance*. IL: Homewood.

Shaher, T.A., Salem, R., Khasawneh, O. (2012). Predicting corporate failure in emerging market: Empirical evidence from Jordan (2001–2008). *Archives Des Sciences, 65*(10), 34–43.

Shin, K.-S., Lee, Y.-J. (2002). A genetic algorithm application in bankruptcy prediction modeling. *Expert Systems with Applications, 23*, 321–328.

Sun, J., He, K., Li, H. (2011). SFFS-PC-NN optimized by genetic algorithm for dynamic prediction of financial distress with longitudinal data streams. *Knowledge-Based Systems 24*, 1013–1023.

Sun, J., Li, H. (2011). Dynamic financial distress prediction using instance selection for the disposal of concept drift. *Expert Systems with Applications, 38*, 2566–2576.

Sun, J., Li, H., Adeli, H. (2013). Concept drift-oriented adaptive and dynamic support vector machine ensemble with time window in corporate financial risk prediction. *IEEE Transactions on Systems, Man and Cybernetics: Systems, 43*(4), 801–813.

Sun, J., Li, H., Huang, Q-H., He, K-Y. (2014). Predicting financial distress and corporate failure: A review from the state-of-the-art definitions, modeling, sampling, and featuring approaches. Knowledge-Based Systems, 57, 41–56.

Tam, K. (1991). Neural network models and the prediction of bank bankruptcy, Omega 19(5), 429–445.

Tam, K., Kiang, M. (1992). Managerial applications of neural networks: the case of bank failure prediction. *Management Science, 38*(7), 926–947.

Varetto, F. (1998). Genetic algorithms applications in the analysis of insolvency risk. *Journal of Banking & Finance, 22*, 1421–1439.

Wang, Y., Wang, S., Lai, K.K. (2005). A new fuzzy support vector machine to evaluate credit risk. *IEEE Transactions on Fuzzy Systems, 13*(6), 820–831.

INDEX

Milton Keynes UK
Ingram Content Group UK Ltd.
UKHW022251280923
429541UK00002B/20